The Amazon Basin
Pages 252–267

Central Sierra
Pages 186–199

THE AMAZON
BASIN

- Iquitos

- Pucallpa

The Inca Heartland
Pages 156–185

Canyon Country
Pages 134–155

CENTRAL
SIERRA
- Huancayo

- Cusco

THE INCA
HEARTLAND

THE
SOUTHERN
COAST

CANYON COUNTRY
- Arequipa

The Southern Coast
Pages 120–133

- Tacna

0 kilometers 150
0 miles   150

EYEWITNESS TRAVEL

PERU

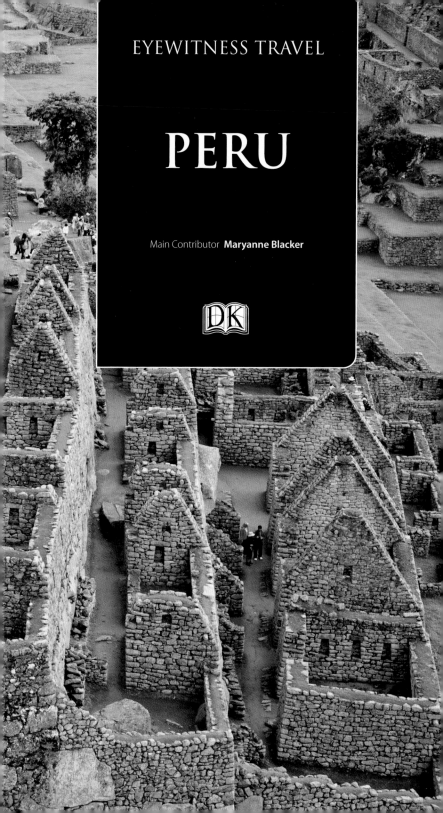

EYEWITNESS TRAVEL

PERU

Main Contributor **Maryanne Blacker**

DK

DK

LONDON, NEW YORK,
MELBOURNE, MUNICH AND DELHI
www.dk.com

Managing Editor Aruna Ghose
Design Manager Priyanka Thakur
Project Editor Shikha Kulkarni
Project Designer Shruti Singhi
Editor Jyoti Kumari
Designers Pooja Badola, Anchal Kaushal
Senior Cartographic Manager Uma Bhattacharya
Cartographer Mohammad Hassan
Senior DTP Designer Vinod Harish
Senior Picture Researcher Taiyaba Khatoon
Picture Researcher Sumita Khatwani
Assistant picture Researcher Shweta Andrews

Contributors
Maryanne Blacker, Jorge Riveros Cayo,
Dominic Hamilton, Rob Rachowiecki,
Joby Williams

Photographers
Demetrio Carrasco, Nigel Hicks, Linda Whitwam

Illustrators
Chapel Design & Marketing Ltd., Chinglemba Chingbham,
Surat Kumar Mantoo, Arun Pottirayil,
T. Gautam Trivedi, Mark Arjun Warner

Printed and bound in China by L. Rex Printing Co. Ltd

First American Edition, 2008
14 15 16 17 10 9 8 7 6 5 4 3 2 1

Published in the United States by:
Dorling Kindersley Publishing, 345 Hudson Street, New York, New York 10014

Copyright © 2008, 2014 Dorling Kindersley Limited, London
A Penguin Company

Reprinted with revisions 2010, 2012, 2014

Published in Great Britain by Dorling Kindersley Limited

A catalog record for this book is
available from the Library of Congress.

ISSN 1542-1554

ISBN: 978-1-4654-1176-1

MIX
Paper from
responsible sources
FSC
www.fsc.org   FSC™ C018179

**The information in this
DK Eyewitness Travel Guide is checked regularly.**
Every effort has been made to ensure that this book is as up-to-date as possible at
the time of going to press. Some details, however, such as telephone numbers,
opening hours, prices, gallery hanging arrangements and travel information are
liable to change. The publishers cannot accept responsibility for any consequences
arising from the use of this book, nor for any material on third party websites, and
cannot guarantee that any website address in this book will be a suitable source of
travel information. We value the views and suggestions of our readers very highly.
Please write to: Publisher, DK Eyewitness Travel Guides, Dorling Kindersley,
80 Strand, London, WC2R 0RL, UK or email: travelguides@dk.com.

Front cover main image: A llama grazing at the pre-Columbian ruins of Machu Picchu

◀ The Inca ruins of Machu Picchu, a UNESCO World Heritage site, El Valle Sagrado

Inhabitants of Islas Uros, Lake Titicaca

Contents

Introducing Peru

Nazca ceramic bottle with stylized patterns

Brightly painted plates at a local market, in Chinchero

Strikingly carved blue balconies, Cusco

Golden pectoral of the Lord of Sipán

San Francisco Church and Convent, Lima

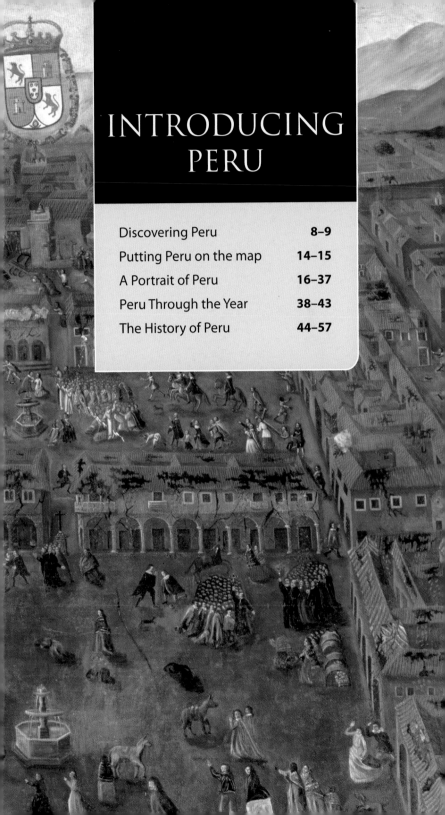

INTRODUCING PERU

DISCOVERING PERU

The following itineraries have been designed to include Peru's main highlights, while keeping long-distance travel manageable. The itineraries include a two-day tour of Lima, Peru's bustling capital, and a two-day tour of Cusco, which was the centre of the Inca empire. There is a one-week tour of northern Peru, where there are opportunities to wander among ancient archaeological ruins, surf Pacific waves, and visit the site where a small group of Spanish conquistadors captured the head of the Inca empire in the 16th century. A two-week tour of southern Peru offers a visit to the country's top attractions, including the ruins of Machu Picchu and Cusco. The tour also includes a visit to floating islands on Lake Titicaca and a flight over the Nazca Lines – giant geoglyphs sketched into the desert. Finish up with a few days contemplating the wonders of the Amazon rainforest.

One Week in Northern Peru

- Stroll through the streets of **Trujillo**, visiting elegant colonial mansions.
- Wander through the ruins of **Chan Chan**, once the world's biggest adobe city with a population of 100,000.
- Visit **Huaca del Sol**, a pre-Inca site built by the Moches in around AD 500.
- Surf the waves near the beach resort **Huanchaco**.
- Visit the modern museum of **Museo Tumbas Reales de Sipán**.
- Check out Cajamarca's **Ransom Chamber**, which was filled with gold by Inca ruler Atahualpa to try to win his release from the Spanish conquistadors.
- Relax like an Inca at the thermal baths of popular resort **Baños del Inca**.

Chan Chan
A UNESCO World Heritage site, this former pre-Columbian metropolis features a complex of sunken plazas, chambers, and temple cloisters.

Lima
Tourists take a break on the steps outside the Palacio Arzobispal on Lima's Plaza Mayor. The building is famed for its Moorish-style carved balconies and ornate façade.

Two Weeks in Southern Peru

- Hike to the ancient Inca ruins of **Machu Picchu**.
- Stroll the streets of **Cusco**, where Spanish churches are built on top of Inca walls.
- Shop for arts and crafts at the lively **Pisac** indigenous market in the **Sacred Valley**.
- Fly above the mysterious **Nazca Lines**.
- Watch colorful wildlife along the shores of the **Río Tambopata** or **Río Madre de Dios**.
- Watch giant condors soar above the **Cañón del Colca**.
- Learn about life on the islands of **Lake Titicaca**.
- Enjoy a world class meal in **Lima**.

Spectacular scenery in the Sacred Valley near Cusco, Peru's Inca heartland
Formed by the Río Urubamba, the Sacred Valley or Urubamba Valley is close the Inca capital of Cusco and the ancient city of Machu Picchu.

UCAYALI

MADRE DE DIOS

CUSCO

Rio Madre de Dios

Puerto Maldonado

Río Tambopata

Machu Picchu • Inca Trail

Cusco

APURIMAC

PUNO

AREQUIPA

BOLIVIA

Cañón del Colca

Isa Taquile

Puno

Lake Titicaca

Arequipa

MOQUEGUA

TACNA

0 kilometers   200
0 miles   200

Key
— One week in Northern Peru tour
— Two weeks in Southern Peru tour

Two Days in Lima

Peru's capital is a bustling metropolis within an ancient setting, complete with pre-Inca ruins, colonial churches, world-class restaurants and lively nightlife.

- **Arriving** The Jorge Chavez International Airport is in Callao, located directly west of Lima. There are several taxi companies at the airport.

- **Moving on** Several flights leave daily from Lima's Jorge Chavez to airport. Buses traveling the 20-plus hours to Cusco also leave daily.

Day 1
Morning Get a taste of Lima's colonial history with a walk through the city center. Head to the **Plaza Mayor** (p 64), which is surrounded by the **La Catedral** (p 66), the **Archbishop's Palace** (p 65) and the **Government's Palace** (p 62). Walk a few blocks to visit the **Monasterio de San Francisco** (p 66), best known for its catacombs. Head to **Casa de Aliaga** (p 66), a colonial mansion considered to be the oldest home in South America. Take a taxi to Miraflores or San Isidro for lunch.

Afternoon Visit **Museo Larco** (p 98) and its collection of pre-Columbian ceramics, including a gallery of erotic pottery, all housed in an 18th-century mansion. Stop by the **Museo Nacional de Antropologia, Arqueologia, e Historia del Peru** (p 100), which was the former home of independence fighters José San Martín and Símon Bolivar. If you have time, take a taxi to **Huaca Pucllana** (p 84), a pre-Inca adobe pyramid. Stay in Miraflores for dinner.

Day 2
Morning Start with an early morning walk along **Miraflores's Malecon** (p 83), where lush parks are perched on top of cliffs overlooking the Pacific Ocean. Walk up to **Parque Kennedy** (p 82), where artists sell their paintings

Ancient Inca terracing at Ollantaytambo fortress citadel, in the Sacred Valley near Cusco

on the weekends. Go to the **Museo de la Nacion** (p 99) and visit the Yuyanapaq exhibit, a powerful collection of photos depicting Peru's internal conflict during the 1980s and 1990s.

Afternoon Take a taxi to Lima's bohemian district of **Barranco** (p 89), and stroll among the early 20th-century mansions. Walk over the **Puente de Suspiros** (p 93) and then check out the art collection at the **Museo Pedro de Osma** (p 94). Barranco is Lima's most trendy neighborhood at night. Check out some live music and dancing at one of the many **Peñas** (p 95). Or, head back to Miraflores and treat yourself at one of Lima's finest restaurants.

Two Days in Cusco

The main draw to the former Inca capital is Machu Picchu, but travelers should spend a couple of days exploring Cusco's cobblestone streets and its outlying attractions.

- **Arriving** The Alejandro Velasco Astete International Airport is located on the outskirts of Cusco. Taxis are available to the city center. Bus terminals are located outside of the city center.

- **Moving on** There are several daily flights between Lima and Cusco. There are also direct flights to Puerto Maldonado. A number of bus companies travel from Cusco to Lima, Puno, and other cities.

Day 1
Morning Start with a walking tour on the Plaza de Armas. First stop is **La Catedral** (p170), where construction began in 1560 on top of an Inca palace. Inside the cathedral, look out for the painting of the Last Supper with roasted guinea pig on the table. Later, head over for a quick tour of the **Museo de Arte Religioso** (p167), where paintings from the Cusco School are on display. Check out the **12-sided Inca stone** (p164) that is part of the museum's exterior wall. Before lunch, stop off at **Koricancha** (p167), which was at one time the richest Inca temple in the empire, complete with gold plated walls.

Afternoon Take a taxi or hike up to **Sacsayhuamán** (p172) and spend the afternoon exploring this former Inca fortress overlooking Cusco. The impressive ruins contain massive stone walls, some of which weigh up to 350 tonnes. Return to Cusco and wander the cobblestone streets of the **San Blas District** (p167), which is full of shops selling handcrafted items.

Day 2
Morning Just outside Cusco, explore the lush Sacred Valley, which is full of Inca ruins and indigenous villages, by first heading to **Pisac** (p177). Here you will find a famed artisans market, which is held three days a week. After perusing the colorful market stalls, head to the nearby hilltop ruins that once held Inca military, religious, and residential buildings.

Afternoon Continue into the Sacred Valley to **Ollantaytambo** *(p176)*, considered to be the last living Inca town. The village includes an Inca fortress, where Manco Inca won a battle against the Spanish conquistadors.

> **To extend your trip...**
> Visit the **Salinas de Maras** *(p176)*, pre-Columbian salt mines where workers are still seen toiling today, and wander the streets of the quaint village of **Chinchero** *(p176)*, which is known for its handicrafts market.

One Week in Northern Peru

- **Airports** Arrive at Trujillo's Capitán FAP Carlos Martínez de Pinillos International Airport and depart from Cajamarca's Mayor General FAP Armando Revoredo Iglesias Airport.
- **Transport** This trip is best done by bus.
- **Booking ahead** Chaparri reserve (www.chaparri.org).

Day 1: Trujillo
On your first day, explore the brightly colored mansions and churches in **Trujillo's** colonial center *(p226)*. Afterwards wander through **Chan Chan** *(p231)*, the biggest adobe city in the world and the former capital of the Chimú empire.

Day 2: Huanchaco
In the morning, visit the **Huaca del Sol** *(p231)*, the largest

pre-Columbian adobe structure in the Americas. It was built by the Moche civilization, as was the nearby **Huaca de la Luna** *(p231)*. Spend the night in **Huanchaco** *(p231)*, a laid back beach town with a fishing village ambiance just outside Trujillo.

The next morning, practice surfing or just relax on the beach. After lunch by the seaside, visit the **Complejo Arqueológico El Brujo** *(p231)*, a Moche complex known for its mural paintings and the discovery of a 1,500-year-old mummy.

Day 3: Chiclayo
After a three-hour bus trip north to **Chiclayo** *(p231)*, spend most of your day exploring the magnificent **Museo Tumbas Reales de Sipán** *(p232)*. This three-story modern museum displays finds from the **Lord of Sipán's** burial chamber *(p239)*, one of Peru's most important archaeological discoveries in over 50 years.

> **To extend your trip...**
> Travel further north along the coast and relax for a few days on the sandy white beaches near **Mancora** *(236)*, hang out at **Cabo Blanco** *(p237)*, where Ernest Hemingway fished for marlins, or visit the **Santuario Nacional Manglares de Tumbes** *(236)*, a red mangrove forest.

Day 4–6: Cajamarca
Travel by bus from Chiclayo to **Cajamarca** *(p246)*, a journey that

Cajamarca, a provincial Andean capital laid out in a traditional Spanish grid plan

takes about 6 hours. Walk along the city's cobblestone streets where Spanish conquistadors captured the Inca emperor Atahualpa in the early 16th century. The **Ransom Chamber** *(p246)*, which Atahualpa allegedly filled once with gold and twice with silver to try to win his release from the Spaniards, is located just off the Plaza de Armas and is well worth a visit.

Next, head to the **Ventanillas de Otuzco** *(p250)*, the ancient cemeteries carved into a cliff of volcanic rock, located 5 miles (8 km) outside Cajamarca. Walk back and stop off at the **Baños del Inca** *(p250)*, the thermal baths that were used by Atahualpa and his Inca army.

Day 7: Cumbemayo
Check out **Cumbemayo** *(p250)*, a collection of 2,000-year-old aqueducts carved out of rock. Nearby is a man-made cave with petroglyphs believed to be 3,000 years old. Return to Cajamarca and catch a flight back to Lima.

Máncora Beach, in the northern beaches, a popular destination for surfers

Two Weeks in Southern Peru

- **Airports** Options include Lima's Jorge Chávez International Airport, Arequipa's Rodríguez Ballón International Airport, Cusco's Alejandro Velasco Astete International Airport, and Padre Aldamiz International Airport in Puerto Maldonado.

- **Transport** To save time, travel by plane on certain parts of the trip. The remaining travel can be done by bus. There is the option of taking the train between Puno and Cusco. Part of the trip to Machu Picchu from Cusco is by train.

- **Booking ahead** Tours to Machu Picchu and a visit to a jungle eco-lodge.

- **For a shorter trip** Start your tour in Arequipa, spending one day there before heading to Puno, on the bank of Lake Titicaca. Follow the remainder of the itinerary from there.

Day 1: Lima
Choose one of the days as detailed in the two-day visit to Lima above.

Day 2: Paracas
Take a bus (3 hours) south to the town of Paracas, which sits on a bay that is popular with kite surfers due to the strong winds and calm water. If you prefer, break up your trip to Paracas with a brief stop in **Chincha Alta** *(p128)*, the hub of Afro-Peruvian culture. Here you can tour the **Hacienda San José** *(p128)*, a former sugar plantation built in the 17th century.

Day 3: Reserva Nacional de Paracas and Islas Ballestas
Visit the **Reserva Nacional de Paracas** *(p131)*, a protected area where jagged desert cliffs meet Pacific waters teeming with flamingos and pelicans. Afterwards, jump on a boat and tour the **Islas Ballestas** *(p129)*, which are home to Humboldt penguins and sea lions. After lunch, take a bus to Ica and stay in one of the hotels at the **Huacachina** oasis *(p129)*.

Day 4: Huacachina
Jump in a dune buggy for an exhilarating ride up and down the sand dunes surrounding **Huacachina** *(p129)*. Test your balance and ride the dunes on a sand-board. Later, tour one of the several wineries and **pisco bodegas** *(p130)* around Ica. In the evening, take a bus to Nazca (2 hours).

Day 5: Nazca
Fly over the **Nazca Lines** *(p134)*, the giant, mysterious geoglyphs

Brightly colored Peruvian handicrafts for sale at a stall in Lima

that were etched into the desert floor hundreds of years ago. After a quick lunch, jump on a bus for the 9-hour trip to Arequipa, which is known as the "white city" because many buildings are constructed with sillar from the nearby volcanoes.

Day 6: Arequipa
Explore Arequipa's **colonial center** *(p138)*, including the elegant **Plaza de Armas** *(p139)*, colonial mansions, and the **Monasterio de Santa Catalina** *(p142)*, a monastery founded in 1580 by a rich widow. Try local cuisine like *rocoto relleno* (stuffed pepper) or *chupe de camarones* (shrimp soup) at one of the typical *picanteria* restaurants.

A cloister in the Monasterio de Santa Catalina, Arequipa

For practical information on travelling around Italy, see pp324–29

Stone terraces of mist-cloaked Machu Picchu in El Valle Sangrado, in the Inca Heartland

Day 7–8: Cañón del Colca

Leave Arequipa for a two-day tour into the **Cañón del Colca** (p146), one of the deepest canyons in the world where condors glide high above the valley floor on thermal currents. At night, relax in the **La Calera** hot springs (p146). On returning to Arequipa, take a 5-hour night bus to **Puno** (p149).

Day 9: Lake Titicaca

From Puno, jump on a boat and head out onto **Lake Titicaca** (p150) to explore the floating **Islas Uros** and **Isla Taquile** (p154), which is the home of some 350 Quechua-speaking families known for their arts and crafts. Upon return to Puno, catch a night bus to Cusco.

To extend your trip...
Spend a night on Isla Taquile to learn more about the unique island way of life, or rent a kayak and guide for a multi-day tour of the lake's islands.

Day 10–11: Cusco

See the two-day Cusco itinerary.

Day 12: Machu Picchu

Visit the spectacular Inca citadel of **Machu Picchu** (p180), a UNESCO World Heritage site perched on top of a mountain surrounded by tropical forests. At Machu Picchu take in the superb Inca stonework at the **Temple of the Sun** (p184), while wandering among its terraces cut into the mountain. Book your trip to Machu Picchu well in advance. At the end of your visit, make the return journey to Cusco by train.

To extend your trip...
Spend four days and three nights hiking the **Inca Trail** (p174) from Cusco to Machu Picchu. Hikes on the Inca Trail need to be booked in advance.

Day 13–14: Río Tambopata or Río Madre de Dios

Catch an early morning flight (30 mins) to Puerto Maldonado, where you can then travel up either the **Río Tambopata** or **Río Madre de Dios** (p266) to the jungle lodge of your choice. Here, you'll see, and hear, a wide variety of wildlife including colorful macaws, capybaras, howler monkeys, river otters and even piranhas. During your stay, visit indigenous shamans to understand the relationship locals have with the rainforest. On your last day, return to Puerto Maldonado and fly back to Lima.

To extend your trip...
Add an extra day or two at your jungle lodge, providing a better chance of seeing wildlife. Travel from Cusco by road and boat into the **Reserva de la Biosfera de Manu** (p265), one of the most biologically diverse spots on earth. Visiting Manu can only be done in a guided tour and it is best to visit over five or seven days.

A view of Lake Titicaca, Canyon Country

Putting Peru on the Map

With the Pacific Ocean lapping its 1,500-mile (2,400-km) coast, Peru shares borders with Ecuador and Colombia to the north, Brazil and Bolivia to the east, and Chile to the south. The third largest country in Latin America, its 500,000 sq miles (1,300,000 sq km) encompasses soaring mountains, vast canyons, coastal desert, and lush jungle, with dozens of microclimates in between. Peru has a population of 29 million, more than half of whom live in coastal areas. Lima, the capital, is home to 8 million people, while a million live in Arequipa, the second largest city. Other major cities include Trujillo, Piura, Iquitos, Cusco, Cajamarca, Puno, and Ayacucho.

Key

- Highway
- Main road
- Minor road
- Railroad
- International border
- Regional border

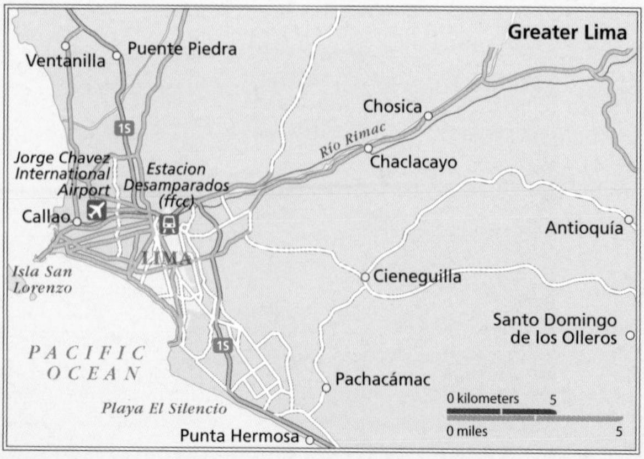

0 kilometers 150
0 miles 100

See inset map below

Greater Lima

0 kilometers 5
0 miles 5

For map symbols *see back flap*

ECUADOR

Santo Domingo de los Colorados · Manta · Quevedo · Guayaquil · Ambato · Golfo de Guayaquil · Cuenca · Machala · Tumbes · Loja · TUMBES · Talara · PIURA · Sullana · Paita · Chulucanas · San Ignacio · Catacaos · Piura · Bahía de Sechura · AMAZONAS · Río Pastaza · Río Santiago · Yurimaguas · Moyobamba · Chachapoyas · Tarapoto · LAMBAYEQUE · Río Marañón · Chiclayo · CAJAMARCA · Cajamarca · SAN MARTÍN · PE · LA LIBERTAD · Trujillo · PANAMERICAN HIGHWAY · ANCASH · Caraz · Tingo María · Chimbote · Huaraz · Huánuco · Cerro de Pasco · Barranca · Churín · Huacho · Huaral · Santa Rosa de Quives · LIMA CITY · LIMA · Chincha Alta · Pisco · Carhua

PACIFIC OCEAN

Ventanilla · Puente Piedra · Chosica · Río Rímac · Chaclacayo · Jorge Chavez International Airport · Estacion Desamparados (ffcc) · Callao · LIMA · Isla San Lorenzo · Antioquía · Cieneguilla · Santo Domingo de los Olleros · PACIFIC OCEAN · Pachacámac · Playa El Silencio · Punta Hermosa

COLOMBIA

Río Curaray
Río Napo
Río Putumayo
Río Japurá
Capana
Río Amazonas
Río Ica
Fonte Boa

Río Tigre
Río Corrientes
Iquitos
Río Amazonas
Amatuará
Río Juruá

L O R E T O
Río Marañón
Nauta
Tabatinga
Río Jutaí

BRAZIL

Rodrigues
Río Ucayali
Río Juruá

R U
Pucallpa
Río Pachitea
Cruzeiro do Sul
364
Feijó

16A
16B
HUÁNUCO
UCAYALI

Central and Southern America

MEXICO
BELIZE
HAITI
GUATEMALA
HONDURAS
NICARAGUA
COSTA RICA
PANAMA
VENEZUELA
GUYANA
FRENCH GUIANA
COLOMBIA
SURINAME
ECUADOR
PERU
BRAZIL
BOLIVIA
PARAGUAY
CHILE
ARGENTINA
URUGUAY
PACIFIC OCEAN
ATLANTIC OCEAN

PASCO

Río Altopurús
Río Iaco
Río Acre

MADRE DE DIOS
Río Manú
Río Piedras
Río Madre de Dios
Riberalta
13
8

Tarma
Río Tambo
JUNÍN
Río Urubamba
3B
35
Huancayo
Huancavelica
HUANCAVELICA
Ayacucho
CUSCO
Ollantaytambo
Puerto Maldonado
26
BOLIVIA
8

Andahuaylas
Cusco
Río Apurímac
35
Sicuani
Río Inambari
PUNO
16

Ica
AYACUCHO
APURIMAC
ICA
Nazca
26A
15
Juliaca
30
Huancané
3

PANAMERICAN HIGHWAY
Río Ocoña
AREQUIPA
30A
Puno
Lake Titicaca
32N
Huarina
26

Aplao
30B
Arequipa
Mazo Cruz
35
La Paz

Camaná
15
30
MOQUEGUA
Cochabamba

Mollendo
15
Fundición
34
TACNA
El Ayro
Oruro
1
4

Boca del Río
17
Tacna

A PORTRAIT OF PERU

Peru conjures up images of the Inca citadel of Machu Picchu, but there's much more to see. Besides archaeological sites, there are several natural treasures, including the world's deepest canyons and the highest navigable lake. Peru is also a racial melting pot, a mix of indigenous peoples, mestizos, and African, Chinese, and Japanese migrants, whose profound cultural influence is everywhere.

Even before the Spanish arrived in the 1500s, Peru was a collage of cultures determined by its geography. Anthropologists and analysts have likened it to an archipelago, with population pockets scattered across the diverse and isolated regions. The soaring Andes exert the greatest influence on climate, topography, flora and fauna, and best illustrate the division in society: the mountains remain a refuge for impoverished indigenous peoples, who practise subsistence farming.

Dozens of rivers flow from the Andes down to the narrow ribbon of desert coastline but only about a third of them contain water year-round, thus emphasizing the importance of seasonal rains. The coast is wealthier, has better infrastructure, and is more industrialized and urbanized. This glimmer of opportunity has led to an influx of rural poor from the highlands, generating *pueblos jovenes,* or young towns, around Lima which usually lack water, electricity, and other basic services.

The Amazon accounts for more than half of Peru's territory, and one-quarter of the world's jungle. Towns are few and rivers are the thoroughfares. An estimated 5 percent of the population lives in the jungle, with 55 ethno-linguistic groups.

Striking, blue-painted carved balconies, Cusco

◄ Locals enjoying a meal during Holy Week, Ayacucho

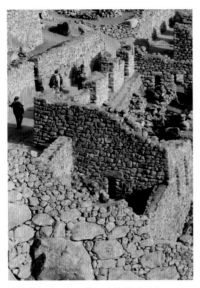

Machu Picchu, the most popular tourist destination in Peru

The Economy

To a large extent the economy reflects Peru's geography – mineral-rich mountains and coastal waters brimming with sea-life. Mining and fishing, as well as agriculture and tourism, dominate and account for most of the employment and investment. Mining supplies almost half of export earnings. Antamina in Ancash is one of the world's biggest copper-zinc mines and Peru is the world's fifth largest gold producer. It is the world's second largest fishing nation after China, and the leading fishmeal producer. Thirty-three percent of the population is employed in agriculture. Tourism is booming with some 1.5 million tourists visiting Peru each year. Machu Picchu remains the main attraction, PromPeru, the tourism and marketing board, is promoting other destinations too. Today, nature tourism draws ever increasing numbers. Peru is home to 84 of the earth's 114 life zones, while almost 10 percent of the world's mammals and 20 percent of birds are found here. The country has 25,000 species of plants, 30 percent of which are found only in Peru.

Politics

The president, who is head of both the state and the government, is elected for a five-year term and cannot be re-elected for a second consecutive term. The government is divided into three branches: the Executive, comprising a Council of Ministers appointed by the president, the Congress, which consists of 120 representatives, and the Judiciary. Peru is divided into 24 departments (*departamentos*), sometimes referred to as regions, and one constitutional province (*provincia constitucional*), Lima-Callao. Regional authorities, including prefects and governors, and the

Agriculture provides the majority of employment in Peru

President Alan Garcia with his supporters in 2006

became the first democratically elected president of Quechua descent. Both Toledo and Fujimori owed their election to their position as outsiders, untainted by the political system.

The People

Peru has a clear-cut class structure with indigenous peoples at the bottom, and the descendants of the Spanish at the top. The rich are very rich, and the poor very poor. A middle class is only just beginning to evolve. Political and economic power has been in the hands of a small white and Mestizo (of mixed European and indigenous descent) elite for centuries.

Almost half the population is indigenous and poor. The majority speak Quechua, although Aymara is spoken near Lake Titicaca. There are different languages in the Amazon. Sixty-four percent of rural residents live in the sierra, which has 10 of Peru's 12 poorest provinces. In the central regions of Huancavelica, Ayacucho, and Apurímac 44 percent live in extreme poverty. The indigenous communities were hardest hit by the armed conflict that plagued Peru for

administrative system, come directly under the Executive. Political parties form around individuals and rarely last longer than the person's political career. The one exception is the left-leaning Alianza Popular Revolucionaria Americana (APRA), Peru's oldest and best-established political party founded in 1924.

With President Belaunde Terry's election in 1980, Peru returned to democratic leadership after years of military rule. In 1985, the 36-year-old Alan Garcia became the region's youngest leader and was dubbed the "Latino Kennedy," because of his charisma. He inherited a country in deep economic crisis and in the grip of a guerrilla war waged by the Maoist Shining Path. By the time Garcia left office in 1990, inflation was rampant at 7,500 percent, the insurgents' campaign had intensified, and poverty had soared.

Traditionally dressed indigenous man

Alberto Fujimori's presidency ushered in a decade that saw a dramatic upturn in the economy and significant curbing of guerrilla activity. However, his increasingly authoritarian stance, an economic slump in the late 1990s, and allegations of corruption led to his ousting. In 2001, Alejandro Toledo, the shoeshine-boy-turned Stanford-educated economist,

Women selling vegetables at a local market

almost two decades. From 1980 to 1990, an estimated 200,000 people were driven from their homes, and an estimated 70,000 were killed, many in the department of Ayacucho.

By and large, the people are friendly and enormously patriotic. Participants in an annual poll conducted around Independence Day unfailingly rejected the idea of having another nationality, with 90 percent declaring themselves happy to be Peruvian. Corruption tops the list of what they are most ashamed of, with poverty coming fourth or fifth.

Visitors enjoying breakfast in a Peruvian hotel

Peruvians will hustle for any advantage and they are persistent. At the same time, they are reserved and polite. Family is sacred, often united economically and socially. Grandparents, married daughters, sons, and their children often share the same house. A nanny or servant is the norm in middle and upper class households. Despite its complex multicultural mix, or perhaps because of

Large statues of saints are carried through Cusco's streets during the Corpus Christi procession

it, discrimination is not uncommon. Upscale bars in Lima and some country clubs have been known to refuse admission to non-whites or members of a particular race or religion. Nicknames, such as negro (black), gringo (white skinned), chino (Asian), and cholo (Indian) exist, and can be used affectionately or as put-downs. In addition, there are local identities, such as a Limeño from Lima, a Cuzqueño from Cusco, and a Huaracino from Huaraz.

Although Roman Catholicism is the official religion, the constitution permits the practice of any religion. Nine out of ten people regard themselves as Catholic. No village, no matter how remote or tiny, is without a church. Peruvian Catholicism, however, does incorporate Andean elements. When conversions first began, churches were often built on ancient foundations and many Christian holidays were made to coincide with existing festivals.

Education

There is widespread belief among the young that worthwhile education can only be obtained overseas. As a result, more than 400,000 Peruvians leave the country each year, most between the ages of 15 and 29. Primary education is free and compulsory, but in many rural areas textbooks and desks are scarce and parents struggle to provide their children with pen or notepad. Private schools are out of reach for most due to the high fees.

Most urban youth are likely to finish secondary education, but the vast rural majority does not. By law each provincial capital must have a public secondary school, yet the best are concentrated in the major cities, particularly Lima. Not surprisingly, a relatively high percentage of urban youth attend post-secondary school.

Arts and Sports

Peruvians have a rich tradition of expression. Ancient cultures transmitted their stories orally, often through song. Since the 19th century, however, writers have felt compelled to put pen to paper and scrutinize society. These include Ricardo Palma *(see p82)* and Clorinda Matto de Turner (1852–1909), whose controversial *Aves sin nido (Birds without a Nest)* focused on the love affair between a white man and an indigenous woman. Many regard Cesar Vallejo as Peru's finest poet and Mario Vargas Llosa as its best novelist, but there are others, such as Jose Maria Arguedas, Manuel Scorza, Jaime Bayly, and Diego Trelles Paz.

Formal works of art by Cusco School painters and modern artists such as Fernando de Szyszlo, Joaquin Roca Rey, and Victor Delfín constitute only a part of Peru's artistic traditions. Just as vibrant are expressions of folk art that testify to the peoples' creativity and ability to make the most of natural elements.

The easily recognizable and restful Andean flute music (the famous "El Condor Pasa") has drawn fans from across the globe. Also popular is the up-tempo Afro-Peruvian music of

Shipibo artisan working on pottery design

Susana Baca and Eva Ayllon, which has its roots in the communities of black slaves brought to coastal Peru in the 1500s.

Like their Latino neighbors, soccer is a national obsession, even though the team hasn't qualified for the World Cup since 1982. Several Peruvians play in the European League including Claudio Pizarro and Nolberto Solano.

As popular is women's volleyball, and Peru is today ranked number 12 in the world, and second in South America.

Bullfighting has gripped the imagination since it was introduced in 1542. More than 500 festivals are held every October all over Peru, with Lima's Lord of Miracles being the largest and most important. No patron saint's day is complete without *la corrida de toros*.

Native musicians playing traditional instruments

Claudio Pizarro, a popular soccer player

Peru's Landscape & Wildlife

Peru is located in the heart of the richest and most diverse region of the world, the Tropical Andes, which contains about a sixth of all plant life in less than one percent of the world's land area. Very few countries can rival the immense diversity of flora and fauna that lies within its borders, spread out between 11 eco-regions with a unique combination of climate, geographic conditions, and wildlife. The country is home to 84 of the world's 114 Holdridge life zones. Peru has two ecoregions that are almost exclusively located in its territory and are difficult to find elsewhere – the Peruvian Cold Ocean Current and the Coastal Pacific Desert. The Equatorial Dry Forest, unique to Africa and South America, is also found here.

Huascarán, part of the western Andes, is the highest peak in Peru and the fourth highest in South America.

Peruvian Cold Ocean Current

The Humboldt Current extends 621 miles (1,000 km) off the coast of Peru, bringing cold, nutrient-rich water up to the surface of the sea, creating one of the most productive marine systems in the world.

Guano birds, producers of guano fertilizer, are the Peruvian pelican (right), Peruvian booby, and guanay cormorant.

Seals, such as the Juan Fernandez fur seal and South American fur seal, and sea lions are common.

The Humboldt penguin is an endangered species that breeds in coastal Peru. It nests on the islands and rocky coasts by burrowing holes in guano.

Puna or High Andean Plain

Located at over 12,500 ft (3,800 m), the plains are classified into three types – wet puna, located mainly in nothern Peru and along the eastern Andes, moist puna, found in most of Peru, and dry puna in south Peru.

Vicuña have been protected since Inca times. They produce small amounts of very fine wool which is highly sought after.

Queñual are the highest growing trees in the world. Their copper-colored bark continually peels off.

Andean condors are the largest flying land birds in the Western Hemisphere with a wingspan of more than 10 ft (3 m).

Coastal Pacific Desert

One of the driest spots on the planet, this strip of desert is brought to life by moisture carried in fog and low-lying clouds each winter. It has a highly seasonal ecosystem that adapts to severe dry conditions during summer and humidity in winter.

Sechura fox, also called Peruvian desert fox, is the smallest of the South American *zorros*.

Peruvian thick-knee, commonly known as *huerequeque*, is a large, unmistakable nocturnal bird.

Reserva de Lomas de Lachay Nacional was established in 1977 and is the only protected area in the coastal hills of Peru. It is home to 74 plant and 55 bird species, some on the verge of extinction.

Montane Cloud Forest

This tropical ecoregion lies on the eastern side of the Andes between 11,500 ft (3,500 m) and 1,900 ft (600 m). Cloud and mist frequently come in contact with vegetation, allowing mosses, ferns, and orchids to flourish.

Cock of the Rock, locally known as *tunky*, are found close to rocky areas, where they build their nests. The males have orange or reddish colors.

Hummingbirds are tiny, nectar-drinking birds. Peru has 127 species that range from sea level to 15,000 ft (4,500 m).

The Andean spect-acled bear is South America's only bear species. Locally known as *ucumari*, this endangered animal normally lives in the mountain forest.

Amazon Rainforest

Peru's Amazon jungle encompasses almost 60 percent of its territory. With an average temperature of 65–97º F (18–36º C), and wet climatic and geographical conditions, the forest has incomparable biodiversity.

Paiche is the world's largest freshwater fish reaching lengths of more than 10 ft (3 m). It weighs up to 441 lb (200 kg) and is a prize catch.

Macaws and parrots in Peru make up 49 species of the world's 354 Psittacidae bird family members, including the beautiful blue-and-yellow macaw.

The red uakari monkey is an arboreal creature that lives mainly in the primary forests. It has been spotted on the border of Peru and Brazil.

The Biodiversity of Peru

A paradise for nature-lovers, Peru's biodiversity is guarded through the 71 national parks, reserves, sanctuaries, and other categories of natural protected areas that have been created throughout the country. Peru holds world records in highest diversity for birds (1,816 species), butterflies (3,532 species), and orchids (3,500 species). The country also has a huge number of mammals (462 species), and amphibians (379 species). There are at least 6,288 endemic species of plants and animals.

Key

- Amazon Rainforest
- Cloud Forest
- Equatorial Dry Forest
- Highlands and Puna
- Coastal Desert

Santuario Nacional Manglares de Tumbes, on the Ecuadorian border, covers the coastal mangrove area. It is the only place in Peru where American crocodiles are found.

Reserva de Biósfera del Noroeste covers four protected areas: Santuario Nacional Manglares de Tumbes, Reserva Nacional de Tumbes, Parque Nacional Cerros de Amotape, and Coto de Caza El Angolo *(see p237),* which protects the biggest Equatorial Dry Forest in the world.

Parque Nacional Tingo Maria

Reserva Nacional Junin

Parque Nacional Huascarán *(see pp206–7)* protects the Cordillera Blanca, the highest tropical mountain range in the world. Peru's highest mountain, the Huascarán (22,200 ft/6,768 m) is also located here. Created in 1975, the park protects 50 snowcapped peaks, 663 glaciers, 296 lakes, and 41 rivers.

Reserva Nacional de Paracas *(see p127),* created in 1975, is the country's only protected area that encompasses both terrestrial and marine ecosystems. It features unique flora and fauna such as 216 bird, 19 mammal, 52 fish, and 6 reptile species. It is a haven for a variety of migratory birds and is recognized by the Ramsar Convention as a wetland of international importance.

Reserva Nacional Pacaya-Samiria *(see p259)* is the largest conservation area in Peru. It can be reached from Iquitos by boat. Among the protected wildlife here are 449 bird, 102 mammal, and 256 fish species.

Unsurpassed Delights

Peru, with its world records in orchid, bird, and butterfly species is perfect for ecotourism. New species are continually being discovered every year in the cloud forests, Amazon jungles, and the Andes. The protected areas provide opportunities for visitors to observe them.

Orchids are found all over Peru but mainly in the Montane Cloud Forest ecoregion. They grow at altitudes of 328 ft (100 m) to 16,000 ft (4,800 m). *Phragmipedium peruvianum*, discovered here, is considered the greatest orchid find in the last 100 years.

Butterflies in Peru make 20 percent of the world's species. Pakitza in Parque Nacional Manu, with 1,300 species, is the world's richest butterfly community.

World records for the maximum number of birds in one place (650) and the greatest number seen in a single day (361), were recorded in Reserva Nacional de Tambopata *(see pp266–7)* and Parque Nacional Manu respectively.

Parque Nacional Cordillera Azul has the highest number of habitats with around 6,000 species of plants and animals.

Curaray

Río Amazonas

Río Ucayali

Río Alto Purús

Río Urubamba

Río Madre de Dios

Parque Nacional Manu

Parque Nacional Bahuaja-Sonene

Parque Nacional Titicaca

Reserva Nacional de Tambopata is a lowland reserve with diverse plants and animals.

Santuario Histórico de Machu Picchu *(see pp180–81)* is not just famous for its Inca sites. It also has 10 percent of Peru's total biodiversity, including 9 Holdridge life zones and 200 orchids, and an average of 90 tree species per hectare.

| 0 kilometers | 300 |
| 0 miles | 200 |

Indigenous Peoples of Peru

Peru has the largest indigenous population of South America, with almost half its nearly 29 million people being of native descent. Living in the Amazonian Basin or in remote mountain villages, they still dress in their traditional style, observe ancient customs, and continue to speak Quechua, Aymara, or other languages. The Ashaninka, Aguaruna, and Shipibo-Conibo, who developed elaborate shamanistic traditions, are the main ethnic groups of the Amazon. The Quechua, Q'eros, and Aymara, who were great builders, live in the Andean region.

Shipibo woman sewing patterns on to a cloth. The graphic designs are said to be inspired by impressions induced by ayahuasca, a hallucinogenic drug used by shamans. They work with cotton muslin usually in black, white, and beige.

Musicians with flutes and drums accompany the dancers.

The Shipibo People

The Shipibo have been living in the Amazon for over a 1,000 years. Their universe is a highly patterned one. The intricate geometric designs, which appear in their textiles, pottery, homes, tools, and even body-art, are believed to be spiritual in origin and a manifestation of shamanic visions.

Handpainted skirts, with a distinct vine pattern, are worn by the women.

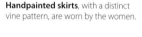

The Aymara Nation is the second largest Andean ethnic group. About 2.3 million live in the southeastern region of Peru in the Altiplano and around Lake Titicaca, Bolivia, northern Chile, and northeastern Argentina. The Aymaras are presumed to descend from the Tiahuanaco, a technologically-advanced culture that flourished during the Middle Horizon period (AD 600–1000).

Ashaninka is the biggest indigenous nation in the Amazon, with 65,000 people living in the central jungle region of Peru. They have a long history of struggle against colonization, slavery, and the *Shining Path Maoist* group.

Pachamama (Mother Earth), wife of Pachacamac (Earth-Maker), being worshiped with varied offerings. She has been the supreme deity of the Andean indigenous communities since Inca times and is also worshiped in Bolivia, Ecuador, northern Chile, and northwestern Argentina.

Q'eros inhabit the northeast of Cusco at a height of almost 16,000 ft (5,000 m). Living in isolation, they have preserved the Inca traditions for almost 1,000 years.

Quechua is the largest indigenous group, about 13 million, living in the Andean region. It is also the name of Peru's second official language spoken by no less than 3 million. Its origins trace back to the Inca period.

Lamas is situated 13 miles (20 km) northwest of Tarapoto. This small settlement in the high jungle is home to the descendants of the Chanca tribe that escaped from the Andes in the 15th century after having been defeated by the Incas. Also called Quechua-Lamistas, they have a distinct lifestyle, a mix of jungle and Andean culture.

Fight sequences are an integral part of all Shipibo dances.

Importance of Plants

Various plants have been used in Peru over the centuries in religious ceremonies as offerings to gods, as medicines, as well as in shamanistic rituals. The Andean people have traditionally used the sacred coca leaves, also known for making cocaine, as a natural energizer and for its curative qualities. Brews made with *ayahuasca* contain hallucinogenic and purgative properties.

Mapacho (black jungle tobacco) smoke is said to be the food of the plant spirits. The shaman heals by blowing smoke over a patient.

Ayahuasca (the rope of the dead) is a giant vine used by shamans for medicinal and religious purposes.

Coca leaves have been used since pre-Columbian times as offerings to different deities, and to cure diverse ailments such as altitude sickness.

The Culture of the Incas

At its height in the 15th and 16th centuries, the Inca Empire encompassed thousands of square miles, stretching almost the entire length of the Andes. The Incas were audacious engineers, building spectacular mountain-top citadels. They developed elaborate farming terraces, sustaining their crops by canal and drainage systems. Their social structure was extremely rigid with the emperor enjoying absolute power, and revered as a living god. The Incas worshiped the sun, moon, earth, and mountains. Animals, such as the condor and puma, were also considered sacred.

The Incas' sun and moon calendar provided timings for agriculture

Cult of the Sun

The Incas revered Inti, the Sun God, who nourished the earth and controlled the harvests. The emperor, believed to be the son of the Sun God, made offerings to the sun during religious ceremonies.

The red macaw, a commonly depicted figure.

Inti Raymi (Festival of the Sun) was celebrated annually on June 21, the winter solstice in the Southern Hemisphere. Mummies of nobles were brought into Cusco's main plaza to witness the event. It is still held on June 24 at Sacsayhuamán.

Ancestors were worshipped with offerings of food and drink. Inca mummies were lavishly dressed.

Sacrifice of animals was practised periodically by the Incas. Human sacrifice was reserved for special occasions and only the most beautiful children from the most powerful families were chosen to be sacrificed.

The lower band shows mainly harvesting or floral motifs.

Infusions of ayahuasca and coca leaves were integral to all ceremonies.

Divination played a large part in religious life. Everything, from treating illness to determining the correct sacrifices, was performed by the high priest consulting the oracles, observing the path of a spider in a dish, the position of scattered coca leaves, or by drinking ayahuasca (see p27).

Canal systems were used to divert water from rivers, sometimes many miles away, to the fields. Channels along the terraces directed the rainwater.

Farming

The Incas carved up mountains into vast terraced farmlands. The banks of the terraces were held up by stone walls. In 1500 there was more land in cultivation in the Andes than there is today. They cultivated corn and potatoes, and raised llama and alpaca for food and as pack animals.

The crop terraces at Moray are like an agricultural laboratory in which the Incas experimented with different varieties of plants to help improve their production.

The top section usually depicts a narrative scene which could also be a representation of a real historical event.

The central band comprises a of series of geometric patterns.

Keros (Inca Cups)

These drinking vessels were made of ceramic or wood and were used during ceremonies to drink chicha (corn beer). Their decoration is usually in three distinct bands, each with its own iconography, and with a limited palette of black, red, white, yellow, and orange.

The food technology of the Incas was innovative. They developed the earliest type of freeze-drying: potatoes were left out at night to freeze in the frost and when the water evaporated during the day a dry potato pulp remained, called *chuño*.

Record Keeping

It is believed the Incas had no formal writing tradition. No documents, letters, books, or evidence of libraries have been uncovered. However, anthropologists have found many *quipus*, strings which were used as a record-keeping device through a complicated system of knots. Made of wool or cotton strings fastened at one end to a cross cord, each *quipu* was different from the other in size or color. The simple or compound knots and their size and colors represented details of crop measures, thefts, and debts, and possibly events. This device was perhaps inherited from the Wari.

Keeping records with the help of the *quipus*

Traditional *quipu*

Architecture in Peru

Peru's greatest architectural heritage can be seen in its Inca ruins, most famously at Machu Picchu, but there are many other distinctive historical styles. Pre-Inca civilizations have also left their architectural legacy, visible in many archaeological sites around the country. With the arrival of the Spanish came European architectural influences and the building of ornate Colonial churches and mansions that continue to dominate many of the country's urban centers. Lima's cityscape has changed significantly due to the growth of contemporary architecture in its financial and port districts.

The ruins at Sacsayhuamán show the stone blocks used by the Incas

The Post-Classical period saw the Chimú (AD 1000–1470) create northern Peru's architectural marvel: Chan Chan's enormous adobe compound *(see p227)*.

Pre-Inca

Monumental ceremonial mounds dating from as far back as 2500 BC have been found at various sites on the coast, and also at Kotosh *(see p200)*, in the Northern Highlands, where terracing and temple structures were discovered.

Spiral access leading down to the underground aqueducts.

Stone and flat rock have been used to build this complicated sub-terranean system.

The Nazca Civilization built many aqueducts for irrigation purposes and some are still in use. The Cantalloc Aqueduct is the most famous.

Huaca de la Luna's Moche pyramid *(see p227)* has some wonderful examples of intricate polychrome murals and reliefs.

Inca

The Incas set themselves apart with their superior architectural stonework, city building, and landscaping. The undecorated and precise style is characterized by immense stone foundations and mortarless walls.

Trapezoidal window directs the sun's light.

Walls made of stone blocks snugly fitted together.

The many-sided stone blocks fit together like a jigsaw without use of mortar

The Temple of the Sun, Machu Picchu *(see p184)* is tapered so that on the winter solstice, the sun's rays illuminate the central stone through a window.

Colonial

Once the Spanish conquistadores had established their military might, they ordered the construction of churches in praise of God instead of the Inca pagan figures, thus creating places of worship for their new converts. Concurrent with these religious imperatives was the establishment of grand mansions, with cloistered courtyards and high ceilings, for the wealthy European settlers. Many of these architectural styles can be seen in Lima, Cusco, Arequipa, and Trujillo among other cities.

Iron House, designed by Gustave Eiffel, was built out of steel in Paris before being shipped to Iquitos in 1890.

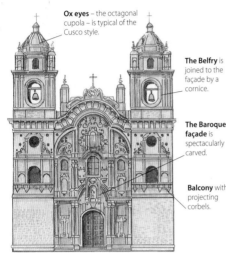

Ox eyes – the octagonal cupola – is typical of the Cusco style.

The Belfry is joined to the façade by a cornice.

The Baroque façade is spectacularly carved.

Balcony with projecting corbels.

Iglesia de la Compañía *(see p161)* shows the influence of the Cusco School, a 17th-century movement that blended European and indigenous elements to create a new decorative style.

Monasterio de Santa Catalina *(see pp142–5)* is a beautiful example of Jesuit religious architecture, which displays a notably Spanish Mudéjar influence in its shady courtyards and cupolas.

Contemporary

Although most emphasis, as well as finance, is placed on the restoration of older buildings in Peru, some new designs are springing up, particularly in Lima's financial district of San Isidro and the port area of Miraflores.

Blue glass is used on the façade.

The 25-story hotel has great ocean views.

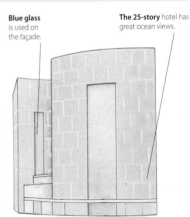

Larcomar *(see p83)* in Lima is a large and modern shopping mall with terraces carved out of the side of the Miraflores cliffs.

Lima Marriott *(see p275)* is the city's tallest building. With its glass façade it is, along with other buildings, helping to transform the skyline of this urban coastal area.

Music and Dance

Music and dance are an essential feature of life in Peru; local and national festivals are celebrated with the lilting, infectious beat of the *huayno* or the teasing and coquettish national dance, the *marinera*. The style of music and dance, as well as the instruments used, varies regionally and reflects the landscape and way of life. Generally speaking, an aural distinction can be made between the melancholy, wind-based music of the sierras and the lively, drum-based rhythms of the coast. But, within these geographical areas there are many more localized variations.

Música Criolla has a mix of African and Spanish elements

The marinera mimics the mating ritual of birds. A female dancer marks the beat with a white handkerchief held above her head, and shakes the folds of her skirt, while a suitor struts around her.

Huayno

Though the *huayno* developed in the rural Altiplano, it has now spread nationwide. The lively rhythms encourage couples to dance through the streets and can be very raucous when accompanied by alcohol.

Costumes, colorful and traditional, include skirts for girls and caps for boys.

Couples perform movements such as the *zapateo*, a rhythmic footwork to mark time.

Musical Instruments

Many Peruvian instruments have pre-Columbian roots – evidence of pipes, thought to date back thousands of years, has been found in coastal areas. Before the conquest there were only wind and percussion instruments; with the Spanish, came stringed instruments such as the guitar.

Ocarina is an oval whistle flute made of clay, stone, wood, and large seeds. It produces a haunting sound and can imitate bird calls.

Zampona in Spanish or *sicu* in Quechua, is the Andean panpipe. Comprising any number of reed tubes, each with a different octave, it is bound together by a knotted string or a strap. The two rows of pipes are open at one end and closed at the other.

Charango is a small mandolin created by the indigenous population of Peru and Bolivia in the early Colonial days of the 1500s. It is still very popular throughout the southern Andes, including Argentina and Chile.

Son de los Diablos, or the Devil's Dance, is a popular Afro-Peruano dance performed with much gusto during the Carnaval in Lima and the surrounding areas. It symbolizes cultural resistance. The accompanying orchestra plays the guitar, *cajón*, and the *quijada* or donkey's jaw.

Costumes comprise smocks, trousers, masks with feathers, tails, cord shoes, cloak, and numerous bells.

Susana Baca, whose song on a 1995 compilation album, *The Soul of Black Peru* produced by David Byrne of Talking Heads, caused an international sensation.

Eva Ayllon, one of the foremost Afro-Peruvian musicians, began singing in school competitions and later on radio and television. Today, she is a composer and singer of international acclaim. She has over 25 albums to her credit.

Musica afro-peruano

The country's black population largely resides in the central coastal region and produces some of the most captivating music. It has become an essential part of Peruvian culture, thanks to its lively rhythms and strong percussion.

Cajón, crafted from a wooden box with a sound hole at the back, provides another percussion element to the music of the coast. The musician sits on top and beats on the front surface with the palms.

Andean harp is a 36-stringed instrument with a large boat-shaped and half-conical sound box. It creates a uniquely rich and powerful bass. It is an essential part of most bands in the highlands.

Quena, a delicate, reed-like, notched flute, is a versatile instrument. Once made from llama or condor bone, today it is often made from wood or bamboo. It produces a distinctive melancholic tone.

Art and Literature

Little evidence of pre-Columbian literature or fine arts remains, thanks to the dominance of the oral tradition in Inca society and to the obliteration of Inca culture by the Spanish. However, native Peruvians gradually began to appropriate European artistic and literary styles in order to resist their Colonial oppressors. After independence, these art forms were increasingly used to analyze issues of race and identity. Peruvian art and literature is a combination of its diverse culture, and today, a rich and varied body of work reflects the changing sentiments with regard to national identity, politics, and issues related to ethnicity and gender.

Cusco School painting of Saint Joseph with the young Christ

Art

When the Spanish arrived in Peru during the 16th century, they brought with them a number of European artists who were commissioned to undertake religious works to adorn the interiors of churches and monasteries throughout the country. A number of examples of these works of art can still be seen, particularly in cities such as Lima, Cusco, and Arequipa.

As demand increased, the colonizers began to teach their techniques to local indigenous artists and there began a new pictorial interpretation of Peruvian life, dominated by Catholic and regal imagery. In the 17th century, a group of largely anonymous native artists, which later became popularly known as the Cusco School (see p171), began to blend this religious iconography with indigenous motifs to create a new and popular art form. Initially, under the tutelage of the Spaniards, these artists painted devotional scenes, using classical Spanish and Flemish techniques, and incorporated Andean flora and fauna, customs, and traditions. The Cusco School went on to dominate the Peruvian artistic tradition for the next 200 years.

The early 20th century saw artists such as Francisco Fierro (1807–79) and José Sabogal (1888–1956) contribute to a new Indigenista movement, which recognized the importance of Andean culture and sought to portray typical events and customs of contemporary Peru. Later in the century artists returning from Europe began to combine national themes with more international styles as is evident from the works of Fernando de Szyszlo (b.1925), who combined abstract expressionism with pre-Columbian motifs and iconography – thereby pushing the Peruvian world of art towards modernism.

The country's current economy has allowed the arts to flourish and several Peruvian painters have achieved international acclaim. They include Gerardo Chávez, Fernando de Szyszlo, and Ramiro Llona, as well as the sculptor Victor Delfín, whose gigantic sculpture, *El Beso*, is a highlight of the Parque del Amor (see p83) in Lima's Miraflores district.

El Beso, the giant kissing statue by Victor Delfín in Lima's Parque del Amor

Painting titled *Arcoiris* by Pablo Amaringo

Usko Ayar School of Art

Established in 1984, by Pablo Amaringo, a self-taught artist from the Amazon region, the Usko Ayar has been recognized as a Not-for-Profit Cultural Organization (with some financial help from the Finnish government). Under his own roof, Amaringo – a former shaman – has given free instruction to more than 700 students who create unusual, vibrant and visionary paintings depicting the landscapes, myths, as well as the diverse flora and fauna of the jungle in colorful and meticulous detail.

Peruvian author and Nobel Prize winner, Mario Vargas Llosa

Literature

The tradition of Colonial literature in Peru began with the arrival of Garcilaso de la Vega from Spain. He chronicled his impressions of the New World and Inca Empire in *Royal Commentaries of the Incas* (1609). Later that century, a different perspective was presented in *Nueva Cronica y Buen Gobierno*, an account of Spanish abuses on the continent, written to King Philip III of Spain by Guaman Poma de Ayala, a native descendant of the Incas from the Huamanga region in the southern Peruvian Andes. The persuasive 1,200-page tract, with full pages of intricate illustrations, sought to convince the Spanish to rethink their devastating methods of colonization.

The late 19th and early 20th century saw many educated Peruvian writers, often urban and socially privileged, taking up the cause of the indigenous population, whose oppression was the focus of the works of Ciro Alegría (1909–67). Alegría's novel *El Mundo es Ancho y Ajeno*, written in 1941, analyzed the humiliations suffered by the Latin American indigenous population. Clorinda Matto de Turner (1852–1909), who embraced indigenous culture, spoke out on behalf of women. Her 1889 novel *Aves sin Nido* (*Birds Without a Nest*) dealt with a love affair between a white man and an indigenous woman, and was considered to be extremely controversial. The short stories and poems of José Maria Arguedas – who was brought up in an indigenous community – explore the conflict between the Hispanic community and traditional native cultures.

The 1960s saw open social exploration and criticism of national cultural identity. Alfredo Bryce Echenique expressed the sensibilities of a culturally conflicted generation of educated and liberal minded young Peruvians in the 1970s with *Mundo Para Julius*, which exposed the social differences between classes in Peruvian society.

The most famous Peruvian author, Mario Vargas Llosa (b.1936), awarded the Nobel Prize in Literature in 2010, is considered one of the front-runners of Latin America's literary boom (which also includes writers such as Carlos Fuentes and Gabriel García Márquez from Mexico and Colombia respectively). His novels present a social critique of racial and social hierarchies in the country. His most famous works include *La Ciudad y Los Perros*. Written in 1963, this novel is an account of life in a military academy. The 1969 book *Conversación en la Catedral* deals with life in Peru under the dictatorship of Manuel Odría during the 1950s. Llosa also ran for the country's presidency in 1990 and was defeated by Alberto Fujimori. Another popular contemporary novelist, Beto Ortiz (b.1968), lived in the US for many years after openly criticizing the Fujimori government. His novel, *Maldita Ternura*, written in 2004, gives an inside view of the media world.

Writer Alfredo Bryce Echenique

Popular Titles

La Ciudad y Los Perros by Mario Vargas Llosa was made into a movie of the same name in 1985.

Aves sin Nido, a two-part novel, is the first of three novels written by Clorinda Matto de Turner.

Maldita Ternura, a novel by Beto Ortiz, portrays the area around Parque Kennedy of the 1980s.

Craft and Textiles

Peruvian craft and textiles reflect the diverse identities that evolved from the country's complex cultural and historical formation. Pre-Inca cultures, such as the Chavín, Moche, Nazca, and Chimú, displayed a high quality of craftsmanship in their pottery, sculpture, and textiles. The Incas further developed these skills when they came to dominate the continent. Cultural stories were expressed through artistic means, in ceramic design and weaving, in the absence of the written word. Pre-Columbian traditions survived the conquest and have been appropriated by contemporary artists, thus preserving the indigenous culture. These crafts and textiles add to the mystical nature of the area.

Alpaca and Andean llama wool is woven using traditional pre-Columbian looms, although European spinning wheels are now used commercially.

Chimú textiles were adorned by geometric and zoomorphic designs similar to the wall relief found in Chan Chan (see p227).

Unku or tunic, worn by Inca men, was usually in bright colors and decorated with geometrical motifs.

Traditionally woven rugs are popular souvenirs.

Textiles

Both practical and illustrative, textiles and clothes can communicate status as well as identity. Beautifully woven and using natural dyes, ponchos and belts can indicate a woman's marital status or the standing of a man's family within the community.

Jewelry

Indigenous peoples manipulated the abundant precious metals with great skill, and the Spanish brought with them new techniques.

Metalworking, to create jewelry and other artifacts, dates back to pre-Columbian Peru.

Threads, beads, shells, bones, and seeds, were some of the natural materials used to make jewelry amongst pre-Columbian cultures.

Silver filigree was introduced with the arrival of the Spanish and is still popular.

Ceramics

Peru has produced some of the finest pottery in the world. The excellent pre-Columbian Art Museum in Cusco shows how their aesthetics still pleases the eye.

Traditional Nazca pottery is polychromatic and characterized by birds and animals with mainly feline features.

Miniature clay churches, painted with corn and flowers, are a famous craft of Ayacucho *(see pp196–7)*.

Moche ceramics are delicately painted with extraordinary detail. Some "portrait vessels" have different male faces that are amazingly realistic.

Clay bulls, made in Pucara, are often flasks too and were used during ritual ceremonies conducted by priests.

Artifacts

Regionally distinctive artifacts, such as engraved gourds, gilt-edged mirrors, woven baskets, and hats can be found throughout the country.

Engraved gourds, dating back over 4,000 years, have been found on the southern coast. They were used in ritualistic ceremonies by the Incas.

Peruvian dolls are bright, colorful, and mostly dressed in traditional clothes.

Woodwork

Carved wooden objects are ubiquitous, varying from drums to masks to magical sticks and the intricate *tablas*.

Wooden masks, both humorous and sinister, are painted in bright colors and used during festivals and carnivals.

Tablas, or colorful painted boards showing everyday life and rural activities, are mainly made in Ayacucho.

Wooden plate with intricate Nazca symbols painted in bright natural dyes.

PERU THROUGH THE YEAR

It appears that every day is cause for celebration in Peru, with its estimated 3,000 festivals each year. Although most derive from the Christian calendar introduced by the Spanish, indigenous Andean beliefs are also woven into the fabric of worship. Celebrations honoring patron saints sit side-by-side with fertility and harvest rituals. Marinera, the national dance, along with the Paso horse, the sun, spring, and all manner of saints are celebrated. The religious festivals include processions with masks and colorful costumes. Peru has two distinct seasons. The dry season is more popular with visitors. Although festivals are common to the country during the wet season, the sierra and the jungle see fewer visitors.

Wet Season

December to April are the wettest months though early rains begin in November. Roads and trails in the Andes become impassable. By contrast, the coast is hot and dry, making city dwellers head for the beach. Beaches near Ecuador are warm enough to swim year-round. Day and night temperatures are mild in the mountains. Most mornings are dry with downpours in the afternoons. Frequent showers swell waterways and the Amazon River can rise up to 50 ft (15 m) in the rains. The jungle gets more rain in the dry season than the mountains in the wet season.

November

All Saints' Day and Day of the Dead (Nov 1), Cajamarca. Families bring paper flower crowns to cemeteries, clean their relatives' gravestones, and share food and drink with the departed. In Piura, families illuminate the graveyard with candles and hold a wake until dawn. Parents who have lost a child go to the main plaza and give sweets to children. Across the country, *guaguas* (bread shaped like dolls and horses) are baked for children.

Founding of Puno *(1st week)*. Students organize dances and street parades. On November 5, people act out the Inca Empire's creation, when Manco Capac and Mama Ocllo emerged from the lake.

Orchid bloom

Festival de la Orquídea *(1st week)*, Moyobamba. The festival showcases the orchids of Moyobamba, which has 10 percent of the 3,500 catalogued species.

December

Homenaje a la Libertad Americana *(Dec 2–9)*, Huamanga Province. Athletes from South America descend

Enacting the creation of the Inca Empire, Founding of Puno

for games to celebrate the defeat of the Spanish in the 1824 Battle of Ayacucho.

Yawar Fiesta *(1st week)*, Apurímac region. As part of the Blood Fiesta, a condor representing Andean defiance is tied to a bull's back for a fight unto death.

Feast of the Immaculate Conception *(Dec 7–10)*, Chivay. After the procession celebrating Jesus' conception, men in women's clothing perform a dance in which they abduct the women.

Santurantikuy *(Dec 24)*, Cusco. Meaning "saints for sale," this is one of Peru's largest arts-and-crafts fairs. Artisans gather to sell nativity scenes, religious carvings, and pottery in the main plaza.

Festival of the Negritos *(Dec 24–Jan 19)*, Huánuco. The Brotherhood of the Slaves of Huánuco dance through the streets and wait at the nativity for the arrival of baby Jesus,

Families offering flowers to their loved ones on All Saints' Day

commemorating the day in 1648 when a Spanish noble freed his black slaves.

January
Founding of Iquitos *(Jan 5)*. Day of civic parades and parties that everyone can attend.
Marinera Festival *(Jan/Feb)*, Trujillo. Couples of all ages compete to be named Peru's best *marinera* dancers.

February
Virgen de la Candelaria *(Feb 2–20)*, Puno. This is the most important religious celebration. Masses, dance contests, banquets, and a procession featuring remarkable masks and costumes are spread over 18 days. The festival is also linked to the pre-Hispanic agricultural cycles of sowing and harvesting, as well as mining activities.
Carnaval *(Feb)*. Across Peru costumed revelers dance and feast throwing water buckets and balloons in the lead up to Lent. In most highland towns, people dance around a *yunza*, an artificially planted tree trunk filled with gifts, trying to chop it. The couple that fells the tree gets to be next year's organizer.

March
Festival de la Vendimia *(2nd week)*, Ica. The Harvest Queen and her handmaidens stomp grapes in a vat and throw

Candles and white roses used as decorations for Semana Santa

grapes to the crowd. There are floats, music, and Afro-Peruvian dancing.
Fiesta de la Cruz *(Mar/Apr)*. Processions of crosses, along with music and dancers, are held across Peru commemorating ancient agro-astronomical rituals. In Porcón (near Cajamarca), 100 reed and palm crosses decorated with mirrors – the souls of the dead – are paraded. On Palm Sunday the crosses are led into the church, along with a female donkey signifying Jesus' entry into Jerusalem.

April
Semana Santa *(Easter week)*. Ayacucho stages Peru's most elaborate Easter procession. Cross processions occur many times a day and differ each day. On Good Friday the figure of Señor del Santo Sepulcro (Lord of the Holy Sepulcher), is borne

on a litter adorned with white roses and thousands of candles from the Santa Clara Monastery. It is followed by an image of the grieving Mary (Virgen Dolorosa) and lines of people with candles. The main plaza's lights are turned off and candles illuminate it. There is dancing as well as fireworks on Saturday night. On Sunday the resurrected Christ is brought from the cathedral, mounted on a huge structure and paraded around the square.

In Tarma and Ica, streets are carpeted with flowers and decked with blooming arches for the processions.
Peruvian Paso Horse National Show *(mid- to late Apr)*, Lima. Distinguished by its unique gait, the Peruvian Paso horse is recognized as a "cultural patrimony" of Peru. It is hailed as one of the world's most elegant steeds.

Colorful procession at the Virgen de la Candelaria Festival

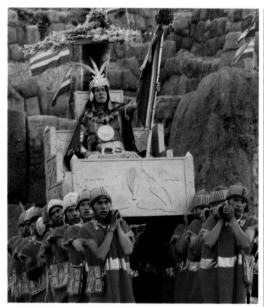

Inca chief at the Inti Raymi celebrations at Sacsayhuamán

Dry Season

May to October is cooler, drier, and ideal for visiting most of Peru. It is the time for outdoor activities such as climbing, hiking, and mountain biking. In the highlands, days are clear and sunny from June to September, although temperatures can plummet at night. Hikers planning on doing the Inca Trail should aim for these months. This is also a good time to visit the jungle as both mosquito and river levels are down. Lima is blanketed in a grey haze during this period, with high humidity making the days and nights chilly. The waters of the Pacific are too cold for swimming.

May

Corpus Christi (end May/early Jun), Cusco. This is the most impressive Corpus Christi procession. Statues of 16 saints are carried to the cathedral to greet "the body of Christ", a consecrated wafer held in a 57-lb (26-kg) gold tabernacle. The Andean and Spanish worlds merge here as the Incas too carried their sovereigns' mummified remains in processions at the same time of year. At night, typical dishes including guinea pig with hot peppers, *chicha*, and corn bread are served. At sunrise the parade moves around the main plaza and enters the cathedral.

June

Qoyllur Rit'i (1st week), Cusco region. More than 10,000 people gather at Sinakara at the foot of Mount Ausangate (20,870 ft/6,362 m) at a shrine bearing a painting of Jesus as a child. According to popular belief the infant Christ appeared to a native boy here. A group of Q'eros, hailed as Peru's purest Quechua community, ascend to the summit searching for the buried Qoyllur Rit'i (Star of the Snow). They haul massive blocks of ice on their shoulders back to their communities for the symbolic watering of their lands with holy water from Ausangate.

Inti Raymi (Jun 24), Sacsayhuamán. The Festival of the Sun celebrates the winter solstice and honors the Sun God worshipped by the Incas. An Inca chief presides over the ceremony, a llama is sacrificed to the sun, and at dusk the ceremony finishes and the music and dancing begins.

Day of Saint John the Baptist (Jun 24). Religious services, dancing and musical celebrations, and craft fairs take place across Peru to mark the feast day of this saint. In the Amazon the event takes on special significance due to the connection with water.

Chaccu Ceremony (end Jun), Lucanas (Pampa Galeras National Reserve, Ayacucho). The communal herding and shearing of the vicuña, whose ultra fine wool was worn by Inca royalty, was revived in 1992 to revitalize local cultural practices. People from across the region gather as a human chain is formed around the wild vicuñas to herd them into a pen. An Inca king blesses the ceremony, recites a prayer in Quechua and the shearing begins.

People gather at Sinakara, Cusco, during Qoyllur Rit'i celebrations

July

Virgen del Carmen (Jul 15–16), Paucartambo (near Cusco). Musicians play, choirs sing in Quechua and groups act out events in history as a tribute to Virgin del Carmen, patroness of the mestizo people. Elaborately dressed dancers accompany the procession with the Virgin blessing the faithful. As a finale, a war is waged and the virtuous triumph over the demons.

Eco-tourism and Coffee Festival (Jul 25–30), Oxapampa. An opportunity to explore ecotourism circuits and coffee plantations run by indigenous people.

Fiestas Patrias (Jul 28–29). The whole country celebrates July 28, the day Peru gained its independence from Spain in 1821. All buildings are required to fly the Peruvian flag at this time.

Apurímac Tourist Week (Jul 31–Aug 3), Andahuaylas, Apurímac, and Abancay Provinces. Festivities include paragliding, white-water rafting, mountain biking contests, a cockfighting championship, and a hiking competition at Ampay Sanctuary.

August

Pachamama Raymi (Aug 1), Cusco. The ritual offering of *pagapus* (gifts) to Pachamama (Mother Earth) is an age-old Andes tradition. Offerings, such as *chicha*, coca leaves, *huayruro* (mystical jungle seeds), and wine, are made to her for good harvests and fortune. It marks the beginning of the Andean New Year.

Yaku Raymi (Aug 20–26), Ayacucho. An ancient ceremony cleanses the water in the canals and offerings are made to Pachamama. There is a competition of dances such as Danzantes de Tijera (Scissors Dance).

Santa Rosa de Lima (Aug 30), Lima. Believers flock to the sanctuary of America's first saint, asking for miracles in letters dropped into the well in which she reportedly threw her chastity belt's key.

Dancers with masks at the Virgen del Carmen festival

September

Ruraltur (1st weekend), Huayllay National Sanctuary, Pasco Province. Festivities include Andean gymkhana, offerings to Pachamama, llama load-carrying contests, wool spinning competitions, pottery demonstrations, rock-climbing contests, and hiking.

Spring Festival (Sep/Oct), Trujillo. Spring is celebrated all over Peru but Trujillo's festivities are the most impressive, with flower-decked houses, floats, and a procession with a beauty queen flanked by drum majorettes from the world over. Horses perform the *marinera* at the Peruvian Paso Horse Contest.

October

El Señor de los Milagros (Oct 18–28), Lima. Tens of thousands of penitents in purple robes solemnly follow an image of the Lord of Miracles on a two-ton (2,000 kg) litter carried on the shoulders of believers on a 24-hour journey from the church of Las Nazarenas to La Merced. Some women wear purple garments for a whole month.

Bullfighting Season (mid-Oct–end Nov), Lima. International matadors come to Lima to compete in the Lord of Miracles bullfights.

Día de la Canción Criolla (Oct 31). A day for celebrating Peruvian Creole music, with street musicians, and concerts in bars, restaurants, and *peñas*.

Procession of El Señor de los Milagros, Lima

The Climate of Peru

There are two main seasons in Peru – wet and dry. Arid deserts line the coast courtesy of the icy Humboldt Current, which causes clouds to release moisture before they reach land. While it rarely rains here, mist and *garúa* (light drizzle) are common in winter (May–Oct), except in the far north, where it is sunny year round. Lima, by contrast, is blanketed in grey gauze for seven months. Inland, temperatures get colder as the altitude increases – in the Andes it can drop from 20°C (68°F) to 2°C (36°F) in one day. In the tropical jungle, summer (Dec–Sep) means hot, sunny days. River levels swell in the rainy season causing flooding.

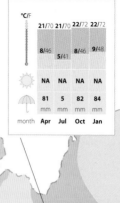

CAJAMARCA

°C/F				
	21/70	21/70	22/72	22/72
	8/46	5/41	8/46	9/48
	NA	NA	NA	NA
	81 mm	5 mm	82 mm	84 mm
month	Apr	Jul	Oct	Jan

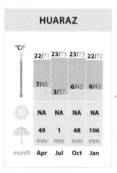

TRUJILLO

°C/F				
	23/73	20/68	20/68	24/75
	19/66	17/63	16/61	19/66
	NA	NA	NA	NA
	0 mm	0 mm	0.2 mm	1.4 mm
month	Apr	Jul	Oct	Jan

— Average daily maximum temperature
— Average daily minimum temperature
— Average daily hours of sunshine
— Average monthly rainfall

NA: Data not available

Key

- Semi-arid areas: sunny all year round with low rainfall
- Desert regions: dry and mild with cool, cloudy winters
- Grasslands: dry and temperate climate with cold nights
- Highlands: colder conditions with higher rainfall in winters
- Tropical: humid with distinct dry and wet seasons

• Cajamarca
• Trujillo
Huaraz •
• Lima

HUARAZ

°C/F				
	22/71	23/73	23/73	22/72
	7/45	3/37	6/43	6/43
	NA	NA	NA	NA
	49 mm	1 mm	48 mm	106 mm
month	Apr	Jul	Oct	Jan

Snow-capped peaks of Huascarán, Cordillera Blanca

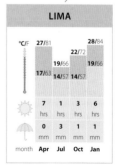

LIMA

°C/F				
	27/81		22/72	28/84
	17/63	19/66 14/57	14/57	19/66
	7 hrs	1 hrs	3 hrs	6 hrs
	0 mm	3 mm	1 mm	1 mm
month	Apr	Jul	Oct	Jan

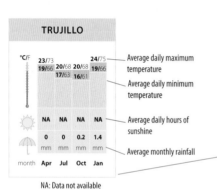

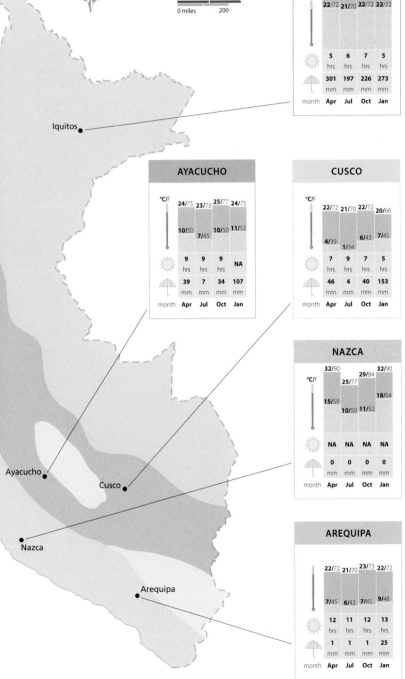

IQUITOS

°C/F	**31**/88	**30**/86	**32**/90	**32**/90
	22/72	**21**/70	**22**/72	**22**/72
	5 hrs	6 hrs	7 hrs	5 hrs
	301 mm	197 mm	226 mm	273 mm
month	**Apr**	**Jul**	**Oct**	**Jan**

AYACUCHO

°C/F	**24**/75	**23**/73	**25**/77	**24**/75
	10/50	**7**/45	**10**/50	**11**/52
	9 hrs	9 hrs	9 hrs	NA
	39 mm	7 mm	34 mm	107 mm
month	**Apr**	**Jul**	**Oct**	**Jan**

CUSCO

°C/F	**22**/72	**21**/70	**22**/72	**20**/68
	4/39	**1**/34	**6**/43	**7**/45
	7 hrs	9 hrs	7 hrs	5 hrs
	46 mm	4 mm	40 mm	153 mm
month	**Apr**	**Jul**	**Oct**	**Jan**

NAZCA

°C/F	**32**/90	**25**/77	**29**/84	**32**/90
	15/59	**10**/50	**11**/52	**18**/64
	NA	NA	NA	NA
	0 mm	0 mm	0 mm	0 mm
month	**Apr**	**Jul**	**Oct**	**Jan**

AREQUIPA

°C/F	**22**/72	**21**/70	**23**/73	**22**/72
	7/45	**6**/43	**7**/45	**9**/48
	12 hrs	11 hrs	12 hrs	13 hrs
	1 mm	1 mm	1 mm	25 mm
month	**Apr**	**Jul**	**Oct**	**Jan**

0 kilometers 200
0 miles 200

Iquitos

Ayacucho

Cusco

Nazca

Arequipa

THE HISTORY OF PERU

The origins of civilization in Peru can be traced back 20,000 years before the Incas, making the country one of the cradles of ancient cultures along with Mesopotamia, Egypt, India, and China. Today, Peru stands as the result of a collision between the Western and the Andean world, a process that began with the arrival of the Spanish in 1532. After independence, Peru set about forging its own identity, a complex process that continues even today.

Peru's earliest settlers are thought to have arrived via the Bering Strait, crossing from Asia (present day Russia) to North America during the last Ice Age between 20,000 and 40,000 years ago. Another theory, based on Thor Heyerdahl's raft expeditions in the last century, suggests that early migration may also have been possible from the Pacific and the Atlantic Oceans.

The first evidence of human civilization dates back probably to 20,000 BC, to Pikimachay Cave near Ayacucho where remnants of the first nomads, including human and animal skeletons and stone tools, have been found. Stone blades, hunting knives, human remains, and cave paintings have also been uncovered in Paiján, La Libertad; Guitarrero, Ancash; Lauricocha, Huánuco; and Telarmachay, Junín.

These cultures probably began domesticating Andean camelids (llama, alpaca) and *cuys* (guinea pigs) as early as 7000 BC, moving on to establish small hunter-gatherer villages around 6000 BC. The nomadic tribes followed animal migration patterns, swapping mountain winters for the milder coast. Towards 2900 BC, they began to plant crops such as manioc, corn, quinua, lima beans, and cotton, thus establishing Peru's long- standing agricultural tradition. Scientists believe the potato, Peru's staple, was first cultivated around 8,000 years ago by farmers living near Lake Titicaca.

Fishing, agriculture, and trade formed the economic base of the Preceramic Period (2700–1800 BC). Cotton was used to weave fishing nets and to make ceremonial paraphernalia. Small amounts of obsidian, a glassy volcanic rock used to fashion stone tools that occurs naturally over 13,000 ft (4,000 m), has been found on the coast, indicating an active exchange of goods between the coast and highland communities. These people worked collectively, with a sense of communal ownership. This, and the control of critical resources, resulted in the development of the first cities along the coast and the highlands.

20,000 BC Nomadic tribes cross the Bering Strait from Asia to the Americas, gradually spreading south

Stone tools used for hunting

8000 The Paiján Man, a consummate hunter with highly developed tool craftsmanship, lived in the Northern Desert coast

20,000 BC	16,000 BC	12,000 BC	8000 BC	4000 BC

11,000 First nomadic tribes roam the Peruvian highlands hunting giant animals such as the megatherium, an elephant-sized ground sloth

7000 Domestication of animals and agricultural cultivation begins

Megatherium, giant sloth

◀ A tile design in Cajamarca showing the 13th Inca, Atahualpa

View of the temple and amphitheater excavated at the sacred city of Caral

Caral: the Mother City

The biggest and most impressive example of monumental architecture during the Formative Period (2700-1000 BC) is Caral, dubbed the oldest city in the New World. The discovery of 5,000 year-old Caral provides indisputable evidence that a complex urban center formed in the Central Andes at the same time as those in the Old World of Egypt, Mesopotamia, India, and China were developing – 1,500 years earlier than previously believed. Radiocarbon dating of plant fibers indicate that Caral, which is just one of 18 sites attributed to the Caral-Supe culture, was built in 2627 BC, 1,000 years before the Olmecs established settlements in Mesoamerica.

Discovered in 1905, the site was overlooked for almost a century because it failed to yield any gold or ceramics. However, dogged research by Peruvian archaeologist, Ruth Shady, since 1994, has unearthed 20 stone-built structures featuring six pyramids and many artifacts including woven religious offerings known as *ojos de Dios* (God's eyes).

The huge structures at Caral were built in a short period of time, indicating complex planning, centralized decision-making, and the mobilization of a large labor force. Society was hierarchical; religion was used as a means to ensure social cohesion and control. According to estimates, about 3,000 people lived here at its height and the varying sizes of the homes indicate clear class distinctions within the society. This sacred mother city served as a model for other religion-inspired urban centers in Peru.

While it is true that other villages in Peru were occupied before 2600 BC, some of which had small scale platforms or ceremonial structures, they are dwarfed by the size of Caral and its monuments. Caral appears to have been abandoned after some 500 years of permanent occupation, with scientists speculating that a drought may have led to the people's departure.

The concentration of urban settlements along the valley with such monumental architecture is unparalleled anywhere in the world at that time.

2627 Caral, the oldest city of the New World, is built in the Supe valley

Flutes made from pelican and animal bones, engraved with the figures of birds, found at Caral

3000 BC   **2500 BC**   **2000 BC**

Cotton cultivated by 2900

2500 First fragments of cotton textiles found at Huaca Prieta in Chicama Valley

2000–1500 Temple of Kotosh constucted near the Andean town of Huánuco

The Rise and Fall of Chavín

The best known of the early Peruvian civilizations, the Chavín culture is considered the South American counterpart of China's Shang or Mesopotamia's Sumerian civilizations. Chavín flourished around 900 BC in what is known as the First or Early Horizon (1000 BC–AD 200) era, emerging after the societies responsible for building the monumental complexes on the coast began to collapse.

Stone carvings on a wall at Sechín in the Casma Valley

The Chavín culture managed to unite coastal, highland, and eastern lowland societies with its powerful religious ideology. They constructed an ornate stone temple at Chavín de Huántar, in the Northern Highlands of Peru, filling it with finely carved stone sculptures and elaborate iconography. The iconography of the Raimondi Stone and Lanzón monolith depicts their worship of a supreme feline deity in the shape of a stylized jaguar head, as well as other natural spirits.

Stylized jaguar carving, a feature of the Chavín

Some archaeologists have suggested that Chavín de Huántar was an Andean oracle controlled by a powerful high-priest elite that relied on San Pedro cactus and other hallucinogens to interact with supernatural forces. Rivaling other sanctuaries such as Kunturwasi in Cajamarca or Sechín in the Casma Valley, it presumably attracted travelers and pilgrims from Ecuador in the north as well as the southern Andes. The discovery of strombus shell trumpets and spindle shells found only in tropical waters off the coast of Ecuador add weight to this hypothesis.

The Chavín were also innovative metallurgists, potters, and weavers. Sometime around 300 BC Chavín's influence began to wane but its adroitness in unifying communities through religion resonates even today.

The Chavín de Huántar ruins at the base of the Cordillera Blanca

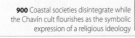

Detail on a Paracas textile

600 The temple complex of Sechín built in the Ancash region

700 Paracas civilization emerges, producing vividly colored textiles

300 Chavín's sphere of influence disintegrates

1500 BC	1000 BC	500 BC

900 Coastal societies disintegrate while the Chavín cult flourishes as the symbolic expression of a religious ideology

Carved Chavín feline god

Depiction of a Moche pyramid under construction

Regional Development

With the demise of Chavín, numerous regional cultures began to emerge generating an epoch known as the Regional Development Period or the Classical Era (200 BC–AD 900). During this time, cultures including the Moche (northern coast), Recuay and Cajamarca (northern highlands), Lima (central coast), Nazca (southern coast), Wari and Tiahuanaco (southern highlands) established strong regional states each with unique features.

The Moche (220 BC–AD 600) was a militaristic society that expanded along Peru's northern coast. They were skillful engineers building large scale adobe pyramids such as the Huaca de la Luna and the Huaca del Sol as well as an impressive network of desert irrigation canals. They are also famed for their finely crafted metallurgy

and ceramics, the best examples of which are the Lord of Sipán's tomb, and the tomb of a tattooed female mummy at the Huaca Cao Viejo at El Brujo. Both provided archaeologists with unprecedented evidence that the Moche was one of the most sophisticated civilizations in pre-Columbian Peru. It is believed that drought was a factor in their demise.

Around the same time, the Nazca (100 BC–AD 700) were displaying remarkable inventiveness in their textiles and ceramics. The Nazca are thought to be the perpetrators of the desert drawings known as the Nazca Lines, and they also constructed Cahuachi, a temple and burial complex that became the main pilgrimage center for the region around AD 100.

Farther inland, near Lake Titicaca, the Tiahuanaco culture (AD 200–1000) built Tiahuanaco, an urban and ceremonial center that flourished for close to a millennium and was home to an estimated 40,000 people. The Tiahuanaco developed a specialized system of farming, which meant they could grow crops despite the icy temperatures of the altiplano.

Nazca textiles with stylized motifs

220 Moche culture flourishes

Moche head sculpted in gold

450 The Lady of Cao, presumably a female warrior or high-priestess, dies at 25 and is buried in El Brujo complex

650 Beginning of the Wari-Tiahuanaco period

200 BC	AD 1	200 AD	400 AD	600 A

100 AD Cahuachi, the pilgrimage center of the Nazca, becomes the most important site in the region

200 Tiahuanaco city is built on the southeastern shore of Lake Titicaca.

Moche earrings

600 Decline of the Moche Empire begins

The Wari (AD 600–1100) built a city near Ayacucho that thrived for some 300 years and was thought to have a population of 70,000. By AD 650 both the Wari and Tiahuanaco Empires had expanded sufficiently so as to share common boundaries. Archaeological evidence indicates there was interchange between the two cultures – both shared intriguing similarities in

Inca construction blends architecture with terrain, Machu Picchu

their iconography on stone sculptures and motifs in ceramics and textiles. While the Wari-Tiahuanaco Empire grew to encompass almost all of Peru, its inability to contain emerging tribal warfare along the coast resulted in its downfall.

Conquering Kingdoms

Around AD 900 the Andean region underwent radical political reorganization. During this period, known as the Conquering Kingdoms (AD 900–1532), two powers emerged on the northern coast: the Sicán in La Leche Valley, and the Chimú (or Chimor) in the Moche Valley. The Sicán, who were descendants of the Moche, constructed adobe pyramids at Bátan Grande while the Chimú built Chan Chan, the largest adobe city in the world. At its zenith around AD 1400 the Chimú kingdom extended from the northern Tumbes area to southern Chancay.

Other important cultural centers sprang up on the coast, including Chancay to the north of Lima, and Ychma at Pachacamac, to the south. Pachacamac had previously been a Wari religious and political center, uniting the Rímac and Lurín Valleys. Farther south lay the Chincha (Ica culture) domain.

Between 1200 and 1400 many small kingdoms emerged in the highlands but only two obtained the same level of political complexity and territorial control as the coastal empires. The Chachapoyas built huge fortresses and cities in the northern jungles in San Martín, with Kúelap being the most famous. The second was an assemblage of forceful groups based in the Cusco Valley, birthplace of the Incas.

The Incas

The Incas (1197–1532), who created Peru's first multicultural society, descended from the families based around Cusco, the heart of a confederation of tribes in 1197. Around the 13th century, they began a slow expansion but it wasn't until the 15th century that they exerted their full dominance, subjugating surrounding territories under the leadership of emperor Pachacútec. The empire, Tahuantinsuyu (Land of the Four Quarters), at one time covered more than a third of South America.

Chimú ceremonial gold knife

Manco Cápac, the legendary founder of the Inca Empire

1200 Mythical foundation of Cusco by Manco Cápac

1400 Maximum expansion of the Chimú kingdom

1438 The 9th Inca, Pachacutec's 33-year reign begins

800 AD   **1000**   **1200**   **1400**

900 Twenty pyramids are built at Batán Grande by the Sicán people

1375 Chimú occupy Túcume

1450 Incas conquer the Chimú kingdom and occupy Chan Chan and Túcume

The Inca Empire

In a relatively short space of time – barely a century – the Incas built not only the largest empire in pre-Columbian America but also one of the largest in history. Their vast domain encompassed dramatic contrasts, from icy peaks to coastal desert and the Amazonian jungle, with the high-altitude city of Cusco at its center. Prior to the arrival of the Incas in the central Andes, which some estimates put as early as AD 1000, the area was home to a host of diverse, and often hostile, cultures. The conquering Incas united the region under one social system and language, but did adopt aspects of the cultures they absorbed.

Inca Expansion

- ▨ Under Pachacútec, 1438–71
- ▫ Under Tupac Inca, 1471–93
- ▨ Under Huayna Cápac, 1493–1527

The Inca Rulers

Inca history divides into two stages: the Legendary and Historical Periods. The Incas' oral history lists 13 emperors (Incas) with the first six from Manco Cápac to Viracocha being mythical. Events from Pachacútec to Atahualpa's reign are more precisely recorded.

Bridges were made from plaited grass and roads were paved with stones.

Manco Cápac, the first Inca, is said to have emerged from Lake Titicaca or a cave at Pacariqtambo and led his *ayllu* (clan) to found the city of Cusco. He married one of his sisters, Mama Ocllo, to establish the royal Inca bloodline.

Pachacútec Inca Yupanqui (1438–71), the ninth Inca who many consider to be the first true Inca. He was also their greatest ruler. He transformed Cusco into an empire, implementing a comprehensive code of laws to reign over his far-flung domain.

Atahualpa (1502–33), the 13th and last emperor, was the illegitimate son of Huayna Cápac. When the old emperor died, the kingdom was divided between Atahualpa, who ruled from Quito, and Huáscar, the legitimate heir, who ruled from Cusco. Atahualpa defeated his half-brother in a ruinous civil war over control of the kingdom.

Conquest and assimilation was achieved due to the Incas' highly developed social and economic system. They expanded through political alliances and conquest.

Lure of Gold

Gold was the "sweat of the sun" for the Incas and by law it belonged only to the emperor. It was the legend of this gold and silver that brought the Spanish conquistadores to the Inca land. They collected 11 tons in gold artifacts alone as ransom for the release of Atahualpa.

Gold pieces from a belt

Decorated headpiece

A pair of llamas

The Incas created walls without mortar, and they have withstood centuries of earthquakes.

Power Center

Power was centered in Cusco and a strict social structure was imposed. To ensure complete control, entire populations were moved so as to destroy any local power base. The empire, a theocracy, was ruled by the Inca, who was considered divine.

The Cápac Ñan (Royal Road)

Roads were crucial to Pachacútec's program of unification. Under his reign alone, the Incas constructed some 2,500 miles (4,000 km) of tightly packed stone roads, some scaling heights of more than 16,500 ft (5,000 m). This impressive Cápac Ñan network of roads, about 3 ft (1 m) wide, connected all four regions of the empire, running from Quito in Ecuador, past Santiago in Chile and La Paz in Bolivia to Tucuman in Argentina.

Message to the king delivered on a *quipu*

The Conchucos-Jauja section of the road is considered the most well-preserved stretch along the Cápac Ñan.

The fish trail enabled fresh fish to reach Cusco in less than two days.

The Spanish arrival was viewed by Atahualpa as a curiosity rather than a threat. Pizarro's men ambushed Atahualpa, held him for ransom and finally executed him in 1533. His enemies aligned with the Spanish to avenge their former oppressors.

Exploration and Conquest

In 1524, the conquistador Francisco Pizarro, along with the soldier Diego de Almagro, and the priest Hernando de Luque, set out to explore and conquer "Birú", a legendary kingdom rich in gold and silver situated south of present-day Colombia and Ecuador.

Although the first expeditions resulted in high casualties, Pizarro returned to Spain with impressive stories and booty to prove the existence of the fabulous yet undiscovered "El Dorado". In 1529, Charles I authorized him to conquer Peru and appointed him Governor and Captain-General. When Pizarro landed in Tumbes in 1532, the Inca Atahualpa was involved in a war with his brother Huáscar over succession, a situation Pizarro felt he could exploit.

The Spanish invasion was one of the first and bloodiest clashes between the Old and the New Worlds. Pizarro easily entered Cajamarca and captured and later executed Atahualpa, in an act of great treachery. With the Inca's death, Pizarro was able to conquer the leaderless empire with the support of the regional kingdoms of Chimú, Huanca, and Chanca. Huáscar's younger brother, Túpac Huallpa, was crowned to legitimize Pizarro's plans to seize and sack Cusco. When he was poisoned, another brother, Manco Inca, became the puppet emperor.

Pizarro asking Charles I for the authority to conquer Peru

Humiliated after the fall of Cusco, Manco Inca led a revolt in 1536 that almost annihilated the Spaniards defending the city. Manco later took advantage of the rivalry between Pizarro and Almagro to establish a parallel court in the inaccessible mountains of Vilcabamba. After his death in 1544, the rebel Inca state passed on to his sons.

The Colonial World

Political turmoil and rivalry did not stop with the execution of Almagro in 1538, which led to the assassination of Pizarro in 1541 by Almagro loyalists, including his son Diego, who was proclaimed the new governor. However, within a year an emissary from the court of King Charles I, Cristóbal Vaca de Castro, aided by a pro-Pizarro army, crushed the Almagrists at Chupas in 1542.

The Spanish conquest and colonization (1532–1821), driven by the lure of gold and evangelical zeal, tore apart the society and

Inca Atahualpa captured by Spanish soldiers

1525 Huayna Cápac dies and his son, Huáscar succeeds; war with Atahualpa

1533 Atahualpa tried and executed; Cusco sacked

1541 Almagro's son kills Pizarro

1572 After fierce fighting Túpac Amaru I is captured, tried, and executed

Potosí mines

1500   **1550**   **1600**   **1650**

1532 Pizarro lands in Tumbes with 168 men, meets Atahualpa and captures him

1535 Pizarro founds Lima on January 18

1600 Potosí mines reach population peak with 160,000 people

Francisco Pizarro

created a divide between the victorious colonizers and defeated natives. The conquistadores introduced the language and religion that most Peruvians still speak and adhere to, and the economic classes they established survive to this day.

The feudal *encomienda* system they introduced resulted in colossal abuses and produced immense inequalities. To curtail the abuses by the conquistadores the Spanish king issued new laws. From 1542 to 1548 the new colony was in the throes of a civil war between the conquistadores, who saw their livelihoods under threat, and the Viceroyalty. Viceroy Francisco de Toledo reintroduced the Inca *mit'a* tax in 1574, forcing Indians to work unpaid, to their death, in mines such as the Huancavelica mercury mine and Potosí silver mine. Mindful of an Indian rebellion, Toledo had Manco Cápac's son executed in 1571. Two hundred years later Túpac Amaru II, a descendant of the last Inca, Atahualpa, staged an uprising which spread throughout Peru. Though he was captured and executed in 1781, the Indians continued their fight against the Spanish until 1783.

José de San Martín
(1778–1850)

Peruvian Independence

With the abdication of Spain's King Charles IV in the early 1800s, thoughts of independence spread throughout South America. In 1821, José de San Martín, who liberated Argentina and Chile, defeated the royalist forces in Peru and proclaimed its independence on July 28, 1821. San Martín then met Venezuelan general Símon Bolivar, liberator of Venezuela, Colombia, and Ecuador, and ceded control. Peru finally gained complete independence from Spain in 1824 after crucial battles in Junín and Ayacucho.

Cross border bickering put an end to Bolivar's vision of a union of states, though Peru and Bolivia did form a confederation from 1836–39. In the 40 years after independence, the presidency changed hands 35 times and 15 different constitutions were produced. Only four presidents were constitutionally chosen during the time.

Despite the political mayhem, there was money to be made. Humble dried seabird droppings (guano) became big business. It was the main export to America and Europe and even sparked the Peruvian-Spanish War in 1866 when Spain occupied the guano-rich Chincha Islands. Peru was again at war in 1879, but this time with Chile, a conflict that saw parts of the country occupied and some territory lost.

Guano being loaded on boats at Chincha Island

Túpac Amaru II

1780-82 Túpac Amaru II rebels, is executed

1821 San Martín proclaims Peru's independence

1824 Battle of Ayacucho; Gen. Antonio José de Sucre defeats the Spanish

Battle of Ayacucho

1700	1750	1800	1850

1742 Juan Santos Atahualpa proclaims himself Inca and rebels

1767 Jesuits expelled from Spanish Empire

1814 Revolution breaks out in Cusco

1879–83 War of the Pacific

The War of the Pacific (1879–83)

The Guerra del Pacifico was sparked off by a dispute over control of the nitrate-rich beds of the northern Atacama Desert on the Pacific coast. It was fought between Chile and the joint forces of Bolivia and Peru, and it remains a thorny issue, dividing historians, politicians, and ordinary citizens even today. The price which Chile extracted from its defeated neighbors has perpetuated a bitter rivalry and dislike among the affected nations. Bolivia lost its sea access leaving it landlocked, while Peru ceded substantial territory and endured widespread pillaging by the conquering Chilean forces. The rivalry was most apparent with pisco, a brandy over which both countries claimed exclusive rights to produce until 2005 *(see p287)*.

Bust of Admiral Miguel Grau, the "Knight of the Seas"

The Battle of Iquique (then in Peru, now in Chile) caused Peru to suffer a huge loss on May 21, 1879, when its warship, the *Independencia*, was sunk.

Capture of Lima

On January 17, 1881, when Chilean forces captured the capital, looting followed and much of Chorrillos and Miraflores was set on fire. Chilean soldiers took thousands of Peru's most valuable books from the National Library back to Chile where they remain even today.

The Heroic *Huáscar*

Victory in the War of the Pacific was contingent on the command of the seas, and the Chilean fleet was considered superior to the Peruvian. With the loss of *Independencia* in the Battle of Iquique, the iron-clad warship *Huáscar* was all that stood between Peru and Chilean domination. Refusing to

The battle between the Peruvian battleship *Huáscar* and the Chilean forces

concede that Peru was facing naval defeat, the commander of the ship, Admiral Miguel Grau, launched a series of daring raids against the Chilean fleet. He broke through the Chilean blockade of Callao three times, capturing transport ships and severely interrupting Chile's communication lines. Chilean ships pursued the *Huáscar* and finally, on October 8 near Punta Angamos, the Chilean fleet surrounded the Peruvian ship, opened fire and destroyed the bridge, killing Grau. The Chileans prevented the surrendering officers from sinking the *Huáscar* and instead had the boat repaired and refitted, using it to attack the Peruvians at Arica in February 1880.

The Saltpetre War was fought for control of nitrate fields, including sodium nitrate (saltpetre) and guano, operated by Chile in Peruvian and Bolivian territories. In the 1870s, with the rising demand for nitrates, a key ingredient in fertilizers and explosives, Bolivia tried to tax the Chilean companies operating in Bolivia. When Chile refused, Bolivia declared war in 1879 and asked Peru for aid.

Fallen heroes from the War of the Pacific are buried in the Panteón de los Próceres in Lima's Presbitero Maestro cemetery. Over its entrance are the words "La Nación a sus Defensores" (From the Nation to its Defenders).

Disputed Territory

- Returned to Peru 1929
- Awarded to Chile 1929
- Awarded to Chile 1883
- Bolivia awards to Chile 1883
- Bolivia awards to Chile 1874
- — Present international boundary
- · – Disputed area boundary

Tense relations with Chile continue. In 1975, Peruvian president General Juan Velasco Alvarado was close to declaring war on Chile in order to regain the two lost Peruvian territories – Arica and Tarapacá. The two nations are currently embroiled in a dispute over fishing waters in the Pacific.

Victor Raúl Haya de la Torre, founder of APRA

Democracy & Dictators

After the War of the Pacific, Peru oscillated between democracy and military dictatorship. In 1920, Augusto Leguía, who had assumed the presidency in a coup in 1919, introduced a new constitution which gave the state wide-ranging power and also allowed him to run unopposed for re-election. His crackdown on worker militancy coupled with the Russian and Mexican Revolutions spawned dissent, prompting exiled political leader Victor Raúl Haya de la Torre in 1924 to form the Alianza Popular Revolucionaria Americana (APRA), a workers' party which today still exerts tremendous influence on politics.

General Juan Velasco Alvarado seized power in 1968 and immediately suspended

Alan Garcia with his party (APRA) flag

the constitution, nationalized mines, banks, factories, oil companies, and the media, and pushed for a more independent foreign policy. Intending to impose a "controlled revolution," he confiscated large privately-owned land holdings (haciendas), transferring them to worker co-ops as part of a wide-ranging *Reforma Agraria*. He also proclaimed Quechua as the official second language. This restructuring, however, wreaked havoc on the economy and led to his ousting in 1975.

In 1980, the first fully democratic election in Peru brought Fernando Belaúnde Terry to power for a second time. Intent on privatizing industry and boosting exports, Belaúnde's term was severely hampered by high inflation, rising drug trafficking, and the threat of guerrilla movements.

Accumulated inflation and corruption too plagued Alan Garcia's presidency (1985–1990). Accused of embezzlement, Garcia fled Peru in 1992 exiling himself to Colombia and then France.

Guerrilla Tactics

The growth of the Maoist terrorist movement Sendero Luminoso and the Marxist Movimiento Revolucionario Túpac Amaru (MRTA) led to a bloodthirsty internal war between 1980 and 2000. According to the Truth and Reconciliation Commission, some 70,000 Peruvians were killed during this period by both the terrorists and the military forces fighting them. When two car bombs exploded in Lima's middle-class Miraflores in July 1992, the Fujimori government stepped up its anti-terror crackdown. Within two months, Abimael

1919–30 Leguía's 11-year civil dictatorship, marked by strong foreign investment and restriction of civil rights

Peruvian soldiers, led by Luis Sanchez Cerro, revolted against Leguía's reign in 1930

1955 Women get to vote for the first time

1900　　**1920**　　**1940**　　**1960**

1914–18 World War I affects Peru's economy, brings in recession

1941 Peru enters a seven-week war over disputed border territories with Ecuador

Guzmán, Sendero Luminoso's founder, was captured and tried by a military court behind closed doors. The sentence of life imprisonment he received was sanctioned by a civilian court in 2006.

On December 17, 1996, the MRTA seized the Japanese Embassy in Lima and took 452 guests hostage, including President Fujimori's brother and other officials. Over the months several hostages were released. Finally, on April 22, 1997, all but one of the 72 remaining hostages were rescued in a dramatic raid by Peruvian commandos.

MRTA, behind the Japanese Embassy hostage crisis

The Rise and Fall Of Fujimori

Guzmán's capture and the successful release of the hostages increased Alberto Fujimori's popularity, who became president in 1990. Under his stewardship inflation dropped to 20 percent, the currency stabilized, and a series of arrests decimated Sendero Luminoso. Fujimori took office for an unprecedented third time in 2000. However, when a bribery scandal involving his former spy chief came to light, he fled and faxed through his resignation as president from Japan. In 2007, Fujimori was extradited to Peru to face charges of corruption and human rights abuses. He was tried and sentenced to 25 years in prison.

Alejandro Toledo, first president of native descent

Peru Today

In 2001, Alejandro Toledo defeated Alan Garcia to become the first elected Peruvian president of Indian descent. Taking over a country mired in political scandal, the former shoe-shiner turned World Bank economist steered Peru to strong economic growth and an export boom. Toledo's five-year term, however, was dogged by scandals.

When ex-president Alan Garcia returned to power in 2006, a period of strong economic growth made Peru one of the most successful economies in the region. Although poverty was reduced, it still remained high however, and social conflicts increased amid corruption scandals.

In 2011, nationalist Ollanta Humala, was elected president by a narrow margin on a platform of social reform, social inclusion, and a greater government role in development. In 2013 a number of demonstrations took place in Lima in which protestors' called for greater social reform. They urged that a bigger portion of the profits made in the economic boom should to be shared with those living in poverty. The next election is due in 2016.

Shining Path founder, Abimael Guzman

1980 Belaúnde is re-elected; Shining Path initiates the guerrilla struggle

2000 Fujimori flees the country and resigns via fax, after a bribery scandal

President Ollanta Humala

2016 Next Parliamentary elections

1980

2000

2020

1968–80 Twelve years of military dictatorship

1985–90 Alan Garcia's first administration marked by rising guerrilla activity

1990–2000 Fujimori elected president for an unprecedented three terms

2011 Ollanta Humala elected president

2007 Major earthquake in the Ica region

LIMA AREA BY AREA

Lima at a Glance

Lima is a city of contrasts, culture, and commotion. Jugglers, fire-eaters, and street-sellers scamper through traffic that idles down streets flanked by Colonial mansions, pre-Inca ruins, historic churches, and museums full of treasures. Long maligned as nothing more than the gateway to Peru, Lima is a fascinating destination in itself. Central Lima is the city's pounding heart, Barranco is the bohemian barrio, Miraflores is a restaurant, hotel, and club haven, and San Isidro is the elegant business district complete with an ancient olive grove.

Locator Map

La Catedral *(see p66)*, considered a master-piece of Colonial architecture, has been re-constructed several times since the 16th century due to earthquakes.

AV. AREQUIPA

CENTRAL LIMA
(See pp62–77)

AV. JAVIER PRADO OESTE

MIRAFLORES & SAN ISIDRO
(See pp78–87)

PACIFIC OCEAN

Farther Afield, Lima
(see pp96–103)

Museo Larco Harrera *(see p98)* has more than 40,000 ceramics, including erotic Moche creations.

Museo de la Nación *(see p99)* features re-creations of the magnificent Lord of Sipán tombs, as well as ceramics and textiles from different civilizations.

| 0 kilometers | 10 |
| 0 miles | 10 |

◀ City Hall on the Plaza Mayor (Plaza de Armas), Lima

San Francisco church and convent *(see pp68–70)* was developed by the Spanish as a place for worship and education. The 17th-century structure houses famous paintings including a *Last Supper* with guinea pig and "Passion of Christ" series by Rubens. The main attraction is the catacombs where city residents were buried until the early 1800s.

Huaca Pucllana *(see pp84–5)* is the site of the remains of a pre-Inca adobe pyramid complex and includes a museum of Wari culture.

Parque Kennedy *(see p82)* is famous for the market set up by artists who come here to sell their wares. The park is also a favorite meeting place for locals at the weekend.

BARRANCO
(See pp88–95)

0 kilometers 3

0 miles 3

Parque Municipal *(see p92)* is known for the striking Biblioteca Municipal, its beautiful marble statue of the Daughter of Venus, and a lively, bohemian nightlife of bars and discos.

CENTRAL LIMA

Founded by Francisco Pizarro in 1535, Lima was the capital of the Spanish Empire in South America for almost two centuries. Dubbed the City of Kings, it was at the time the most important metropolis in the region, the center of power and wealth. Its coat of arms bears three crowns, representing the three kings of the nativity, and the motto proclaiming, "this is truly the sign of kings." Based on a Roman plan, the original 117 city blocks radiate out from Plaza Mayor, where the imposing presence of both church and state accent its pivotal role. Centuries-old streets house buildings dating mainly from Colonial times as an earthquake in 1746 razed most original structures. Private homes have since morphed into museums or government offices. Fervent devotion to the Catholic doctrine, introduced by the Spanish, means there is a Baroque-, Renaissance-, or Rococo-inspired church or convent on almost every street corner.

Sights at a Glance

Historic Buildings
2 Palacio de Gobierno
3 Casa de Aliaga

Churches and Monasteries
1 La Catedral
4 *San Francisco pp68–70*
6 San Pedro
7 Santo Domingo
9 Convento de los Descalzos
10 Las Nazarenas

Squares and Parks
5 Parque de la Muralla
11 Plaza San Martín

Museums and Galleries
8 Museo Taurino
12 Museo Andrés del Castillo
13 Museo de Arte Italiano
14 Museo de Arte
15 Museo Nacional de la Cultura Peruana

| 0 meters | 750 |
| 0 yards | 750 |

See also Street Finder pp108–115

◀ The cathedral and Archbishop's Palace, Plaza Mayor

For map symbols *see back flap*

Street-by-Street: Plaza Mayor

Formerly called the Plaza de Armas, it was here that Francisco Pizarro founded Lima. Major institutions such as La Catedral, the Palacio Arzobispal (Archbishop's Palace), the Municipalidad (Town Hall), and the Palacio de Gobierno (Government Palace) were established here and today they form the city's historic center. The plaza has witnessed many significant historical events including the first bullfight, the execution of those condemned by the Spanish Inquisition, and the declaration of Peru's independence in 1821. The large bronze fountain in the center, erected in 1651, is the square's oldest feature.

❷ Palacio de Gobierno
The president's residence was remodeled and inaugurated in 1938.

❸ Casa de Aliaga
This oldest piece of family-owned real estate on the continent was built on top of an Inca shrine in 1535.

Municipalidad

★ Casa Riva-Agüero
Named after the original owner, writer Don José de la Riva Agüero, this 19th-century *casa* houses archives, a fine library, and the Museo de Arte Popular (Folk Art Museum). It is now run by Lima's Catholic University.

The bronze fountain was commissioned by the Count of Salvatierra, and Viceroy of Peru, in 1650.

JIRÓN DE LA UNIÓN

JUNIN

| 0 meters | 100 |
| 0 yards | 100 |

Jirón de la Unión links Plaza Mayor with Plaza San Martín via a busy pedestrian thoroughfare.

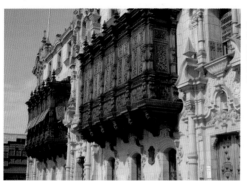

★ **Palacio Arzobispal**
Home to the Archbishop of Lima, the Archbishop's Palace was reconstructed in 1924. It is famed for the Moorish-style carved balconies that decorate its imposing and ornate façade.

The Museum of Religious Art and Treasures is in the Cathedral.

❶ ★ **La Catedral**
Ambitious building plans combined with earthquakes saw the rebuilding of Lima Cathedral several times, until it was finally reconstructed in 1758. The choir chairs are one of the greatest works of Peruvian art.

LAMPA

Museo Del Banco Central de la Reserva
Specializing in pre-Columbian archaeology, the museum displays 19th- and 20th-century Peruvian art. There's also an exhibition of Peru's currency.

UCAYALI

MIRÓ QUESADA

Iglesia de la Merced is where Lima's first Latin mass was held.

Palacio Torre Tagle
Considered the best representation of 18th-century Lima architecture, it was built in 1735. It is famed for its carved wooden balcony and finely worked stone entrance.

Key

━ Suggested route

La Catedral dominates the east view, Plaza Mayor

❶ La Catedral

Plaza Mayor. **Map** 1 F1. **Tel** 01 427
9647. **Open** 9am–5pm Mon–Fri,
10am–1pm Sat, 1–5pm Sun. 🅿 🄫
♿ 📷 with flash. 📷 🄫 Corpus
Christi (9th Thu after Easter).

With its imposing twin towers,
the Cathedral dominates the
eastern side of Plaza Mayor.
Conquistador and founder of
Lima, Francisco Pizarro (1478–
1541) carried the first log for the
construction of the original
adobe wall and the straw roof
structure on this site in 1535.
Construction began on the
current Baroque-Renaissance-
style structure in 1564. However,
work stalled due to lack of funds
and the devastating earthquakes of 1687 and 1746. The

reconstruction ended in 1758,
but it had to be rebuilt after the
destructive earthquake of 1940.
The Cathedral has five naves
and 10 side chapels, with the
smaller ones dedicated to
religious figures. The chapel of
John the Baptist has a carving
of Jesus, said to be the most
beautiful in the Americas. The
remains of Francisco Pizarro lie
in the mosaic-covered chapel
to the right of the entrance. A
headless body thought to be
his languished in the crypt
until tests in 1990 proved
that wrong remains were
on display.
The ornate choir stalls, carved
by 17th-century Spanish
sculptor, Pedro Noguera, are a
highlight, along with the gold-
leaf altars and religious museum
with its collection of art.

❷ Palacio de Gobierno

Plaza Mayor. **Map** 1 F1. **Tel** 01 311
3900. 🛈 PR office, Jirón de la Unión.
Open 9am–10:30am Sat & Sun by
prior registration. Changing of the
Guard 11:45am daily.

Known as the Casa de Pizarro,
the Government Palace was
built by Pizarro on the land once
owned by Taulichusco, a pre-
Hispanic chief of the Rimac

Valley. It has been the seat of
political power in Peru ever
since, undergoing major
reconstruction in the 1920s
and 1930s following a fire.
Inaugurated in 1938, the
palace is a grand example of
Colonial affluence. Rooms are
festooned with mahogany and
cedar carvings, French glass,
Carrera marble, and Czech
crystal. A marble staircase
dominates the Grand Hall,
which is flanked by busts of key
figures in Peru's history.
The gilded Salon Dorado
(Golden Room) is modeled on
Versailles Palace's Hall of Mirrors,
while the dining hall takes its
cue from local life.

❸ Casa de Aliaga

Jirón de la Unión, 224. **Map** 1 F1.
Tel 01 427 7736. **Open** 9:30am–1pm,
2:30–5:45pm daily. 🄫

The *quincha* (earthquake
resistant material) mansion was
built by Jerónimo de Aliaga, one
of Pizarro's lieutenants. It is the
oldest and best preserved
home in the continent and is
owned by the same family
17 generations later.
The ornate balcony offers the
only clue to the lavish 66-room
house. Marble stairs lead to the
second floor patio and the main
entrance. The part open to the
public showcases Colonial art
and decor from the 16th to 18th
century such as Louis XIV mirrors
and furniture, family portraits,
and Cusco School paintings. One
of the two Andalusian patios has
a bronze fountain.

Intricately carved wooden portable
altar, La Catedral

Paintings and Seville tiles adorn the interior
of Casa de Aliaga

Colonial Architecture

Spanish and indigenous design often merges in Colonial architecture, resulting in a kind of Creole style. The Moorish influence, which crossed into Spain from North Africa and was then transplanted to the Americas, is discernible in the Mudéjar style (Arabic patterns that appear in decorative details). Two such impressive Colonial buildings are the Casa de Aliaga, built by Jerónimo de Aliaga, and the Santo Domingo church *(see p71)*, built by friar Vicente de Valverde. These two friends of Pizarro were with him on his conquest of Peru and he bestowed on them the choicest plots of land near Plaza Mayor. The old quarter of the city originally mapped out by Pizarro – *el damero de Pizarro* (Pizarro's chessboard) – is now a UNESCO Mankind Heritage Site.

Casa de Aliaga

Dating back from 1535, this mansion displays an outstanding array of Colonial art and decor.

Paintings from the Cusco School are interspersed with Aliaga family portraits.

Arabesque-style tiles add color and detail to the second floor balcony.

Furniture, paintings, and porcelain from Spain, Asia, and Peru add to the elegance of the mansion's decor.

Tiles were always used in the patios, modeled after Seville houses.

Courtyards commonly featured a second floor wooden balcony.

The Dining Room has a coffered ceiling with intricately carved squares. It also showcases original period furniture and artwork.

Features of Colonial Architecture

Enclosed wooden balconies are very much a trait of Colonial Lima, along with ornamental doorways, painted façades, glazed Seville tiles, high ceilings, imposing stairways, and an inner courtyard.

Palacio de Torre Tagle, built in 1730, features two intricately carved wooden balconies made of Nicaraguan cedar and a Panamanian stone entrance.

Casa de Osambela Oquendo, with its four levels, is Colonial Lima's tallest house. Built between 1803 and 1807, its elaborate street-front balconies reflect the Mudéjar style.

Iglesia San Pedro offers the best preserved example of early Colonial religious architecture.

❹ San Francisco

The striking yellow and white Colonial complex of San Francisco comprises a church, a convent, the chapels of La Soledad and El Milagro, and eerie catacombs. The original mud and wood church constructed in 1557 was destroyed in the 1656 earthquake, and the rebuilt church was completed in 1672 by Portuguese architect Constantino de Vasconcellos. The façade is one of the best examples of 17th-century Baroque architecture in Peru. Original blue tiles from Seville decorate the convent cloisters and patio, and the library is home to centuries-old manuscripts and books.

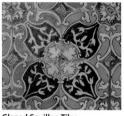

Glazed Sevillan Tiles
Lima's largest collection of blue tiles from Seville, dating back to 1620, line the cloisters.

Convent Cloister and Garden
The tiled patio has a machimbrado ceiling (wooden pieces fitted together without nails) made from mahogany, and the walls are painted with frescoes.

★ Baroque Church Façade
Two towers flank a stone altarpiece-portal, a lavish mass of sculptures, frontispieces, niches, windows, and pilasters dating from 1664.

★ Convent Library
This 17th-century library houses more than 20,000 books from the 15th–18th centuries including many first editions and parchments.

For hotels and restaurants in this area see pp274–9 and pp288–97

The High Altar
Designed by the renowned Spanish architect, Presbítero Matías Maestro, this impressive structure, entirely carved in a Neo-Classical style, is complemented by the Mudéjar ceiling.

★ **Catacombs**
The church is built on a network of inter-connected underground tunnels or catacombs which were used as a cemetery during the Colonial period.

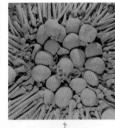

KEY

① **Fountain**

② **The wooden dome** was constructed in 1625.

③ **The convent cloisters** feature a wall fresco on the life of Saint Francis of Assisi.

④ **Earthquake-resistant quincha** – a mix of rushes, mud, and plaster – was used to construct the entire church.

⑤ **The Church interior** features three 7-span aisles, a transept, and a presbytery.

Painting of the *Last Supper*
The 1656 painting of the *Last Supper*, with the apostles supping on guinea pig *(see p70)* and drinking from golden *keros* (Inca cups), adorns the Dining Hall.

Exploring San Francisco

In 1535, Emperor Charles I ordered Francisco Pizarro to put aside two sites in Lima so that the Franciscans could build a church and convent. Located on the banks of the Río Rimac, the sites were approximately one eighth the area of the city, the largest in the New World. The best artists of the day, from silversmiths to sculptors to woodcarvers, were brought in to add decoration. A factory was organized to produce *azulejos* (painted tiles).

Interior of the church of San Francisco

Church and Convent

With the exception of the stone altarpiece-portal and the lateral portal, the church is made of the earthquake-resistant *quincha* (a mix of rushes, mud, and plaster). The architectural layout is simple, with three 7-span aisles, a transept, and a presbytery. Detailed decorative patterns can be seen on the altarpieces, façade, domes, and towers.

The carved saints and lectern in the friar's choir are superb examples of Baroque sculpture.

Being the preferred place of worship for the Spanish viceroy and his court, the church received generous donations, especially from the gold and silver mines of Peru that were under Spanish control. Thus, San Francisco amassed a valuable collection of treasures.

Unfortunately, some of these vanished during the wars of independence in the 19th century, though some remarkable works of art, architecture, and literature remain. The first dictionary published by the Real Spanish Academia is housed in the convent library. The beautiful courtyards with tiled walls, frescoes, paintings, and ornate woodwork are highlights of the convent.

Religious Museum

The Religious Museum has a series of the "Passion of Christ" paintings from the workshop of 17th-century Flemish painter, Peter-Paul Rubens, in Antwerp. Portraits of the apostles from the studio of Francisco Zurbarán, the famous Spanish painter, hang in the Zurbarán Room.

Though the Catholic church was vicious in its suppression of indigenous religious icons, insisting local artists copy European images, some distinctly Andean touches can be seen in the works of art.

The Catacombs

The bone-packed crypt, the site of an estimated 70,000 burials, features rows of bones, along with a circle of skulls and femurs deep in a well. Bodies were laid on top of each other, dusted with lime, and once decayed, the bones were sorted and stored.

Azulejos on a wall of the convent cloister, San Francisco

Guinea Pig Supper

Guinea pigs are integral to Peruvian life and millions are eaten every year. No special occasion is complete without one and evidence shows that guinea pigs were domesticated in Peru as far back as 2500 BC. Guaman Poma de Ayala (1550–1616) reported that the Incas sacrificed 1,000 guinea pigs and 100 llamas in Cusco's plaza each year for the safety of their fields. When Spanish priests ordered Geronimo de Loayza, Lima's first bishop (1545–75), to conduct an extermination of guinea pigs he refused, fearing a rebellion. Small wonder that San Francisco's *Last Supper*, painted by Marcos Zapata, shows Jesus and his 12 disciples sitting down to *cuy chactado* (roast guinea pig), with papaya and *chicha* (corn beer) in Inca cups.

Last Supper by Marcos Zapata (18th century)

❺ Parque de la Muralla

Jirón Amazonas and Av. Abancay.
Map 1 F1. **Tel** 01 427 2617.
Open 9am–10pm daily. 🅿️ ♿ 📷

Situated behind the Iglesia San Francisco, next to the river Rimac, this park exhibits the remains of a 17th-century wall that once protected the city from pirates and enemies of the Spanish crown. The park also contains a small exhibition of maps, prints, and artifacts, as well as a statue of Francisco Pizarro.

❻ San Pedro

Jirón Ucayali, 451. **Map** 1 F2.
Tel 01 428 3017. **Open** 9:30–11:45am,
5–8pm daily. 🛐

The only church in Lima with three entrances (normally a feature of cathedrals), the small church of San Pedro is considered to be one of the finest examples of early Colonial architecture in the city. Built in 1636, it was consecrated two years later. Inspired by the Jesuit's Church of Jesus in Rome, it has three naves.

The restrained exterior sits in stark contrast to the interior, which is opulent. It is adorned with Churriguresque (Spanish Baroque) and gilded altars, along with gilded carvings of the founders of various religious orders, and Moorish balconies. The side chapels, with their superb glazed tiles, are awash with paintings from the Lima, Quito, and Cusco Schools.

Glazed tiles, San Pedro

The impressive golden main altar, designed by priest Matías Maestro (1760–1835), features columns, balconies, and sculpted figures.

A painting of the coronation of the Virgin Mary by Bernardo Bitti (1548–1610), who worked with Michelangelo in Italy and supervised the construction of San Pedro, hangs in the beautifully tiled sacristy.

Santa Rosa de Lima (1586–1617)

The Americas' first saint, Lima-born Isabel Flores de Oliva was nicknamed "Rose" due to her beauty. Isabel used pain to focus solely on God and rubbed hot peppers on her cheeks to make herself less attractive. She joined the Third Order of St Dominic and her penance became more persistent. She fasted constantly and reportedly slept on a bed of broken glass, wore a spiked metal crown covered by roses, and an iron chain around her waist. Working tirelessly for Lima's poor, she advocated rights for indigenous people. Sanctuario de Santa Rosa de Lima, built near the house she was born in, has a chapel, a lemon orchard, and the well where she threw the key of the chain she always wore. Thousands flock here on August 30 tossing letters into the well, asking for her help.

Statue of Santa Rosa de Lima

❼ Santo Domingo

Cnr of Conde de Superunda and Camaná. **Map** 1 E1. **Tel** 01 734 1190.
Open 8:30am–noon, 1–5:30pm daily.
Tower **Open** 11am–4pm daily.
🅿️ 📷 🛐

Construction of the Santo Domingo church began in 1540, a few years after Francisco Pizarro granted the land to Dominican friar Vicente de Valverde, who was with him during his conquest of Peru. Pizarro had sent Valverde to meet the Inca ruler Atahualpa *(see p50)* in Cajamarca as he wanted him to try and convert the Inca to Christianity or face a war with the Spanish. However, Valverde failed.

Work was not completed on the church until the late 16th century.

The church features superbly carved cedar choir stalls, an imposing dome, and the Retablo de las Reliquias, an altar with relics of three Dominican Peruvians who attained sainthood – Santa Rosa de Lima, San Martin de Porras (1579–1639), and San Juan Masias (1585–1645). The alabaster statue of Santa Rosa was presented by Pope Clement in 1669. To the right of the church tower are the chapel and the convent cloisters, said to be the best preserved in Lima.

The **Universidad Nacional Mayor de San Marcos** (the San Marcos University), the first in South America, was founded here in 1551. It still has a campus in downtown Lima.

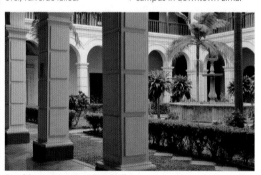
View of the convent's courtyard, Santo Domingo

Colonial painting of the Three Kings, Convento de los Descalzos

❽ Museo Taurino

Hualgayoc 332. **Tel** 01 482 3360.
Open 8:30am–4:30pm Mon–Fri.

Lima's main bullring, the Plaza de Acho, was founded in 1768 by Viceroy Amat y Juniet and is the oldest bullring in the Americas. Naturally enough, the Museo Taurino, located next to the plaza, pays tribute to centuries of clashes between man and the horned beast.

There are brave bull's heads mounted on walls, photographs of matadors flourishing their capes perilously close to the animals, a bloodstained costume worn by a Spanish matador who was gored to death in the Lima ring, swords, capes, matador suits, and posters. Also of interest are the numerous *toro*-centric (bull)

paintings and drawings, which include works by Goya as well as Picasso, a bullfight fanatic.

❾ Convento de los Descalzos

Alameda de los Descalzos. **Tel** 01 481 0441. **Open** 9:30am–12:30pm, 2–5:30pm 2–5:30pm Tue–Sun. 🚫 for a tip.

The Convent of the Shoeless Ones, named after the barefooted Franciscan monks who originally lived here, was founded in 1592 by the Corsican priest, Andres Corso.

The Franciscans lived a silent, spartan life in this spiritual retreat relying on donations to meet their needs. Missionaries, who took over the convent in 1852, said it breathed "poverty, orderliness and thrift, in contrast

to the ostentation of other religious establishments."

Today, it is home to a priceless collection of religious and Colonial paintings from the 17th and 18th centuries, which includes a Murillo (1617–82) of Saint Joseph with Jesus.

The chapel has a gold leaf altar, kitchen with winemaking equipment, a refectory, an infirmary, and monks' cells. Seville tiles adorn the patio walls and Cusco School *(see p171)* paintings hang in the chapel dedicated to Nuestra Señora de la Rosa Mística.

Take a taxi and make it wait as this area is very poor and assaults have been known.

❿ Las Nazarenas

Cnr of Jirón Huancavelica and Av. Tacna. **Map** 1 E1. **Tel** 01 423 5718. **Open** 6am–noon, 4–8:30pm daily. ✝ 🎭 El Señor de los Milagros (Oct 18, 19, 28).

The Church of the Nazarene was built in the 18th century outside the city's walls in Pachacamilla, a neighborhood then inhabited by freed black slaves from Angola and Pachacámac Indians. It was constructed around a local slave's painting of Christ on an adobe wall, El Señor de los Milagros (Lord of Miracles), which inexplicably survived the massive 1655 earthquake when every other wall crumbled. The major earthquakes of 1687 and 1746 also caused it no harm. Sensing a miracle, people began to flock to see the painting, and the church sprang up at the site.

Today, behind the altar, on the still-standing adobe wall, is an oil replica of *The Purple Christ*, as it is also known.

A copy of the image is paraded through Lima streets on a one-ton silver tray during the El Señor de los Milagros procession in October *(see p41)*.

The procession, which takes different routes on three different days, draws thousands of devout believers, all dressed in purple robes.

Traditional Chinese celebration in a Lima neighborhood

Chinatown

Between 1849 and 1874, about 100,000 Chinese immigrants arrived in Peru to replace African slave labor on coastal cotton and sugarcane plantations. As their contracts ended many moved to Lima settling around Calle Capón, which became known as Barrio Chino, one of the Western Hemisphere's earliest Chinatowns. They fiercely guarded their cultural identity and traditions, opening small businesses, including eateries serving Cantonese food. Now, Peru has more than 2,000 Chinese restaurants, called *chifas*, meaning "eat rice" in Mandarin. Their influence on local cuisine is significant – the Peruvian classic *lomo saltado*, a beef stir-fry, is served with both rice and potatoes.

The Bullfighting Season

Lima's first bullfight took place in the Plaza Mayor in 1538, organized by city founder Francisco Pizarro, who set in motion Limeños' passion for the spectacle. The South American circuit kicks off in Peru in late-October, and sweeps through Colombia and Ecuador, ending in Venezuela in February. In Lima, the Feria Taurina del Senor de los Milagros (Bullfighting Festival for the Lord of Miracles) follows the centuries-old Spanish tradition of combining a public display of bullfighting with a saint's feast day or a village fiesta. Peruvian writer Mario Vargas Llosa reportedly never misses a bullfight during the October fair.

Bullfighting season

The Lima season starts in late October and runs until early December. Celebrated matadors from the americas and Europe fly in to flaunt their skills in Spanish-style contests – meaning that the bull is killed as a finale.

Posters such as this one dating back to 1918 can be seen at the Museo Taurino.

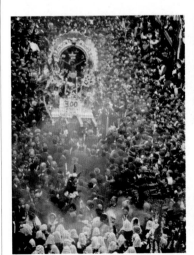

The Lord of Miracles procession, on October 18, coincides with the start of the bullfighting season in Lima. Both events are extremely popular and attract large and enthusiastic crowds.

Plaza de Acho, Lima's main bullring, has a perimeter of 804 ft (245 m), a diameter of 256 ft (78 m), and can seat 13,000 people.

Picadores goad the bull with steel pointed lances, testing its bravery. The lances weaken the animal's shoulder muscles.

⓫ Plaza San Martín

Map 1 E2. 🚹

Built to commemorate 100 years of independence, Plaza San Martín was opened in 1921. At its center is a statue of the Argentinian liberator of Peru, General José de San Martín *(see p53)*, crossing the Andes on horseback. A statue of Madre Patria, the symbolic mother of the country, stands beneath the nation's protector and sports a rather bizarre headdress. She should have been adorned with a crown of flames, known as *llama* in Spanish. Instead she has a little Peruvian llama – the animal – sitting on her head. The double meaning of the word was obviously lost on the artist who crafted the image in Spain.

The plaza has a distinct French architectural influence which can be seen in the exclusive men-only Club Nacional and the Gran Hotel Bolívar *(see p270)*, built in 1924 to accommodate the visiting heads of state and other dignitaries who came to Lima for the celebrations of the centenary of the Battle of Ayacucho.

The pedestrianized Jirón de la Unión, lined with shops and restaurants, connects Plaza San Martín with the eastern side of Plaza Mayor.

Statue of General José de San Martín in Plaza San Martín

⓬ Museo Andrés del Castillo

Jiron de la Unión 1030. **Map** 1 E2. **Tel** 01 433 2831. **Open** 9am–6pm Wed–Mon. 🚹 🚹 🔲 🎦
W madc.com.pe

Located in Casa Belén, this beautifully restored 19th-century house is home to a private museum set up in memory of Andrés del Castillo, a young student of mining engineering who died tragically in 2006. The museum has three separate exhibitions, reflecting Andrés' studies and interests. A unique and vast collection of crystallized minerals from the Peruvian Andes incorporates cabinet specimens and beautiful, museum-quality pieces, while a display of exceptional Chancay ceramics dating from AD 900 to 1400 includes many sculptures and pots. In the fascinating collection of pre-Hispanic clothing and accessories, the robes, corsets, shoes, belts, hats, wigs, and jewelry demonstrate the use of plant fibers, animal hair, human hair, feathers, and natural dyes.

⓭ Museo de Arte Italiano

Paseo de la Republica 250. **Map** 1 E3. **Tel** 01 423 9932. **Open** 10am–5pm Mon–Fri. 🚹 🚹 🎦

Designed by the Milanese architect, Gaetano Moretti (1860–1938), the Italian Art Museum was gifted to Peru, in 1921, by the Italian community living in Lima to mark the centenary of the country's independence. Inaugurated two years later, the museum has a grand white Renaissance-style façade that features the coats of arms of major Italian cities and reliefs made of marble. There are two detailed mosaic panels on the façade which depict some of the illustrious figures from Italian history.

Earthquakes in Lima

Peru is prone to earthquakes due to its location on a geological fault that spans the entire length of the country and Lima has endured its fair share of earthquakes over the centuries. The worst one occurred on October 28, 1746, when a colossal tremor rattled the country. The ground shook for four minutes – more than 15,000 people died in the capital, many vanishing in the tsunami that swallowed Callao, sinking all the boats in the harbor and reportedly carrying one vessel as far as 1 mile (2 km) inland. Lima was in ruins, with each of its 74 churches, 12 monasteries, and all except 20 of the 3,000 private houses, severely damaged. In the aftermath of the quake, one account said of Lima's 40,000 survivors that "it was not life they were living but death they were enduring." The church sent out priests exhorting citizens to "take advantage of such terrible punishment to reconcile themselves with God through penitence," while the viceroy authorized the police to hang anyone found looting or robbing. However, Lima recovered and was quickly rebuilt and most of the Colonial buildings seen today date from after 1746. Lima's last major earthquake of May 1940, demolished 23 percent of its buildings.

San Francisco church and convent, rebuilt after the 1652 earthquake

Inside, there are decorative details inspired by the great Italian masters such as Donatello, Michelangelo, and Botticelli. More than 300 works by about 100 Italian artists of the 20th century are also represented here. These include a broad selection of paintings, engravings, sculptures, and drawings, as well as ceramics.

⑭ Museo de Arte

Paseo Colón 125. **Map** 1 E3.
Tel 01 204 0000. **Open** 10am–8pm Tue–Fri & Sun, 10am–5pm Sat. 🎨 🎫 💻 📷 **w** mali.pe

Nestled in the Parque de la Exposición and surrounded by statues and gardens, the Neo-Renaissance Palacio de la Exposición (the Palace of the Exhibition) was built in 1872 for the big industrial expo held in the city. The palace, once at the heart of Lima's most important 19th-century urban projects, is home to the city's Art Museum. It has a collection of Peruvian art, ranging from ancient ceramics and textiles to jewelry, furniture, and paintings from the last 3,000 years.

The Colonial Art Gallery on the second floor has several fascinating exhibits. Some of the highlights include paintings by Juan de Santa Cruz Pumacallao, Diego Quispe Tito, and Juan Zapata Inca. These paintings of the Cusco School *(see p171)* combine Andean mythology with Catholic symbols and contrast marvelously with the conventional religious parables depicted by Bernardo Bitti (1548–1610). The collection includes painted Nazca ceramics, Inca cups, and flouncy Colonial dresses. Also on view are portraits of wealthy 19th-century families by José Gil Castro (1785–1841)

Intricate detail on Colonial-style cupboard, Museo de Arte

and Carlos Baca Flor (1867–1941), renowned for his paintings of eminent people such as Pope Pius XII, US banker J.P. Morgan, and famous fashion designer, Worth. Challenging contemporary works by 1960s vanguardists, such as Jesus Ruiz Durand, are also on display in this popular museum.

Parque de la Exposición, also known as the Parque de la Cultura, provides a welcome respite from the noise and bustle of Lima's traffic. The park houses an amphitheater, a children's puppet theater, and other performance areas, to give citizens free access to various cultural events taking place. The grounds also have a peaceful Japanese garden and an artificial lake dotted with paddle-boats. Monuments, such as the Chinese fountain, Seismograph, the Bizantino (Byzantine) Pavilion, and the pretty Morisco (Moorish) Pavilion, all celebrate Peru's centenary of independence.

Exercise caution here as thieves have been known to frequent the park. Avoid visiting after dark.

Amphitheater in Parque de la Exposición, home to free cultural events

⑮ Museo Nacional de la Cultura Peruana

Av. Alfonso Ugarte 650. **Map** 1 D1.
Tel 01 423 5892. **Open** 10am–5pm Tue–Sat. 🎨 🎫 **w** museode lacultura.perucultural.org.pe

Founded in 1946, the National Museum of Peruvian Culture was set up to conserve Peru's ethnographic heritage. The building's design was inspired by the iconography of the Tiahuanaco culture, which flourished around Lake Titicaca in 300 BC.

Folkloric and ethnographic exhibits have been gathered from all over the country, and have been divided into four sections. The one on the Amazon includes objects from the 42 different groups that inhabit the Peruvian jungles, while the Andes section displays works from Ayacucho, Cusco, Cajamarca, and Puno. The other two sections are devoted to functional and traditional objects, including a display of musical instruments. Folk art lovers should not miss the miniature *retablo* depicting the *marinera*, Peru's national dance, by Joaquín López Antay (1897–1981). The engraved gourds, particularly the donkey pen by Alicia Bustamante, and the geometric designs on the ceramics of the Shipibo people, are also spectacular.

MIRAFLORES & SAN ISIDRO

Founded in 1857, Miraflores today is Lima's prosperous commercial hub, boasting shopping zones, theaters, art galleries, cinemas, and the city's highest concentration of cafés. Vestiges of the area's ancient past remain, however, in the form of the Huaca Huallamarca and the Huaca Pucllana, ancient adobe pyramids dating back to AD 200 and 500 respectively. Miraflores is also known for its flowery parks, which regularly host craft and food markets. Despite concerns about water cleanliness, the beaches that line Miraflores' Costa Verde or Green Coast draw hordes each summer, and wet-suited surfers all year round. San Isidro is the city's garden district and features an olive grove which was established in 1560. The area is the preferred address of Lima's upper echelons.

Sights at a Glance

Historic Buildings
❷ Casa Ricardo Palma

Museums and Galleries
❻ ICPNA
❼ Museo Amano
❽ Museo Enrico Poli

Parks and Other Areas
❶ Parque Kennedy
❸ Miraflores Clifftops
❹ Larcomar
❾ Bosque El Olivar

Archaeological Sites and Ruins
❺ *Huaca Pucllana pp84–5*
❿ Huaca Huallamarca

See also Street Finder
maps 2, 3, 4

Street-by-Street: Miraflores

When feminist and grandmother to Paul Gauguin, Flora Tristán, visited Lima in the 1830s, she wrote that Miraflores was "the most beautiful village" she had visited in South America. Some of the village atmosphere still remains, particularly around Parque Central, a key gathering place for locals and visitors. Between the main shopping artery, Avenida Larco, and traffic-heavy Diagonal, the park offers space for quiet contemplation. Miraflores earned the tag Ciudad Heroica (Heroic City), which appears on vendor carts and signs, after the War of the Pacific fought against Chile in 1881 *(see pp54–5)*.

Avenida Larco is the area's commercial hub, housing boutiques, cafés, cultural centers, galleries, and casinos.

Municipal Palace

Luis Miro Quesada Garland Art Gallery, which opened in 1984, exhibits interactive installations and contemporary paintings.

The amphitheater plays host to dancing couples on Sundays.

★ **Iglesia de la Virgin Milagrosa**
Built on the old San Miguel de Miraflores church, this Church of the Miraculous Virgin dates from 1939. It is the work of Polish architect Ricardo de Jaxa Malachowski.

This avenue is named after one of Peru's favorite sons, writer Ricardo Palma.

AVENIDA LARCO

AVENIDA RICARDO PALMA

OLAYA

AVENIDA JOSE PARDO

Paseo de los Pintores
Artists set up their easels on this pedestrianized street to show off completed works focusing on Peruvian landscapes and people. A sculptor is usually present and can be seen carving out images from wooden blocks.

Artisans from Cusco region selling their handicrafts in Parque Kennedy

0 meters   50

0 yards   50

Key

— Suggested route

❶ ★ Parque Kennedy

With its shady benches, food vendors, craft market, and dancing couples, Parque Kennedy is the area's most popular park and attracts a large number of people.

Calle de las Pizzas

The Pizza Alley or San Ramon houses myriad bars, cafés, and restaurants, touting varied menus and specialties. Locals and tourists alike congregate on the pavement terraces.

Municipal Palace

This building was opened in July 1944 and houses the town council. It was designed by architect Luis Miro Quesada Garland and has paintings and murals by famous artists.

Paintings by local artists for sale at Parque Kennedy

❶ Parque Kennedy

Cnr of Av. Benavides & Calle Schell, Miraflores. **Map** 4 B1. ♿

The shady, tree-lined Parque Kennedy and the adjoining Parque 7 de Junio offer a welcome escape from Lima's jostling crowds and lurching traffic. Its modern playground with numerous swings and slides is a bonus for families traveling with children.

Local artists line the pedestrianized street in front of the Virgen Milagrosa church, proffering color-saturated canvases of Peru's landscapes and street scenes. Throughout the day food vendors and shoe-shiners can be seen plying their trade across the park.

The weekends are even more lively with all kinds of entertainment. A small but colorful craft market springs up in the center of the park in the Rotonda de los Artesanos. Innumerable stalls are set up to sell a wide variety of Peruvian crafts, including jewelry, antiques, as well as garments. Occasionally, artisans are brought in from various parts of rural Peru for week-long craft fairs.

The small amphitheater in the park is transformed into a dance arena on the weekends. Couples take to the floor sashaying to everything from robust salsa beats and Andean pipes, to brash Latino music.

❷ Casa Ricardo Palma

General Suarez 189, Miraflores.
Map 4 B1. **Tel** 01 445 5836.
Open 9am–12:45pm, 2:30–5pm
Mon–Fri. **Closed** pub hols. 🎨 🖼
in Spanish only. ♿ ✉

Peruvian writer Ricardo Palma's witty historical anecdotes or *tradicións* have won him a prominent place in Latin American literature. His love for writing and books was reflected in his efforts to rebuild Lima's National Library. He was director of the library from 1884 until his retirement in 1912. It is said that he recovered several books dumped by Chilean soldiers from some street vendors he happened to pass one day.

Built at the beginning of the 20th century, the house where Palma spent his last years celebrates his life and works. Palma became such an institution in Lima that a pilgrimage to his home was deemed essential for connoisseurs of Latin-American literature. Even though Palma has been dead for over eight decades, his desk, favorite chair, manuscripts, letters, and photographs have been preserved for posterity.

Visitors can wander around the music room, study, and bedroom to get a glimpse of Ricardo's life and his possessions. His binoculars and books set aside for reading can be seen exactly where he left them.

Ricardo Palma (1838–1919)

Ricardo Palma, one of Latin America's most popular writers, was also a naval officer, journalist, politician, and historian. He is renowned for rebuilding the National Library of Lima into one of the finest in Latin America, after it was destroyed during the War of the Pacific. Some of his historical sketches, called *Tradicións Peruanas*, have been translated into English as *The Knights of the Cape*, and have won him many accolades. These imaginative tales of pining monks, corrupt conquerors, lovers, magistrates, and all manner of foolish folk in Colonial Peru are part fiction and part reconstruction of history. Palma called himself a good tailor, artfully sewing together different stories. His funeral on October 6, 1919, was an elaborate affair with a procession of white robed priests and a military escort for his hearse.

Author and historian, Ricardo Palma

❸ Miraflores Clifftops

Malecon Cisneros & Malecon de la Reserva. **Map** 4 B2. ♿ ▣ in Parque del Amor.

The clifftops, overlooking the Pacific Ocean, are one of Lima's most popular outdoor destinations. The weekends are particularly busy with strolling families, picnickers, skaters, paragliders, kissing couples, ice-cream vendors on bicycles, and rehearsing musicians and dancers. People eager for a bird's-eye view of Lima's coastline opt for paragliding from Raimondi Park, which is a focal point for visitors. These tandem or solo paragliders race the oceanfront bluffs, hovering just meters above the heads of the promenading public.

At the northern end, colorful flower beds in the shape of the Nazca Lines, the mysterious Peruvian "drawings" in the desert (see pp130–1), dominate the view at the Parque Grau. On Sundays, during the summer, tango dancers gather on a paved area overlooking the sea to show off their skills.

Southward is the black-and-white striped La Marina lighthouse. It is located in Parque El Faro, or the Lighthouse Park, which commemorates 100 years of navigation. The lighthouse is a beacon for children, along with the adjacent playground.

The nearby skate park, with 1.6 miles (2.6 km) dedicated to ramps, tracks, and sandy hills, swarms with padded-up BMX bikers, boarders, and bladers on the weekends.

The pretty Parque del Amor, or Love Park, inaugurated on February 14, 1993, is devoted to the old Peruvian custom of courting in public gardens. In the center of the park is a colossal statue of a kissing couple, El Beso, or The Kiss, by sculptor Victor Delfín, which is perhaps a source of inspiration for the couples who come here. A serpentine mosaic bench, recalling Gaudí's

View of the seaside from the terrace of Larcomar, Miraflores

Parc Güell in Barcelona, is embedded with names and notes of love.

Across the Puente Villena Rey bridge is the imposing Intihuatana statue by abstract artist Fernando Szyszlo, celebrating the Incas' sacred stone (see p180). Intihuatana in Quechua translates as "hitching post of the sun," an apt premise for a coastline that is blanketed in gray and mist for more than half a year.

Love-themed mosaic bench at Parque del Amor

❹ Larcomar

Av. Malecón de la Reserva 610, Miraflores. **Map** 4 B2. **Tel** 01 625 4343. **Open** 11am–10pm. ♿ partial. ▨ ▣ ▨ W larcomar.com

Built in 2002, Larcomar, a shopping mall, comprises three terraces carved into the Miraflores cliffs. It has boutiques specializing in Peruvian handicrafts, a 12-screen cinema complex, cafés, bars, clubs, restaurants, a bowling alley, and gaming arcade. Limeños are in two minds about the mall. Some lament that it replaced a park, bringing traffic and noise into a once-tranquil area, while others consider it a great addition to the neighborhood.

Whatever they think of it, most locals find themselves here during the week. Some come to shop, others to admire the ocean views.

Victor Delfín (b.1927)

Victor Delfín studied painting and drawing at the School of Fine Arts in Lima and, on graduation, directed the Regional Schools of Art in Puno and Ayacucho. His monumental sculptures which adorn several public spaces – a dove in Piura, a condor in Quito, and El Beso in Lima – owe much to Peru's rich folk art traditions. Delfín believes that you have to "put your eyes in the earth to discover your roots." His imaginative sculptures are made from ceramics, concrete, tiles, and metal. His passion for Peruvian culture is visible in all his works. Delfín's vibrant tapestries often depict birds inspired by the traditional mantels of the Paracas culture and Incan symbols.

Victor Delfín at work

❺ Huaca Pucllana

More than 10,000 years ago, nomadic fishermen and farmers built camps in the area now known as Miraflores. The villages expanded and an adobe-brick administrative and ceremonial center covering 15 acres (6 ha) was built. The complex was a meeting place where produce was exchanged and religious ceremonies held. Around AD 700 the center was abandoned, probably due to the influx of new religions and ideas, and the Wari took over, transforming the center into a cemetery for its elite. Over time it became a place for offerings and was worshiped as a *huaca* or shrine. Pucllana was the Quechua name given to the site in the 16th century.

Workers at Huaca Pucllana
Mannequins are used to display scenes from daily life within this adobe ceremonial center.

Main Plaza is located at the tip of the pyramid. It features abode walls up to 13 ft (4 m) high. Access is via a ramp on the side of the pyramid.

Mannequins with Ceramics
These recreate the ritual offering of ceramics to the gods. It was believed that breaking the jars and sacri-ficing children and women helped to maintain cohesion within the community.

★ **Pyramid**
Religious rites and ceremonies, including human sacrifices, were performed at the pyramid and plazas by the priests, who functioned as local governors.

★ **Ceramics**
The ceramics in the museum are mainly sea-dominated. The waves symbolize movement while the two-headed shark is considered the bringer of life and death.

★ **Wari Mummy**
The dead were buried in a sitting position, wrapped in elaborate bales of fabric and tied with rope made of vegetable fiber. The oldest mummy found in Lima is 1,300 years old.

MIRAFLORES & SAN ISIDRO | **85**

Huaca Pucllana with the city in the backdrop, contrasting old and new

VISITORS' CHECKLIST

Practical Information
Calle General Borgoño, block 8.
Map 2 C4.
Tel 01 617 7138.
Open 9am–5pm Wed–Mon.

Detail of Sun-Dried Bricks
Small handmade adobe bricks were arranged like books in shelves to build walls and platforms for the main pyramid and adjacent plazas.

Wari Textile
The Wari fabrics were characterized by geometric and animal shapes. Wari textiles are among the most vibrant and finely woven in the world. Intricately patterned tunics were worn for ceremonial occasions.

Plan of Site

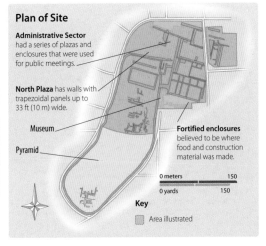

Administrative Sector had a series of plazas and enclosures that were used for public meetings.

North Plaza has walls with trapezoidal panels up to 33 ft (10 m) wide.

Museum

Pyramid

Fortified enclosures believed to be where food and construction material was made.

| 0 meters | 150 |
| 0 yards | 150 |

Key
Area illustrated

On-Going Excavation
Work began on the site in 1967 and continues today with the help of specialists.

Woven Chancay textile on display at Museo Amano, Miraflores

❻ Instituto Cultural Peruano Norteamericano

Av. Angamos Oeste 160, Miraflores.
Map 3 D5. **Tel** 01 706 7000.
Open 11am–8pm Tue–Sun.
📷 varies. 🖥 🌐 icpna.edu.pe

The Peruvian–North American Cultural Institute (ICPNA) has a long tradition of promoting the arts in Lima. It was founded in 1938 by a group of Peruvian and North American writers, intellectuals, and scientists. The ICPNA organizes exhibitions ranging from photography, painting, and printing to sculpture, ceramics, and installations featuring local as well as international artists.

Every three years, the ICPNA holds the International Sculpture Encounter attracting sculptors from across the world. In a period of one week, each artist creates a piece which is later exhibited in the ICPNA galleries.

The Institute's widely-known engraving and watercolor competitions have been in existence since 1965 and 1971 respectively.

Classical, acoustic, and Peruvian music concerts are also staged here, along with plays, ballet, and modern dance performances, all of which are usually held in the evenings, starting at 7pm. The Institute has five branches in different parts of the city.

❼ Museo Amano

Retiro 160, Miraflores. **Map** 2 B5.
Tel 01 441 2909. **Open** Mon–Fri by appointment only. 📷 by donation.
📷 3pm & 4pm in Spanish; 3:30pm & 4:30pm in Japanese. 📷

The house of Yoshirato Amano (1898-1982), and his collection of exhibits, was opened to the public in 1964 as the Museo Amano. It houses one of the most comprehensive private collections of pre-Hispanic textiles and handicrafts in Lima. The ceramics section has objects from the Kotosh, Moche, Chimú, Cupisnique, and Nazca cultures and charts the development of pottery in Peru through the ages.

The exhibits are organized chronologically, illustrating the differences and the advances made, between one culture and the next. It reveals how people in the north, such as the Moche, focused more on sculptural images, while those in the southern areas, the Nazca for example, used vibrant and vivid colors.

However, the section dedicated to pre-Hispanic textiles is what draws the crowds. On display, among others, are beautiful woven pieces by the Chancay people, some of which resemble fine lacework, and an ancient Incan

quipu, their unique system of recording events and keeping track of livestock with multicolored threads and knots.

❽ Museo Enrico Poli

Lord Cochrane 466, Miraflores. **Map** 2 B5. **Tel** 01 422 2437. **Open** Mon–Fri by appointment only. 📷 📷 only in Spanish. 📷

Among the many private collections of pre-Columbian art in Peru, Enrico Poli's is considered the finest, hailed by *National Geographic* as one of the world's "25 great adventures." Of Italian descent, Poli moved to Peru in the 1950s, and amassed an astonishing number of treasures. The museum, inside his villa, is full of Cusco paintings, Colonial silver, and furniture dating to the 15th and 16th centuries. There is a spectacular display of pre-Columbian artifacts, comprising gold objects from the Moche royal tombs in Sipán, discovered in 1987 *(see pp232–3)*. There are also exquisite gold masks, jewels, textiles, sculptures, mummified heads of Inca nobility, and erotic figurines.

Poli, associated with many archaeological expeditions in South America, acts as the tour guide.

Silver artifact in Museo Enrico Poli

❾ Bosque El Olivar

Av. La Republica, San Isidro.
Map 2 C3. ♿

Spread over a large area in central San Isidro, the beautiful Bosque El Olivar (Olive Grove) was declared a national monument in 1959. Antonio de Rivera, a former mayor of Lima, introduced the olive tree to Peru in 1560. Of the numerous saplings he brought from Seville, only three survived the journey. He planted these in the middle of San Isidro.

By 1730, when Nicolas de Rivera, a descendant, decided to build his hacienda – Los Condes de San Isidro – among the olive trees, with a grinding mill and an olive press, the number of trees had swelled to over 2,000. In 1828, there were 2,831 trees in the garden.

Rufous-collared sparrow

Today, the garden contains over 1,500 olive trees, many of them centuries old. The grove is also home to around 15 species of birds. San Isidro Council organizes birding tours for school children to encourage awareness of habitat conservation.

Spending a lazy day under the sprawling branches is a favorite with picnickers and couples. The trees also provide an ideal backdrop for wedding photographs. The central pathway, spanning several blocks, is perfect for a leisurely evening stroll.

❿ Huaca Huallamarca

Nicolás de Rivera 201, San Isidro.
Map 2 B3. **Tel** 01 222 4124.
Open 9am–5pm Tue–Sun.
Closed pub hols. 📷 🎫

Also known as the Sugar Loaf or Pan de Azucar, the Huaca Huallamarca is a fully restored ancient adobe pyramid dating from AD 200 to 500. In the Quechua language, *marca* denotes "region or town" and consequently, *huallamarca* means the "place or residence of the Hualla people."

Experts believe it to be a ceremonial center. The floors show little sign of wear, indicating that it was used only by the religious elite.

The tombs uncovered in the *huaca* (shrine) show the changes in funerary practices from AD 300 up to the 15th century, when the center was finally abandoned. During the Early Intermediate Period (AD 200–600), bodies were laid on their backs on reed

Well-preserved mummy at Huaca Huallamarca, San Isidro

mattresses. Later, the dead were put in a fetal position and wrapped in fine fabrics. During the Middle Horizon (AD 600–900), burials became more elaborate and wrapped bodies had a mask of wood or painted fabric placed over the head.

Archaeologists have recovered farming tools, children's games, crockery, woven cotton, and sewing baskets from the tombs. The presence of the latter emphasizes the importance of women within these ancient communities.

Some of the mummies, as well as the artifacts found with them, are on display at the on-site museum. The ceremonial platform located on top of the *huaca* provides a vantage point for an excellent view of San Isidro.

Centuries-old olive trees line the pathway in Bosque El Olivar, San Isidro

BARRANCO

Just a stone's throw from Miraflores, Barranco is located on the cliffs at the southern tip of Lima Bay. It divides neatly into three parts: the bustling working-class neighborhood, the center sporting elegant 100-year-old villas, and the coast lined with modern apartment blocks. It was a quiet windmill-dappled hamlet until the 19th century, when Lima's elite moved in and began to build grand summer mansions, spurred on by the new fashion of bathing in the sea. Small colonies of Europeans, mainly English, French, and Italians, settled here, adding their own stylistic traits to local architecture. The Parque Municipal retains a hint of the refined airs of days gone by. Many of Barranco's cafés, restaurants, and bars are located around here, and in nearby Bajada de los Baños, which runs below the Puente de los Suspiros, or Bridge of Sighs, down towards the ocean.

Sights at a Glance

Bridge
❸ Puente de los Suspiros

Church
❹ La Ermita

Museums and Galleries
❷ Museo de la Electricidad
❺ Museo Pedro de Osma
❻ Museo de Arte Contemporáneo

Park
❶ Parque Municipal

See also Street Finder pp108–115

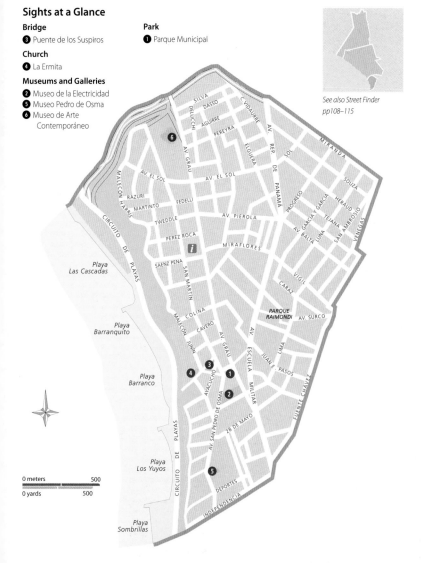

Street-by-Street: Barranco

It is easy to visualize Barranco's previous life as an aristocrat's playground, while wandering along the stately Avenida Sáenz Peña, past mansions that dot both sides, or are hidden away on nearby leafy streets. Some, however, are crumbling and Barranco has launched an "Adopt a Façade" program to promote private investment as a means of restoring the neighborhood's beauty. Colorfully painted façades along Calle Junín, Avenida Grau, and Bajada de los Baños merge the past with the present.

Avenida Sáenz Peña is lined by graceful old mansions with their sepia, rose, ochre, or lapis lazuli painted façades that recall the bygone era of pomp.

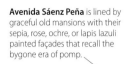

❸ ★ **Puente de los Suspiros** This emblematic symbol of romantic Barranco was remodeled in 1921. Legend has it that anyone who crosses this bridge for the first time while holding their breath will be granted their wish.

★ **Bajada de los Baños**
The present-day *bajada* (slope) corresponds with the path of a stream once followed by local fishermen down to the ocean. Over time it has morphed into a lane of elegant summer homes.

❹ **La Ermita**
The devastating 1940 earthquake considerably damaged the church; the disintegrating roof is a reminder of the tremor's ferocity.

Key

— Suggested route

426–428 Avenida Grau: Rancho Rosell
This lavish summer house, built in the early 1900s, was once the setting for opulent balls. After a period of neglect it has now been restored and is once again used for special private and public events.

Iglesia Santisima Cruz
Following the destruction of La Hermita in 1940, prominent local parishioners asked the Archbishop of Lima to authorize the building of a new parish church in the municipal plaza. The first stone was laid in 1944 and the Santisima Cruz church was finally consecrated in 1963.

★ Biblioteca Municipal
The Municipal Library, which opened in 1922, functioned as the Barranco Town Hall for many years. The columns at the entrance and along the façade are repeated on each side of the elongated windows.

AV GRAU

AV SAN MARTIN

To Sanchez Carrion

Puente de los Suspiros

Sanchez Carrion This pedestrainized street, famed for its bars and clubs, including multi-level, multi-faceted La Noche, is loved by night owls.

Clock tower of the Biblioteca Municipal, Parque Municipal

❶ Parque Municipal

Av. Grau. **Map** 5 D5. ♿

Inaugurated in February 1898, Barranco's Parque Municipal, with its wooden benches, towering palms, and colorful flower beds, is a favorite stop for locals, especially after mass in the nearby Santísima Cruz church.

During the late afternoon, resident artists often display their canvases under the watchful gaze of the Cararra marble statue of *La Donaide*, or *Daughter of Venus*. She floats languidly over the clear waters of the central pool alongside two small angels or puttis. An exquisite original Etruscan vase – Barbenini's *Candelabro* – also in marble, sits nearby.

The striking crimson-colored **Biblioteca Municipal**, constructed between 1895 and 1899 and opened in 1922, dominates this popular park. The tower, that was added in 1911, displays the Barranco crest and a clock. Designated a "historic monument of exceptional worth" by Peru's Ministry of Culture, the Biblioteca organizes regular lectures in Spanish, on diverse topics ranging from Peruvian identity and gastronomy to art and theater.

On weekends, a food market takes over the plaza opposite the park, with Peruvian cooks showing off their baking, roasting, frying, and selling skills.

❷ Museo de la Electricidad

Av. Pedro de Osma 105. **Map** 5 D5. **Tel** 01 477 6577. **Open** 9am–5pm daily. 📷 book ahead.

Most people come to this museum not to learn about the history of electricty in Peru, or to gaze upon an old Wurlitzer jukebox or ancient television models, they come instead to ride the tram.

Lima's tram cars were built in the 1920s in Italy and operated in the center of the city, while larger carriages serviced Barranco. In 1997, some 30 years after the last tram stopped running in Lima, the museum rebuilt a car that it found abandoned in a city scrapyard. It was placed back in service on a six-block section of track down Avenida Pedro de Osma in Barranco. It bears the number 97 in honor of the year it was restored. The tram runs on all days of the week from 10am to 5pm, except Mondays.

Today, this quaint tram car, using mechanical parts imported from France, gives its enthralled passengers a chance to enjoy a mode of transport once so common in Lima. Officially known as Vagón del Recuerdo, or the Car of Memories, this unusual tram is double-ended. It has doors, lights, and controls at both ends for the motor and brakes. The seats can be flipped around according to the direction the tram is heading. Perfectly customized to cope with Lima's extremely narrow streets, the trams were designed with doors on both sides, so that commuters could conveniently board or disembark on either side of the line.

Inside the museum there are some photographs of other trolleys that once plied the streets of Lima. Today, it may seem very hard to believe that Lima's public transport during those early days had such an advanced and efficient system of trolleybuses and trams.

Also on display are a wide array of electrical appliances and machines that have been used over the years by the people of the area.

The old tram rebuilt by the Museo de la Electricidad

❸ Puente de los Suspiros

Between Calles Ayacucho and La Ermita. **Map** 5 D5. ♿

The 19th-century "Bridge of Sighs," which survived the earthquake of 1940, is steeped in legend. It derived its name from the thwarted love of a beautiful girl who lived on the Bajada de los Baños. She fell in love with a lowly street sweeper, but her father forbade her to see the boy and she spent the rest of her days gazing out of the window hoping for a glimpse of him. People crossing the bridge used to hear her sighing for her lost love.

The Bajado de los Baños, a pretty walkway which was built in 1870, slopes gently to the sea connecting the streets of Ayacucho and La Ermita. It is flanked on both sides by grand old homes that were once shaded by leafy olive and fig trees and framed by colorful French bougainvillea. Reflecting the times, the façades were brightly painted, moving away from the favored rich brown of the Colonial era. Today, most of them have been transformed into quality cafés, bars, and restaurants but their balconies and carved ceilings are a reminder of their former Colonial grandeur.

Visitors crossing the Puente de los Suspiros

During the late 19th and early 20th centuries, Barranco was transformed into a fashionable summer address for upper-class Peruvian families. Many of them built fancy country homes here. Wooden baths were used in 1876, and rebuilt in 1906 following their destruction during the War of the Pacific (*see pp54–5*). Unfortunately, the baths were demolished in the 1960s to make way for a coastal road.

❹ La Ermita

Jirón Ermita. **Map** 5 D5. **Closed** to the public.

The façade of the Church of the Hermitage is a famous Barranco landmark. According to legend, a group of fishermen, lost in a winter mist blanketing Lima's coast, prayed to be rescued. They rowed towards a glow that suddenly appeared in the distance and, once on land, they found only a wooden cross in the place from where the light had emanated. Believing divine intervention had spared them, the fishermen erected La Ermita on that same spot.

In front of La Ermita is a statue commemorating Peruvian singer Chabuca Granda, most famous for her tribute to Barranco's bridge known as the Puente de los Suspiros (*see p93*).

A pathway bordering the side of the church, built in 1988, leads past colorful houses and cafés to El Mirador Catalina Recavarren, a lookout point offering panoramic ocean views.

Barranco, the Seaside Resort

In 1876, President Ignacio Prado spent the majestic sum of 15,000 soles to build a path from the Barranco clifftop down to the beach. That same year, wooden baths were constructed for summer holidaymakers on what was then known as the Baño de Pescadores, or Fishermen's Bath. Five years later the baths were destroyed during the war with Chile. In 1906 they were rebuilt, this time with a large pier stretching into the sea, 400 changing rooms, and a huge restaurant with a dance floor that played host to the best orchestras of the day. Barranco, thus, was transformed from a simple seaside hideaway into the most popular summer address for aristocratic Peruvians and expatriates escaping Lima's heat. Postcards from 1915 show women in expansive hats and white dresses promenading on the pier, escorted by men in straw boaters and crisp, pressed suits. Windmills, used to draw water for the houses, dot the area. A funicular, inaugurated in 1895, ferried patrician families around.

Visitors on a Barranco beach during the mid-20th century

The beautiful French-influenced architecture of the Museo Pedro de Osma

5 Museo Pedro de Osma

Av. Pedro de Osma 423. **Map** 5 D5.
Tel 01 467 0141. **Open** 10am–6pm
Tue–Sun. 🖼 🎦 🎦 🖼 with flash.
🚾 **museopedrodeosma.org**

This sugar-white structure is one of Barranco's oldest mansions, erected in the early 20th century for the distinguished Osma family, who were natives of the region of La Osma Riojana in Spain. The main building houses a fine collection of Colonial art and furniture, amassed from the top cultural centers of the time.

Paintings from the Cusco School, melding Spanish Baroque with Andean imagery, offer fascinating examples of subversion, such as the Virgin Mary portrayed with dark Andean hair. Outstanding religious sculptures, many from the Lima School, also line its walls. Of particular interest are the bleeding head of John the Baptist and Adam and Eve reaching for the apple.

The second building, set amongst palm trees, geranium beds, and marble sculptures in the back garden, was originally the dining room. It now houses photographs and dinnerware belonging to the Osma family. A third building is home to an impressive collection of silverware.

6 Museo de Arte Contemporáneo

Av. Grau 1511. **Map** 4 C3.
Tel 01 652 5100.
Open 10am–5pm Tue–Sun. 🖼
🖼 with flash. 🚾 **mac-lima.org.pe**

This modern, glass-walled museum set within a public park houses a permanent collection of more than 120 contemporary paintings, sculptures, and installations by some of today's leading Peruvian and Spanish-American artists, including Fernando de Szyszlo, Ramiro Llona, Oswaldo Guayasamin, Sonia Praga, Lika Mutal, and José Tola. The museum also hosts temporary exhibitions and events, and has a research library. Visitors to the museum also have access to the gardens, where sculptures are displayed. The popular "Art in the Park" program offers weekend art workshops for all ages.

Bohemian Barranco

Barranco has long been a popular spot with artists and intellectuals. From 1913 through to the 1950s, it saw many days of memorable partying, especially during Carnaval which took over the streets for days with revelers in dazzling costumes and masks. One of Peru's most beloved singers, Chabuca Granda, lived here, singing its praises thus: *"there is an age-old belief we Barranquinos have, that the founder of Barranco was none other than God."* Today, it is Lima's evening haunt, with music spilling out of hole-in-the-wall bars, posh nightclubs, and a number of busy *peñas*. Gian Marco, local pop hero and popular Latin music composer, honed his skills here with bar gigs, and after a stint abroad returned to live in his favourite *barrio* (district). While writer Mario Vargas Llosa's seafront house has been replaced by an apartment block, other homes remain, such as that of renowned sculptor and artist Victor Delfin *(see p83).*

Statue of Chabuca Granda

Peñas: Peru's Music Clubs

Peñas originated in the *callejones* (tenements) of central Lima, traditional home to immigrants and the rural poor. They began as small, informal clubs for family and friends, united in their love of a particular kind of folk music. Like Peruvian cuisine, the music is a product of its Andean, African, and Spanish roots with the African slaves contributing percussion instruments. Lima's *peñas* generally focus on folkloric or *criolla* (Creole) music, though some cross all borders. Fans may argue that today's *peñas,* with their all-singing, all-dancing performances, are more variety shows than traditional clubs, where participation and knowledge-sharing is the goal, but the bottom line is that they are very popular.

Spanish influences from the 16th century introduced the harp and the guitar. Until then, pre-Hispanic Andean music mostly consisted of wind instruments and small drums.

Musica *criolla* is a blend of African music with Spanish and Andean rhythms. It has a Creole version of Spanish guitar and *cajon* drum.

A lively evening at a popular Peña

Far from the intimacy of a traditional *peña*, today's clubs provide energetic singing and dancing performances while encouraging participation from a willing audience. Modern *peñas*, such as La Candelaria, offer a taste of culture showcasing dances from several regions of the country.

Dances that are performed in a *peña* range from the *marinera* from the north to Cusco's *huayno*, Puno's *tuntuna*, and *diablada*.

Musicians dressed in colorful costumes play traditional music, and the revelers, fueled by pisco sour, can't help but take to the dance floor.

Retablo detail depicts musicians playing various Andean instruments. South Andes is famous for the *huayno*, a mestizo chant of melancholic vocals, the harp, and *charango*.

FARTHER AFIELD

Beyond the key areas of Central Lima, Miraflores, and Barranco, the sights of interest are somewhat dispersed. The village-like suburb of Pueblo Libre to the south of Central Lima, is home to a number of museums. Museo Nacional de Arqueologia, Antropologia e Historia del Peru, and the privately run Museo Arqueologico Rafael Larco Herrera are people-friendly spaces that chronicle Peru's intriguing past. Far away from the confines of museum walls is Pachacámac, a couple of adobe pyramids, which at one

time hosted both Wari as well as Inca cultures and was renowned as the site of a powerful oracle. Evidence of Peru's strategic importance in the region during the time of the Spanish colonization is displayed at the Fortaleza del Real Felipe, a fortress built in the 18th century on the port of Callao. The Museo Naval nearby also showcases and celebrates Peru's maritime prowess. Stately mansions in the nearby district of La Punta are a reminder of the area's popularity with Lima's aristocracy in the 19th century, and again, in the 1930s and 1940s.

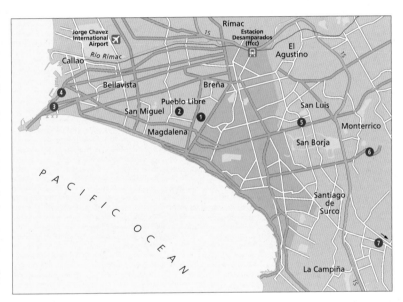

Sights at a Glance

Historic Buildings and Sights
❸ Fortaleza del Real Felipe
❼ Pachacámac

Museums and Galleries
❶ *Museo Nacional de Arqueologia pp100–101*
❷ Museo Arqueológico Rafael Larco Herrera
❹ Museo Naval del Peru
❺ Museo de la Nacion
❻ Museo de Oro del Peru

Key
▨ Central districts
═ Highway
━ Major road
═ Minor road

0 kilometers 3
0 miles 3

◀ Gulls and black skimmers at the Pantanos de Villa nature reserve

For map symbols *see back flap*

Bright blooms adorn the façade of Museo Arqueológico Rafael Larco Herrera

❶ Museo Nacional de Arqueología

See pp100–101.

❷ Museo Arqueológico Rafael Larco Herrera

Bolivar 1515, Pueblo Libre.
Tel 01 461 1312. **Open** 9am–10pm daily.
W museolarco.org

A grand 18th-century mansion built on a pyramid dating back to the 7th century provides more than a fitting home for 3,000 years of ancient history. The Larco Herrera Museum, founded in 1926, houses the biggest private collection of Peruvian pre-Columbian art – 45,000 pieces – amassed by sugar baron Rafael Larco Hoyle.

The Culture Hall, divided into North Coast, South, Center, and Highlands, is a good starting point as it gives a comprehensive view of the cultures that existed from 7000 BC to the 16th century.

In the Andean world, the beauty and durability of metals gave objects an almost divine value. They were designed to be offered to the gods. The Incas, as representatives of the gods, wore them or took them to their grave on their way to the other world.

The gold and silver collection, which is nothing short of heavenly, comprises head-dresses, beads the size of golf balls, and chest plates inlaid

with precious stones. Enormous ear "plugs," nose ornaments, crowns with quartz and turquoise, funerary masks, and a shirt made of gold discs are also displayed.

There are ancient textiles, including a fragment from a Paracas weaving showing 389 threads to 1 inch (3 cm) – a world record. Other exhibits range from a Wari loom-woven wall-hanging made from parrot feathers, to an Inca *quipu*, the ancient way of recording facts and events with colored threads and knots *(see p29)*. The museum also showcases tools, kaolin, clay, molds, paints, as well as unbaked ceramics.

Separate from the main house is a gallery of erotic art, with myriad vessels depicting the sex lives of ancient Peruvians. They were made by Larco Hoyle in the 1960s, based on his research on Peruvian pre-Columbian art.

❸ Fortaleza del Real Felipe

Plazuela de la Independencia, Callao.
Tel 01 429 0532.
Open 9am–4pm daily.
Closed pub hols.

The stone-walled Royal Felipe Fort is one of the largest forts built by the Spanish in the 18th century. Of interest to both the visitor and the historian, it was

designed by Frenchman Luis Gaudin and inaugurated in 1774 by Viceroy Amat. The fort was named in honor of Felipe V, the first Bourbon king of Spain, who died in 1746.

The austere, pentagon-shaped fort was intended to defend against pirate attacks. During the 19th century, Callao *(see p102)*, where the fort stands, was considered to be the most powerfully protected port on the west coast of South America. Real Felipe had been "war-ready" since Colonial times, and had repelled many attacks. The fort had been besieged five times but never conquered. It also played a pivotal role in Peru's War of Independence *(see p53)*, acting as the first line of defense.

Covering more than 84,000 sq yards (70,000 sq m), the fort contains brass and iron cannons, military tanks, the Governor's House, Towers of the King and Queen, as well as the Museo del Ejército (Military Museum), with its impressive collection of weapons, documents, military uniforms, and relics dating back to 1730.

Golden neck-piece, Museo Larco Herrera

Environs
Two islands visible from the fort are **San Lorenzo** and **El Frontón**. San Lorenzo, Peru's largest island, was said to be a pirates' lair in Colonial times. Dutch pirate, Jacob the Hermit, who died in 1624, is buried here. The Spanish Armada also used the island as a refuge during the Battle of Angamos in 1879.

The history of El Fronton (Island of the Dead) is less romantic. It operated as a political prison during Colonial times but later became a jail for common criminals. The nearby **Cabinzas Islands** are a haunt of sea birds, while **Palomino Island** is home to sea lions, some weighing up to 660 lb (300 kg).

Boat tours for the islands depart from the Muelle de Guerra in Plaza Grau.

❹ Museo Naval del Peru

Av. Jorge Chavez 123, Callao.
Tel 01 429 4793. **Open** 9am–3pm
Tue–Sun. 🅿️ 📧
🇼 **museonaval.com.pe**

The Naval Museum, near the Fortaleza del Real Felipe, is a key site for seafaring history buffs. Instigated by Capitán de Navío Julio J. Elías Murguía, a Peruvian naval hero, the museum has an important collection of historical, naval documents, oil paintings, uniforms, and relics from the 1879–83 War of the Pacific (see pp54–5). Also included are many personal objects of those involved in the conflict, photographs, weapons, and navigational instruments.

Prized items are those that belonged to one of Peru's great military heroes, Admiral Miguel Grau, who died in the Battle of Angamos. Also known as the Caballero de los Mares (Gentleman of the Seas), his letters, navigational charts, and medals, as well as a sarcophagus with a fragment of his shinbone, his only remains found after the battle, are displayed here.

One room is devoted entirely to model ships, showcasing vessels from different eras and countries.

❺ Museo de la Nacion

Javier Prado Oeste 2465, San Borja.
Tel 01 476 9878. **Open** 9am–5pm
Tue–Sun. **Closed** Jan 1, Easter Thu & Sat, May 1, Jul 28 & 29, Dec 25. 🅿️
🎫 📧 🖥️ 📷

Although this imposing concrete building embodies the architecture of Peru's military government of the 1970s, the exhibits inside celebrate Peru's rich archaeological past.

Opened as a museum in 1990, the collection highlights Peru's history dating back to its prehistoric cultures. It includes extensive displays of Chavín stone carvings, Wari textiles, and Paracas and Chancay weavings.

Extensive display of ceramics at the Museo de la Nacion

Moche ceramics, wooden idols, and a sarcophagus from the Amazon, are also on view. The museum gives an insightful overview of Peru's past, which will be of interest to visitors about to tour the country's main sites. Entire floors are given over to ancient ceramics: huge glass cases showcase Nazca pottery adorned with pumas and condors, the distinctive white, cream, and black Chancay pottery, as well as the yellow and white designs favored by the people from around Cajamarca.

Nazca pottery, Museo de la Nacion

Also displayed are good models of Peru's most famous ruins – Machu Picchu (see pp180–5), the Nazca Lines (see pp130–31), and the Lords of Sipán tomb (see pp232–5); the latter hailed as one of the greatest discoveries in Latin American history.

In a separate section of the museum there are interesting displays of traditional costumes from across Peru, as well as a selection of popular regional art.

The museum hosts various temporary exhibitions and is also a venue for dance and theater performances.

Rafael Larco Hoyle (1901–66)

Born on a sugar plantation in Trujillo, Rafael Larco Hoyle rose to be one of Peru's most noted businessmen, with a sharp eye for the country's ancient crafts. His passion saw the family hacienda break sugar production records when he mechanized it after completing his studies in the USA. In 1926, he opened a museum on his plantation and dedicated it to north Peruvian pre-Columbian pottery. He continued to collect the rarest and finest of the arts, at one point commandeering the largest swimming pool on the hacienda to remove salt from a newly acquired 8,000-piece collection. Don Rafael also began to explore and excavate sites in northern Peru collecting artifacts, pottery, and vessels. He moved the entire collection to Lima in 1958.

Rafael Larco Hoyle studying an artifact

❶ Museo Nacional de Arqueología, Antropologia e Historia del Peru

This comprehensive collection of Peruvian historical artifacts is displayed in Casa Huerta, a mansion used by Peru's liberators José de San Martín and Símon Bolivar. Thousands of objects chart the country's history, from pre-Hispanic to the Colonial and Republican times. It boasts the largest collection of ceramics, the most important collection of ancient human remains, including mummies, and *fardos funerarios* (wrapped bodies), as well as a series of Viceroy portraits from the 18th and 19th centuries.

Textile with geometric iconography typical of the Paracas culture

Café

Moche Ceramics
Moche potters used a molding technique to produce bottles with spouts and handles as well as musical whistling bottles depicting men, women, animals, and deities in realistic activities such as hunting, fishing, or fighting.

★ Mummies
The Paracas culture buried their dead in a sitting position, wrapped in layers of fabric. Their mummies are said to be the best pre-served in the world due to the freeze-drying effect of the arid climate there.

Principal entrance

★ Estela Raimondi
This enomorous stone obelisk was recovered from Chavín de Huántar ceremonial center. Carved with intricate images of snakes, condors, jaguars, and the Staff God, it is one of the most important pieces in the museum.

Obelisko Tello, named after the archaeologist who discovered it at Chavín de Huantár, was used to mark the beginning and end of the agricultural year by projecting shadows in certain areas.

The Lithics Gallery
Comprising 18,250 stone artifacts
(lithics) from all over Peru, some
dating from 12,000 BC.
The display includes
knives, axes, hammers,
grinding stones,
sculptures, beads,
and bowls.

VISITORS' CHECKLIST

Practical Information
Plaza Bolívar, corner of San Martín
& Vivanco, Pueblo Libre.
Tel 01 463 5070.
Open 8:45am–4pm Tue–Sat,
8:45am–3pm Sun & public
holidays.

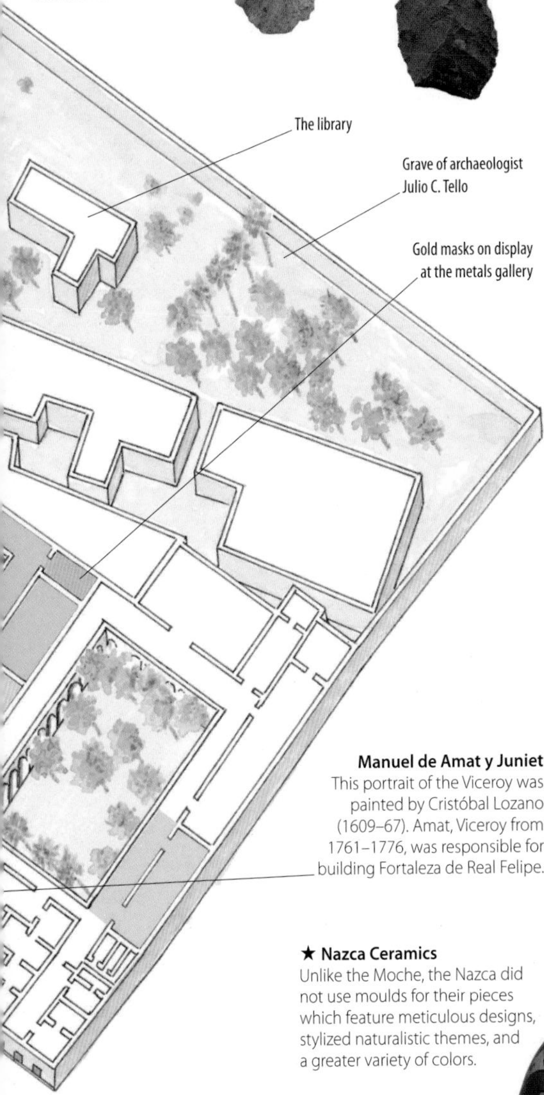

The library

Grave of archaeologist
Julio C. Tello

Gold masks on display
at the metals gallery

Key

Metals
Temporary Exhibitions
Wari Gallery
Chimú
Inca
Moche
Paracas
Formative
Origins Gallery

Manuel de Amat y Juniet
This portrait of the Viceroy was
painted by Cristóbal Lozano
(1609–67). Amat, Viceroy from
1761–1776, was responsible for
building Fortaleza de Real Felipe.

★ Nazca Ceramics
Unlike the Moche, the Nazca did
not use moulds for their pieces
which feature meticulous designs,
stylized naturalistic themes, and
a greater variety of colors.

Gallery Guide

*Beginning at the left of the main entrance, exhibits are
displayed chronologically in a series of connecting rooms
on one level, each devoted to a specific period. The main
house, Casa Huerta, is accessed via the final gallery to the
right of the entrance.*

➏ Museo de Oro del Peru

Alonso de Molina 1100, Monterrico-Surco. **Tel** 01 345 1292/345 1271.
Open 10:30am–6pm daily.
Closed Jan 1, May 1, Jul 28 & Dec 25.
🏛 🅿 ♿ 🚻 📷
W museoroperu.com.pe

One of Lima's top attractions, Miguel Mujica Gallo's massive private Gold Museum displays numerous ceremonial knives and vases studded with turquoise. Ornate funerary masks, crowns, helmets, figurines, earrings, necklaces, an impressive gold ceremonial bag, and a tunic appliquéd with gold are also on view.

In addition, there are ceremonial objects, a Nazca poncho woven with parrot feathers, "hats" made of human hair, a feathered headdress, tapestries, ceramics, and mummies, some even with tiny babies. Labeling on the exhibits is unfortunately poor, with inadequate explanation in Spanish, and almost none in English, making an audio guide essential.

Windowed patio of the House of the Chosen Women, Pachacámac

Chimú mask, Museo de Oro del Peru

The building's upper floor is set aside for Armas del Mundo (Arms of the World), a vast collection of ancient firearms and military paraphernalia. On view is an 1812 sword of Russian Tsar Alexander, and the pistol that belonged to Chilean President Salvador Allende. In 2001, the museum was rocked by scandal with the National Institute of Culture and the Tourism Protection Bureau declaring that almost all its estimated 7,000 pieces were fake. However, the owners claim to have only genuine gold pieces on display.

➐ Pachacámac

Panamerican Highway South, KM31.5, Lurín. **Tel** 01 430 0168 or 01 430 2115.
Open 9am–5pm Tue–Sat. 🏛 🅿 ♿
🚻 in museum. 🅿 📷

Dating from AD 200, this complex of adobe pyramids rising out of the Lurin Valley was a key pilgrimage center on Peru's central coast, and home to a much venerated oracle. It flourished through the centuries and pilgrims traveled great distances to pay homage to God Pachacámac (He who Enlivens the Universe and Everything).

Pachacámac was expanded by the Wari and their designs can be seen on the ceramics and textiles found here. However, most of the compounds and pyramids date from after their downfall.

When the last Inca king, Atahualpa, was imprisoned by Pizarro, he complained that the oracle had falsely predicted his victory. His account of gold at the site led soldiers there but they were disppointed by the "ugly" idol they found instead.

The Incas built five separate complexes, including the Templo del Sol (Temple of the Sun) and the Palacio de Las Mamaconas (House of the Chosen Women), with stonework on its entrance gate, a rarity on the coast.

The on-site museum houses a collection of pre-Hispanic relics, including Paracas textiles, ceramics, and a two-faced image of Pachacámac.

Environs
The **Pantanos de Villa**, a wetland area 11 miles (18 km) south of Lima, is one of the main coastal refuges for more than 150 bird species, including the majestic white heron. With its *totora* reed-lined pools, it is Lima's last remaining natural reserve. There are signposted trails and lookout towers for bird-lovers.

Callao's Battles

As a leading commercial port, Callao was the site of many battles

Founded in 1537, Callao became the leading port for Spanish commerce in Latin America. Its colorful history saw attacks by pirates and buccaneers, including Sir Francis Drake, who seized all the valuables from the anchored Spanish ships and sank them in 1574. Later, the earthquake and tsunami of 1746 destroyed the entire port. Battles were waged here during the independence and the Pacific wars, and it was occupied by Chile for three years.

Lima's Beaches

With more than 1,156 miles (1,860 km) of shoreline, Peruvians have long worshipped the Pacific. Wave-riding is documented in friezes in the 2,000-year-old archaeological complexes on the coast. Beaches, headlands, and coves are plentiful, providing lots of opportunity for keen surfers and swimmers. Come December, when Lima's grey haze finally lifts, Limeños head south for weekends. On Sundays, the Panamerican Highway back to Lima can become so clogged that it reverts to one-way, with outgoing traffic diverted to another road. By January, most city-dwellers move for the summer to one of the string of beaches stretching down the coast.

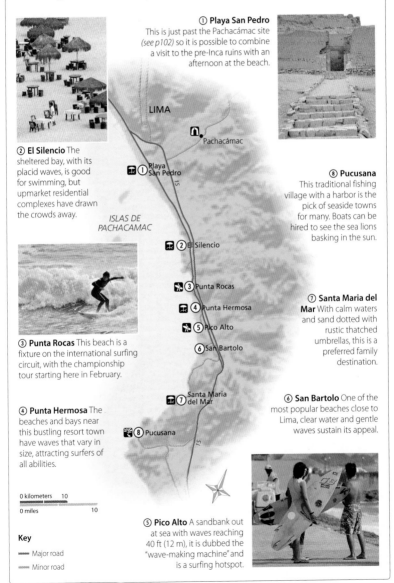

① **Playa San Pedro**
This is just past the Pachacámac site (see p102) so it is possible to combine a visit to the pre-Inca ruins with an afternoon at the beach.

② **El Silencio** The sheltered bay, with its placid waves, is good for swimming, but upmarket residential complexes have drawn the crowds away.

③ **Punta Rocas** This beach is a fixture on the international surfing circuit, with the championship tour starting here in February.

④ **Punta Hermosa** The beaches and bays near this bustling resort town have waves that vary in size, attracting surfers of all abilities.

⑧ **Pucusana**
This traditional fishing village with a harbor is the pick of seaside towns for many. Boats can be hired to see the sea lions basking in the sun.

⑦ **Santa Maria del Mar** With calm waters and sand dotted with rustic thatched umbrellas, this is a preferred family destination.

⑥ **San Bartolo** One of the most popular beaches close to Lima, clear water and gentle waves sustain its appeal.

⑤ **Pico Alto** A sandbank out at sea with waves reaching 40 ft (12 m), it is dubbed the "wave-making machine" and is a surfing hotspot.

LIMA
Pachacámac
Playa San Pedro
ISLAS DE PACHACAMAC
El Silencio
Punta Rocas
Punta Hermosa
Pico Alto
San Bartolo
Santa Maria del Mar
Pucusana

0 kilometers 10
0 miles 10

Key

━━━ Major road
━━━ Minor road

SHOPPING IN LIMA

If you missed buying those blankets from the weavers near Lake Titicaca, the odds are that you will find the same in Lima. The shops here are stacked with handicrafts from different regions of Peru. Silver aficionados can sate their appetite on Avenida La Paz, which is lined with sparkling shops, while souvenir hunters are spoilt for choice at Lima's indigenous markets. Specialist shops and galleries stock myriad handmade folk art objects and upmarket items. Although Lima is not a fashion capital, the city's largest mall, Jockey Plaza, does have some designer label boutiques, along with department stores stacked high with locally made jeans and outfits. Remember it is illegal to take historical artifacts out of Peru; visitors need to be extra careful while shopping.

Pottery, Ceramics, Art, and Crafts

Mari Solari's shop-gallery, **Las Pallas**, is a Peruvian treasure trove. You can find anything from hand-painted masks to engraved gourds and from pottery to amulets – some masquerading as funky fridge magnets. *Retablos*, hinged wooden boxes containing painted figures crafted from dough, are also available. If you are in luck, Solari might even allow you a glimpse of her private collection of Inca *keros* (cups).

Housed in a mansion on Barranco's designer store strip, **Dédalo**'s maze of rooms brims with Peruvian homewares, Spanish-language books, toys, furniture, clothes, handbags, ceramics, jewelry, and glassware crafted by local artisans.

The **Galería del Barrio** is located in a beautiful old Casona Chorrillana dating from

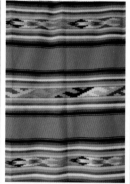
Colorful fabric with traditional pattern for sale

the mid-19th century. This historic site, with brass ceilings and a stained glass dome, houses an art gallery and an arts and handicrafts shop selling a wide variety of items, including paintings, sculptures, and photographs. Recycled furniture, old cameras, toys, and more are available in the gallery's vintage store.

Galería Lucia de la Puente's main objective is to promote both renowned Peruvian visual artists and young talent in contemporary art. The gallery gives professional advice on the purchase of contemporary art in all its forms – painting, sculpture, printmaking, film, photography, and more.

Representing the work of Peruvian artists that specialize in drawing, painting, sculpture, and photography, **Wu Galería** is also devoted to discovering young talent. It has a permanent display of its own prints, as well as pieces from other workshops.

Fabrics

Kuskaya works with artisans across Peru to preserve handicraft traditions while modernizing them. Cotton table linen and pillows are produced by the Callua weavers in Cajamarca, feather-soft scarves woven from Suri alpaca by Puno artisans, and cotton handbags are embroidered in the jungle. In addition, alabaster-like napkin rings are sculpted in Ayacucho and decorative ceramics come from the northern Chulucanas. Kuskaya also tailor-makes pieces to match your existing decor.

For clothes, **Alpaca 111** has a reputation as the place to shop for alpaca, with downy baby alpaca jumpers, coats, capes, and vicuña scarves and shawls on sale. Vicuña, a tiny distant cousin of the llama, is said to produce the world's finest wool, boasting a diameter of 11–13 microns, against 16 microns for cashmere, 17–19 microns for alpaca, and 30 microns for sheep wool. Prices are a little higher than normal but then so is the quality.

Wooden angel playing music

Silver

Argentinian-born designer **Ester Ventura**, who sees customers by appointment only, combines objects and fragments from centuries-old pre-Columbian cultures with silver for her exclusive jewelry. Chunky silver

Ceramic churches from the owner's collection, Las Pallas

bands or delicate mesh are entwined with Chavín beads, and Paracas or Nazca textiles. Elongated shell beads, mother-of-pearl, coral, turquoise, and ceramic shards are used to create exquisite one-off pieces.

Necklaces at **Ilaria** range from chic silver bands and sparsely threaded beads to elaborate amethyst, turquoise, and other stone-studded pendants. Silver tableware is a specialty and decorative pieces such as polished wooden angels with silver wings are also appealing.

Camusso is a bastion of traditional silverware. Founded in 1933 by an Italian immigrant Carlo Mario Camusso, it boasts some 3,600 pieces in its collection, ranging from cutlery to cocktail shakers. Tours of the factory can be arranged.

A host of silver shops proffering frames, vases, trays, plates, and jewelry are concentrated around Avenida La Paz in Miraflores. Prices don't differ that much, but most merchants are willing to reduce from the price tag.

Markets

Avenida Petit Thouars is lined with handicraft markets and the unassuming **Mercado Indio**, with its 100 or so stalls offering

Peruvian handicrafts shop, Larcomar Shopping Mall, Miraflores

items from all over Peru, is a good place to start. Although most items are mass produced, you can stumble on some unique pieces, including colorful hand-woven baskets and elaborate wooden candle-sticks and mirrors in the Cusco style. You can haggle, but prices are pretty much standard.

The covered **Mercado Surquillo** is one of the most interesting places in Lima to shop for food. Stocked with fruit, vegetables, fish, cheese, and meat from all over Peru, the market is a favorite with Peruvian super-chef Gaston Acurio. However, you need to be beware of pickpockets.

Malls and Department Stores

Opened in 1997, **Jockey Plaza** in Monterrico is Lima's largest mall, housing big stores such as Ripley and Saga Falabella. It has a movie theater, food court, fashion stores including Hugo Boss, along with home decor specialist Casa y Ideas. The mall also has some books and CD shops, and there is a supermarket as well as a hardware store.

Larcomar *(see p83)* in Miraflores is a good one-stop shop for local handicrafts, quirky accessories, designer sun-glasses, swim- and surfwear, cigars, and books.

DIRECTORY

Pottery, Ceramics, Art, and Crafts

Dédalo
Paseo Sáenz Peña 295,
Barranco.
Tel 01 652 5400.

Galería del Barrio
Bernardino Cruz 148,
Chorrillos.
Tel 01 251 9111.

Galería Lucia de la Puente
Paseo Saenz Peña 206,
Barranco.
Tel 01 477 9740 or
01 477 0237.

Las Pallas
Calle Cajamarca 212,
Barranco.
Tel 01 477 4629.

Wu Galería
Paseo Saenz Peña 129,
Barranco. **Tel** 01 247 4685.

Fabrics

Kuna (Alpaca 111)
Av. Larco 671, Miraflores.
Map 4 B2. **Tel** 01 447
1623. w kuna.com.pe

Kuskaya
Av. Conquistadores 556,
San Isidro. **Map** 2 C4.
Tel 01 222 0625.
w kuskayaperu.com

Silver

Camusso
Jr. Camino Real 1801, Int
A-08B, Parque Industrial
San Pedrito, Surco.
Tel 01 637 5140.

Ester Ventura
Tel 01 251 3953 or 998
241 915.
w estercventura.com

Ilaria
Av. Dos de Mayo 308,
San Isidro.
Map 2 B2.
Tel 01 512 3530.

Markets

Mercado Indio
Av. Petit Thouars 5245,
Miraflores.
Map 3 D5.

Mercado Surquillo
Paseo de la República,
Cnr of Angamos Este.
Map 3 D5.

Malls and Department Stores

Jockey Plaza
Javier Prado 4200,
Surco/Monterrico.
Tel 01 716 2000.
w jockey-plaza.com.pe

Larcomar
Avenida Malecón
de la Reserva 610,
Miraflores.
Map 4 B2.
Tel 01 620 6000.
w larcomar.com

ENTERTAINMENT IN LIMA

Peru has a rich tradition of dance and music reflected by Lima's *peñas (see p95)*, proudly flying the red and white flag, encouraging crowdsof locals and tourists to try their hand and feet at local dances. Movies are another popular pastime and the city has more cinemas than the rest of Peru combined. There is also a small but active theater scene, although most productions are in Spanish, naturally. Bar-hoppers and live music fans flock to Barranco, while Miraflores also has its share of pubs and dance clubs. Come October, Limeños are out in droves for the annual bullfighting season, which features world-renowned matadors.

Enraptured viewers with a mural in the backdrop at La Candelaria, Barranco

Peñas and Salsodromos

Peru has two main types of music – *folklórico* and *criollo*. Folkloric is from the Andean highlands while Creole is more coastal. Whatever the musical theme, a *peña (see p95)* is a recipe for a rowdy night aided by helpings of Peruvian food, pisco, and beer.

Creole **Peña Del Carajo** often features well known Creole performers such as Arturo "Zambo" Cavero and Pepe Vásquez, while **Dama Juana** is a restaurant that serves up a creole buffet and showcases a display of traditional Peruvian dances. **La Candelaria** has a little bit of everything, offering dances from coast and mountain, as well as from the jungle.

As the name implies, *salsodromos* pulsate to the sound of salsa and Caribbean music. Weekends at **El Pizzotón** are dedicated to Puerto Rican and Cuban sounds; rhumba and Afro-Peruvian music feature on other nights. **La Casa de la Salsa** hosts some of the best salsa bands and the huge dance-floor is always teeming.

Bars, Clubs, and Discos

Barranco is the place for bars and clubs. Since everything is within walking distance, just a few steps can mean a change of pace from electronica at **La Noche** to live rock and roll in an English pub-style setting at the **Lion's Head Pub**. **Posada del Ángel** offers cold beer and Latino-style troubadors, while **El Dragon** is an underground jazz club with live music and cool decor. The classy **Ayahuasca Bar** offers a colorful selection of cocktails and snacks. Miraflores discotheque **Gótica** features international DJs and is always jam-packed. Pubs such as **O'Murphy's** draw Limeños and expats with its on-tap Guinness, wide choice of imported and local beers, and pool table.

Cinema and Theater

Lima has a huge number of multiplex cinemas, mostly showing Hollywood blockbusters, often in English with subtitles. Children's films, however, are always dubbed. For those who prefer classic or independent films, there's the **Centro Cultural de España**. Lima theaters host a number of productions during the year, with all offerings listed in *El Commercio* newspaper.

The restored **Teatro Municipal de Lima** offers a varied program of theater, ballet, and opera. **Teatro Marsano** is known for light comedy. **Teatro Segura**, which hosted its first performance in 1615, presents classical and contemporary works including musicals and ballets. The **Teatro Británico** occasionally stages plays in English. Film festivals, concerts, and exhibitions as well as theater and dance events are held regularly in cultural centers such as **Instituto Cultural Peruano Norteamericano (ICPNA)**, **Central Cultural PUCP**,

Musicians performing at the Estacion del Barranco

A bullfight in full swing at the popular Plaza de Acho bullring

and **Alianza Francesa**. The Museo de la Nacion (see p99) is often used as a venue for a variety of events, from children's plays to international dance and circus performances.

Casinos

Lima is awash with casinos but the most reputable ones are located in major hotels, such as the **Sheraton Lima**, the **JW Marriott**, and **Los Delfines**. Slot machine fans be aware that Lima's one-arm bandits have a reputation for paying out very little, if anything.

Spectator Sports

Fútbol (soccer), is the national sport and **Estadio Nacional** is the venue for most big matches. The bullfighting season, which runs from October to the end of November at the **Plaza de Acho** bullring, coincides with Lima's biggest festival, Feria Taurina del Señor de los Milagros (see p73). Famous matadors from Spain and France take part, along with local luminaries, and tickets for events in the oldest bullring in the Americas are sold well in advance. Prices for the seats in *la sombra*, or the shade, are the most expensive, while seats in *el sol*, the sun, are cheaper. The tickets are available from TeleTicket counters in the Wong and Metro supermarkets.

DIRECTORY

Peñas and Salsodromos

El Pizzotón
Calle de las Pizzas 290.
Map 4 B1.
Tel 01 9330 0829.

La Candelaria
Av. Bolognesi 292.
Tel 01 247 1314/2941.

La Casa de la Salsa
Av. Bausate y Meza 169.
Map 1 E3.
Tel 01 331 1510.

Las Brisas del Titicaca
Heroes de Tarapacá 168.
Map 1 D3.
Tel 01 715 6960.

Peña Del Carajo
Catalino Miranda 158.
Map 5 D3.
Tel 01 247 7023.

Bars, Clubs, and Discos

Ayahuasca Bar
Prolg. San Martín 130.
Map 5 D4.

El Dragon
Nicolas de Piérola 168.
Map 5 D4.
Tel 01 477 5420.

Gótica
Larcomar Commercial Centre, Level 5, Malecon de la Reserva 601.
Map 4 B2.
Tel 01 242 7869.

La Noche
Av. Bolognesi 307.
Map 5 D4.
Tel 01 247 1012.

Lion's Head Pub
Av. Grau 268.
Map 5 D5.
Tel 01 247 1499.

O'Murphy's Irish Pub
Schell 619. **Map** 4 C1.
Tel 01 650 8267.

Posada del Ángel
San Martín 157.
Map 4 C4.
Tel 01 247 5544.

Cinema and Theater

Alianza Francesa
Av. Arequipa 4595,
Miraflores. **Map** 3 D4.
Tel 01 610 8000.
w alianzafrancesa lima.edu.pe

Central Cultural PUCP
Av. Camino Real 1075, San Isidro. **Map** 5 E5.
Tel 01 616 1616.
w cultural.pucp.edu.pe

Centro Cultural de España
Natalio Sanchez 181, Santa Beatriz. **Map** 1 E4.
Tel 01 330 0412.

ICPNA
(see p86).

Teatro Británico
Bellavista 531,
Miraflores. **Map** 4 B1.
Tel 01 615 3610.

Teatro Marsano
General Suárez 409,
Miraflores. **Map** 3 F4.
Tel 01 445 7347.

Teatro Municipal de Lima
Jr. Ica 377.
Map 1 E1.
Tel 01 315 1300.

Teatro Segura
Huancavelica 265.
Map 1 E1.
Tel 01 315 1451.

Casinos

JW Marriott
w marriott.com

Los Delfines
w losdelfineshotel.com

Sheraton Lima
w sheraton.com.pe

Spectator Sports

Estadio Nacional
Via Expressa.

Plaza de Acho
Hualgayoc 332, Rimac.
Tel 01 481 1467.

STREET FINDER

The map below shows the area covered by the maps on the following pages. All map references given with sights, entertainment venues, and shops described in the Lima section of the guide refer to the Street Finder maps in this section. Map references are also given for Lima hotels and restaurants as well as for useful addresses

in the Travelers' Needs and the Survival Guide sections at the back of the book. The main sights in the Central Lima area can be found on page 111 and those in San Isidro on pages 112 and 113. The main attractions of Miraflores are on pages 112–115, while Barranco's are shown on the maps on pages 114 and 115.

Key to street finder

- Major sight
- Place of interest
- Other building
- Railroad station
- *i* Tourist information point
- Police station
- Church
- Highway
- Railway line

Scale of Maps 1–5

0 meters 500
0 yards 500

Street Finder Index

4

ENRIQUE PALACIOS

2 DE MAYO

2 DE MAYO

MIRAFLORES

AV. JOSÉ PARDO

COLINA

Casa Ricardo
Palma

AV. PALMA

SAN DIEGO

AV. CÁCERES

PLAZA
MORALES
BARROS

BERLÍN

LEÓN

BONILLA

ESPERANZA

PARQUE
CENTRAL

VARGAS MACHUCA

PARQUE
LAS TRADICIONES

1

BERLÍN

JOSE GALVEZ

AV. COMANDANTE ESPINAR

RECAVARREN

BEL LA VISTA

Parque
Kennedy

i

AV. LARCO

DÍEZ CANSECO

SILVA

ALFARO

AV. AVIACIÓN

FRANCIA

BOLOGNESI

GRAU

SCHELL

AV. LA PAZ

AV. CASIMIRO U

MADRID

PARQUE
EL FARO

ITALIA

AV. O. BENAVIDES

PORTA

AV. A. BENAVIDES

PARQUE
REDUCTO

TRIPOLI

BOLÍVAR

15 DE E

PASEO DE

2

Playa Makah

VENECIA

LAVALLE

SAN MARTÍN

AV. 28 DE JULIO

SOLAR

AV. REDUCTO

GONZÁLES

MANCO CÁPAC

PORTA

FANNING

AV. LARCO

FERRÉ

DALIAS

ALCANFORES

SANTA ISABEL

SAN FERNANDO

AV. NÚÑEZ DE BALBOA

Playa
Costa Verde

CIRCUITO DE

MALECÓN DE LA RESERVA

Larcomar PARQUE
SALAZAR

AV. ARMENDÁRIZ

ACACIAS

PLAYAS

Nstra.Sra.
de Fátima

3

Playa
Redondo

PARQUE
DOMODOSSOLA

MALECÓN HARRIS

Museo de Arte
Contemporáneo

AV. EL SOL OESTE

RAZURI

MARTÍN

Playa
La Estrella

4

P A C I F I C

O C E A N

Playa
Las Piedritas

CIRCUITO

MALECÓN SOUZA

PEREZ ROCA

SAENZ PEN

MA

MALECÓN PAZOS

DE

Playa
Las Cascadas

PLAYAS

Playa
Barranquito

Muse
Galería Ar

5

Playa
Barranco

Playa
Los Yuyos

PERU REGION BY REGION

Peru at a Glance

The massive Andes mountain range divides the country down the middle, with dense jungle on one side covering 60 percent of Peru's landmass, and sandy desert edging the coast on the other side. Unique animal and plant life flourish across all regions, which are also dotted with magnificent examples of ancient civilizations including the Nazca Lines, Chan Chan, Chavín de Huántar, and Machu Picchu. The Colonial monasteries and churches evoke the Spanish conquest in myriad towns and isolated villages.

Kuélap *(see pp248–50)* is an imposing pre-Inca walled city perched above Río Utcubamba.

Museo Tumbas Reales de Sipán *(see pp232–5)* showcases the amazing archaeological finds of the Royal Tombs of Sipán, dubbed "the richest tomb of the New World" for all the beautifully crafted artifacts unearthed there.

Chavín de Huántar *(see pp212–13)* is one of the best preserved Chavín sites and provides an insight into their sophisticated construction and artistic skills.

Piura   San Ignacio

The Northern Desert
(see pp218–37)

Chachapoyas

Chiclayo

The Northern Highlands
(see pp238–51)

Tara...

Trujillo

Caraz

Huaraz

Poz...

Cordillera Blanca
(see pp200–217)

Lima
(see pp58–115)

Imperial

Reserva Nacional de Paracas *(see p127)* is the country's largest area of protected coastline, teeming with wildlife. Towering cliffs fringe the beaches along some of the richest seas in the world.

◀ Aerial view of the canyon country surrounding Colonial Arequipa

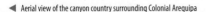

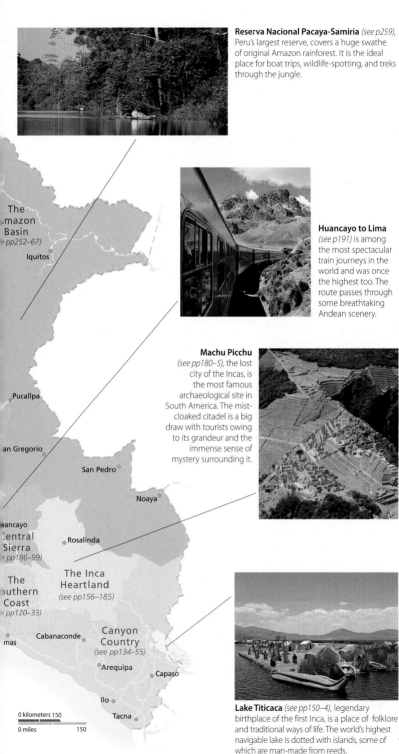

Reserva Nacional Pacaya-Samiria *(see p259)*, Peru's largest reserve, covers a huge swathe of original Amazon rainforest. It is the ideal place for boat trips, wildlife-spotting, and treks through the jungle.

Huancayo to Lima *(see p191)* is among the most spectacular train journeys in the world and was once the highest too. The route passes through some breathtaking Andean scenery.

Machu Picchu *(see pp180–5)*, the lost city of the Incas, is the most famous archaeological site in South America. The mist-cloaked citadel is a big draw with tourists owing to its grandeur and the immense sense of mystery surrounding it.

The Amazon Basin *(pp252–67)*

Iquitos

Pucallpa

San Gregorio

San Pedro

Noaya

Huancayo

Central Sierra *(pp186–99)*

Rosalinda

The Southern Coast *(pp120–33)*

The Inca Heartland *(see pp156–185)*

mas

Cabanaconde

Canyon Country *(see pp134–55)*

Arequipa

Capaso

Ilo

Tacna

0 kilometers 150

0 miles 150

Lake Titicaca *(see pp150–4)*, legendary birthplace of the first Inca, is a place of folklore and traditional ways of life. The world's highest navigable lake is dotted with islands, some of which are man-made from reeds.

THE SOUTHERN COAST

Peru's southern coast is a strange mix of barren desert and teeming sea. It is a parched landscape left arid by the icy air of the Humboldt ocean current, a phenomenon which contrastingly endows the water with an opulent supply of marine life, much of which is protected in coastal wildlife reserves.

Boobies, penguins, and flamingos fluff feathers, while sea lions bounce off rocks to swim in the chilly waters. Even the Andean condor, lured by the promise of abundant food, makes an appearance.

Remains uncovered in this dry tract reveal a fascinating blend of cultures, dating back at least 5,000 years. The Paracas civilization fashioned textiles in 300 BC with an artistry that still resonates today.

The Nazca people created their mysterious giant drawings in the desert some 2,000 years ago, and the purpose of these enormous geoglyphs puzzles experts to this day. Aqueducts which they built remain in use, and the ceramics they produced are among the finest of the pre-Columbian era.

African slaves, brought to local plantations by the Spanish conquistadores in the 16th century, sowed the seeds within their close-knit communities for the Afro-Peruvian music now venerated across the country.

Despite the aridity of the land, agriculture thrives here thanks to the centuries-old systems of irrigation that use underground water supplies. The Spanish first introduced grape stocks in the 1550s and such was the success that the district around Ica is now Peru's wine basin and home to the national drink, pisco.

The region also played an instrumental trading role in the 19th century due to its island deposits of guano (bird droppings), then a sought-after fertilizer. Nowadays, the local economy is powered by grapes, cotton, olives, fruits, and nuts.

Even the desert has its own appeal. Dunes whipped into peaks by strong winds attract sand-boarders and dune buggy riders, and hidden in the sands are the remains of prehistoric pelicans and whale-eating sharks.

Pink-walled Colonial hacienda of Bodega Tacama, the oldest vineyard in Peru

◀ Sand dunes stretching into the distance, Nazca Desert

Exploring the Southern Coast

Sand dunes, wineries, and the enigmatic Nazca Lines are the tourist magnets of this region. The city of Ica is the ideal departure point for a marine fossil hunt through the desert in four-wheel drives – two million years ago there was an ocean here – or a leisurely pisco tasting in one of more than 80 vineyards. Tambo Colorado displays the Incas' building prowess, while the pyramids at Cahuachi are a souvenir of the earlier Nazca culture. Chincha is famed as the center of Afro-Peruvian music and traditions, with the nearby Hacienda San José providing an insight into plantation life in the 17th century. The Paracas National Reserve and the Ballestas Islands are sanctuaries for bird and other wildlife; the islands have been dubbed the "Peruvian Galapagos".

Owl Man geoglyph, Nazca Lines

La Caravedo organic winery, Ica

Sights at a Glance

Towns and Cities

1 Chincha Alta
2 Pisco
5 Ica
9 Nazca

Archaeological Sites and Ruins

3 Tambo Colorado
8 *Nazca Lines pp130–1*
10 Cahuachi
11 Cementerio de Chauchilla

Areas of Natural Beauty

4 Islas Ballestas
7 *Reserva Nacional
de Paracas p127*

Tour

6 Pisco Bodegas

Cliffs and clay beach at Reserva Nacional de Paracas

Getting Around

Nazca has a domestic airport for charter flights from Lima. The Panamerican Highway South links Lima with Ica and Nazca and there are regular daily bus services, though crime has been reported on some budget routes. Minibuses and *colectivos* operate from Ica to Nazca and Pisco. Boats leave from Pisco or Paracas for tours to the Ballestas Islands. Taxis can be hired in Ica for visits to Lake Huacachina or winery tours.

Key

═══ Motorway

─── Main road

═══ Minor road

▪▪▪ Untarred main road

▫▫▫ Untarred minor road

--- Track

═══ Regional border

Chiara

Casacancha

Vilcanchos

Cangallo

Paccha

Vilcashuamán

Sarhua

Huancapi

Carhuanca

Hualla

Huanca
Sancos

Sacsamarca

Querobamba

Soras

Putaccasa

Santa Ana de
Huaycahuacho

AYACUCHO

Andamarca

Chipao

:oca

Lucanas

26A

Río Huanca

Cordillera de Huanzo

nbo
emado

Puquio

allhua

*Reserva Nacional
Pampa Galeras*

San Pedro

Río Calpamayo

Saisa

Chaviña

Santa Lucía

San Javier
de Alpabamba

Río Acari

Sancos

Chumpi

Pararca

Lampa

Huanca

Río Yauca

Púllo

Incuyo

Pausa

Bella Holanda

*Laguna
Parinacochas*

0 kilometers   50
0 miles   50

For map symbols see back flap

❶ Chincha Alta

Road Map C5. 124 miles (200 km) S of Lima. ⛰ 58,250. 🚌 from Lima 🎭 Verano Negro (last week Feb), Fiestas Patrias (Jul 28 & 29), Virgin del Carmen (Dec 27).

Up to the 14th century when the Incas arrived, Chincha had been the domain of the small Chincha Empire, the ruins of Tambo de Mora attesting to their presence. Nowadays, home to one of the country's largest black communities, it is renowned across Peru as the hub of Afro-Peruvian music, along with nearby El Carmen.

Slaves were originally brought to the area to work on the large sugar and cotton plantations congregated here; a census of 1570 registered more blacks than Spanish living in coastal Peru.

The blacks guarded their music and traditions as best they could, passing them down over the centuries but also melding them with indigenous and Spanish elements.

In February, the Verano Negro (Black Summer) festival showcases all aspects of Afro-Peruvian culture including food, music, dance, and storytelling, drawing large local and international crowds.

Environs

Originally built by Jesuits and currently being rebuilt after extensive earthquake damage, **Hacienda San José** began as a sugar plantation in 1688. It was at one time the richest hacienda, with 1,000 slaves. With its founders' portraits and cell for runaway slaves, it gives a glimpse of 17th-century life on both sides of the fence.

Chapel façade at Hacienda San José prior to earthquake damage

❷ Pisco

Road Map C5. 155 miles (250 km) S of Lima. ⛰ 56,300. 🚌 from Ica 🚤 boat tours of Paracas Bay and Islas Ballestas. 🛈 Municipalidad (Town Hall) on main plaza.

Founded in 1640, Pisco, a quiet city of farmers and fishermen, was unable to withstand the earthquake that rocked the area on August 15, 2007. Three-quarters of the town was lost as historic buildings around the plaza crumbled, tens of thousands of adobe homes collapsed and hundreds of people died. The statue of liberator, José de San Martín in the main plaza was left to survey the ruins including the 18th-century San Clemente

Statue of José de San Martín, Pisco

church, which caved in during mass, killing a number of worshippers. Boats bound for the Ballestas Islands still depart from the port.

❸ Tambo Colorado

Road Map C5. Los Libertadores Highway, opposite Panamerican Highway South, KM229. Taxi from Pisco, negotiate half-day rate. **Open** 9am–4pm daily. 📷 🎫 take a tour from an agency in Pisco.

Once a significant Inca administrative center, Tambo Colorado sits at the base of steep foothills in the Pisco river valley. It was a connecting point on the Inca road joining Ayacucho with the coast, making it ideal for overseeing the flow of people and produce. It is thought that the ninth Inca, Pachacútec, lived here at one time. Despite its lack of roofing, it is one of the best preserved adobe ruins in Peru. Niches in the stucco outer walls bear traces of the red and yellow pigment used to decorate them, and alcoves are adorned with carvings of human figures.

The Inca ruins of Tambo Colorado with traces of red paint just visible

For hotels and restaurants in this region see pp274–9 and pp288–97

❹ Islas Ballestas

Road Map C5. 162 miles (261 km) S of Lima. 🚌 from Pisco or El Chaco port, Paracas. **Open** 8:30am–10:30pm daily. 🎫 💷 can only be visited as part of organized tour from agencies in Pisco, Paracas, and Paracas hotels.

The Ballestas Islands are among the most popular draws on the Southern Coast. It is possible to take a boat tour around the islands, but visitors are not allowed to disembark.

A series of arches and caves provide shelter for more than 160 species of marine birds, including Humboldt penguins, boobies, and pelicans, as well as immense numbers of sea lions, incessantly barking, biting, basking, and throwing their hefty bodies into the sea. Dolphins and whales sometimes appear, too.

Old factory remains on the islands are a throwback to the 19th century when guano (mineral-rich bird droppings) was an important fertilizer and provided a vital source of revenue for the country.

General San Martín landed his army here in 1820 before disembarking on the nearby mainland to secure Peru's independence from Spain.

Look out for the startling Candelabra geoglyph *(see pp116 and 123)* visible on the way to and from the islands. Some say it was a navigational aid while others claim it is a pirate's sign. Do take warm clothing and sun protection as the boats are not covered.

The desert oasis of Huacachina, ringed by palm and *huarangos* trees

❺ Ica

Road Map C5. 200 miles (325 km) S of Lima. 🚐 122,376. 🚏 charter services from Lima. 🚌 from Lima 🎉 Vendimia (Grape Harvest, first 2 weeks Mar), El Señor de Luren (3rd Sun of Oct). 🌐 **muniica.gob.pe**

Founded by the Spanish in 1563 as Villa de Valverde, the village was relocated and renamed in 1640, and is now Peru's premier wine center with vineyards dating back to the 16th century.

The city was badly affected by the 2007 earthquake, Peru's worst since 1974. A chapel in the Neo-Classical Sanctuario del Señor del Luren collapsed during evening mass, killing several people and injuring dozens. The church, named for Our Lord of Luren, the city's patron saint, was among an estimated quarter of the buildings that were damaged. Over 2,800 pre-Hispanic artifacts in museums across the Ica region suffered irreparable damage during the earthquake. Ica's **Museo Regional Adolfo Bermúdez Jenkins**, which houses an interesting collection of Paracas, Nazca, Ica, Huari, and Inca artifacts including mummies and skulls showing evidence of ancient surgical techniques, escaped relatively unscathed.

Environs

A green lagoon amidst towering dunes, the oasis of **Huacachina** is just 3 miles (5 km) from Ica. Swimming is allowed (although the water is not that clean) but most come to sand-board or ride the dunes.

🏛 **Museo Regional Adolfo Bermúdez Jenkins**
Av. Ayabaca 8va. **Tel** 056 234 383. **Open** 8am–7pm Mon–Fri, 9am–6pm Sat & pub hols, 9am–1:30pm Sun. 🎫 💷 ♿ 📷 charge for cameras and video recorders.

El Carmen

From the 16th to 18th centuries, slaves from all over West Africa made their homes in El Carmen. With no common language or tribal leader, they developed a distinctive style of music to help them unite.

Boys playing Afro-Peruvian music

Combining African, Andean, and Spanish elements, Afro-Peruvian music is known for its use of traditional instruments like the *cajón*, a wooden box drum, and *quijada de burro*, a percussion instrument made from a donkey's jaw bone. The music moved mainstream in the 1970s, when the group Peru Negro and singers such as Chabuca Granda embraced it. Today, it is the pride of Peru. El Carmen is also famous for 24-hour partying come festival time, especially around Christmas.

A nesting colony of Peruvian boobies, Islas Ballestas

❻ A Tour of Pisco Bodegas

Peru's first vineyards were planted near Ica in the 1550s, using vines brought by the Spanish conquistadores. The industry flourished until the 17th century when Spain banned the exportation of Peruvian wine because it was damaging their own economy. Wine-makers then turned their full attention to making a clear grape brandy, which came to be known as pisco. Today, the major producers and small artisans are still based around Ica, Peru's pisco capital.

Tips for Visitors

Getting there: If you don't have your own transport, some bodegas can be reached by *combis*, or you can hire a taxi
When to visit: Most are open year round for tours. The harvest festival (Vendimia) is in March.

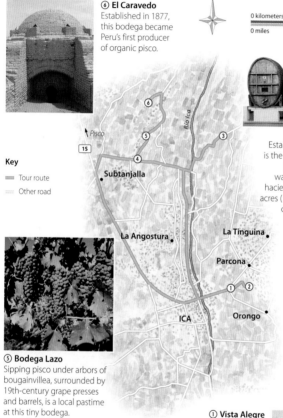

⑥ El Caravedo
Established in 1877, this bodega became Peru's first producer of organic pisco.

0 kilometers 3
0 miles 3

③ Bodega Tacama
Established in 1540, Tacama is the oldest vineyard in Peru. A bell tower, part of the watermelon-pink Colonial hacienda, overlooks 450 lush acres (180 ha) planted with 20 different grape varieties.

Key

━━ Tour route
══ Other road

Pisco

Río Ica

Subtanjalla

La Angostura

La Tinguina

Parcona

Orongo

ICA

② Bodega Lovera
The Lovera family have been making pisco since 1867. Today, a sixth generation of producers combine their age-old artisanal methods with more advanced technology to create some award-winning pisco.

⑤ Bodega Lazo
Sipping pisco under arbors of bougainvillea, surrounded by 19th-century grape presses and barrels, is a local pastime at this tiny bodega.

① Vista Alegre
Founded by the Jesuits, it was taken over in 1857 by Italian Emmanuel Picasso and his brothers, and today remains in the hands of the same family. Peru's largest vineyard, it can distil up to 15,000 liters of pisco a day.

④ El Catador (Tres Esquinas)
Come harvest time, visitors to family-run El Catador are invited to join in treading grapes underfoot. Crushed grapes are still pressed in a vast adobe platform weighed down by a 19th-century tree trunk.

❼ Reserva Nacional de Paracas

The desert meets the sea in dramatic fashion at the Paracas National Reserve, Peru's largest piece of protected coastline, with towering cliffs fringing beaches swarming with wildlife. The reserve is home to more than 1,800 species of plants and animals, and provides a habitat for both resident and migratory waterbirds, including flamingos, Humboldt penguins, pelicans, sanderlings, moorhens, boobies, cormorants, and terns. On occasions, condors can be seen circling overhead, along with ferocious-looking red-headed vultures.

Sights at a Glance

① Isla San Gallán
② La Catedral
③ Paracas Necropolis and Museo
④ El Candelabro
⑤ Lagunillas

Key

═══ Minor road

– – Track

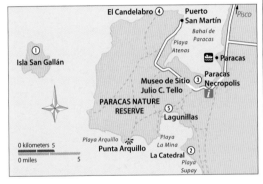

VISITORS' CHECKLIST

Practical Information
Road Map C5. 177 miles (285 km) S of Lima. 🅸 Open 7am–6pm daily. 🏕️ 🚌 arrange agency tour in Pisco. 🅿️ Lagunillas and Playa Atenas. E Museo de Sitio Julio C. Tello: Bahía de Paracas. Open 9am–5pm Tue–Sun. 🏕️

Transport
🚐 from Pisco.

The **San Gallán** and **La Vieja Islands**, which lie just off the coast, are the only places for the endangered *potoyunco* (Peruvian diving petrel) to reproduce in Peru.

Marine mammals also abound including sea lions, seals, sea turtles, marine otters, dolphins, and the endangered *chinguno* (sea cat). **La Catedral**, a rock formation created by centuries of pounding from ocean winds and tides, was badly damaged in the 2007 earthquake but still provides one of the few homes to the *chinguno* in the area.

The cliff lookout of **Punta Arquillo** allows for views of a sea lion colony on the rocks below, which teems with the beasts during the December to March mating season. Unfortunately, several viewing areas were affected by the devastating earthquake. The reserve has archaeological significance too. Behind the visitors' center is the **Paracas Necropolis**, burial ground of the Paracas people (700 BC), who buried their dead in elaborate funerary bundles of colorful embroidered textiles. They are considered the finest examples of pre-Columbian textiles in the country, though most are now housed in museums in Lima.

Museo de Sitio Julio C. Tello, named for the archaeologist who discovered the mummies, contains a small display of textiles, ceramics, and skulls.

The bay in front of the museum is home to flamingos. A trail leads down to a lookout with a great view of the scarlet-and-white birds that inspired the Peruvian flag. Liberator José de San Martín landed nearby and was supposedly impressed by them.

Beyond the museum, a trail off the road to Puerto San Martín leads to the three-pronged **El Candelabro**, a 490- ft- (150-m-) high geoglyph stamped into the desert hillside. Some say it was a navigational aid, but more likely it's a Nazca ritual symbol.

Scuba diving, swimming, and kite- or windsurfing are possible off beaches but be warned there are stingrays and jellyfish. The tiny village of **Lagunillas** comprises pretty beaches and fish restaurants.

The distinctive red-brown sands of a beach near Lagunillas

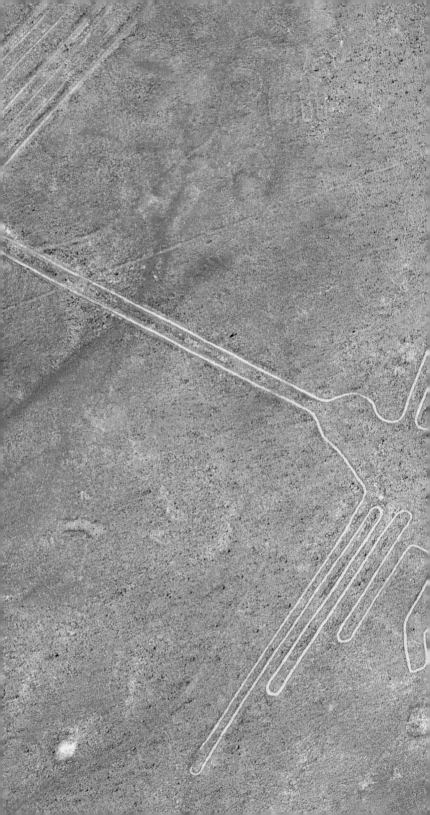

❽ Nazca Lines

It never rains on the Peruvian coast which is why the remarkable Nazca Lines have survived so many centuries, preserving the secrets of an ancient culture. Dispersed over the high desert plateau between the towns of Nazca and Palpa, this collection of geoglyphs, comprising more than 70 human figures and stylized animals, and 10,000 lines, was first noticed from the air in 1927. Etched into the plains between 500 BC and AD 500, they were declared a UNESCO World Heritage Site in 1994. Debate continues about their original purpose – giant astronomical calendar, ceremonial center, or alien landing strip – ensuring they remain one of the world's great archaeological mysteries.

Flying the Lines
The graphic beauty and sheer complexity of the lines can best be seen from the air.

★ The Hummingbird
Measuring 315 by 217 ft (96 by 66 m), this is one of the best-known geoglyphs. The Nazca believed hummingbirds were messengers between the worlds of men and condors, which they considered to be gods.

★ The Monkey
The monkey was regarded as a divine being. This image has only nine fingers and Maria Reiche suggested it may have been made to mark the equinoxes. The monkey also appears on Nazca ceramics.

Río Nazca

Trapezoids
Researchers assumed the trapezoid figures in the desert were used for ceremonies, others have fancifully speculated they were runways for alien spaceships.

KEY

① Viewing platform

② Nazca town

◀ Ancient trapezoids and lines drawn in the desert near Nazca

★ The Spider

The spider is identified as being both a symbol of rain and fertility, and a representation of the soothsayers, who used the creatures to predict the future.

The Tree

The Tree is one of only a few figures visible from the viewing platform. The Nazca may have made the lines to worship Kon, a flying god of water, which explains why they were probably designed to be seen from above.

Panamerican Highway South

Airport

Viewing the lines

There's a free viewing platform at KM420 but the best way to see the lines is from one of the 3–9-seater planes flying out of Nazca airport. Flight prices vary from company to company but range between US$30–51 for a 30- to 45-minute trip. Flights leave in the morning and early afternoon, weather permitting, with the best time usually between 8–10:30am, though it can be hazy in the early morning. Be sure to fly with a reputable air carrier

Maria Reiche (1903–98)

German mathematician and astronomer, Maria Reiche, began studying the Nazca Lines in the 1940s and devoted her life to uncovering their mysteries. As the giant, perfectly proportionate geoglyphs seemed to be pointing to the stars, she believed they were sophisticated astral charts. Before her death in 1998, she concluded they were part of a huge astronomical calendar to commune with the gods, and thus secure water and blessings for crops. She believed the lines were created by tying a chord to an axis, just as a compass is used to draw a circle.

Maria Reiche

The Whale

The first geoglyph to be discovered, it probably depicts a killer whale or orca.

Adobe pyramid at Cahuachi, built by members of the ancient Nazca community

❾ Nazca

Road Map C5. 285 miles (460 km) S of Lima. 🚐 26,000. ✈ from Lima and for Nazca Lines. 🚌 from Lima. 🚌 from Ica. 🛈 in Town Hall.

The discovery of the Nazca Lines put the sun-baked town of Nazca on the map, and that is the main reason most people visit the area.

The **Museo Antonini**, however, makes a worthwhile stop. It displays many of the finds from the Cahuachi site made by Italian archaeologist, Giuseppe Orefici. The collection gives an insight into all aspects of Nazca society, and includes mummies and distorted heads – the Nazca wrapped the heads of their newborns in leather or wood bands. It also has an important collection of ceramic *antaras* (pan flutes), and ceramics, portraying sea creatures and gods, and textiles, including one festooned with iconic birds gobbling serpents and four-legged animals.

The archaeological park behind the museum features a scale model of the Nazca Lines, a replica of a Nazca tomb, and the pre-Columbian Bisambra Aqueduct.

Nazca bowl, Museo Antonini

🏛 **Museo Antonini**
Av. de la Cultura 600. **Tel** 056 523 444.
Open 9am–7pm daily. 📷
🌐 digilander.libero.it/MD Antonini/English.htm

❿ Cahuachi

Road Map C5. 11 miles (17 km) NW of Nazca. **Open** no set hours. 📷 organized tour from Nazca.

Cahuachi, an enormous Nazca ceremonial center, reached its zenith more than 2,000 years ago. Extending across 370 acres (150 ha), it is dominated by a 100-ft (30-m) high central pyramid and plaza. Forty other pyramids were sculpted from the landscape with massive mud-brick adobe walls applied over them. Some 5,000 tombs have been identified but, sadly, Cahuachi has suffered from looting.

Archaeologist Giuseppe Orefici has been excavating the site for decades and has concluded it was home to priests who conducted public ceremonies and rituals to thank the gods for water. The site's numerous treasures can be seen at the Museo Antonini, and should help to unravel the secrets of the Nazca Line builders.

⓫ Cementerio de Chauchilla

Road Map C5. 18 miles (29 km) S of Nazca. Taxi from Nazca, negotiate half-day rate. **Open** 8am–6pm daily. 📷 best to visit on an organized tour.

Chauchilla Cemetery, naturally enough, is full of graves dating back to the Chincha period (AD 1000–1400). At one stage mummies were scattered across the site, courtesy of tomb-raiders who fleeced the bodies of valuables and discarded textile scraps, bones, and carcasses in the desert. From an archaeologist's point of view, they effectively robbed the bodies of their identities and in doing so hindered researchers' ability to piece together the history of the people found here.

There are thousands of graves but only 12 have been restored and they show carefully positioned, shrouded mummies in squatting positions with bleached skulls and long matted hair. There is also a children's-only grave.

Normally the mummies would have been well preserved because the arid sands are rich in salt and nitrates, but their exposure to the elements destroyed the mummified skin and faded the bones.

Squatting mummies in a restored tomb, Cementerio de Chauchilla

The Southern Beaches

The asphalt ribbon of the Panamerican Highway South carves through Peru's coastal desert, making beach-hopping an easy pursuit. The northern beaches might be more famous, but the southern coast has its own different attractions: archaeological ruins, rugged cliffs, rampant marine and bird life, along with the more traditional pleasures such as fishing and swimming. Most fishing villages have boats for rent, or locals who are happy to ferry visitors around for a small price. Secluded beaches dot the coast but be warned the water is cold and lifeguards rare. On remote or isolated beaches, campers should always camp in groups.

① Punta San Fernando
The Humboldt Current flows close to the shore here, guaranteeing a rich supply of marine life which attracts the Andean condor.

② Punta San Juan de Marcona
This protected zone provides refuge to almost 75 percent of Peru's Humboldt penguin population and 50 percent of its pure-bred sea lions.

Chauchilla

① Punta San Fernando
Marcona
San Nicolás
26
San Juan ② Punta San Juan de Marcona
Magdalena
Mina Acarí
Acarí
Bella Unión
Jaqui
Lomas ③
Parcoy
Yauca
Tócata
Tanaka
Cháparra
Puerto Inca
Ayparipa ④ ⑤ Chala
Pascana

HUMBOLDT CURRENT

0 kilometers   25
0 miles   25

③ Las Lomas
A small fishing village with a beach that is ideal for pelican watching. Good, too, for sole and sea bass fishing.

④ Puerto Inca
These pre-Columbian ruins are thought to be the starting point for one of the most important Inca trails (see p51). Fresh fish were dried and then transported to Cusco by a network of runners. The crescent-shaped beach is popular for swimming and fishing.

⑤ Chala
This tumbledown fishing village with a lighthouse is a favorite stop-off point for a bite of super-fresh seafood. Boat rental is also available if you want to go seal spotting.

CANYON COUNTRY

Nowhere else in Peru is the air so clear and the sunlight so radiant as here in its folkloric heart. The Colonial city of Arequipa, with its stately mansions, churches, and cloisters, sits in stark contrast to its untamed surrounds, where high altitude deserts, active volcanoes, and yawning canyons – particularly Colca and Cotahuasi, reputed to be the deepest in the world – abound.

This area embodies nature at its most spectacular. Majestic condors soar above the Colca and Cotahuasi Canyons and villages with thatched houses. Rock art found here is testimony to a civilization dating back more than 8,000 years, while lush 2,000-year-old agricultural terraces recall the ingenuity of the Collagua people.

In the 14th century, Inca leader Mayta Cápac sealed his victory over the Collagua by marrying the daughter of a local chief and building her a house made of copper. This same mineral wealth – gold, silver, lead, copper, quartz – drew the Spanish conquistadores in the 16th century. The Colonial heritage is on full display in the Baroque churches that dominate villages such as Chucuito.

The Colca River, which stretches from Peru's southern highlands through the western Andes and on to the Pacific Coast, courses through the Colca Canyon, providing adventurers with countless white-water rafting opportunities. Mount Ampato, near Arequipa, where the mummified body of Juanita, the Ice Maiden, was discovered, attracts climbers. Farther east lies the sapphire expanse of Lake Titicaca, hailed in Inca mythology as the birthplace of their civilization. Legend has it that Manco Cápac, the son of the Sun, and Mama Ocllo, the daughter of the Moon, emerged from the lake to found the Inca Empire. The world's highest navigable lake is shared with Bolivia, as is the local language, Aymara.

Ancient settlements of weavers, fishermen, and farmers still ply their trade around the shore and on near and far islands, including the famous floating isles made entirely from reeds.

A group of local women and children in colorful traditional attire, Chivay

◀ The Neo-Classical cathedral on Plaza de Armas, Arequipa

Exploring Canyon Country

The classic starting point for touring this area is Arequipa (7,660 ft/2,335 m), a Colonial jewel built on the slopes of a volcano and the commercial hub of southern Peru. Travelers often stop here en route to Lake Titicaca to get acclimatized to the altitude. The canyons of Colca and Cotahuasi, north of Arequipa, abound with hiking, rafting, and mountain biking opportunities. There is also ample scope to view diverse species of birds and herds of alpaca and vicuña. Near Lake Titicaca, the city of Lampa hosts a replica of Michelangelo's *La Pieta* while tiny Juli is replete with Colonial churches. In between lies Sillustani, with its burial towers, and Puno, the departure point for the islands dotting the lake. Along the lake, women in multi-colored, layered skirts can be seen knitting.

Fountain in the cloisters courtyard,
La Compañia, Arequipa

A view of Río Colca meandering through the valley

Key

— Main road

=== Minor road

--- Untarred main road

=== Untarred minor road

--- Track

— Railroad

▬▬ International border

▬▬ Regional border

△ Peak

Sights at a Glance

Towns and Cities

1. *Arequipa pp138–45*
4. Puno
5. Lampa
8. Juli

Areas of Natural Beauty

2. *Cañón del Colca pp146–7*
3. Cañón de Cotahuasi
6. *Lake Titicaca pp150–55*

Archaeological Site and Ruin

7. Sillustani Burial Towers

Parque Nacional Baltuaja-Sonene
San Gabán
Zona Reservada Tambopata Candamo
Río Inambari
Río Guacamayo
Laniacuni Bajo
Ollachea
Ayapata
30C
Alincápac 18,848ft/ 5,745m
Oroya
Río Huari Huari
Pilcopata
Cura Alegre
Usicayos
San Juan Del Oro
Antauta
Rosario
PUNO
Aricoma
Río Carabaya
Cuyocuyo
Siná
Nuñoa
San Antón
Cordillera Apolobamba
Trapiche
Ayaviri
Azángaro
Putina
Cojata
Pucará
Ocuriri
Huancane
Palca
Reserva Nacional Titicaca
Moho
LAMPA 5
Pusi
Juliaca
Paratía
Coata
30A
SILLUSTANI BURIAL TOWERS 7
Isla Amantani
Paucarcolla
Isla Taquile
30B
LAKE TITICACA 6
PUNO 4
Ancora
Pilcuyo
Yunga
Loripongo
32N
JULI 8
Pomata
Ubinas 18,602ft/ 5,670m
PUNO
Sorapa
Altiplano
35
Matalaque
Zepita
34B
MOQUEGUA
Río Huenque
24C
Zona Reservada Aymara-Lupaca
Mazo Cruz
Chillihua
Humajalso
Pisacoma
Tutupaca 18,963ft/ 5,780m
Tacalaya
Viluta
Capaso
Moquegua
Toquepala
Susapaya
Barroso 18,835ft/ 5,741m
Mirave
Río Locumba
TACNA
Desierto de la Clemesi
Quilla
Las Yaras
17
40
36
Pachía
Boca del Río
Tacna
15A
La Yarada
Concórdia

Woman making handicrafts on the floating Isla Uros, Lake Titicaca

Getting Around

Arequipa has a domestic airport with flights to and from Lima, Cusco, Juliaca, and Tacna. There are also flights to and from La Paz, Bolivia. The airport servicing Puno is located in Juliaca, 23 miles (44 km) north, and has flights to Lima, Cusco, and Arequipa. *Combis (see p329)* are a cheap option between Juliaca and Puno. The roads between Arequipa and Puno are paved and efficient coach services operate between the two cities as well as on the Panamerican South highway to Lima. A train runs between Puno and Cusco. Boats from Puno leave regularly for various islands on Lake Titicaca. Bolivia is linked by bus only. Taxis can also be hired in Puno.

For additional map symbols *see back flap*

❶ Street-by-Street: Arequipa

Basking in the shadow of the snow-capped Misti, Chachani, and Pichu Pichu volcanoes, Arequipa is built almost entirely from *sillar*, a white volcanic rock, and thus its nickname – *la ciudad blanca*, or the white city. According to legend the city was founded when the fourth Inca, Mayta Cápac, camped here. After some of his soldiers asked permission to stay back, he responded in Quechua *"ari, quepay"* (yes, you may stay). In 1540, the Spanish re-founded the city and the Neo-Classical Cathedral, the Baroque churches, and the lordly mansions show their influence. Monasterio de Santa Catalina is the city's most amazing sight *(see pp142–5)*.

★ **Cathedral**
The Cathedral is one of the city's first 17th-century religious monuments. It has survived many earthquakes.

Casona Iriberry, an 18th-century mansion, is now a cultural center.

To Monasterio de Santa Catalina

★ **Casa del Moral**
This 18th-century house is one of the oldest and best examples of Arequipa's Baroque style, with the façade featuring carvings of iconic pumas and serpents.

BOLIVAR

SAN AGUSTIN

SUCRE

MERCAD

LA MERCED CATALINA

Iglesia San Agustín
Although the church was built in 1575, the mestizo façade dates back from the early 18th century. Made of *sillar* stone, San Agustín contains a striking dome, Neo-Classical altars, and impressive gilded carvings.

| 0 meters | 750 |
| 0 yards | 750 |

Casa Tristán del Pozo
Built in 1738, this mansion is a classic piece of Colonial architecture. The frieze above the door depicts medallions of Jesus, Joseph, and Mary.

VISITORS' CHECKLIST

Practical Information
Road Map D6. 627 miles (1,009 km) SE of Lima.
🚗 894,944. 🛈 iPeru, Plaza de Armas, 054 223 265, 9am–6pm daily. 🚫 🏢 🏛 🚲 🎭 Semana Santa (week before Easter), Anniversary of Arequipa (Aug 15).

Transport
✈ 🚌 from Cusco. 🚌 from Puno & Lima.

Museo Arte Textil is dedicated to textiles of the region.

★ La Compañia
Built to house the Jesuits as well as provide them with a spiritual center, this 17th-century church features carved wooden altars with gold leaf. The cloisters were added in the 18th century.

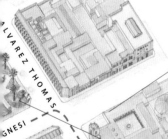

Plaza de Armas
Tuturuto, the statue that sits in the plaza's center, is a representation of a 16th-century soldier whose job it was to inform citizens of news and events.

Casa Goyeneche houses sculptures from the 17th-century Granada School and works from the Cusco and Arequipa schools.

Key
— Suggested route

Exploring Arequipa

Earthquakes have rocked Arequipa over the centuries due to a geological fault line known as *cadena del fuego* (chain of fire). However, most Colonial buildings have weathered the assaults, aided by Arequipeños' unwavering determination to retain their heritage. Today the city has been listed as a UNESCO World Heritage Site. It is Peru's second largest city and has a long history of commercial repute as a hub for sheep and alpaca wool exports, which still thrive today. Bordered by an impressive two-towered Cathedral and stately symmetrical colonnades, Arequipa's Plaza de Armas is one of Peru's finest.

Intricately carved stone façade of Casa del Moral

A view of the white *sillar* Cathedral from Plaza de Armas

🏛 Cathedral

Plaza de Armas. **Tel** 054 232 635.
Open 7–11:30am & 5–7:30pm Mon–Sat, 7am–1:30pm & 5–7pm Sun.
🎫 for a tip. 🔔 during masses.
🔔 7 & 8:30am, 5, 6 & 7pm daily; 4pm Thu (vigil).

Originally constructed in 1621, the indomitable Cathedral was damaged during a series of earthquakes and fire. It was rebuilt by local architect Lucas Poblete in 1868. The cathedral, which is made of *sillar* (white volcanic stone), is regarded as the most important Neo-Classical religious building in Peru. Flanked by two arches, it is the country's only cathedral that stretches the entire length of a plaza. The main altar is made of Carrara marble as are the 12 columns which represent the 12 apostles. The carved wooden pulpit held aloft by a devil with a serpent's tail was made in France, and the tower clock was made in England.

🏛 Casona Iriberry

Cnr of Santa Catalina & San Agustín. **Tel** 054 204 482. **Open** 9am–1pm, 4–8pm daily. ♿ downstairs only.
📷 🏛

Built in 1793, the volcanic rock walls of the Casona Iriberry, also known as Casa Arróspide, are thought to be the thickest in Arequipa.

Formerly a private home, it is now the Cultural Centre Chavez de la Rosa, and part of the University of San Agustín. Rooms, where art and photography exhibitions are held, open on to a series of charming stone patios. There are messages and monograms carved out in Spanish above the doorways. The top terrace has great views of the beautiful Cathedral located nearby.

🏛 Casa del Moral

Calle Moral 318. **Tel** 054 210 084.
Open 9am–5pm Mon–Sat.
Closed 1pm on pub hols. 📷 🏛 ♿
The 18th-century Casa del Moral is named after an ancient *mora* (mulberry) tree that is still standing in its central patio.

Intricate carvings, in *sillar*, of puma heads with snakes emerging from their mouths adorn the stone gateway, along with a crown suspended above a coat of arms held up by two angels. Inside, there are displays of furniture from Colonial and Republican times, Cusco School *(see p171)* oil paintings and 16th-century maps. The view from the rooftop of this home looks out over the towering volcanoes that surround the city.

🏛 Convento de la Recoleta

Jirón Recoleta 117. **Tel** 054 270 966.
Open 9am–noon, 3–5pm Mon–Sat.
📷 🏛 for a tip.
Situated in the Antiquilla neighborhood, a ten-minute walk from the main plaza, the Recoleta convent was founded by the Franciscans in 1648. Its enchanting four cloisters, featuring tranquil gardens and *sillar* columns, are a fine example of Arequipa's old Colonial style. Re-modeling campaigns have seen the addition of various architectural styles from Romantic and Neo-Gothic to 1940s modern.

Stone fountain in the cloister garden, Convento de la Recoleta

🏛 Museo Histórico Municipal

Plaza San Francisco. **Tel** 054 204 801.
Open 9am–5pm Mon–Fri, 9am–3pm Sat. 📷

The history of Arequipa is the focus here, with photographs of the old city, maps, historical documents, portraits of the city's nobles, and a number of archaeological pieces on show.

For hotels and restaurants in this region see pp274–9 and pp288–97

Also highlighted are Arequipa's heroes including painters, writers, and poets. A series of satirical caricatures and works by famous artist, Jorge Vinatea Reynoso (1900–31) are very insightful. The naval museum displays objects relating to various conflicts, including items from the 1860s Arequipa Revolution and the historic Dos de Mayo combat with Chile. Arequipa was a bastion of nationalism during Peru's struggle for independence from Spain in the early 19th century, and during the War of the Pacific (see pp54–5) with Chile.

⛪ Iglesia San Francisco

Calle Zela. **Tel** 054 223 048. **Open** 7–9am, 5–8pm Mon–Sat, 7am–8pm Sun; Convent: **Open** 9am–12:30pm, 3–5pm Mon–Sat. 🔲 for convent. 📷 for a tip. 🚫 in the church. ⛪

Despite being battered by numerous earthquakes, the 16th-century San Francisco church is still standing, albeit with a few scars including a crack in the cupola. The church features an unusual brick entrance-way, a bas-relief Baroque pulpit and a main altar with a solid silver façade. The convent contains paintings from the Cusco School including one of The Last Supper.

⛪ Iglesia La Merced

Cnr of Calle Merced & Tristán. **Tel** 054 21 3233. **Open** 8am–1pm, 4–7pm Mon–Fri, 8am–noon Sat. 🚫 with flash.

Construction began in 1551 and was completed in 1607. The side entrance of this *sillar* church features the image of the Virgin Mary with two "saints of mercy." A series of paintings portraying the Virgin de la Merced are on display. The convent has a library too.

🏛 Casa Tristán del Pozo

Calle San Francisco 108. Tel 054 212 209. **Open** 9:15am–12:45pm & 4–6pm Mon–Fri, 9:30am–12:30pm Sun. 🚫

This grand Colonial home takes its name from General Domingo Tristán del Pozo who commissioned the house in 1738. Built

Baroque detail above entrance and windows, Casa Tristán del Pozo

of white volcanic stone, its façade features intricately carved Baroque details above the windows and entrance. Inside, there are arched roofs and expansive patios. Today, the house is home to a bank, as well as a small museum and an art gallery.

⛪ Iglesia de la Compañía

Cnr of Calle General Morán & Álvarez Thomas. **Tel** 054 212 141. **Open** 9–11am, 3–6pm daily. 📷 for chapel. 📷 🚫 with flash. ⛪ 🏛

Built between 1595 and 1698, the Jesuit church of La Compañía is one of the city's oldest. Originally designed by Gaspar Baez in 1573, the first structure was flattened by an earthquake in 1584. Profuse mestizo ornamentation incorporating flowers, faces, spirals, and the completion date of the work, are engraved into the volcanic rock façade. Inside, the main altar is carved in the

Artifact from La Compañía

Churrigueresque style – Spanish Baroque with a Latin twist, involving gold leaf and cherubs with Inca faces. La Compañía is also home to more than 60 canvases from the Cusco School, including works by Bernardo Bitti and Diego de la Puente. The cloisters now house shops.

🏛 Museo Santuarios Andinos de la Universidad Católica de Santa Maria

La Merced 110. **Tel** 054 21 5013. **Open** 9am–6pm Mon–Sat, 9am–3pm Sun. 📷 📷 tips expected. ♿ 🚫 with flash. 📷 🌐 ucsm.edu.pe/santury/

The museum's most famous exhibit is Juanita, la Dama de Ampato (the Lady of Ampato). Alongwith Juanita, there are other mummies that were discovered in Ampato. All children, they were found with textiles, gold and silver figurines, dolls, and ceramics in their mountain tombs.

Juanita – the Ice Maiden

A last-minute decision to photograph an erupting volcano gave anthropologist Johan Reinhard (b.1943) the find of his life – the Andes' first frozen female mummy. Reinhard and his assistant found "Juanita" bundled in alpaca wool lying near a 20,700-ft- (6,310-m-) high peak. The Ice Maiden is considered one of the world's best-preserved mummies. Sacrificed by Inca priests high on Mount Ampato, she was buried with wooden and gold figurines, and assorted items she would need in the afterlife. Carbon dating has shown that she died between 1440 and 1450. Her remarkable preservation has allowed researchers to gain amazing insights into Inca culture.

Juanita, one of the world's best preserved mummies

Arequipa: Monasterio de Santa Catalina

Taking up an entire block of the city, the Monastery of Santa Catalina was founded in 1580 by Doña María de Guzmán, a rich widow who became a nun. The first to join the Order of Saint Catherine of Siena were poor Creole women, daughters of *curacas* (local Indian chiefs), and women from upper-class families. The wealthy novices brought along home comforts including servants, living as they had previously, even hosting parties. The monastery underwent reform in the 1870s when Sister Josef Cadena, a Dominican nun, replaced the hedonistic lifestyle with religious austerity.

★ Pinacoteca
The portrait of St Jeronimo by Diego Quispe Tito is one of the highlights of the two-room Religious Art Gallery.

Claustro los Naranjos
The Orange Tree Cloister takes its name from the orange trees planted there. Three crosses are stationed in the middle of the cloister.

★ Iglesia de Santa Catalina
The white *sillar* dome of the church dominates the monastery. It has a long aisle and dates back to 1660.

KEY

① **Architecture** is a fusion of indigenous and Spanish, using *sillar* (local volcanic stone).

② **Calle Córdova**

③ **Plaza Zocodovar** is where the nuns met on Sundays to exchange items they had made.

④ **Nuns' cells** were furnished frugally or lavishly according to their family circumstances.

Fresco in Claustro Mayor
The Main Cloister is the largest in the monastery. It was built between 1715 and 1723 and is decorated with 32 frescoes, 26 of them depicting Mary's life and 9 showing the public life of Jesus.

★ **Calle Sevilla**
With its terra-cotta walls and bright flowers, Seville Street is one of the prettiest in the complex. Flying buttresses straddle the walkway and the old church of Santa Catalina, which was later converted into a kitchen, can be seen at the end of the street.

Lavanderia
Water for the communal laundry, built in 1770, ran through a central channel into 20 earthenware jars which served as washing troughs.

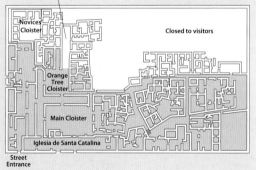

Floorplan of Monasterio de Santa Catalina

Calle Córdova
Novices' Cloister
Closed to visitors
Orange Tree Cloister
Main Cloister
Iglesia de Santa Catalina
Street Entrance

Key
Area illustrated

Cocina
The kitchen was probably designed as a chapel, given its high roof. The walls are blackened with soot from the coal and wood burning stove. The original utensils now sit unused.

Exploring Monasterio de Santa Catalina

Resembling a small town, the monastery comprises 100 rooms, lined along six streets, three cloisters, a church, and a gallery full of superb Colonial paintings. In its heyday it housed 450 people, a third of them nuns and the rest servants. The servants were freed under the direction of Sister Josef Cadena in 1871 and many of them joined the order. The convent was opened to the public in August 1970, since tourism was thought to be the best option to raise the funds required to install electricity and running water. Today, more than 20 nuns live in the complex, in an area that is off-limits to visitors.

Statue of St Catherine at the entrance to the monastery

Three crosses standing in the colorful Claustro los Naranjos

Claustro los Naranjos

The three crosses stationed in the Orange Tree Cloister are used by nuns in the monastery to re-enact the Passion of Christ, or the final days of Jesus' life, on Good Friday every year. Unfortunately, the public cannot view this ancient tradition, since the monastery is closed on that day, recalling the days when the order was completely cloistered from the world.

Lavanderia

The communal laundry was built at a time when Arequipa's only water source was a series of small canals. The 20 huge earthenware jars, earlier used to hold grain or store wine, doubled up as wash basins.

The water for washing was channeled through a central canal, with offshoots leading into individual jars. At the bottom of each jar was a plug which was removed once the washing was finished. This helped in draining

all the dirty water down to an underground canal which was connected to the river.

The laundry is located at the end of a long boulevard called Calle Toledo.

Iglesia de Santa Catalina

Dating back to 1660, the Church of Santa Catalina has been reconstructed several times after a number of earthquakes

in the region caused serious damage to the structure. However, the original design of the chapel has been retained.

The long aisle leads to the main silver altar, which is heavily embossed with religious motifs. This altar is positioned under an impressive dome.

There is also an altar dedicated to Sister Ana of the Angels, a former Mother Superior. A grand European organ takes pride of place in the high choir.

Pinacoteca

When restoration began on the monastery before it was opened to the public in the 1970s, workers uncovered a cache of religious paintings dating back to the Peruvian Viceroyalty (see pp52–3). Experts restored the 400 artworks, many of which were hailed as the most important examples of religious art on the continent.

These works are displayed in the Religious Art Gallery which is housed in two large rooms in the shape of a cross with

Painting of *Sor Ana de los Angeles* in the Religious Art Gallery (Pinacoteca)

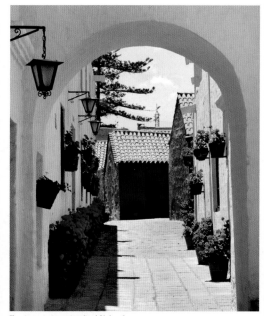
The picturesque geranium-lined Córdova Street

exposed block walls made of *sillar*. This space was once used as a shelter for homeless widows and single mothers. There are numerous paintings from the admired Cusco School *(see p171)* including the *Divine Shepherdess*, believed to be the work of Marcos Zapata *(see p70)*. There is a depiction of St Michael, dressed in Spanish armor, complete with a feathery helmet, as well as a portrait of St Catherine, or Santa Catalina, with a description of the scene written on a panel that is held by an angel.

Bell on the steeple facing the street

Calle Córdova
Córdova Street, as the name implies, is inspired by the architecture of Andalusia. Terra-cotta pots filled with geraniums line the gleaming white walls, which trap the sun all year round.

The 18th-century wall on the right is made from volcanic stones from Arequipa. These *sillar* blocks each measure 18 in by 16 in (45 cm by 40 cm).

The 20th-century building on the left side of the street is out of bounds for visitors. The area forms part of the complex in which the nuns live today.

Torre del Campanario
Built in 1748, the steeple has four bells facing the streets around the monastery. The oldest bell is towards the south, facing Ugarte Street and bears the inscription "Santa Catalina Ora Pronobis 1749." The bell facing Bolivar Street on the west has "R.M. Maria de Villegas 1787," while other bells bear no inscriptions.

Claustro Mayor
The Main Cloister is bordered by five confessionals on the left side, ensuring the nuns retain a degree of privacy during their declarations.

Thirty-two beautiful frescoes decorate the cloister walls. The majority of them show biblical scenes depicting the life of Virgin Mary, while the remainder portray the life of Jesus.

Sor Ana de los Angeles Monteagudo
Santa Catalina was also home to Sor Ana de los Angeles Monteagudo (1602–1686), who was beatified by Pope John Paul II in 1985.

Sister Ana of the Angels was educated in the monastery until she was about 11 years old. She returned to join the order after having a vision of Santa Catalina in which she showed Sister Ana a Dominican nun's habit.

She was eventually elected Mother Superior but it was not a unanimous decision. According to reports, some of the nuns questioned the appropriateness of the choice given Sister Ana's inability to read and write and three attempts were made to poison her. She survived and went on to establish a reputation as a miracle-worker. It was said her "close relationship with the souls in Purgatory" enabled her to predict both death and disease.

She was also a healer, with nuns writing of cases where ailing patients miraculously recovered after touching her possessions. It is said that a stricken painter, who made the only known portrait of Sister Ana, was completely cured of all his ailments when he finished the painting.

Sister Ana was buried in the monastery. Her humble cell and the utensils she used more than 300 years ago are on display in her rooms.

Stairs leading to one of the five confessionals, Claustro Mayor

❷ Cañón del Colca

Reaching a depth of 11,155 ft (3,400 m), the 62-mile (100-km) long Colca is one of the deepest canyons in the world, along with neighboring Cotahuasi Canyon *(see p148)*. The valley was home to the Cabana and Collagua people almost 2,000 years ago, who built a system of terraces that trap melting run-off water from nearby snow-capped volcanoes. The *colcas* (grain storehouses) are testament to their presence. When the Spanish arrived, they put the farmers to work in the mines and moved the scattered Collagua community into 14 villages, each with a main plaza and handsome Colonial church.

Sumbay cave paintings showing a group of camelids

★ La Cruz del Condor
Located on the canyon's highest point, it offers a vista of giant Andean condors wheeling over the valley. The lookout is jam packed with tourists and buses most mornings.

Collagua People
Originally inspired by the petticoats of Spanish women, the Collagua still embellish their clothing with colorful embroidery. The women wear two or three skirts, and beribboned or brightly stitched hats.

La Calera
Just outside Chivay are the sulphur and iron-rich waters of La Calera, said to help in the treatment of rheumatism and arthritis.

For hotels and restaurants in this region see pp274–9 and pp288–97

Reserva Nacional Salinas y Aguada Blanca
Covering a huge area, the reserve shelters a variety of plants and animals. Camelids such as llamas, alpacas, and vicuñas are bred to help the sustainable development of villages.

Yanque Town
Iglesia de la Inmaculada Concepción has a glorious mestizo façade covered in saints and a 16th-century processional silver cross inside.

★ **Collagua Terraces**
Nearly 2,000 years ago, the Collagua and Cabana people carved out a huge area of terracing in an effort to control irrigation and erosion, and in order to grow crops. Today, the communities living in the valley still use the terraces for cultivation.

Condor

The condor (*Vultur gryphus*) is the world's largest flying bird, standing up to 4-ft (1.2-m) high with a wingspan of 10 ft (3 m). Despite weighing up to 27 lbs (12 kg), the condor can fly for hours without using its wings, simply gliding on thermal currents. The condor feeds on carrion or newborn animals which it can identify from the air thanks to its heightened sense of smell and remarkable eyesight. The birds sleep on the canyon walls at night. Considered a sacred bird by the Incas, it was once a common sight in the Andes but is now listed as "vulnerable" by the World Conservation Union due to centuries of hunting, habitat loss, and the rampant use of pesticides by farmers.

Condors perched atop a cliff in the canyon

Rafting on Río Colca
The river is famous for its 300 rapids, with the best known rafting route starting at Chivay and running some 25 miles (40 km).

❸ Cañón de Cotahuasi

Road Map D5. 124 miles (200 km) NW of Arequipa. 🚌 🚐 in Cotahuasi, Liucho, and Alca.

At 11,560 ft (3,535 m), Cotahuasi is reportedly the deepest canyon in the world and twice as deep as America's Grand Canyon. In Quechua *cota* means "union" and *huasi* is "house" thus Cotahuasi means "united house," or in this case "united community."

The impressive landscape of the canyon combines sheer shadowy cliffs rising out of riverbanks, towering snow-capped mountains, terraced citrus groves, fields of corn, stands of eucalyptus, adobe villages, and hot springs.

The canyon was an important route in the Inca times, connecting the Pacific Coast with Cusco. Remnants of these roads still link many of the traditional villages here.

There are ruins from the Wari culture and the unmistakable imprint of the Spanish conquistadores in the entire area. Every settlement has a chapel and belfry, and sometimes even a bullring.

Nearby villages have their own attractions. **Liucho** has soothing hot springs while **Sipia**'s charm is the 197-ft- (60-m-) high waterfall of Cataratas de Sipia.

❹ Puno

Road Map E6. 27 miles (44 km) SE of Juliaca. 🚹 129,000. ✈ in Juliaca. 🚉 from Cusco. 🚌 from Arequipa. 🅹 Plaza de Armas. 🎉 Fiesta de la Virgin de la Candelaria (Feb 2).

Viceroy Conde de Lemos founded the city in 1668, naming it San Carlos de Puno. The Spanish converted the indigenous people to Christianity and built several churches.

The Baroque-style **Catedral de Puno** on Plaza de Armas was designed by the 18th- century Peruvian architect Símon de Asto. The **Iglesia de San Juan Bautista** on Parque Pino is the sanctuary of Mamita Candelaria, Puno's patron saint, and is famous for its carvings.

Salmon colored houses of Lampa, the pink city

Parque Huajsapata, which is located on the hilltop, honors Puno's pre-Hispanic past with a statue of Manco Cápac, the first Inca. Legends claim there are tunnels in the hill that connect Puno with the Koricancha Temple in Cusco.

Museo Carlos Dreyer houses pre-Hispanic and Colonial art-works collected by the German artist Dreyer, including Moche ceramics, Inca silverwork, Paracas textiles, and religious objects. Striking gold pieces found at Lagarto *chulpa* in Sillustani are also displayed.

🏛 **Catedral de Puno**
Plaza de Armas. **Open** 7am–noon, 3–7pm daily. 🏛

🏛 **Iglesia de San Juan Bautista**
Parque Pino, Av. Independencia. **Open** 7am–noon, 3–7pm daily. 🏛

🏛 **Museo Carlos Dreyer**
Calle Conde de Lemon 289. **Open** 9:30am–7:30pm Mon–Sat. 🚫 📷 📹 🌐 dreyer.munipuno.gob.pe/

Details on the façade of Puno's cathedral

❺ Lampa

Road Map E5. 50 miles (80 km) N of Puno, 22 miles (35 km) N of Juliaca. 🚹 12,000. 🚌 from Juliaca. 🎉 La Fiesta de Santiago Apóstol (Jul 26).

Known as La Ciudad Rosada meaning "the pink city," the dusty salmon- and maroon- tinted roofs and walls of Lampa add a welcome splash of color to the surrounding golden grass plains.

The city's other main attraction is the **Iglesia de Santiago Apóstol**. The church is made from river stones and lime mortar and dates back to the 1650s.

Local luminary and mining engineer, Enrique Torres Belón, who was responsible for the restoration of the church in the 1950s, added a marble-covered chapel and crowned it with a replica of Michelangelo's statue *La Pietá*. The Vatican provided a plaster mold of the famous statue, which, instead of being destroyed after casting as agreed, is now on display in the Town Hall.

Torres Belón, who was also the president of Peru's Congress in 1957, was buried in the chapel along with his wife and his mother. In a rather macabre display, hundreds of bones removed from the catacombs during restoration of the building hang on the walls around them.

The church also has a fine collection of beautiful Colonial paintings from the famous Quito and Cusco Schools (*see p171*) and an elaborate carved pulpit.

Puno: Peru's Folkloric Capital

Puno melds the two ancient Andean civilizations of the Aymara from the south and the Quechua from the north with Colonial influences. The result is a rich diversity of high-spirited folkloric festivals, often hailed as the best in all of Peru. More than 300 dances have been catalogued in the region. Some satirize the Spanish, some celebrate Andean beliefs, while others are pure religious revelry. The most important event in Puno is the festival of the Virgin of the Candles in honor of Mamita Candelaria. Groups with more than 100 dancers each, perform in dance contests held during the 18 days of festivities. The festival also has pre-Hispanic origins which relate to agricultural cycles of planting and harvesting.

Diablada mask represents the devil.

Waca Waca, parodies the iconic Spanish bullfight. The men wear colorful costumes and a bull-shaped headpiece.

Dazzling suits of lights are common.

A heart on the blouse is a part of the costume during the Love Dance.

The Diablada, which symbolizes the victory of good over evil, is Puno's most famous dance. A devil is pursued by angels, skeletons, and other characters.

The Aymara Love Dance represents a courting ritual, where rows of women wildly flick their layered skirts, as groups of whistling bachelors twirl around them.

The Festival of the Virgin of the Candles in February, draws thousands of locals to toast Puno's patron saint.

Llamerada, an Aymara dance, pays tribute to llama herders with dancers dressed in silver-and-gold-threaded ponchos imitating the rhythmic gait of the animals.

⑥ Lake Titicaca

At an elevation of 12,500 ft (3,800 m), Lake Titicaca is the highest lake of its size in the world. South America's second largest lake, it covers 3,210 sq miles (8,300 sq km), is 120 miles (194 km) long and 50 miles (80 km) wide at its broadest point. Its water level fluctuates according to the seasons, receding slightly in winter. Numerous islands are sprinkled across the lake, and the inhabitants cling to a traditional way of life centered around fishing, farming, and weaving. The Uros people live closest to Puno, on floating islands, like huge straw-like nests. They describe their buoyant life as living "between water and heaven" *(see pp154–5)*.

★ **Reed Boats**
Totora reeds are used to build the boats, known as *caballitos*.

The Yavari
This 19th-century gunboat, anchored in the Bay of Puno, houses a museum and a bed-and-breakfast taking seven guests.

★ **Isla Taquile**
The island's red soil contrasts with the deep blue color of the lake. One of the most industrious islands, its walled paths are crowned with rustic arches and dotted with Inca and pre-Inca ruins.

KEY

① **Puno** provides the easiest access to the lake, with boats operating tours throughout the day.

② **Isla Amantani**, the lake's largest island, has religious centers dating back to the Tiahuanacos (500 BC–AD 900).

③ **Isla Soto** lies close to where the lake reaches its greatest recorded depth of 920 ft (280 m).

④ **Juli**, with its four impressive Colonial churches, confirms its past as a key religious center for Jesuits.

⑤ **Pomata** houses a church founded in 1700 and built from pink granite.

★ **Islas Uros**
There are more than 40 floating islands made by layering *totora* reed atop root clods. New reeds are laid weekly as those below decompose.

The blue of Lake Titicaca highlighted against the mountains

VISITORS' CHECKLIST

Practical Information
Map E6. 🛈 in Puno. 🚤 fee for
private boat, organized tour. 🅿️
🛟 on some boats. 🚻 in Puno &
Isla Taquile. 🏪 in Puno. 🏠 in
Puno & Isla Taquile. 🍴 in Puno,
Taquile, Suasi, Amantaní, &
Anapia Islas.

Transport
✈️ from Juliaca. 🚂 from Cusco.
🚌 from Arequipa. 🚢 from Puno
or through hotel; early morning
tour (7:30am) recommended.

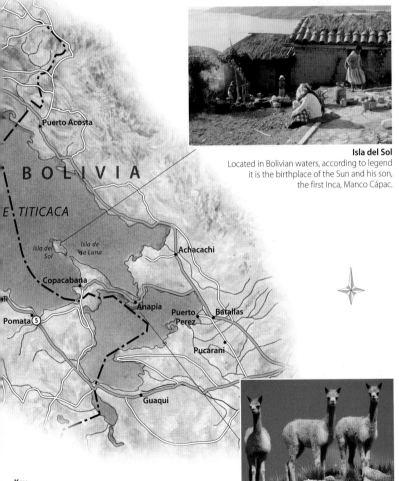

Isla del Sol
Located in Bolivian waters, according to legend
it is the birthplace of the Sun and his son,
the first Inca, Manco Cápac.

Isla Anapia
Located on the Bolivian border, the
islanders use the neighboring island,
Yupisque, for agriculture. It is inhabited
by wild vicuñas.

Key

══ Major road
── Minor road
── Railroad
▬ ▪ International border

0 kilometers 25
0 miles 25

For map symbols *see back flap*

Sunrise in Puno, on the banks of Lake Titicaca ▶

Exploring Lake Titicaca

Enveloped in mythology, Lake Titicaca encapsulates the age-old traditions that have molded and defined the Andean region. For thousands of years, islanders have been growing potatoes and quinoa on tiered hills, fishing, weaving magical textiles, and herding llama – a lifestyle still carefully preserved. Woven textiles are the main source of income. Prices are set and profits from handicraft sales are pooled and shared by the islanders. Staying with a family on an island offers a unique opportunity to experience their traditions. Archaeological sites dot the islands with the most notable on Islas del Sol and de la Luna. Ruins of an ancient temple and crop terraces, dating back 1,500 years, were discovered in the lake's waters in 2000.

Reed boats and the floating islands of the Uros people

Islas Uros

4 miles (6 km) from Puno. 2,000. for organized boat tours.

The Uros developed their unique floating islands centuries ago to escape hostile cultures on the mainland. They consider themselves to be "the oldest people on earth." Legend says they existed before the sun, and could not drown or be struck by lightning. Mixing with the Aymaras and other tribes lost them their super-being status. They speak Aymara today.

The largest of the floating islands is estimated to be 160 years old, housing a meeting hall and a school. The islanders use the ubiquitous *totora* (a reed-like papyrus) for food and firewood – fires are carefully built on a layer of stone – as well as to make their boats, houses, and handicrafts. Most islanders earn a living from fishing and tourism.

Isla Taquile

22 miles (36 km) from Puno. 2,000. San Diego (St James's Day, Jul 25).

Some 350 Quechua-speaking families still live here following the Inca creed of *Ama suwa, Ama quella, Ama llullav* (do not steal, do not be idle, do not lie). There is no police force – a reflection of their belief in honesty – and problems are solved by elected community leaders at the Sunday meetings. The people wear colorful handwoven clothes. Red knitted caps distinguish married men from bachelors who don red and white. Señoritas wear multicolored pompoms, while married women wear bright red ones on their heavy, layered skirts. With no cars, donkeys or llamas, residents carry supplies on their backs up 545 steep steps from the jetty to the hilltop village.

Isla Amantaní

25 miles (40 km) from Puno. 5,000.

Amantaní islanders are famous for their baskets woven from *ichu* (a native grass) and granite carvings. Sacred Inca sites crown the island's peaks. Local shamans read the future in coca tea leaves, so be sure to have a translator on hand.

Isla Suasi

43 miles (70 km) from Puno.

The only building on this small island is a luxury ecolodge which mimics traditional architecture with its thatched roof and stone walls. It runs solely on solar power. There are protected areas for birds, as well as wild vicuñas, centuries-old tracts of natural vegetation and cultivated plots of herbs.

Isla del Sol

9 miles (14 km) from Copacabana, Bolivia. 5,000. to Copacabana. from Copacabana.

Famed as the birthplace of the Incas, the Island of the Sun is actually in the Bolivian waters of the lake. Close to the ruin of mazes called Chinkana, is a sacred rock carved into the shape of a puma. Farther along are two large footprints, supposedly made when the Sun came down to earth to give birth to the first Incas – Manco Cápac and Mama Ocllo. An Inca stairway leads up from the water's edge at Yumani to what is known as a fountain of youth, fed by three springs. A short walk away from the steps is Plikokayna, a fortress that was probably used to watch over the Virgins of the Sun on Isla de la Luna.

Isla de la Luna

4 miles (7 km) from Isla del Sol.

The *aqllawasi* (monastery) is the most important archaeological site on the Island of the Moon. In Inca times, the island housed the "chosen women," who took part in special ceremonies dedicated to the sun. The main palace, which was rebuilt in the 1960s, has some 30 rooms centered around a courtyard.

For hotels and restaurants in this region see pp274–9 and pp288–97

An Incan rock carving of a face near Chucuito, Puno

Chucuito

12 miles (19 km) S of Puno. 🏔 10,000. 🚌 Taxi from Puno 🕭 for Inca Uyo. 🛇🛇🛇🛇

The town of Chucuito was capital of the province and the main tax collection center during Colonial times.

It boasts of two magnificent Colonial churches – **Nuestra Señora de la Asunción**, built in 1601 and adorned with a Renaissance façade, and **Santo Domingo** with its single stone tower, carved stone arches, and beautiful golden altar.

The walled complex of **Inca Uyo** is often described as a fertility garden. Tales abound of women sitting on top of these stones for hours in an attempt to improve their fertility. Sceptics hint that the garden is more a marketing tool than an ancient Inca relic.

🏛 Iglesia Santiago Apóstol de Pomata

67 miles (108 km) S of Puno. 🚌 from Puno **Open** 8am–4pm daily. 🛇

This Dominican church surveys both town and lake from its hilltop position. Built in pink granite, it is known for its intricate sandstone façade, fusing indigenous symbols with Baroque. It is one of southern Peru's most beautiful churches. Inside are windows made from *huamanga* stone, a towering gold leaf altar adorned with coiled columns, and Cusco School paintings.

❼ Sillustani Burial Towers

Road Map E6. 21 miles (34 km) N of Puno. 🚌 Taxi from Puno. **Open** 7am–5pm daily. 🛇 🛇 organized tours from Puno. 🛇

Standing on the shores of the pristine Laguna Umayo, Sillustani is famous for its *chulpas* (circular burial towers), some of which are more than 39 ft (12 m) high.

The Collas, who dominated the area before the Incas, buried their leaders in towers that are wider at the top than at the base. The Lagarto and Intiwatana *chulpas* are the best examples. Experts have long deliberated whether the Collas built the towers to show off their dexterity with stone, to deter tomb-raiders, or simply to honor the dead nobility.

The inside of the tombs are said to be shaped like a woman's womb with the corpses mummified in a fetal position. Some tombs have carvings of lizards, a symbol of life due to their ability to regrow their tails. Blocks and a ramp used to hoist them up demonstrate the difficulty of constructing the towers.

Traditional weaver hard at work

A museum displays pieces from the Colla, Tiahuanaco, and Inca cultures.

❽ Juli

Road Map E6. 49 miles (79 km) S of Puno. 🏔 27,000. 🚌 Taxi from Puno. 🕭 Thu.

The Dominicans founded Juli in 1534 and turned the settlement into their most important religious hub, a center for training missionaries for Bolivia and Paraguay.

The presence of four Colonial churches, constructed to convert the indigenous locals, has earned the town the nickname of "Little Rome."
San Juan Bautista de Letrán dates from 1570 and has dozens of Cusco School paintings depicting the life of John the Baptist and Saint Teresa.

Iglesia de San Pedro Mártir, completed in 1560 and remodeled in the 20th century, combines a Renaissance façade with a Baroque altarpiece and paintings by Bernardo Bitti (1548–1610). It once boasted a 400-strong Indian choir.

Island Homestays

Villagers on the islands of Taquile, Amantaní, and Anapia happily share their homes and lives with visitors. Tourism on Anapia is community-based; all the money goes back into the island to improve education and strengthen local culture. Visitors help in everyday tasks – harvesting, fishing, minding cattle, building houses, or attending the local community council meeting. They may also take part in *casarasiri* (a traditional marriage ceremony) that lasts three days, or sample *huatia* (potatoes roasted in a mud brick oven along with fish or lamb). Amantaní and Taquile islands are closer to Puno and thus easier to reach. Travelers are usually welcomed with a traditional dance and eat with the family.

Visitors and their homestay hosts on Amantaní island

THE INCA HEARTLAND

The Incas' innate ability to build in harmony with the environment is more than apparent in this picturesque Andean province. The Sacred Valley, which they took to be a representation of heaven on earth, has many Inca temples and fortresses. Northwest of this valley, in a tropical mountain forest, lies the spectacular Machu Picchu, a UNESCO World Heritage Site.

For two centuries, Cusco and its environs were the homeland of the Incas. Myths enfold its founding as the dynasty's capital. It is said that Manco Cápac and Mama Ocllo, the children of the Sun and the Moon, set out on a quest to find a place to establish their kingdom. When they reached the valley of the Río Huantanay, Manco Cápac was able to thrust his staff into the ground until it vanished, a divine sign indicating that this was the site for the Inca capital.

Although the area was occupied by other cultures for several centuries before the Incas arrived, including the Wari in the 8th and 9th centuries, it was under Inca control that Cusco reached its peak as an administrative, religious, and military hub.

According to the 16th century writings of Garcilaso de la Vega, the son of an Inca princess and a Spanish conquistador,

13 Inca emperors ruled over the valley from the 12th to the 15th century. From here, they built the Inca Empire in less than a century. Pachacútec, the ninth Inca (r.1438–71) and a construction visionary, was responsible for fashioning Cusco into a shape resembling the sacred puma.

In 1533, Francisco Pizarro and the Spanish arrived in Cusco and following the crushing defeat of the Incas, founded their own city, turning pre-Hispanic structures into Colonial mansions. Gradually, Cusco and its surrounds became a symbol of mestizo, a blending of Colonial Spanish with Andean elements, both architecturally and culturally.

Once Pizarro left, the province reverted to being just another calm Andean domain. The rediscovery of Machu Picchu in 1911 set in motion the transformation of this remote Inca outpost to sightseer central.

Terracing under an Inca fortress, on a hillside above Pisac

◀ Elliptical terraces at Moray archaeological site, Cusco

Exploring the Inca Heartland

Cusco, now Peru's tourism capital, was once the majestic mountain capital of the Incas. Today, it is the ideal base to explore the various sites located in the aptly named Sacred Valley such as Pisac, Ollantaytambo, Tipón, and Rumicolca. These sites and Machu Picchu, "the city in the clouds", all showcase the Incas' amazing grasp of architecture and hydraulics. The circular terraces at Moray testify to their aptitude for agriculture, while the meticulous positioning of the giant granite blocks at Sacsayhuamán exemplifies their precise masonry skills. Spanish influence too is on display, especially in San Pedro de Andahuaylillas, a UNESCO World Heritage listed church.

Locator Map

Area illustrated

Sights at a Glance

Towns and Cities
1 *Cusco pp160–7*
10 Chinchero
11 Calca
12 Pisac

Archaeological Sites and Ruins
2 Sacsayhuamán
4 Tipón
5 Pikillacta and Rumicolca
7 Raqchi
8 Ollantaytambo
9 Moray and Salinas de Maras
14 *Machu Picchu pp180–5*

Tours
3 *Tambomachay Tour p169*
13 *Inca Trail pp174–7*

Church
6 San Pedro de Andahuaylillas

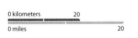

| 0 kilometers | 20 |
| 0 miles | 20 |

Colonial buildings with carved wooden balconies surround the Plaza de Armas, Cusco

For hotels and restaurants in this region see pp274–9 and pp288–97

Key

— Main road

=== Minor road

--- Untarred main road

=== Untarred minor road

--- Track

⊶ Railroad

— Regional border

△ Peak

Meticulously placed limestone blocks at the ruins of Sacsayhuamán

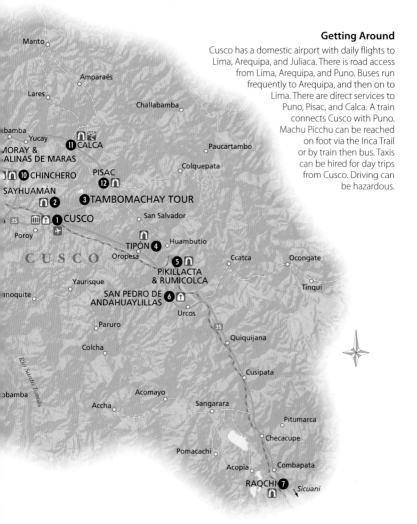

Getting Around

Cusco has a domestic airport with daily flights to Lima, Arequipa, and Juliaca. There is road access from Lima, Arequipa, and Puno. Buses run frequently to Arequipa, and then on to Lima. There are direct services to Puno, Pisac, and Calca. A train connects Cusco with Puno. Machu Picchu can be reached on foot via the Inca Trail or by train then bus. Taxis can be hired for day trips from Cusco. Driving can be hazardous.

For additional map symbols see back flap

❶ Street-by-Street: Cusco

Filled with Spanish arches and squares, and wooden balconies jutting over narrow cobbled streets, the picturesque town of Cusco was declared a UNESCO World Heritage Site in 1983. Women in layered skirts, wearing stovepipe hats over long black plaits, chat in Quechua on the Cathedral steps, both fragments of the past hovering in the present. Shining examples of Spanish conquest abound in the Colonial architecture, while the precise stonework of the ancient walls is a reminder that the Incas founded the city. Despite high tourist traffic, the indigenous people ensure its Andean atmosphere is retained.

★ Museo de Arte Religioso
On the exterior of the museum, once an Inca palace, is the famed 12-sided stone fitting flawlessly into the wall.

★ La Catedral
The commanding Cathedral pays tribute to the Renaissance on the outside and Baroque on the inside *(see pp166–7).*

Museo Inka, or the Admiral's Palace, is devoted to Inca artifacts rather than naval souvenirs. It was damaged in the 1650 earthquake and was restored by a Spanish count.

TUCUMAN

PLATE

| 0 meters | 50 |
| 0 yards | 50 |

Corpus Christi Festivities
The week-long celebrations include street events when the effigies of the saints are paraded through the city.

Ceramic wall mural depicts iconic Cusqueña crafts and landmarks

Inca-built walls

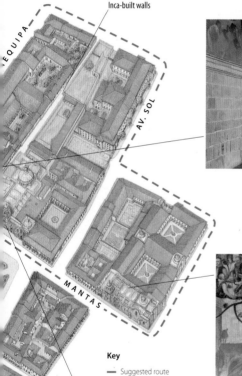

Santa Catalina
Built over the Inca ruins of the Acllawasi
(House of the Chosen Women), this convent
opened in 1610; its museum opened in 1975.

Key
 Suggested route

Iglesia La Merced
Cusco's third most important church, founded
by Riña Sebastián de Castañeda in 1535
on land donated by Pizarro, was handcrafted
by local stonemasons.

★ Iglesia de la Compañía
Originally intended to be Cusco's grandest
church, the Jesuits' lofty plans were thwarted
when the bishop insisted that it not surpass the
majesty of the Cathedral. Its ornate façade,
however, belies its secondary role.

Exploring Cusco

In the earthquake of 1650 most of Cusco's Spanish structures were damaged but the Inca foundations remained, and under the patronage of Bishop Manuel de Mollinedo y Angulo the city was rebuilt. He also developed the Cusco art style, which can be seen in the local churches and museums. Artisans in the San Blas quarter still practice traditional kinds of handicrafts, and the churches and museums brim with centuries-old Cusco School paintings. Starting from the Plaza de Armas, Cusco's heart, all of the city's sights are in easy walking distance.

Visitors and locals relaxing at Plaza de Armas

⊞ Plaza de Armas

In Inca times, the square was mainly used for ceremonial purposes and was known as Huacayapata, meaning Warriors' Square or Square of Regrets. Inti Raymi, the Festival of the Sun, was celebrated here each year. On occasions, the mummies of the dead Incas were placed here so people could venerate them. It is said that the plaza was once covered with white beach sand, transported from the coast by llamas for the emperor's pleasure. It was then studded with tiny gold and coral sculptures to represent all the provinces.

Francisco Pizarro (see p52) claimed Cusco for Spain at the Plaza de Armas, and Túpac Amaru II (see p53), the leader of the indigenous uprising, was beheaded here in 1781.

The stone arches which grace the plaza are a reflection of the Spanish influence, along with the Cathedral and the Jesuit church of La Compañia. The latter is often mistaken for the more famous Cathedral due to its elaborate façade.

Two flags fly in the plaza, the red-and-white Peruvian national flag and a rainbow colored flag said to be the banner of the ancient Inca Empire, Tahuantinsuyu.

⊞ Museo Inka

Cuesta del Almirante 103. **Tel** 084 237 380. **Open** 8am–6:30pm Mon–Fri, 9am–4pm Sat. 🅿 🆔 with flash.

Built on the top of Inca foundations, the museum is also known as the Palacio del Almirante (Admiral's Palace). It is named after the original owner, Admiral Francisco Aldrete Maldonado, and is one of the finest Colonial homes in all of Cusco.

The exhibition is a must for all Inca-philes. It comprises mummies, ceramics, textiles, jewelry, metal, and gold objects. Of particular interest is the assortment – reputed to be the world's largest – of keros, (Inca wooden drinking cups) many of which are richly painted.

While the collection of Inca artifacts is the prime motivation for a visit, the display of textiles

and ceramics belonging to earlier civilizations, a reminder of the area's long Andean history, are a bonus.

⊞ Museo de Arte Precolombino

Plaza Nazarenas 231. **Tel** 084 233 210. **Open** 9am–10pm daily. 🅿 🆔 🔁 with flash. 🅿 📷 🆆 map.org.pe

The former Inca ceremonial court, Kancha Inca, was transformed into a mansion for the Spanish conquistador, Alonso Díaz, in 1580. In 1850, the Earl of Cabrera took up residence here, and in 2003 it was converted into the Museum of Pre-Columbian Art.

The 11 rooms are now filled with 450 masterpieces dating from 1250 BC to AD 1532. The collection was chosen by Peruvian painter Fernando de Szyszlo and historian Cecilia Bákula from the thousands of artifacts kept in the Museo Arqueologico Rafael Larco Herrera (see p98) in Lima.

The Mochica gallery contains standout ceramic pieces. Also on display are geometrically decorated, sculptural ceramics by the Wari, and aribalos (monumental containers) made by the Incas. Other rooms are devoted to wooden sculptures, silver, jewelry, and gold. The museum has an impressive collection of funerary ornaments.

Colonial courtyard of the Museo de Arte Precolombino

🏛 Museo de Plantas Sagradas, Mágicas y Medicinales

Calle Santa Teresa 351. **Tel** 084 222 214 . **Open** 8am–9pm Mon–Sat, 8am–6pm Sun. 🖼

🌐 **museoplantascusco.org**

This unique museum contributes to the conservation of South American flora, especially herbs and plants used for human wellbeing, and the long-standing indigenous knowledge of the use of plants as medicinal resources. Six halls are divided into three sections – the History of Indigenous Medicine, Shamanic Traditions, and Medicinal Plants and the Challenge of Bio Piracy. An excellent café serves snacks, herbal teas, and other refreshments.

🏛 Calle Hatunrumiyoc

The street of Hatunrumiyoc is named after the famous 12-angled stone which is perfectly fitted into the right-hand side of the wall. The stone was taken from the wall of the palace of Inca Roca, the sixth Inca emperor. It is now a part of the Archbishop's Palace.

The wall is a brilliant example of the Inca's skill in polygonal polished stone masonry which they used to construct support walls.

🏛 Museo de Arte Religioso

Cnr Calles Hatunrumiyoc & Herrajes. **Tel** 084 222 781. **Open** 8–12:30am, 3–6pm Mon–Sat, 2–5:30pm Sun. 🖼 Boleto Turístico valid. 🖼 with flash.

Housed in the Palacio Arzobispal (Archbishop's Palace), the museum displays religious paintings from the 17th and 18th centuries, including works by Diego Quispe Tito, regarded as the master of the Cusco School (see p171) painters.

The palace itself boasts carved cedar ceilings, Moorish-inspired doors and balcony, stained-glass windows, and a room displaying life-size models of Cusco's archbishops.

The house, which once belonged to Marquis de San Juan de Buenavista, is built on top of the ancient Inca Roca palace.

Detail on the doorway of an artist's workshop in San Blas District

🏛 San Blas District

Iglesia de San Blas Open 10–11:30am, 2–5:30pm Fri–Wed. 🖼 Boleto Turístico valid. 🖼 🖼 with flash. 🖼

Dotted with Colonial houses featuring Inca stone walls, San Blas is also known as the craftsmen's district. Once the domain of Quechua nobility, its network of narrow streets are now home to the workshops of Cusqueña artists who practice metalwork, and stone- and woodcarving.

Iglesia de San Blas, built in 1563, is Cusco's oldest parish church. Its ornate pulpit features fine Baroque woodcarving.

🏛 Koricancha and Santo Domingo

Plaza Intipampa, cnr Av. El Sol & Calle Santo Domingo. **Tel** 084 254 234. **Open** 8:30am–5:30pm Mon–Sat, 2–5pm Sun. 🖼 🖼 🖼

🌐 **qorikancha.org**

Koricancha, meaning the "golden enclosure," was built to honor Inti or the Sun God. It was the richest Inca temple and had gold plated walls flecked with precious stones. The garden featured life-sized gold and silver statues of animals, local trees, and corn stalks. Mummified bodies of noble Incas were kept here for ceremonies. Sadly, the temple was drained of all its treasures soon after the arrival of the conquistadores.

The church and convent of Santo Domingo were built on top of the Inca shrine. The building brings the two cultures together. It is difficult to imagine how the temple must have looked as so little remains of it now. However, the imposing trapezoidal architecture, pebbled floor, wall niches, and holes that are thought to be either drains or speaking tubes, hint at its past glory.

🏛 Museo de Historia Regional

Calle Heladeros, cnr of Calle Garcilazo. **Tel** 084 223 245. **Open** 8am–7pm Mon–Sat. 🖼 Boleto Turístico valid. 🖼

Cusco's Regional History Museum was originally the home of the 16th-century Inca historian, writer, and poet Garcilaso de la Vega. It exhibits articles spanning the pre-ceramic era to Colonial times.

It has ancient arrowheads, Chavin, Mochica, and Chimú ceramics, a Nazca mummy, Inca musical instruments and tools, and several Cusco School paintings.

🏛 Iglesia de la Compañía

Plaza de Armas. **Open** no set hours. 🖼 🖼 🖼 🖼 with flash.

Constructed in 1571 on the palace of Huayna Capac, the eleventh Inca, La Compañía had to be rebuilt after the earthquake of 1650.

Considered one of the best examples of Colonial Baroque architecture in Peru, it features a spectacular carved stone façade, a 69-ft- (21-m-) high cedar altar covered in gold leaf, huamanga (see p300) stone windows, sculptures, and a number of Cusco School paintings.

View of Cusco with the historic district and Plaza de Armas in the foreground ▶

Cusco: La Catedral

Construction of the Cathedral began in 1560 but took almost 100 years to complete. The church was built on top of the palace of the eighth Inca, Viracocha, using red granite slabs from the fortress at Sacsayhuamán. Two auxiliary chapels sit on either side. To the left is El Triunfo, Cusco's first church, built on top of the main Inca armoury to symbolize Spain's victory over the Incas. The 18th-century Jesús, Maria y José chapel is on the right. The Cathedral's Renaissance façade is in contrast with the lavish Baroque interior containing Colonial gold and silver and over 400 Cusco School paintings.

Iglesia Jesús, María y José
The façade and altar feature images of Jesus, Mary, and Joseph – the sacred family.

★ El Señor de los Temblores
The Lord of the Earthquakes crucifix is said to have calmed the 1650 earth-quake. The figure on the cross, El Negrito, has dark skin which many believe is due to candle smoke.

KEY

① **One of the towers,** according to legend, has an Inca prince enclosed within and when it falls, he will emerge to claim his birthright.

② **The chapel** was built between 1733 and 1735.

③ **Finely carved granite altar**

★ Cedar Choir
The magnificently carved 17th-century choir stalls by Giménez de Villarreal features images of saints and popes.

Main Altar
Fashioned from Bolivian silver, the Neo-Classical main altar weighs more than 885 lbs (400 kg). It was constructed between 1792 and 1803 by the silversmith Pinelo.

★ The Last Supper
Painted by Marcos Zapata *(see p70)* the painting has an Andean touch with Christ and his disciples enjoying a meal of roasted guinea pig, drinking *chicha* (corn beer) from Inca cups.

El Triunfo
The first Spanish church to be built in Cusco, its name itself is a constant reminder of the Spanish "triumph" over the Incas. It has an elaborately carved altar and a crypt that contains the ashes of historian Garcilaso de la Vega.

Main Entrance
These massive doors open for morning services, but the usual entrance is through El Triunfo.

Three tiers of zigzag ramparts built from huge stone blocks, Sacsayhuamán

❷ Sacsayhuamán

Road Map D5. 1 mile (2 km) NE of Cusco. Taxi from Cusco, or walk.
ℹ **Tel** 084 240 006. **Open** 7am–6pm daily. 🎫 Boleto Turístico valid *(see p157)*. ♿ only ground level. 🎭 Inti Raymi (Jun 24).

Sacsayhuamán is an impressive example of Inca military architecture. It is made up of three large terraces which overlap in a zigzag fashion. The enormous granite ramparts stretch about 985 ft (300 m), with stones as high as 17 ft (5 m), some weighing as much as 350 tonnes. So perfectly are the stones aligned that Spanish chroniclers recorded that even a fine knife could not penetrate the joints. No mud mixture was used to bind the stones together.

The ramparts feature 22 salient and re-entrant angles on each level. Such is their design that attackers trying to scale them would expose their flank to the defenders.

Thousands of men were recruited to wrestle the huge stones into place. Legend has it that about 20,000 Indians hauled the largest stone

into position and thousands were crushed to death when it toppled over at one stage.

In designing Cusco *(see pp160–63)*, the Incas imagined it in the shape of a puma; with Sacsayhuamán representing the head and its serrated walls as the beast's teeth. Cusco was the body of the animal, while the temple of Koricancha *(see p163)* represented its tail.

The esplanade which runs in front of the ramparts on ground level probably functioned as a huge ceremonial square for

Gateway made with giant stones slotted together, Sacsayhuamán

religious and military events. Three towers guarded the top of the fortress; the surviving foundations are a reminder of their large size. They were linked by a series of underground passages through which all communication passed. All of Cusco's population could have been housed in the fortress if disaster struck.

During the battle of 1536 the Spanish forced the Incas back to the towers and slaughtered them. Leader Manco Inca escaped, retreating to Ollantaytambo *(see p172)*.

The condors on Cusco's coat of arms are a macabre reference to the battle's body count, immortalizing the birds that came to feed on the dead.

Soon after their victory, the Spanish tore down many of the walls, using Sacsayhuamán as a quarry and taking the white stones to build churches and other structures in Cusco.

Opposite the hilltop fortress is Rodadero Hill, crowned by polished rocks and steps leading to an edifice shaped like a chair. From here, the Incas presided over ceremonies.

❸ Tambomachay Tour

A number of Inca sites lie on the road to Pisac, within easy reach of Cusco. The ruins of Tambomachay, Puca Pucara, Salapunco, and Qenko can be visited in a day, either by bus, taxi, on foot, or on horseback. Each of these locations is different and illustrates the artistic and architectural skills of the Incas. The shrine or *huaca* at Qenko, which is closest to Cusco, consists of a series of tunnels and a cave containing an altar, possibly used for sacrifices. At Tambomachay a spring was harnessed to form fountains, sacred to the Incas.

Tips for Visitors

Tour length: 10-mile (16-km) round trip.
Tickets: Boleto Turístico valid.
Note: Most visitors join an organized tour or hire taxis. Traditionally dressed locals lingering near the sites expect a tip if they are photographed.

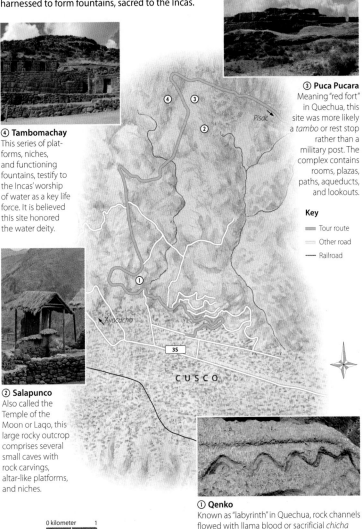

③ Puca Pucara
Meaning "red fort" in Quechua, this site was more likely a *tambo* or rest stop rather than a military post. The complex contains rooms, plazas, paths, aqueducts, and lookouts.

④ Tambomachay
This series of platforms, niches, and functioning fountains, testify to the Incas' worship of water as a key life force. It is believed this site honored the water deity.

Key
━━━ Tour route
═══ Other road
─── Railroad

② Salapunco
Also called the Temple of the Moon or Laqo, this large rocky outcrop comprises several small caves with rock carvings, altar-like platforms, and niches.

① Qenko
Known as "labyrinth" in Quechua, rock channels flowed with llama blood or sacrificial *chicha* (corn beer) during ceremonies honoring the sun, moon, and stars.

0 kilometer 1
0 mile 1

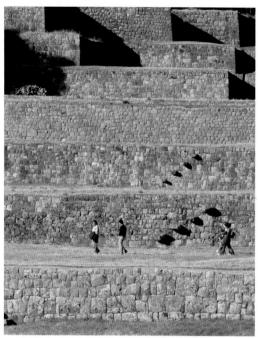

Stone terraces of the Inca ruins at Tipón

original Wari work. These gates acted as a checkpoint for people heading to Cusco, much like a customs office. For the people of the Quechua-speaking world, visiting Cusco was almost like making a religious pilgrimage. Standing at 12 m (39 ft), the gateway is one of the most impressive Inca constructions.

❻ San Pedro de Andahuaylillas

Road Map D5. 22 miles (36 km) S of Cusco. Taxi from Cusco.
Open 8:30am–noon, 2–5pm Mon–Sat, 8:30–10am, 3–5pm Sun.

Nicknamed the Sistine Chapel of the Americas, the simple mud brick façade of this 17th-century church gives no hint of the lavish treasures within.

These include a shimmering gold leaf ceiling, a Baroque cedar and gold leaf altar, wonderful murals, and two restored 17th-century pipe organs, which are the oldest parish organs in the Americas.

❹ Tipón

Road Map D5. 16 miles (25 km) S of Cusco. Taxi from Cusco.
Open 7am–6pm daily. Boleto Turístico valid (see p161).

The picturesque set of stone canals, terraces, and stairways that make up Tipón are said to be part of a royal hacienda built by the eighth Inca ruler, Wiracocha, as a refuge for his father. According to experts, it was once a place of agricultural research and worship. Water is chaneled through stone structures, underground aqueducts, and decorative waterfalls, showcasing the Incas' grasp of hydraulics.

❺ Pikillacta and Rumicolca

Road Map D5. 19 miles (30 km) S of Cusco. Taxi from Cusco.
Open 7am–6pm daily. Boleto Turístico valid (see p161).

Pikillacta, meaning the City of Fleas, was one of the pre-Inca cities built at the peak of the Wari culture. It was so named because of numerous 13-ft (4-m) enclosures that formed a protective garrison. The large complex has hundreds of mud and stone two-story buildings.

Pikillacta has an almost perfect geometrical design, divided into big rectangular blocks with long, straight streets. Walls were originally covered with mud and white-ned with gypsum.

A short distance away are the remains of two imposing Inca gates called Rumicolca. Built on Wari foundations, the Inca blocks are much finer than the

❼ Raqchi

Road Map D5. 73 miles (118 km) SE of Cusco. Taxi from Cusco.
Open 7am–6pm daily.

Located on the Cusco–Puno road, this remarkable 15th-century stone and mud temple to the supreme god Wiracocha still has some walls standing 39 ft (12 m) high. The complex includes housing for the nobility and circular silos that stored food.

Remains of the stone walls of the ancient city, Pikillacta

The Cusco School

Hailed as one of the most important painting movements in the Americas, Escuela Cusqueña or the Cusco School of painting, grew out of the Spanish conquerors' desire to convert locals to Catholicism. Once the victory over the Incas was sealed, various Catholic orders set about winning over people who were, in general, Spanish-illiterate. They imported large numbers of European Renaissance religious paintings, including 16th-century works by Bartolomé Estéban Murillo, Peter Paul Rubens, and Francisco de Zubarán, as well as engravings and illustrations. This demand in turn drew painters to Peru in search of commissions. Representations of the Madonna, the Saints, Christ, and the crucifixion were used by priests as a kind of propaganda to illustrate their sermons.

Indigenous features were introduced in the form of local flora and fauna.

The Nativity is a perfect example of the School's tradition whereby typical Christian images were blended with local Peruvian scenes. This painting is the representation of the birth of Chirst but the landscape is Andean; a llama and indigenous people in native headgear can be seen in the background along with angels.

Cusco School artists who made these paintings were largely anonymous. Paintings were produced in an industrial way, with specific artists for each phase – one for faces and hands, others for landscape and details.

Clothing was studded with decorative ears of corn, a local crop.

Artists depicted the archangels, armed with muskets and clad in Spanish armour, as soldiers of heaven. A symbol of both political and religious victory, the sword of the archangel defends faith but it also symbolizes the Spanish conquest of Peru.

The Virgin of Pomata portrays the Virgin Mary with smooth dark reams of hair like Andean women. She took on a triangular shape to represent the *apu* (*sacred mountain*) or Pachamama (*Mother Earth*), both sacred to Peruvians.

View of town and mountains from Inca terraces, Ollantaytambo

❽ Ollantaytambo

Road Map D5. 60 miles (97 km) NW of Cusco. ⛰ 11,000. 🚌 🚕 Taxi from Cusco. 🎉 Fiesta de Reyes (Jan 6).

Spectacular Ollantaytambo is described as a living Inca town. The residents still strive to maintain ancient traditions such as tilling their fields with foot ploughs. The place takes its name from Ollanta, the Inca general who fell in love with the ninth ruler Pachacútec's daughter. He was forced to flee the city but was united with her after Pachacútec's death. Significant in Peruvian history for the greatest Inca victory over the Spanish, the town was reconquered by the Spaniards in 1537.

People have lived in these cobblestone streets since the 13th century. Originally named Qosqo Ayllu, this Inca town is divided into individual *canchas* (courtyards). Each courtyard has one entrance. A series of carved stone terraces, built to protect the valley from invaders, lead up the hillside to the fortress, **Araqama Ayllu**. The fort comprises the Temple of the Sun, the Royal Hall, or Mañacaray, the Princess' Baths, or Baños de la Princesa, and the Intihuatana, used to trace the sun's path.

Although unfinished, the Temple of the Sun is one of the finest examples of Inca stonework. Six pink monoliths,

designed to glow as the rays of the rising sun hit the structure, fit perfectly together. The T-joints, filled with molten bronze, hold the wall in place, and traces of puma symbols can still be seen on the surface. Stones for the fortress were quarried from an adjacent hillside, moved down one mountain, and up another by ramps.

❾ Moray and Salinas de Maras

Road Map D5. 31 miles (50 km) from Cusco. 🚕 Taxi from Cusco. **Open** 7:30am–5pm daily. 📷 for Moray.

At first glimpse Moray looks like a Greek amphitheater, but closer inspection reveals what researchers believe may have been a crop laboratory used by

the Incas to find the best conditions for allowing particular species to thrive.

There are four overlapping *muyus* (slightly elliptical terraces) with each tier experiencing a different temperature due to varying levels of sun, shade, and elevation, and the largest being 148 ft (45 m) deep. Built on retaining walls filled with soil, and watered by a complex irrigation system, the 7-ft (2-m) high terraces show traces of about 250 cereals and vegetables.

The nearby Salinas de Maras (salt mines), dating back to pre-Columbian times, are in stark contrast. The natural salty water is channeled into 3,000 man-made wells and left to evaporate in the sun. Hundreds of miners work on the site even now, demonstrating their ancient working techniques.

❿ Chinchero

Road Map D5. 18 miles (28 km) NW of Cusco. ⛰ 11,000. 🚕 Taxi from Cusco. 🛒 Tue, Thu, & Sun.

Dubbed the birthplace of the rainbow, Chinchero is perched about 12,375 ft (3,772 m) above sea level on the Anta plain, surveying the Sacred Valley.

The tenth Inca, Tupac Yupanqui, reportedly built his palaces here. In the mid-16th century, Manco Inca, the puppet king appointed by the Spanish conquistador Pizarro, burned down the village thereby cutting off his Spanish pursuers' supply lines. Chinchero

Moray stone circles, believed to be an Inca crop laboratory

Women selling fresh produce at Chinchero market place

did, however, finally succumb to the Spanish by the end of the 16th century. Viceroy Toledo established a plantation here, putting local Indians to work on it, and built an adobe church just above the square over Inca foundations. The ceiling and walls are covered in floral and religious designs.

A massive stone wall in the main plaza, featuring ten trapezoidal niches, recalls the Incas, as do extensive agricultural terraces, seats, and stairways carved into rocks just outside the village.

Quechua-speaking locals preserve the Inca customs, wearing traditional dresses, farming the terraces, and weaving. A colorful handicraft market comes up in the square three days a week. Every Sunday, residents from the surrounding villages gather at the main plaza and exchange their agricultural products and handicrafts using a pure barter system.

Access to the ruins and the main plaza requires a Boleto Turístico, or a Tourism Ticket, available in Cusco. This ticket provides access to 16 historical sights *(see p161)*.

⓫ Calca

Road Map D5. 31 miles (50 km) N of Cusco. 🚹 20,000. 🚌 Taxi from Cusco. 🎉 El Señor de Huanca (Sep 14).

Nestled in the shadow of the Pitusiray and Sawasiray Mountains, Calca was once an important Inca administrative center favored due to its fertile

soil. Today, all that remains are the maize fields and the archaeological ruins of **Huchu'y Qosqo** (Little Cusco), just outside town. Founded by the eighth Inca, Huiracocha, who spent his final days here, Huchu'y Qosqo was named after a tribe that lived here. Despite its name, the adobe brick ruins, including the remains of a three-story building, seem to bear very little resemblance to the real Cusco's streets.

Of special interest are the hot sulphur springs of **Machacancha** and the cold waters of **Minasmoqo**, considered good for health.

⓬ Pisac

Road Map D5. 20 miles (32 km) N of Cusco. 🚹 10,000. 🚌 Taxi from Cusco. 🛒 Tue, Thu, & Sun.

After Ollantaytambo, the most significant Inca ruin is at Pisac. Inhabited since the 10th or 11th century, it became an important regional capital once the Incas arrived.

Researchers believe the town began as a military post to guard against invasion but grew into a ceremonial and residential center. Agricultural terraces and steep paths lead up to the hilltop fort, which has huge walls of polished stone. **Pisac Ruins** comprising military, residential, and religious buildings show that the Incas were masters at architecture, especially building in difficult places.

The site's central element is the Templo del Sol, or Temple of the Sun, an astronomical observatory. The Templo de la Luna, or Temple of the Moon, a ceremonial bathing complex, and the Intihuatana, designed to track the sun's movements, are other highlights.

Pendant from Pisac market

🏛 **Pisac Ruins**
Open 7am–5:30pm daily. 🎟 entry by Boleto Turístico *(see p161)*. 📷

Inca Emperors

Originally, the word Inca was used only to describe the emperor, rather than the people. There were 13 Inca emperors beginning with Manco Cápac, called the Son of the Sun, who founded Cusco in the 12th century. The empire expanded slowly, spreading into the area around Cusco. The ninth Inca, Pachacútec (r.1438–71), pushed the empire down into Chile and captured most of the central Andes. His son, Tupac Yupanqui, extended the territory from Quito in Ecuador to Santiago in Chile. Grandson Huayna Cápac went farther north into Colombia, settling in Quito and making it the northern capital. The Inca civilization, at its peak around 1493, spanned an area of 2,983 miles (4,800 km).

Atahualpa, the last emperor of the Incas

⑬ The Inca Trail

The Incas developed an extensive network of roads, covering about 15,550–18,650 miles (25,000–30,000 km), to connect their wide ranging empire. The Cápac Ñan or Royal Road *(see p51)* comprised stone paths wide enough to accommodate two or three people as well as a llama train. Hanging bridges made of vegetable fiber spanned rivers and steep slopes were surmounted with steps and ramps. The famous Inca Trail, linking Machu Picchu with the Sacred Valley, is the best-preserved of these roads. The present day trail covers diverse landscapes and passes more than 30 Inca sites. Broken up into sections, it takes four days to complete.

① Patallacta
This site on the Inca Trail was once a major agricultural center. The surrounding land is now powder-dry and barren.

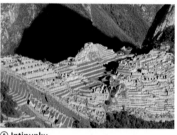

⑧ Intipunku
The Sun Gate is where the Incas controlled access to the city. It offers a 180-degree view of Machu Picchu. Most hikers try to get here in time to see the sunrise.

The Inca tunnel, 66-ft (20-m) long and cut through solid rock, features carved steps and polished walls. It is an amazing feat considering the lack of sophisticated mechanical drills.

Aguas Calientes

Poques 10,758 ft/ 3,279m

Río Urubamba

Machu Picchu Ruins

San Miguel 9,594ft/ 2,924m

Intipata

Río Sayacmarca

0 kilometers 3
0 miles 2

Key

=== Other road
— Railroad
- - Trail
⊢--⊣ Tunnel

⑦ Phuyupatamarca
Stairways connect the four groups of buildings built in the *pirca* architectural style (rough stones set in mud). Six water fountains and crop terraces are highlights.

② Huayllabamba
The largest village on the trail, it is the last place to buy basic supplies such as snacks and bottled drinks. Locally brewed *chicha* (corn beer) is also readily available.

③ Abra de Warmiwañusca
This is the highest point on the trail and the hardest climb because of the lack of oxygen at this altitude. From the pass hikers can look down to the Pacaymayu (Hidden River) Valley and up to Runkurakay, which is the second pass on the trail.

Tips for Hikers

Starting point: Pisacacucho, near Chilca (KM82).
Length: 24 miles (39 km).
Permits: All hikers must go as part of a group with an agency, accompanied by a licensed guide. Bookings must be made well in advance as there is a limit of 500 people a day, including both trekking staff and hikers.
Note: December to April are the wettest months; the trail can be muddy and clouds mar views. The trail is closed for two weeks, sometimes more, due to heavy rains in February.

④ Runkurakay
Opinion is divided on the role of this circular Inca ruin – food storehouse, watchtower, or rest stop. Its commanding position on the edge of the pass overlooking the entire area, however, suggests that it served as a watchtower. It offers superb views across the valley.

⑥ Wiñay Wayna
Resting on a series of terraces are upper and lower house clusters, interconnected by a long, steep staircase. A series of 10 fountains run from the top of the slope to the bottom, perfectly aligning with the agricultural terraces.

⑤ Sayacmarka
Carefully adapted to blend in with the natural mountain forms, this complex is made up of semicircular buildings, with a series of rooms and squares on different levels, narrow streets, fountains, patios, and canals.

For additional map symbols *see back flap*

Exploring the Inca Trail

The city of the Incas, Machu Picchu, is a must on every traveler's list. One of the best ways to reach it is via the ancient Inca Trail. With paved stone paths and stairs cut into mountainsides, the trail passes Inca citadels, such as Runturakay, Wiñay Wayna, and Phuyupatamarca, through cloudforests speckled with orchids, across high Andean plains and up on to the oxygen-starved Warmiwañusca Pass. At a height of 13,780 ft (4,200 m), the pass leaves many a hiker panting for breath. It is worth remembering that the Incas used to run along this trail. They used the trail to send messages across the kingdom. The *chasquis* (dispatch carriers) carried memorized official messages and each could cover over 250 miles (400 km) a day. Ironically, the Spanish used the same roads to infiltrate the country.

Abra de Warmiwañusca or Dead Woman's Pass

🏛 Patallacta

4 miles (6 km) from KM82. 🏔 2,000.

Crop terraces, houses, and other edifices show Patallacta's significance in the region. At 9,843 ft (3,000 m) above sea level, it supplied Machu Picchu with maize, their staple crop.

The stone houses were believed to be occupied by the nobility and religious authorities, while the rest of the people lived in humble mud and cane homes. Pulpituyuj, the large circular tower built on a huge rock, may have served as an altar or prison. Its name comes from the Spanish word *pulpito* (pulpit) and the Quechua word *yuj*, which means a place with a pulpit. Around 15 families still farm the surrounding land.

Huayllabamba

8 miles (13 km) from KM82. 🏔 6,000 (district). 🏛 📅 San Diego (Jul 25).

Huayllabamba, which means "grassy plain" in Quechua, is the largest and the last Andean community found on this trail. At 10,040 ft (3,060 m), the village, located at the foot of a mountain, is set amid terraces where maize and potato crops are cultivated. On clear days, one can see the snow-covered peak of Mount Veronica (18,640 ft/5,682 m) in the Urubamba Cordillera in the distance. Many hiking groups camp here on the first night of the trail. Interestingly, in Colonial times, the village resisted independence.

Andean woman and child at Huayllabamba

Abra de Warmiwañusca

14 miles (23 km) from KM82.

This mountain pass is 13,780 ft (4,200 m) above sea level. According to Inca mythology, the Andes were formed by giants turned into stones. This pass was perceived to be a reclining woman. The Incas believed they had to climb over her stomach to get to the other side. Warmiwañusca translates as "dead woman" in Quechua, hence the name Dead Woman's Pass.

The landscape changes here to barren and cold high plains, with the wind whistling through the pass. Hikers often place a stone on an *apacheta* (mound of rocks) located at the highest points on the trail as a payment to the Pachamama (Mother Earth).

🏛 Runturakay

17 miles (28 km) from KM82.

The ruins at Runturakay, discovered by explorer Hiram Bingham in 1915, have only a single north-facing entrance and exit. Some believe that Runturakay was used as a marker by travelers going to and from Machu Picchu to determine how much traveling time they had left. Others suggest that it was simply a post used to guard the road.

The round shape of the structure apparently inspired the workers employed to clean the site by Bingham to christen it Runturakay, refering to its egg or basket shape.

View of terraces in the ancient town of Patallacta

🏛 Sayacmarka

22 miles (35 km) from KM82.
Perched high on a ridge at a
height of 11,810 ft (3,600 m)
above sea level, Sayacmarka
can only be reached by a
narrow stairway cut into the
mountain. It is thought to have
been a sacred ceremonial
center devoted to astronomy.
Sayacmarka means the "inaccessible town," in Quechua,
but it did have a permanent
supply of water and excellent
food storehouses suggesting
its importance.

Hiram Bingham named the
site Cedrobamba in 1915 after
discovering a cedar wood forest
nearby. It was renamed in 1941
by anthropologist Paul Fejos
to reflect the site more accurately.

Hikers on the narrow stairway cut into
the mountain, Sayacmarka

🏛 Phuyupatamarca

25 miles (41 km) from KM82.
One of the best preserved
towns on the trail, it is called the
"town above the clouds"
because at night the clouds
settle in the ravines and the
complex rises majestically
above them. However, at sunrise the clouds disappear.

Hiram Bingham discovered
the ruins in 1915 and christened
them Qorihuayrachina. Like
Sayacmarka, Paul Fejos renamed
the ruins in 1941.

The curved walls and
geometric terraces superbly
blend with the shape of the
mountains, illustrating the deep
respect the Incas had for their
natural environment. The
ceremonial baths reflect the
Inca mastery at controlling a
natural force, spring water.

Path through the rocky terrain
of Phuyupatamarca

🏛 Wiñay Wayna

27 miles (44 km) from KM82
This impressive Inca complex is
situated at 8,860 ft (2,700 m)
above sea level. The ruins were
discovered in 1941 by, Paul
Fejos, but it was Peruvian
archaeologist, Julio C. Tello, who
named it Wiñay Wayna in 1942.
Meaning "forever young," Wiñay
Wayna is also the name of a
local orchid that blooms
perennially. Its location near a
major access road and the
striking architecture suggests
that Wiñay Wayna was an
important township for the
Incas. The town is divided into
four distinct sectors. There is the
agricultural area with terraces,
the religious or ritual area, the
tower area which boasts some
of the best architecture, and the
urban sector. The latter is made
of rectangular single- and
double-story buildings with
trapezoidal windows, doors
and wall niches, as well as
stairways and fountains.
Significant sections of the
complex illustrate the high-
quality cut stone assembly of
the Incas. It is the last ruin
before Machu Picchu, which is
just 4 miles (6 km) from here.
It offers fantastic views of the
beautiful valley and the
surrounding mountains.

Aguas Calientes

5 miles (8 km) from Machu Picchu.
🏠 2,000. 🚉 to Cusco. 🚌 to Machu
Picchu. 🛈 in Town Hall. 🖂 in
thermal baths.

Aguas Calientes, meaning "hot
springs" in Spanish, is popular
amongst visitors for its natural
pools. Also known as Machu
Picchu Pueblo, it is the last town
for visitors going to the ruins
and the end of the line for
travelers arriving by train from
Cusco (see p180).

The town's economy revolves
around tourism so there are
many hotels, restaurants, and
countless souvenir and
handicrafts stalls. The streets are
filled with vendors touting for
trade. Even the railroad track
changes into an open market
once the train leaves the station.

For hikers with aching
muscles, there are thermal pools
just out of town, including a
bracing one filled with icy
mountain water. The pools were
destroyed by floods but have
been re-built.

Terraced mountainside and buildings at Wiñay Wayna

The astonishing Machu Picchu ruins draped in cloud ▶

❹ Machu Picchu

The mist-cloaked lost city of the Incas is arguably the most famous sight in all of South America. The citadel is built of rock at an altitude of 7,710 ft (2,350 m), on the saddle of a mountain flanked by sheer drops to the Urubamba Valley below. It was never sacked by the Spanish as they failed to find it, instead Machu Picchu was simply abandoned and left to nature to reclaim. The exquisite Inca stonework has withstood the ravages of time, but its function remains baffling. Experts speculate that it served as a place of worship, a sight for tracking stars, and the ninth Inca emperor, Pachacútec's country hacienda.

Sacred Rock is said to have been an altar for mountain and river gods.

★ **Intihuatana**
The stone was used by the Incas as a precise indicator of the two solstices, which they then used to plan agricultural cycles.

★ **Sacred Plaza**
The plaza is flanked by the Temple of the Three Windows on the east, the House of the High Priest to the south, and the back of the Principal Temple to the north. This fine structure was probably used for ceremonial rites.

Visiting Machu Picchu

Trains leave regularly from Cusco and Poroy for Aguas Calientes, a town just below Machu Picchu. Hiram Bingham, the luxury train, leaves from Poroy, a 20-minute drive from Cusco. Backpacker and Vistadome trains (see p326–7), meant for standard tourists, leave from Cusco for a scenic journey through the Urubamba Valley to Aguas Calientes. From here a local bus zigzags up the mountains to the historical Inca site. However, the most satisfying way to visit Machu Picchu is by hiking the Inca Trail.

Train at the Aguas Calientes station

View of Machu Picchu
A spectacular view of the ruins, terraces, and stairways with Huayna Picchu forming the backdrop.

Skilled Architecture
The fine craftsmanship involved in building the structures here is evident: they are made of many-sided stone blocks fitted together flawlessly like pieces in a jigsaw and without mortar.

Agricultural terraces were cut into the mountainside and provided food for up to 1,000 inhabitants.

★ **Temple of the Sun**
Machu Picchu's only round building has two tower windows aligned to the points where the sun rises on the summer and winter solstices.

Exploring Machu Picchu

The remarkable state of preservation of Machu Picchu, with its superb interlacing masonry, satisfies even the most demanding visitor. This Inca city, comprising an upper and lower section with houses, temples, fountains, plazas, and agricultural terraces, clings to a mountain ridge, linked by scores of stairways and paths, and watered by natural springs. No other civilization has managed to assemble so many colossal stone blocks so seamlessly. Cut with stone or bronze tools, the edges of the stones were rubbed smooth until they merged together perfectly, like a jigsaw. Just how the Incas transported the granite they chiseled from the mountain remains a talking point for scholars today.

Water collects in the cut stone base of the fountains

Caretaker's Hut

This small open-fronted hut, with its spectacular view over Machu Picchu, was perfectly positioned to allow the caretaker to observe the access points to the city's south. The hut has been restored with a thatched roof, similar to how it would have appeared when the site was inhabited.

Fountains

The Incas harnessed a natural spring located on a steep slope to the north of Machu Picchu, building a 2,457 ft- (749 m-) long canal to bring the water down to the city. They channeled the water through a series of 16 fountains, often referred to as the "stairway of fountains." The water collects in

the cut stone base of the fountain before going into a circular drain that delivers it to a channel leading to the next fountain. Each fountain featured a rectangular spout fashioned to produce a stream of water tailor-made to fill an *urpu* (a tall-necked, globular clay jug with a flared rim and a pointed base).

Royal Sector

The buildings in the Royal Sector, sometimes called the Group of the King, all feature considerable rock lintels, some weighing as much as three tons. These heavy structures were a feature of imperial Inca architecture. Such characteristic rock lintels along with the

Terraces next to the Caretaker's Hut

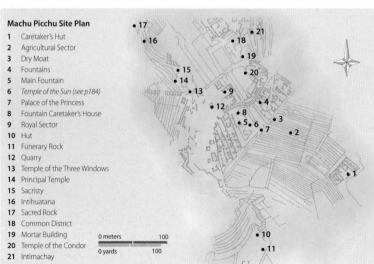

Machu Picchu Site Plan

1   Caretaker's Hut
2   Agricultural Sector
3   Dry Moat
4   Fountains
5   Main Fountain
6   *Temple of the Sun (see p184)*
7   Palace of the Princess
8   Fountain Caretaker's House
9   Royal Sector
10 Hut
11 Funerary Rock
12 Quarry
13 Temple of the Three Windows
14 Principal Temple
15 Sacristy
16 Intihuatana
17 Sacred Rock
18 Common District
19 Mortar Building
20 Temple of the Condor
21 Intimachay

0 meters   100
0 yards   100

abnormally spacious rooms, the high quality of stonework, and close proximity to the Temple of the Sun, the Sacred Plaza, and the first of the fountains, has led experts to surmise that this is where Pachacútec, the ninth Inca emperor, and other members of the Inca court lodged when they were in Machu Picchu. The entrance and exit to the Royal Palace via a single portal also signifies a high level of security. Hiram Bingham believed that the room at the front of the inner patio facing south was the Inca ruler's bedroom. It features 10 trapezoidal niches that would have housed significant ornaments. A room on the other side of the patio, with 12 niches, was thought to be the ruler's workroom.

Funerary Rock

The Funerary Rock, with its curious engraved shapes, is located near the Hut, which provides a great view of the entire area. Researchers believe it may have been used as a sacrificial altar. Llamas, the Incas' favorite offering, were probably sacrificed here. Hiram Bingham, however, suggested it was a mortuary slab on which deceased Inca nobles were laid out in the heat and cold to mummify. Just above the rock lies the upper cemetery of the complex, where Bingham uncovered a significant number of tombs.

Condor-shaped rock at the Temple of the Condor

Temple of the Three Windows

Located on the eastern side of the Sacred Plaza, the rectangular temple comprises large polished blocks flawlessly positioned together. There are three walls and the open side faces the plaza. On the opposite side, the wall has three trapezoidal windows, flanked by two niches. During the winter solstice, the first rays from the sun would come through these windows filling the room with light. At other times, there is a sweeping view on to the ruins below and across the valley. A group of stones in the center of the temple testifies to the presence of a column at some point.

Temple of the Condor

The temple earned its name from the two slabs which form the bird's stylized outspread wings and the head defined by the carved rock on the ground. Hiram Bingham tagged this area as the "prisons" during his expedition because of the dank subterranean dungeons and the niches above the building in which he believed prisoners were held and lashed. Modern day historians, however, believe that the niches were in fact altars on which mummies were placed during the ceremonies that were devoted to the condor, one of the most important Inca deities.

One of the sacred windows at the Temple of the Three Windows

Hiram Bingham (1875–1956)

Explorer, professor, and archaeologist Hiram Bingham set out as the leader of the Yale Peruvian Scientific Expedition in 1911 with a local policeman acting as guide and interpreter. While camped at Mandor Pampa, the expedition met local farmer Melchor Arteaga, who claimed that there were extensive ruins hidden on a nearby mountaintop. Bingham convinced Arteaga to show him the site by offering him one sol for his services. Bingham, Arteaga, and the policeman made the steep climb, eventually coming upon present day Machu Picchu, which despite being covered in centuries of growth, Bingham described as breathtaking.

Hiram Bingham embarking on an expedition

The Temple of the Sun

The temple is regarded by many as having the most sublime stonework in all of Machu Picchu. Built over a large polished rock, the walls of the temple sinuously mimic its natural curve; the entire perimeter wall bends inward. It has compartments for holding offerings or idols. Archaeologists believe it served as an astral observatory, with Inca astronomers gleaning information about their crop cycles from the position of the constellations and the solstices.

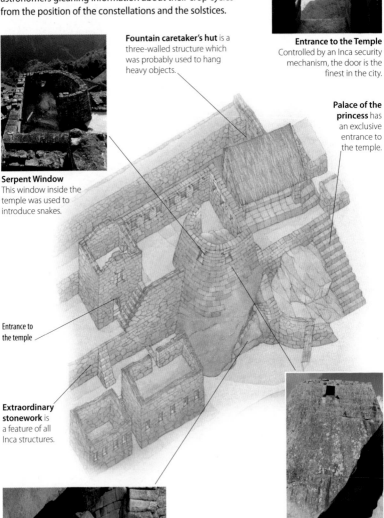

Fountain caretaker's hut is a three-walled structure which was probably used to hang heavy objects.

Entrance to the Temple
Controlled by an Inca security mechanism, the door is the finest in the city.

Palace of the princess has an exclusive entrance to the temple.

Serpent Window
This window inside the temple was used to introduce snakes.

Entrance to the temple

Extraordinary stonework is a feature of all Inca structures.

The Royal Tomb
The steps represent the three levels of existence in the Inca world – the snake (underworld), puma (present), and condor (celestial world).

Window for the Solstices
This is aligned to the points where the sun rises on the summer and winter solstices, the longest and the shortest days.

A grand view of the Royal Sector on left and Temple of the Condor on right, with Common District behind

Sacred Plaza

The Principal Temple, the Sacristy, the House of the High Priest, the Temple of Three Windows, and the Intihuatana make up what Bingham called the Sacred Plaza. The Principal Temple, which faces the House of the High Priest, features the finest architecture. The two side walls have five expertly finished niches, while the back wall contains a small stone altar and seven niches. The Sacristy, which is connected to the Principal Temple, is famed for the two rocks lining the entrance, one of them is said to contain 32 angles. A stairway behind the building leads up to the Intihuatana.

Intihuatana

The Intihuatana stone indicates the precise dates of the solstices and the equinoxes, as well as other important astronomical periods. The June (winter) solstice was said to be the most important day of the year, when the sun is said to cast its longest shadow from the pillar. At this moment the sun is said to be "hitched" to the rock, hence its name "hitching post to the sun." The Incas held ceremonies at

this time, "tying the sun" to halt its northward movement. From this day onward the days become longer meaning more hours of light and more time to work the land and produce more food. Interestingly, the Intihuatana is not completely vertical but tilts 13 degrees to the north, the city's latitude.

Sacred Rock

The enigmatic carved rock, which mimics the shape of a mountain, is believed to have been used as an altar to worship the Apus, the Gods of the Mountain, Water, and Fertility.

Steps lead to the Intihuatana, used for astronomical purposes

Anthropologists believe that the rock mirrors the Pumasillo (Puma's Claw) located in the Vilcabamba Range, a peak revered by Andeans today. The Sacred Rock appeals to the gods whose form it re-creates. It may also have been used as a sacrificial altar to appease the gods.

Common District

Located above the Temple of the Condor is the Common District, also known as Secular District or Industrial Quarter. It was thought to have housed the workers of the realm because the construction is inferior to that of the upper section. Bingham speculated that the two circular rocks which protrude from the floor in one of the buildings were mortars used to crush grain, but as they do not show any wear and are highly polished, this seems unlikely. They may have played a role in a ritual, being filled with offerings of *chicha* or blood, or in an astrological ceremony as the sun, moon, and some stars are reflected when the mortars are filled with water. Their real purpose, however, remains a mystery to archaeologists.

CENTRAL SIERRA

The Central Sierra is an unspoiled area of remote Andean scenery, splendid Colonial towns with an ancient pre-Inca heritage, and traditional rural communities. Despite the wealth of local crafts and lively festivals, this region sees relatively few visitors. Those who do venture here will be amply rewarded by some of Peru's most attractive and pristine landscapes.

Visitors to Peru, lured by the attractions of the Amazon and Cusco regions, largely ignore the Central Sierra. Yet the area's Colonial cities rival Cusco for architecture and charm, especially 16th-century Ayacucho, with its well-preserved churches and grand mansions.

Here, you will also find ancient ruins of the Wari Empire (around AD 600–1100), which dominated the area. The Incas were greatly influenced by the Wari methods of governance and their culture.

Until the early 1990s, this region witnessed the worst of the atrocities committed by the Maoist guerrilla group, the Shining Path (see p199). After the capture of their ringleaders in 1992, the group went into decline and has now all but disappeared. As memories of violence recede, the pretty villages have seen a revival and have now begun to draw

travelers. Today smaller towns, such as Lircay, where the inhabitants still wear distinctive local dresses, and Huancavelica, once a strategic Inca center, are well worth a visit. Another attraction is Huancayo, which plays host to a bustling market every Sunday, where villagers from the surrounding communities display colorful fabrics, handmade wooden ornaments, and produce from their own smallholdings.

The local population – the majority of whom are subsistence farmers – is one of the poorest in the country. Small rural communities are dotted across the neatly cultivated valleys and locals are generally welcoming and friendly. Wandering through the dusty streets and plazas is like taking a step back in time: ancient crafts and traditions are still maintained and there are hardly any tourists in the area.

Well-preserved Colonial buildings line the streets of Ayacucho

◀ Ferrocarril Central Andino train traveling from Lima to Huancayo in the Andes

Exploring Central Sierra

The region provides a fascinating glimpse of rural Peru. Distinctive local artesanía is on show in the adobe villages of the Mantaro Valley, such as Cochas Grande, Hualhuas, and San Agustín. Ayacucho has some wonderful examples of Colonial architecture best seen in its churches, and the Santa Rosa Convent, outside the village of Concepción is also impressive. There is evidence of pre-Inca cultures at the Temple of Kotosh, Huánuco, and the Wari Ruins, outside Ayacucho. These areas are all accessible from the region's commercial hub, Huancayo, where a dynamic Sunday market showcases the agricultural produce and craftwork from nearby villages. Huancayo is also the last stop on one of the world's highest train journeys.

Sights at a glance

Towns and Cities

1 Huánuco
2 Palcamayo
3 Concepción
4 Huancayo
6 Huancavelica
7 Ayacucho pp196–7
9 Quinua

Area of Natural Beauty

10 Pikimachay Caves

Tour

5 Mantaro Valley Tour

Archaeological Site and Ruins

8 Wari Ruins

Brightly-colored façade of the Cathedral in Huancavelica, one of the best examples of Colonial architecture in the region

Key

— Main road

=== Untarred main road

=== Untarred minor road

--- Track

— Railroad

▬ Regional border

For hotels and restaurants in this region see pp274–9 and pp288–97

Andean farmers herding their flock of sheep along a mountainous path in the Huánuco area

Getting Around

There are daily flights from Lima to Ayacucho and to Huánuco. Buses regularly ply the route from Lima to Huancayo (193 miles/ 310 km), Huánuco (230 miles/370 km), and Ayacucho (354 miles/570 km). The roads for the ten-hour journey between Huancayo and Ayacucho and the 92-mile (147-km) stretch between Huancayo and Huancavelica are in very poor condition. It is not advisable to hire a car in Central Sierra. A train also runs from Lima to Huancayo and from Huancayo to Huancavelica.

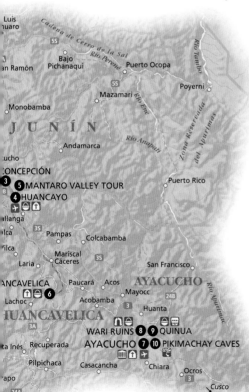

Ornate golden altar of the Cathedral, Plaza de Armas, Ayacucho

Mud moldings of crossed arms from the Temple of Kotosh, Huánuco

❶ Huánuco

Road Map C4. 280 miles (450 km) NE of Lima. 🏙 190,000. ✈ 🚌 from ⋅ Lima. ℹ General Prado 718, 51 2980. 🎭 Town Anniversary (Aug 12–17).

This Andean town, situated at a height of 6,214 ft (1,894 m), has the best climate in Peru. The capital of its department, Huánuco lies on the banks of the Río Huallaga. Founded by the Spanish in 1541, the town still has a few examples of fine Colonial architecture. These include the Cathedral, which contains some pieces from the famous Cusco School paintings *(see p171)*, Iglesia San Cristóobal with intricate woodcarvings, and the grand 16th-century Church of San Francisco. The town also has a natural history museum.

Just outside Huánuco lies the **Temple of Kotosh**, said to be one of Peru's oldest arch-aeological sites, dating from 2000–1500 BC. Although the site was rediscovered in 1935, it was not excavated until 1960, and still little is known about this ancient culture. The most important findings here are the two mud moldings, each depicting a pair of crossed arms in one of the enclosures, believed to be between 4,000 to 5,000 years old. One of these is now on display at the Museo de la Nación *(see p99)* in Lima. The other pair, unfortunately, has been destroyed.

The site, comprising three stone-built enclosures, is a bit overgrown, though there are a number of replicas of the mud moldings in the temple. Local guides willingly take visitors around for a small tip.

🏛 **Temple of Kotosh**
3 miles (5 km) W of Huánuco.
Open 8am–6pm daily. 🚫 📷 ♿

❷ Palcamayo

Road Map C4. 65 miles (105 km) N of Huancayo. 🏙 28,000. 🚌 from Tarma. 🎭 week-long Fiesta Patronal (end of July).

Palcamayo is a small town situated in a green valley. The area's main attraction is the **Gruta de Huagapo**, an enor-mous limestone cave considered the deepest in South America. Although speleologists have explored 9,006 ft (2,745 m) of the cave, its exact depth is still unknown.

The entrance to Huagapo, which means "cave that cries" in Quechua, is through a huge hole on the side of the mountain from which an underground river flows. The entrance leads into a giant chamber that is 99 ft (30 m) high and 66 ft (20 m) wide. Exploring the first 984 ft (300 m) of the cave is fairly straight-forward, but professional equip-ment, including scuba gear, is needed to go farther. The light fades and temperature drops as visitors venture deeper into the cave. Local boys act as guides, providing ropes and torches for a tip.

🏛 **Gruta de Huagapo**
2 miles (4 km) from Palcamayo.
Open 8am–4pm daily. 🚫 🎫 📷 ♿

Ancient cave paintings in Gruta de Huagapo, Palcamayo

❸ Concepción

Road Map C4. 14 miles (22 km) NW of Huancayo. 🏙 63,000. 🚌 from Huancayo.

A sleepy village, Concepción lies in the Mantaro Valley. Just out of town is the 18th-century Franciscan **Convent of Santa Rosa de Ocopa**, which was established as a base for training missionaries heading to the Amazon. The museum in the convent exhibits indigenous artifacts and examples of wildlife, as well as old maps and photographs. The library has a fascinating collection of more than 25,000 volumes, some of which are hundreds of years old. There is also a display of Colonial

Convent of Santa Rosa de Ocopa, Concepción

The library at the Convent of Santa Rosa de Ocopa, Concepción

religious art as well as works by contemporary Huancayo-born artist, Josué Sánchez (b.1945).

The beautiful convent, with its cloisters, stone fountains, and a picturesque garden, is a lovely place to explore. Nuns give hourly tours of the premises to the interested visitors. Unfortunately they only speak Spanish.

⌂ Convent of Santa Rosa de Ocopa
4 miles (6 km) from Concepción.
Open 9am–noon, 3–6pm Wed–Mon.
🗨 Spanish only. ⌂

❹ Huancayo

Road Map C4. 224 miles (360 km) E of Lima. 🚏 430,000. 🚆 🚌 from Lima.
ℹ Casa del Artesano, Calle Real 481.
🎭 Semana Santa (week leading to Easter), Fiesta de las Cruces (May).
🅆 **huancayoperu.com**

Situated at a height of 10,696 ft (3,260 m) in Mantaro Valley, Huancayo is a busy, modern, commercial center. It is also the trade hub for the nearby villages. For a good view of the town, the Cerrito de la Libertad hill is a short distance from the city center. Beyond the hill are the dramatic sandstone towers of **Torre Torre**.

The region is both culturally and agriculturally one of the richest in the Andes. Every Sunday, a huge market attracts villagers from surrounding communities, who come here to sell agricultural produce and local handicrafts. It is perhaps one of the most popular markets in Peru. Huancayo is also a good base from which to visit these rural communities. Each has its own traditional dress and style of dance, and are renowned for their many festivals. This is also the area to savor local culinary specialties such as *pachamanca* (marinated meat, potatoes, spices, and vegetables cooked in a hole dug in the ground and covered by hot stones).

Once home to the Wari culture, around AD 600, Huancayo was absorbed into the Inca Empire in 1460. The Calle Real, which runs through

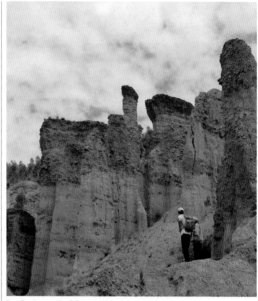
Torre Torre's unusual rock formations, Huancayo

the city, was part of the Cápac Ñan *(see p51)* from Cusco to Cajamarca. The city was founded by the Spanish in 1572, and a few Colonial buildings still remain, the most interesting of which is La Merced. It was in this church that the Peruvian constitution was approved in 1839. It contains a good collection of religious art from the Cusco School.

A big tourist attraction is the **Lima to Huancayo Train**, one of the world's highest train journeys. Conceived by an American, Henry Meiggs, the railroad was built between 1870 and 1908 by more than 10,000 workers, mainly brought over from China. Though passenger service has been disrupted several times, a limited service has now resumed.

Lima to Huancayo Train
Departs: Lima, 7am on last Thu of each month. Returns: Huancayo, 7am & 6pm Sunday. 🗨 🚫 🖥
🅆 **ferrocarrilcentral.com.pe**

The Lima to Huancayo Train

The spectacular journey begins at sea level in Lima's Desamparados Station, and winds its way through 66 tunnels and 59 bridges. At 15,843 ft (4,829 m), the Ticlio Pass is one of the highest railroad passes in the world, and Galera, at 15,686 ft (4,781 m), one of the highest passenger stations. The passenger service is a weekend excursion, on the final weekend of the month. Its daily, regular service is used to transport minerals from Andean mines and agricultural produce from the Mantaro River Valley. This 208-mile (335-km) journey takes about 12 hours, and passes through breathtaking Andean scenery.

Thrilling route of the Lima to Huancayo train

⑤ Mantaro Valley Tour

The Mantaro Valley, through which the Río Mantaro flows, is a beautiful, verdant region of agricultural abundance, producing corn, potatoes, artichokes, and carrots. The area is dotted with small adobe villages and the population is renowned for its distinct craftwork, music, and dance with numerous lively festivals held throughout the year. There are few facilities here, and very little English is spoken, but these communities provide a refreshing glimpse of rural Peruvian life. All the villages are easily accessible from Huancayo.

① Cochas
The pre-Inca tradition of *mates burilados* (engraved gourds) is still practised in the twin villages of Cochas Grande and Cochas Chico. The intricate and detailed carvings depict stories of Andean life.

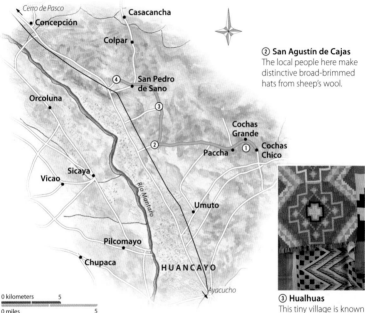

② San Agustín de Cajas
The local people here make distinctive broad-brimmed hats from sheep's wool.

Cerro de Pasco
Casacancha
Concepción
Colpar
④ San Pedro de Sano
Orcoluna
③
Cochas Grande
② Cochas Chico
Paccha ①
Sicaya
Vicao
Río Mantaro
Umuto
Pilcomayo
Chupaca
HUANCAYO
Ayacucho

0 kilometers 5
0 miles 5

③ Hualhuas
This tiny village is known for its beautiful tapestries, blankets, and ponchos. Most are still made from handspun wool and natural dyes.

Key

━━ Tour route
═══ Other road
── Railroad

④ San Jerónimo
Masked dancers participate in the festival of the patron saint of San Jerónimo. The village is renowned for its complex silver filigree jewelry, on sale at the Wednesday market.

Tips for Drivers

Starting point: Huancayo.
Length: 35 miles (54 km).
Stopping-off points: Carry water and snacks as there is little infrastructure along the route. The small roadside stalls sell only agricultural products. Good views of the valley provide lots of opportunities for photo-stops.

Colonial-style buildings in the Plaza de Armas, Huancavelica

❻ Huancavelica

Road Map C5. 92 miles (147 km) S of Huancayo. 🚹 40,000. 🚍 from Huancayo. 🚌 from Huancayo & Lima. 🎭 Semana Santa & Christmas.

This attractive town, the capital of the department of the same name, is located in a high, remote area known for mining and agriculture. At one time a strategic Inca center, the Spanish town was founded in 1571 after the discovery of vast deposits of mercury nearby. They exploited the area's mineral wealth, bringing in slaves to mine for silver and mercury. Due to gradual depletion of resources, the mines were closed in the mid-1970s. At 12,140 ft (3,700 m), the town retains a lovely Colonial atmosphere and has some excellent examples of Spanish architecture. The churches are renowned for their intricate silver altars. Each Sunday a lively market attracts villagers from the surrounding rural communities, who come in their traditional dress.

Environs
Santa Barbara, made famous by the mines nearby, is a good three-hour hike from Huancavelica, up a steep trail that reaches over 13,125 ft (4,000 m) above sea level. The walk to the mines goes over some striking terrain, past herds of alpaca and llama. Carved into a rockface, the old entrance to

one of the original 16th-century mines is still open and unguarded, but it is not advisable to enter.

❼ Ayacucho

See pp196–7.

❽ Wari Ruins

Road Map D5. 14 miles (22 km) from Ayacucho. **Open** 8am–5:30pm Tue–Sun. 🎟

The road from Ayacucho on the way to Quinua passes the Wari Ruins. Built on a hill, at 8,100 ft (2,470 m), it was the capital of

Wari pottery, Wari Ruins museum

the first known expansionist empire in the Andes, and covers an area of around 4 sq miles (10 sq km). Divided into five main sections, it comprises rectangular buildings set out on a grid system, a complex of streets, squares, tombs, paths, and irrigation channels. Very little restoration work has been carried out so far, and the site is therefore not much to look at. The site museum too is usually closed but some of the artifacts from these ruins are displayed at an archaeological museum in Ayacucho.

The Wari (AD 600–1100)

The Wari founded Peru's first militaristic and urban culture, expanding their influence by conquest. They subdued the cultures of those they conquered by enforcing their own customs and forbidding any practice of the former culture. As a result, all trace of the earlier oral traditions has been lost. The Wari Empire *(see pp48–9)* lasted four times longer than that of the Incas, who went on to appropriate their road network and architectural devices, such as an advanced ventilation system and earthquake-proof housing. The reasons for their decline in AD 1100 are unclear, but it is thought that they were replaced gradually by smaller, locally dominant regional groups.

Water channel at the Wari Ruins

❼ Ayacucho

Founded by the Spanish in 1539, Ayacucho lies 8,950 ft (2,750 m) above sea level. A temperate climate, leafy plazas, and beautifully preserved Colonial architecture make strolling around it a pleasure. Ayacucho has a rich tradition of arts and crafts and has retained its charm and Colonial atmosphere which is visible in its wonderful church architecture. During the 1980s the city was isolated and tourism was discouraged due to terrorist activity by the Shining Path. It now plays host to the country's famous Holy Week celebrations, which attract visitors from all over Peru.

Angel adorning the gilt altar inside the Cathedral

The Cathedral located next to the gardens of Plaza de Armas, Ayacucho

⛪ Iglesia de Santo Domingo

Cnr of Bellido & 9 de Diciembre.
Open 6:30–8am daily. ⛪

The church has a Renaissance façade which was later embellished with columns and a balcony. The Spanish Inquisition used this balcony to hang its victims. Inside the church, there is evidence of the fusion of Andean and Catholic influences. There is a portrait of an Inca face on the gold leaf altar, and a hummingbird motif used for decorative purposes. The bells of Iglesia de Santo Domingo were rung to declare independence from the Spanish after Peru's victory at the Battle of Ayacucho in 1824.

🏛 Museo de Arte Popular

Plaza de Armas. **Open** 10:15am–5:30pm Tue–Fri; 9:45am–12:15pm Sun.

This fascinating museum is a showcase for the traditional art of the region. There is a display of *retablos*, Peruvian term for small portable altars once used by mule drivers to bring luck. These wooden boxes have two doors and feature elaborate depictions of religious scenes or laid-back rural Andean life, made from plaster and containing papier-mâché models. Some examples tell the story of political agitation and conflict during the Shining Path era.

There are also exhibits of traditional small clay churches that local women paint with designs of corn and flowers; and several examples of the *tablas de sarhua*, or illustrations on wood, depicting traditional village customs.

⛪ Cathedral

Plaza de Armas.
Open 5:30–7pm daily. ⛪

Located beside the university, on the elegant Plaza de Armas, Ayacucho's 17th-century cathedral has an inauspicious pink and grey façade. The interior is impressive, with a gilded altar and ornately carved pulpit, which is best viewed when it is illuminated during the evening service. The Cathedral is the center of the famous candlelit Holy Week procession, when a crowd gathers here to follow an effigy of Christ that is carried around the city atop a white donkey. There is also a Museum of Religious Art inside the church that exhibits works brought to the country from Rome during the Colonial period.

🏛 Casa Boza y Solís-Prefecture

Portal Constitución, Plaza de Armas.
Open 8am–8pm Mon–Fri.

This two-story mansion, built in 1748, has been turned into government offices, which are

Stone fountain in the courtyard of Casa Boza y Solís-Prefecture

open to the public. The interior courtyard has an original stone fountain and the upper floor is decorated with beautiful glazed Sevillian tiles. Visitors are allowed to see the cell of María Parado de Bellido, a revolutionary hero who was incarcerated here before she was executed by a firing squad in 1822.

🔼 Iglesia San Francisco de Paula
Cnr of Garcilaso de la Vega & Cusco.
Open 6:15–7.30am, 6:15–7:30pm daily. 🔼

This church is in competition with Cusco's San Blas church *(see p163)* for Peru's finest carved pulpit. The altar here is one of the few in the city not covered in gold leaf. It is considered to

Cedar wood altar and decorated pews at the Iglesia San Francisco de Paula

be the finest in the country, made from Nicaraguan cedarwood carved with dozens of angels. The church, built in 1674, also holds a collection of Flemish paintings.

Detail on the limestone façade of La Merced

🔼 Compañía de Jesús
28 de Julio, btwn Lima & San Martín.
Open 9:30am–12:30pm daily. 🔼

This Jesuit church, built in different architectural styles, has a façade of flowers sculpted in red and orange stone. Inside, the gilded altar, carved wood interior, and a good collection of Colonial religious paintings and sculptures are worth seeing. Next door is the Jesuit school where Latin, music, wood-carving, and painting lessons were given to indigenous children, before the expulsion of the Jesuits from Latin America in 1767.

VISITORS' CHECKLIST

Practical Information
Road Map: D5. 357 miles (575 km) SE of Lima, 224 miles (361 km) S of Huancayo. 🚍 92,000.
🛈 Tourist Police, 2 de Mayo 100, 66 761 049. 📷 Semana Santa, Semana de Huamanga (Apr).

Transport
✈ 2.5 miles (4 km). 🚌

🔼 La Merced
Cnr of 2 de Mayo and San Martín.
Open 6:15–7:30am daily. 🔼

Built in 1541, La Merced is the city's second oldest church. It has one nave and a simple Renaissance façade made from fading limestone, which stands in marked contrast to the later elaborate Baroque style, and is a characteristic of many of the neighboring churches. Constructed in a similar modest style, is the adjacent convent, one of the oldest in the country.

🔼 Iglesia y Monasterio de Santa Clara
Between Libertad & Nazareño.
Open 6:30–8am daily. 🔼

The church has a simple limestone exterior and has the effigy of Jesus that is the center of worship during the famous Holy Week celebrations. It also has a beautiful, intricately carved Mudéjar-style wood ceiling.

Ayacucho City Center

0 meters   200
0 yards   200

For map symbols *see back flap*

Semana Santa

The most important event in the Peruvian religious calendar begins on Palm Sunday. Semana Santa, a week of festivities commemorating the trial and crucifixion of Christ, culminates in a joyous celebration of his resurrection on Easter Sunday. Spectacular celebrations are concentrated in Andean towns and villages, where the mixture of Catholic rituals and the pagan beliefs of indigenous communities combine to create a fascinating spectacle. All schools and offices are closed during Holy Week and locals exhibit their religious devotion with processions through the streets, united in impassioned prayer behind an effigy of Christ. These emotional expressions of piety are combined with a celebratory atmosphere filled with folkloric music, dance, feasts, and fireworks. The week-long celebrations present a bewitching fusion of Catholic and pre-Columbian beliefs.

Tarma is famous for its elaborate floral carpets that cover the streets during Semana Santa. Arches, also made from flowers, add to the festive atmosphere.

Ayacucho sees thousands of people descend on the town for Holy Week. City lights are dimmed while a glass coffin containing an effigy of Christ is paraded through streets strewn with roses, followed by a candlelit procession of black-clad worshippers, chanting and praying.

Cusqueñans worship the Christ of the Tremors, which locals believe defended the city from an earthquake in 1650. This painting, commissioned by Alonso Cortes de Monroy, depicts the city after the earthquake and is carried along the streets of Cusco every Easter Monday.

Handmade costumes and elaborate masks with mythological or pre-Columbian themes are common. Some outlandish get-ups are also used to poke fun at the Spanish conquistadores.

An effigy of Christ is central to celebrations all over Peru. Even though each area has its own style of celebrating Semana Santa, all processions have people following the effigy in fervent prayer.

Handmade ceramic church on a roof, Quinua

9 Quinua

Road Map D5. 23 miles (37 km) NE of Ayacucho. [bus] from Ayacucho. [calendar] Sunday. [festival] Independence Day (early Dec).

In the rolling hills 23 miles (37 km) northeast of Ayacucho (see pp196–7) lies Quinua at almost 10,827 ft (3,300 m) above sea level. This beautiful little town has an attractive cobbled plaza and is famous for its ceramic crafts. The roofs of the houses in the region are adorned with small ceramic churches, decorated with painted flowers and corn. These churches are believed to be good luck charms by the locals, and are used to ward off evil spirits.

Local artisans also produce handmade guitars and alabaster figurines featuring comical bands of musicians or groups of gossiping women. The ceramics, made from the rich, red local clay, are on display at workshops and are also sold at the small Sunday market held every week.

Just outside the village lies the **site of the Battle of Ayacucho** (see p53), where Spanish royalist troops were finally defeated, after years of struggle for independence, on December 9th, 1824. This battle brought an end to Colonial rule in the country. The battlefield is a ten-minute walk from the town, and a 132 ft- (40 m-) high white obelisk commemorates the event. There is an annual week-long festival held every December. Locals in Quinua and people all over Peru celebrate with week-long festivities that include feasting, folk music, and dance.

10 Pikimachay Caves

Road Map D5. 15 miles (24 km) W of Ayacucho. [tours] organized tours from Ayacucho.

Situated close to Ayacucho, the cave is hewn out of limestone and is thought to date back to 12,000 BC. It holds evidence of long-term human occupation – the earliest in all of South America. These early inhabitants are thought to have been nomadic hunters and gatherers. Remains of ancient chopping implements, basalt, and blades have been found, along with bones of a giant sloth. It was not until 4,000 BC that agriculture was introduced, and man started cultivating crops such as beans, squash, and chilies.

Beyond the Pikimachay Caves is the **Mirador de Huatuscalla**, a remote viewpoint that looks over the confluence of the Urubamba, Cachi, and Mantaro rivers. Dramatic mountain scenery provides the backdrop to the confluence.

Tour operators based in Ayacucho can arrange personalized packaged tours for visitors going to Quinua, Pikimachay Caves, and Huatuscalla.

The Shining Path

Sendero Luminoso or Shining Path, a Maoist guerilla group, was founded in the 1960s by Abimael Guzmán. It pledged to overthrow the government and return land to peasant farmers. By assassinating unpopular government officials and landowners, the movement gained sympathy initially. However, the 1980s saw a decline in the support due to their activities in rural areas, including brutal "popular trials" and the execution of peasants. By 1992, the group was waging a terror campaign, and had widespread control throughout the countryside of central and southern Peru and in Lima's shantytowns. In 1992, Guzmán was captured and imprisoned for life. Since then the Shining Path has all but disappeared.

Abimael Guzmán, founder of the Maoist Shining Path

View of the valley from the Pikimachay Caves

CORDILLERA BLANCA

The Cordillera Blanca, or White Range, so called because of its perennial ice-capped peaks, has the greatest number of summits over 19,700 ft (6,000 m) outside the Himalayas. These include Peru's highest mountain, Huascarán (22,205 ft/6,768 m), and Alpamayo (19,511 ft/5,947 m), considered one of the most beautiful mountains in the world, thanks to its near-perfect pyramid of ice.

This 112-mile (180-km) range in the heart of the tropical Andes is a breathtaking area of dramatic views, towering peaks, precipitous gorges, sparkling lakes, and abundant wildlife. The range runs parallel to the Cordillera Negra, forming the Callejón de Huaylas, a lush agricultural valley dotted with small villages, known for their arts and crafts, where ancient ways of life persist. Villages such as Chacas, in the neighboring Callejón de Conchucos, are renowned for their woodcarving and carpentry. The valley is also home to natural thermal baths in Monterrey and Chancos, and a number of fascinating Inca and pre-Inca ruins, including the 3,000-year-old archaeological site at Chavín de Huántar, a major ceremonial center of the Chavín people.

Huaraz, capital of the Ancash region, is one of the most important trekking and climbing centers in Peru. Led by local guides, mule-supported treks into the Huascarán National Park are some of the most spectacular that the continent has to offer, with high-altitude camping over vertiginous passes and fantastic views of the surrounding snowy peaks. The dazzling turquoise lakes, such as Parón and Llanganuco, are the highlights of many hikes in the region. The glacial silt collected in these lakes creates a vibrant color that glows in the bright Andean sun.

The region is home to the some unusual flora, such as *Puya raimondii*, a gigantic bromeliad, which takes up to a century to reach its full height, and forests of polylepsis trees, a member of the rose family that flourishes at this altitude. While trekking through the range, visitors may also catch sight of the Andean condor, and the camelid vicuña.

A stone face decoration on the remains of a wall at Chavín de Huántar

◀ Yungay church in Yungay Viejo with the majestic Huascarán, Peru's highest mountain, in the background

Exploring the Cordillera Blanca

Most visitors to the area base themselves in the towns and villages of the Callejón de Huaylas, the valley between the Cordillera Blanca and the Cordillera Negra. Huaraz, Caraz, Carhuaz, and Chacas, in the Callejón de Conchucos, are all home to local festivals, rural produce markets, and arts and crafts. From the valley many of the highlights of the region can be visited on a day trip, including the hot springs at Chancos and Monterrey, the ruins at Chavín de Huántar, the spectacular lakes of Llanganuco and Parón, and Huascarán, a UNESCO Biosphere Reserve. More adventurous travelers can use Huaraz or Caraz as a base from which to hire mules, equipment, and a guide to go for a longer hike into the mountains. The popular choices are the Santa Cruz trek, and the Olleros to Chavín trek.

Sights at a glance

Towns and Cities

1 Caraz

3 Carhuaz

5 Chacas

7 Huaraz

10 Sechín

11 Cordillera Huayhuash

Cemetery

2 Campo Santo, Yungay

Archaeological Sites and Ruins

8 *Chavín de Huántar pp212–13*

9 *Caral p216*

Areas of Natural Beauty

6 Hot Springs of Monterrey

4 *Parque Nacional Huascarán pp206–8*

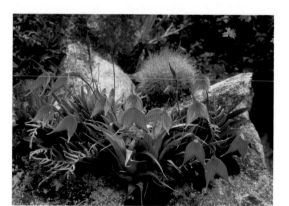

Wild orchids growing on the mountain slopes

For hotels and restaurants in this region see pp274–9 and pp288–97

Key

━━ Moter Way

━━ Main road

═══ Minor road

▬▬▬ Untarred main road

════ Untarred minor road

--- Track

╌╍╌ Railroad

▬▬▬ International border

▬▬▬ Regional border

▲ Peak

An awe-inspiring view of the Cordillera Huayhuash

A guide and trekker on a mule ascending a mountain in the Cordillera Blanca

Getting Around

There is one daily flight to the airport in Anta, 20 miles (32 km) north of Huaraz. Most visitors fly to Lima and then reach Huaraz by road. Frequent buses, *colectivos*, and *combis* make the 42-mile (67-km) journey from Huaraz to Caraz, stopping at villages on the way. Four routes cross the Cordillera, one via Carhuaz to Chacas over the Quebrada Ulta Pass, and another via Chavín de Huántar. The Casma road north to the coast passes the ruins at Sechín and crosses the Punta Callan Pass at a height of 13,850 ft (4,200 m), giving fantastic views. Another road follows the Santa River to Chimbote via the Cañón del Pato.

For additional map symbols *see back flap*

Laguna Parón surrounded by snow-capped mountains

❶ Caraz

Road Map B3. 42 miles (67 km) N of Huaraz, Callejón de Huaylas. ⚑ 16,600. 🚌 frequent colectivos from Huaraz & Yungay. ℹ Municipalidad, Plaza de Armas. 🕒 Wednesday. 🎉 Fiestas Patrias (Jul 28).

A small, pretty town at the end of the Callejón de Huaylas, Caraz has avoided total devastation from the earth-quakes and avalanches that have destroyed so much of the valley. A flower-lined road leads into town, which has a leafy Plaza de Armas.

At 7,450 ft (2,270 m), Caraz is lower than nearby Huaraz (see p206) and has a milder, more agreeable climate. The tourism industry is developing slowly here to accommodate trekkers and climbers – it is the starting point for the panoramic Santa Cruz Trek (see p208) and also for ascents of Mount Alpamayo (see p209).

There are a number of good places in the area in which to stay and eat as well.

Environs

To the north, near Caraz, are the ancient ruins of **Tunshukaiko** – a platform structure thought to date back to the Huaraz culture, around 2000 BC. The setting, in a lush valley with the Cordilleras Blanca and Negra on either side, is spectacular, although there is little to see at the site.

A road runs 20 miles (32 km) east of Caraz through an impressive canyon bordered by 3,280-ft (1,000-m) high granite walls, leading to **Laguna Parón**. This lake is surrounded by snowy peaks, including **Mount Pirámide**, at a height of 19,310 ft (5,885 m). Parón is less-visited but just as spectacular as the Lagunas Llanganuco (see p208).

"Sweet Caraz", icing on the cake

❷ Campo Santo, Yungay

Road Map B3. 7 miles (12 km) from Caraz. 🚌 colectivos run throughout the day from Caraz & Huaraz. **Open** 8am–6pm. 🚻 🍴 📷

The Callejón de Huaylas suffered more than its fair share of tragedy in the last century due to a number of devastating *aluviónes*. When the high-altitude lakes of the Cordillera breach as a result of earth-quakes or excessive snow-melt, they send deadly cascades of water, ice, mud, and debris on to the villages below. In 1970 an enormous earthquake (measuring 7.7 on the Richter scale) rocked central Peru and the resulting *aluvión* wiped out the village of Yungay, burying 18,000 people. When an enormous mass of ice and granite was dislodged from the west face of Mount Huascarán's north peak by the earthquake, it hurtled down towards Yungay at over 190 mph (300 kmph), burying the entire village and sparing only 400 lives. The site, known as Campo Santo or holy ground, is an expansion of where the original cemetery stood. It is open to visitors, and the thick layer of soil that covers the former village is adorned with paths and flowers. It is a poignant and evocative sight;

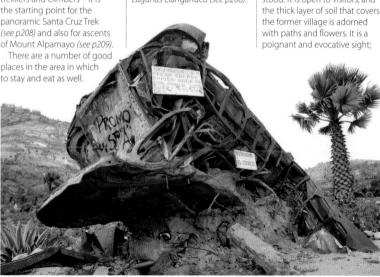

Remains of a bus after the 1970 mudslide in Campo Santo, Yungay

The beautifully maintained gardens of the Plaza de Armas, Carhuaz

the tip of the cathedral's spire and the tops of four palm trees are all that remain of the Plaza de Armas, and there are a number of monuments marking the sites of former homes. A large statue of Christ on a nearby hillside looks over the ruined town. It was to this point that 243 residents managed to climb and escape. Other catastrophic mud-slides in 1941 and 1962 have claimed around 9,000 lives.

❸ Carhuaz

Road Map B4. 20 miles (32 km) N of Huaraz, Callejón de Huaylas. 🏔 13,000. 🚐 frequent colectivos from Huaraz. 🅰 Sunday. 🎭 Virgen de la Merced (end Sep).

This quiet little town in the northern Callejón de Huaylas has a limited tourist infrastructure, although it is a stopping point for trekkers in the Cordillera Blanca. The town lies at 8,655 ft (2,638 m) and has an attractive main square and a bustling market which comes alive every Sunday morning with displays of agricultural produce and crafts from all over the region.

Each September, for ten days Carhuaz comes alive with dancing, drinking, music, and firework displays at the annual celebration of the Virgen de la Merced festival, thought to be the most raucous in the valley.

Environs

A number of good walks from Carhuaz have remained relatively unexplored as visitors favor the longer treks into Cordillera Blanca. A pretty 5-mile (8-km) walk east from Carhuaz leads to the **Baños de Pariacaca**, the bubbling hot thermal waters of the natural rock pools beside a chilly river. For the brave, these are a fun place to swim.

The trail continues to the **Lakes Hike**, a rugged trek that passes between Laguna Rajupaquinan, Laguna 513, and

Condor in flight

Lagunas Auquiscocha. The most spectacular and longest hike is to a small village called **Yanama**. This three-day trip into the Quebrada Ulta (13,780 ft/4,200 m), features fantastic views of the towering peaks of the **Parque Nacional Huascarán** (see pp206–7). Other major treks in Quebrada Ulta can be accessed from Chacas via a paved road through Ulta. Information on these and other good hikes is available at local hostels and trekking shops.

Quispe Sisa

Born in the Ancash region, Quispe Sisa (later known as Doña Inés Yupanqui) was of noble Inca birth. When the Spanish arrived in Peru, her brother, the 13th Inca emperor Atahualpa, "gave" her to conquistador Francisco Pizarro to be his wife. Their union produced what are thought to be the country's first two mestizo children. However, they were the last in the line of Inca nobility because both died childless. The marriage of Pizarro and Quispe Sisa did not last long. He soon found a younger mistress, and she went on to marry another Spaniard and left for Spain with her daughter, who was later legitimized.

Sculpture of Quispe Sisa and conquistador Francisco Pizarro

❹ Parque Nacional Huascarán

Situated in the Ancash region, the Huascarán National Park encompasses almost the entire Cordillera Blanca. This area of glaciers, turquoise lakes, and stunning mountain scenery, has 50 towering snow-capped peaks over 18,700 ft (5,700 m), including Peru's highest mountain, Huascarán *(see pp208–9)*. Declared a UNESCO Biosphere Reserve in 1977, and a World Heritage Site in 1985, the park aims to protect the region's diverse flora and fauna, its geological formations, and archaeological remains. Locals participate in the growing adventure tourism industry so that revenue is channeled to their communities.

Locator Map
▢ Parque Nacional Huascarán

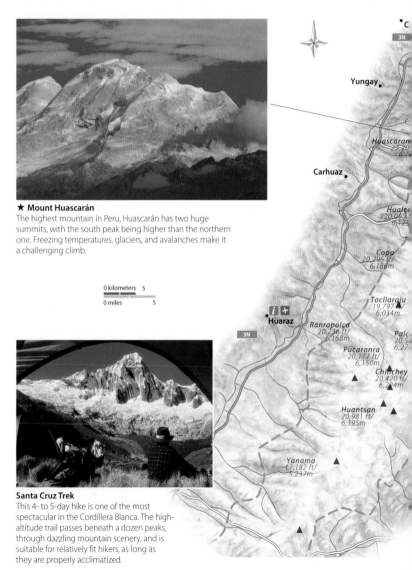

★ **Mount Huascarán**
The highest mountain in Peru, Huascarán has two huge summits, with the south peak being higher than the northern one. Freezing temperatures, glaciers, and avalanches make it a challenging climb.

0 kilometers 5
0 miles 5

Yungay

Huascaran
22,?9?
6,7?

Carhuaz

Huale?
220,00?
6,12?

Copa
20,295 ft/
6,180m

Tocllaraju
19,797 ft/
6,034m

Huaraz

Ranrapalca
20,236 ft/
6,168m

Palc?
20,5?
6,27?

Pucaranra
20,177 ft/
6,150m

Chinchey
20,420 ft/
6,2?4m

Huantsan
20,981 ft/
6,395m

Yanama
17,182 ft/
5,237m

Santa Cruz Trek
This 4- to 5-day hike is one of the most spectacular in the Cordillera Blanca. The high-altitude trail passes beneath a dozen peaks, through dazzling mountain scenery, and is suitable for relatively fit hikers, as long as they are properly acclimatized.

Alpamayo
Once voted the most beautiful mountain in the world. Alpamayo is not the highest mountain in Peru, but the climb to its summit is considered to be one of the most technical.

VISITORS' CHECKLIST

Practical Information
Road Map C4. 13 miles (40 km) from Huaraz. [i] SERNANP, Federico Sal y Rosas 555, Huaraz, 043 422 086. [icons] guide & mule with handler. [icon] hostels & hotels in Yungay, Caraz, and Huaraz. [icon] free camping throughout the park on payment of entrance fee & guide fees. [w] sernanp.gob.pe

Transport
[icon] from Huaraz. Taxi from Huaraz.

Santa Cruz 20,476 ft/ 6,241m
Laguna Jatuncovha
Alpamayo 19,511 ft/ 5,947m
Laguna Parón
▲ *Caraz* 19,767 ft/ 6,025m
Huandoy 20,981 ft/ 6,395m
Chacraraj 19,931 ft/ 6,075m ▲
Pomabamba
unas anuco
▲ **Vaqueria**
Chopicalquiju 20,846 ft/ 6,354m
Piscobamba
Cordillera Blanca

★ **Lagunas Llanganuco**
These two lakes lie in a narrow glacial valley east of Yungay. The dazzling turquoise waters reflect the peaks of Huascarán and Huandoy.

The topography of the area is varied, ranging from snow-capped mountains to glaciers and high-altitude lakes. Hence the diverse flora and fauna.

San Luis
Chacas

Key
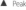 Major road
═══ Minor road
‑ ‑ Santa Cruz Trek
▬ ▬ Park boundary
▲ Peak

ri

Puya Raimondi in Bloom
This extraordinary plant is the world's largest bromeliad and is found in just a few isolated Andean areas.

Spectacled Bear
Ten mammal species, including the spectacled bear, can be found here along with 112 species of birds.

For additional map symbols *see back flap*

Exploring Parque Nacional Huascarán

Gleaming mountain peaks, jeweled turquoise lakes, fascinating archaeological sites, and unusual fauna make the Huascarán National Park an essential part of any visit to Peru. The area is attractive for hikers, climbers, and naturalists alike and is easily accessible from Huaraz *(see p210)* or Caraz *(see p204)*. Both these lofty towns have good hotels, equipment hire shops, and mountain guides, and Huaraz has a lively pre- and post-trek scene. Regular minibuses run between major villages in the valley, and the main road is in good condition. Short trips to the surrounding mountains, or longer hikes for the more adventurous climbers can be organized.

One of the many waterfalls at Lagunas Llanganuco

Santa Cruz Mountain reflected in a lake

🏔 Santa Cruz Trek

Start from Lagunas Llanganuco (see below) or Cashapampa, near Caraz. 🚌 🚶 guides can be hired in Caraz or Huaraz. ⛺

This is one of the most popular treks in the Cordillera Blanca. The high-altitude trail through panoramic mountain scenery passes beneath a dozen peaks which are over 18,700 ft (5,700 m) high.

The trail can begin from Lagunas Llanganuco, which are accessible from Huaraz, Yungay, or from Cashapampa, just beyond Caraz. For those who require mules and handlers to help with the equipment, Cashapampa is a better option.

The path is well defined, and there are a number of long and moderate to difficult ascents along switchback trails, as well as some more level walking alongside rivers and across the verdant meadows in the valley.

The highest pass is Punta Unión at 15,590 ft (4,750 m). Here the Cordillera opens up in front of the trekkers to reveal a breathtaking 360-degree

panorama of snowy peaks and glistening glacial lakes. Camping at this altitude is a chilly but spectacular affair. To wake up surrounded by towering ice-capped peaks and thaw out with hot coffee is a once-in-a-lifetime experience. It is a suitable trek for amateur hikers, providing they are fit, properly acclimatized, and have the right equipment as well as clothing.

🏔 Lagunas Llanganuco

18 miles (28 km) E of Yungay. 🚌 trucks & minibuses leave in the morning from Yungay's main square. 🎟 Huascarán National Park's entrance fee.

These two glacier-fed lakes sit in an awesome glacial valley 12,630 ft (3,850 m) above sea level, with the peaks of Huascarán and Huandoy looming above them, covered by glaciers all year round. Surrounded by the rare polylepis trees, the dazzling turquoise waters glow in the midday sun.

It is best to arrive in the morning as the lakes get shady later and the afternoons often bring clouds and an icy wind. Pick-ups and minibuses from Yungay run throughout the day in the tourist high-season which lasts from May through to September.

Puya Raimondi

Named after the Italian scientist Antonio Raimondi (1826–1890), who discovered it, this extraordinary plant is the world's largest bromeliad and is found in just a few isolated Andean areas such as the Huascarán National Park. One of the most ancient plant species in the world, the spiky and tough *Puya raimondi* has a thick rosette of pliable, cactus-like leaves. It blooms once in its 100-year lifetime. The elongated cluster of flowers grows from a single main stem which can reach 40 ft (12 m) in height. It may yield up to 20,000 flowers, which bloom from May for about three months, before the plant withers and dies. It is often surrounded by hummingbirds.

Puya raimondi, the world's largest bromeliad

Climbing in the Cordillera Blanca

The Cordillera Blanca is a climbers' paradise, with 33 peaks over 19,700 ft (6,000 m). The views afforded by these ascents, over an expanse of pristine snow, are staggering. Most climbers base themselves in Huaraz, where there are many companies who can help plan a trip to the mountains, provide experienced guides, and rent out equipment. However, it is advisable to bring your own gear for the longer expeditions. Huaraz is also a good place for acclimatization hikes, ranging from one day to a week, before any serious climb. There are a number of climbs which are best-attempted only during the dry season, between June and the end of August.

Climbers' Paradise

There are numerous treks in the area which range from short, non-technical ascents to long, highly technical ones meant for experienced and physically fit climbers. Muleteers can be hired locally, but burros carry equipment only until the base camp.

Specialist gear is an absolute necessity as temperatures drop dramatically at sundown and fierce winds are frequent.

Mountain biking, such as the 6-day trip into the Ulta Valley, is both challenging and exhilarating. The highest altitude reached on the route is 16,080 ft (4,900 m).

Spectacular views, especially from some of the mountain summits such as the Pisco, are ample reward for the demanding climbs.

Non-technical ascents of 2–3 days to Urus, Pisco, and Ishinca, with good guides and equipment suit the less-experienced.

Climb	Climb Duration	Height	Areas Covered
Alpamayo	7 Days	11,950 ft (5,947m)	Huaraz, Cashapampa & Llamacorral
Chopicalqui	5 Days	20,850 ft (6,354m)	Huaraz, Lakes Chinancocha & Orconconcha
Huascarán	6 Days	22,210 ft (6,768m)	Huaraz, Musho & Huascarán
Ishinca	3 Days	18,210 ft (5,550m)	Huaraz, Pashpa & Ishinca

Stained-glass window of the Don Bosco School, Chacas

❺ Chacas

Road Map C4. 73 miles (118 km) NE of Huaraz. 🚌 from Huaraz. 🎭 Bullfight (Aug 17–18).

The rural town of Chacas is accessible by a stunning bus journey. The trip starts from Huaraz and passes through a tunnel beneath the spectacular pass at Punta Olímpica (16,044 ft/4,890 m). The pretty Plaza de Armas plays host every August to a bullfight in which townfolk take their chances in the arena. The streets are filled with dancing and music during the festival.

The town is also home to the **Don Bosco School**, the famous woodcarving institute for underprivileged children. This cooperative, established in 1979, teaches poor children the art of woodcarving and carpentry, and the profits are used to fund medical and agricultural projects in the area.

The beautiful designs can be seen in the church, as well as decorating many of the balconies in the village.

❻ Hot Springs of Monterrey

Road Map B4. 3 miles (5 km) N of Huaraz. 🏊 🚻 🍴 🚗

The hot springs of Monterrey are famous for their curative properties. The high temperature of the water in the springs is believed to be good for digestive and other health-related problems. Visitors can immerse themselves in the hot water of the springs. The lower pools, however, are cheaper which is why they are more crowded.

Monterrey is located at a height of 8,868 ft (2,703 m) in the Callejón de Huaylas, the beautiful valley between the Cordillera Blanca and Negra mountain ranges.

Environs
About 22 miles (35 km) farther up the valley is Chancos, located at the foot of Mount Copa. It has a series of small lakes and a steam bath within a cave, as well as a number of private cubicles with saunas.

❼ Huaraz

Road Map C4. 292 miles (470 km) from Lima. 🛬 80,000. 🚌 from Lima. 🈂 Plaza de Armas, 51 043 728812. 🎭 El Señor de la Soledad (around May 3), Semana del Andinismo (Jun). 🌐 centroculturalhuaraz.gob.pe

Huaraz is the capital of the Ancash region and the tourist center for visitors to the Huascarán National Park (see pp206–7) and the Callejón de Huaylas. The city was largely rebuilt after a catastrophic earthquake in 1970, so little Colonial architecture remains, but the setting is spectacular.

The town is situated at an altitude of 10,142 ft (3,091 m) with the colossal peaks of the Blanca and Negra mountain ranges rising on either side. The busy main street, Avenida Luzuriaga, teems with cafés, bars, and shops that rent out hiking equipment. People from nearby communities come into town to sell local products such as cheese, honey, and sweets, as well as handicrafts.

Huaraz is a sociable place with some lively nightspots, hostels, and bars.

Panoramic view of Huaraz with the Cordillera Blanca in the background

Olleros to Chavín Trek

This three-day hike, also known as the Llama Trek, follows an ancient Inca path on its way to Chavín. This area of southern Cordillera is characterized by stunning and varied scenery, from the lush valleys of the eastern slopes of the Andes, to high-altitude savannah, lakes, and snow-capped peaks. There are several passes en route with grand views of the surrounding peaks and valleys. The high point of the trek is the Yanashallash Pass, which, at 15,420 ft (4,700 m), is a tiring but rewarding climb with an inspiring view of the adjacent area. Nights are spent camping, with the imposing Mount Huantsan (20,981 ft/6,395 m) providing a constant backdrop. For information on guides and trek operators see page 307.

Key

— Trail route

Olleros, the starting point of the Llama Trek to the impressive ruins of Chavín, is about an hour's drive from Huaraz. Guides and animal handlers with llamas, to carry the trekking equipment, can be hired from this pretty village.

The trail passes through a marshy valley following, for much of the way, an Inca path alongside the Río Negro. There are a number of other ruins worth exploring en route.

Camping spots that are flat, firm, and grassy are easily located along the trek.

Ruins of Chavín, considered the best remaining example of the Chavín culture, are visible after descending Quebrada Huachesca.

Independent trekkers should carry a good map and keep an eye out for signposts. There are some areas where paths intersect and it is easy to lose the way. Good quality equipment and enough food and water are also important as there is nothing available along the route.

❽ Chavín de Huántar

Located in the Ancash region, halfway between the coast and the jungle, Chavín de Huántar lies at 10,335 ft (3,150 m) above sea level on the Río Mosna. Declared a World Heritage Site by UNESCO in 1985, this major ceremonial center for the Chavín people dates back to around 1300 BC. Displaying a pattern of additions and renovations, there are two distinct parts to the complex, an original temple with underground passageways and carved stelae, and a much larger and later extension, which comprises a mighty, pyramid-like building leading down to the main plaza. The construction is notable for its sophisticated masonry.

View of Chavín de Huántar with Río Mosna in the foreground

★ **El Castillo**
The most important building in the extension of the original temple's right wing, El Castillo is believed to date from 500–200 BC.

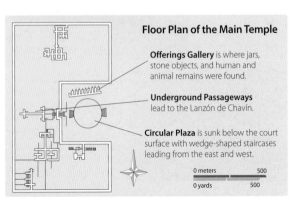

★ **Underground Tunnels**
These incredible passageways are connected by a series of ramps and stairs. They are extremely well ventilated despite there being just one doorway.

Floor Plan of the Main Temple

Offerings Gallery is where jars, stone objects, and human and animal remains were found.

Underground Passageways lead to the Lanzón de Chavín.

Circular Plaza is sunk below the court surface with wedge-shaped staircases leading from the east and west.

0 meters	500
0 yards	500

Porch of Falcons
The black and white portal on El Castillo comprises a large carved lintel spanning the cylindrical columns.

★ Lanzón de Chavín
Located between the subterranean passageways in the Main Temple, this 13-ft (4-m) granite monolith has a carving of the principal deity worshipped by the Chavín culture.

Ceiling Detail
Underground passageways and chambers are roofed with rectangular slabs resting on the top of walls or supported by stones projecting from the walls.

Sunken Plaza
This large central plaza is believed to be where thousands of pilgrims gathered during important fiestas.

The Cult of Chavín (1300–400 BC)

The Chavín, the oldest major culture of Peru, dominated northern Peru with its artistic and cultural conquest more than 2,000 years before the Incas. Due to abundant agricultural production the Chavín used their free time to pursue artistic and religious practices. They had a highly sophisticated artistic style and their principal deities (anthropomorphic feline characters) were represented in stone stelae that can be found at Chavín sites.

A leopard figure etched in stone, Chavín de Huántar

KEY

① **The original temple** buildings sit to the right of El Castillo around the circular plaza.

② **Low platforms** flank each side of the sunken plaza.

❾ Caral

Rediscovered in 1994, Caral is believed to date from 2600 BC, around the same period as the Egyptian pyramids were built, and long before Mexico's Aztec and Toltec structures. It was officially declared the oldest known urban center in the Americas in 2001 *(see p46)* and indicates that an advanced civilization existed in the New World 800 years earlier than previously thought. Archaeologists have unearthed 20 stone structures featuring six pyramids with ceremonial plazas, irrigation channels, and many artifacts.

The sunken circular plaza of the Great Pyramid

Altar of the Eternal Fire
This structure within the walled complex of the amphitheater was used for rituals.

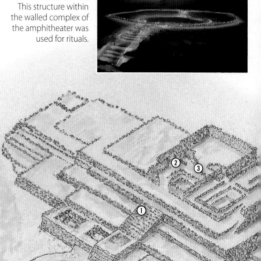

★ Amphitheater
This was one of the main buildings of the city and was used for religious and political functions.

Great Pyramid
The complex has two components, a circular plaza and a pyramid with platforms. The leaders could survey the city from this most impressive building of Caral. It was the center of all activities.

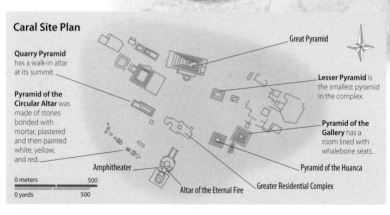

Caral Site Plan

Quarry Pyramid has a walk-in altar at its summit.

Pyramid of the Circular Altar was made of stones bonded with mortar, plastered and then painted white, yellow, and red.

Great Pyramid

Lesser Pyramid is the smallest pyramid in the complex.

Pyramid of the Gallery has a room lined with whalebone seats.

Pyramid of the Huanca

Amphitheater

Altar of the Eternal Fire

Greater Residential Complex

0 meters 500
0 yards 500

★ **Pyramid of the Huanca**
This three-tier structure
has a staircase leading up to
a ceremonial area with a
view of a large obelisk.

⑩ Sechín

Road Map B4. 3 miles (5 km) SE of
Casma. from Casma. **Open** 9am–
5pm daily. in Casma.

Thought to date back to 1600
BC, the ruins at Sechín were
first excavated in 1937 by the
famous Peruvian archaeologist
J.C. Tello (1880–1947). The stone
frieze on the outside wall of
the main temple depicts
a gruesome battle scene:
warriors dressed in loincloths
and carrying staves or clubs
standing over their victims,
who are shown with severed
heads and limbs. It is thought
that the temples were intended
to commemorate an important
battle but it is unknown, as yet,
to which belligerent culture this
complex belonged. Inside the
temple, earlier mud structures
are being excavated even today.

⑪ Cordillera Huayhuash

Road Map C4. from Chiquián or
Huallanca, on the bus route between
Huaraz and Huánuco. guides and
mule handlers can be hired at
Chiquián or Huallanca. free.

Just 19 miles (30 km) long, this
remote and pristine range
incorporates dramatic mountain
scenery, turquoise lakes, and
rolling grasslands. There are
seven peaks over 19,600 ft
(6,000 m), including Yerupaja, at
around 21,765 ft (6,634 m), the
second highest mountain in
Peru, and Siula Grande (20,853 ft/
6,356 m). It was the latter where
the famous motivational

The stunning scenery of
Cordillera Huayhuash

speaker and mountaineer Joe
Simpson (b.1960) along with
fellow climber Simon Yates
(b.1963) famously came
unstuck. Simpson talks about
the mountain in his memoir
Touching the Void. A documen-
tary film of the same name was
shot in the area and was
released in 2003 making the
range famous worldwide.
   There are seven other peaks
over 18,000 ft (5,500 m) high.
Although barely 31 miles
(50 km) away, Huayhuash is
very different from its more
famous neighbor, Cordillera
Blanca. There are no broad
valleys, mountain passes are
higher and more treacherous,
and access is limited. At one
time, the only trekking here
was a 12-day loop of the range
from Chiquián. Today, buses
carry hikers on the dirt road
from Huaraz to Huallanca,
where shorter, five-day trips are
possible. A period of prior
acclimatization is essential.

A head carved in a wall at Sechín

THE NORTHERN DESERT

This is one of Peru's richest archaeological regions. From the Moche Valley to the Túcume Valley, north of Chiclayo, monumental adobe pyramids rise majestically over farmlands. Discoveries over the last few decades have revealed incredible treasures, such as the Lord of Sipán's tomb and Batán Grande, that confirm the historical importance and development of these people in ancient times.

Often described as South America's Egypt, this region was the cradle of the Moche, Sicán, and Chimú kingdoms, highly sophisticated pre-Columbian civilizations that flourished in the heart of one of the world's most arid strips of land. Besides the Lord of Sipán's Tomb, the area is home to many spectacular structures, including Túcume or the Valley of the Pyramids, Huaca del Sol y de la Luna (Temples of the Sun and the Moon), and Chan Chan, the world's largest adobe city and a UNESCO World Heritage Site.

The region's Colonial past can be seen in Peru's second largest city, Trujillo, founded in 1534. An elegant town with well-preserved churches and mansions, the city led the call for Peruvian independence in 1820. In 1931, after the Alianza Popular Revolucionaria Americana (APRA) was outlawed and its leader, Victor Raúl Haya de la Torre, was imprisoned by dictator Sánchez Cerro, Trujillo's middle classes staged an uprising which saw over 6,000 rebels shot dead near Chan Chan.

The Sechura Desert occupies 72,900 sq miles (188,750 sq km) from the northern coast, extending 12 to 62 miles (20 to 100 km) from the shoreline to the secondary ridges of the western Andes. In the north lies the Northwestern Biosphere Reserve, which includes four natural protected areas of red mangrove and Equatorial Dry Forests. To the south are a series of arable valleys that have provided food in this area since pre-Columbian times.

This territory has an exquisite culinary tradition with fish, seafood, and goat as the main ingredients of the varied spicy and richly flavored dishes. It is a prosperous region thanks to its agricultural lands where the best rice, sugar, limes, and mangoes are grown, as well as its thriving rum industry.

Colonial houses in the Plaza de Armas, Trujillo

◄ *Caballitos de totora* (reed boats) on the beach in Huanchaco

Exploring the Northern Desert

This long strip of land stretches from the mangrove forest and sunny beaches of Tumbes to the warm desert valleys south of Trujillo. The city of Trujillo is also the base for visiting sites such as Chan Chan, Huaca del Sol y de la Luna, and Huanchaco. Treasures recovered from the Moche, Sican, and Chimu cultures can also be seen in museums, a highlight being the Museo Tumbas Reales de Sipán in Lambayeque. The Northern Desert is also home to picturesque sea towns such as Huanchaco and Máncora, and Peru's most attractive beaches on the coast off Piura and Tumbes, the country's northernmost region. Here, a number of reserves protect the endangered species that live in endemic and unique ecosystems.

Sights at a Glance

Towns and Cities
❶ Trujillo pp222–5
❹ Huanchaco
❻ Chiclayo
❿ Tumbes
⓫ Zorritos
⓬ Máncora

Museum
❼ Museo Tumbas Reales de Sipán pp232–5

Archaeological Sites and Ruins
❷ Huaca del Sol y de la Luna
❸ Chan Chan
❺ Complejo Arequeológico El Brujo
❽ Túcume
❾ Batán Grande

Brightly painted Colonial buildings, Trujillo

For hotels and restaurants in this region see pp274–9 and pp288–97

Key
— Main road
═ Minor road
--- Untarred main road
=== Untarred minor road
--- Track
▬ International border
— Regional border

Getting Around

The Panamerican Highway is generally in good condition, unless heavy rains occur due to El Niño. Avoid daytime driving when crossing the long desert coast, especially the Sechura Desert located between Chiclayo and Tumbes, since it has high temperatures all year round. There is a network of comfortable overnight bus services that connect all major cities and towns from Lima to the Ecuadorean border. Major airports in Trujillo, Chiclayo, Piura, and Tumbes have daily flights to Lima.

A mural on the walls of Huaca de la Luna (Temple of the Moon)

Small fishing boats woven from *totora* reeds; a practice that has been in use since pre-Inca times, Huanchaco

For map symbols *see back flap*

❶ Trujillo

Ranked as Peru's second largest city, though in constant rivalry with Arequipa for such a privilege, Trujillo's spring-like climate has earned it the title of Ciudad de la Eterna Primavera (the city of eternal spring). The 50 small blocks that make up the Colonial heart of the city, encircled by the Avenida España, contain most of the relevant sites worth visiting, all at walking distance. The city's historic buildings and churches are relatively well preserved. Many have been restored magnificently, highlighting the strong Colonial tones in which they were originally painted, and the blend of local and Colonial architectural styles that justify this city's reputation as the urban jewel of northern Peru.

Bright façade of the Cathedral, Plaza de Armas

🏛 Cathedral

Cnr of Independencia & Orbegoso. **Tel** 044 223 328. **Open** 7:50–9:30am, 5:30–8:30pm Mon–Sat; 7:30am–1pm & 5:15–7pm Sun. 🏛 Museum: **Open** 8am–2pm daily. 📷

On one side of the Plaza de Armas is the Cathedral, also known as the Basilica Menor by the locals. First built in the mid-17th century (between 1647 and 1666), it was destroyed in the 1759 earthquake and then rebuilt. It features colorful Baroque sculptures and paintings from the Escuela Quiteña, a style of painting which originated in 18th-century Quito.

The Cathedral also has a **Museum** with a number of beautiful 18th- and 19th- century religious paintings and sculptures on display.

Giant sculpture, Plaza de Armas

🏛 Plaza de Armas

Also known as Plaza Mayor, some claim it to be the largest main square in Peru. At the center of the plaza is a giant marble and bronze monument dedicated to the heroes of the Wars of Independence. The 85-ft (25-m) high and 100-ft (30-m) wide statue, designed by the German artist, Edmund Moeller (1885–1957), was inaugurated in 1927 to commemorate the city's struggle and independence from Spanish Colonial rule.

Every Sunday, a flag-raising ceremony accompanied by a parade is held on the Plaza de Armas. At certain times *marinera* (see p32) dancers can be seen performing here. The famous Peruvian Paso horses (see p225) can also be seen striding through the plaza.

🏛 Casa Urquiaga

Pizarro 446. **Tel** 044 244 841. **Open** 9:15am–3:15pm Mon–Fri. 📷

This magnificently restored mansion, also known as Casa Calonge, originally belonged to Bernardino Calonge, who founded the city's first bank. The grand Colonial mansion, painted royal blue with white window grills, was bought from the Urquiaga family in 1972 and is now owned by the Banco Central de Reserva del Perú. The 18th-century mahogany desk of Simón Bolívar, who lived in the

0 meters 200
0 yards 200

Trujillo City Center

house after proclaiming Peru's independence in 1821 *(see p53)*, is preserved here.

The building features three interior courtyards. The dining room is decorated with exquisite French porcelain and superb

earthquake it suffered severe damage. The building, with its restored dome, features beautiful and picturesque molded figures representing scenes from the life of Saint Peter Nolasco, the French founder of the

VISITORS' CHECKLIST

Practical Information
Road Map B3. 348 miles (560 km) N of Lima. ⛟ 804,000. ℹ Pizarro 402, 044 294 561. 🎭 Concurso Nacional de Marinera (Jan), Festival de la Primavera (Sep).

Transport
✈ 6 miles (10 km) NW. 🚌 from Lima.

the walls, dating from the time before free-standing altars were used, as well as a priceless Rococo pipe organ.

🏛 Casa de Orbegoso

Orbegoso 553. **Tel** 044 234 950. **Open** 9am–1pm, 4–8pm Mon–Sat.

This outstandingly elegant 18th-century mansion, now the property of the Interbank, is still in perfect condition. Stretching around the block, it has its own plaza facing the Iglesia de San Agustín. It was the residence of Luis José de Orbegoso y Moncada, a well-known general who fought for Peru's independence and later became the President of Peru from 1834–36 and 1837–8. His government marked a low point in the country's history and he disappeared from the political scene to return to his mansion in complete disgrace.

Orbegoso's mansion has an interesting collection of glass, art, silverware, and furniture from that period. It also exhibits the general's relics and personal objects as well as the crypt where he is buried.

Mercedarian congregation. There is also an image of the Virgin of Mercy, patron of the congregation, sculpted by Alonso de Mesa around 1603. Other interesting features include unusual altarpieces painted on

chandeliers, as well as mirrors. It is home to some extremely fine Rococo-style furniture. Several Moche and Nazca ceramics along with many Chavín and Chimú gold ornaments are also on display here.

🏛 Iglesia la Merced

Pizarro 550. **Tel** 044 201 615. **Open** 8am–noon, 5–8pm daily.

This church was designed and built around 1636 by Portuguese artist Alonso de Las Nieves. During the 1970

Musicians outside the 17th-century Iglesia la Merced

Exploring Trujillo

Founded by Diego de Almagro in 1534, Trujillo became the northern coast's most important city in the 16th century. Sugar-cane landlords and rich merchants built opulent mansions during the Colonial era. Due to constant attacks by pirates, a wall was built around the 3-sq mile (8-sq km) city in the late 17th century. In 1820, Trujillo led the struggle for Peruvian independence, and since then, it has been a center of popular rebellion. Today, Trujillo is an oasis of green surrounded by abundant rice and sugar-cane fields, and with fascinating Moche and Chimú archaeological sites nearby.

🏛 Casa de la Emancipación
Pizarro 610. **Tel** 044 207 778.
Open 9:15am–12:45pm, 4–6:30pm Mon–Fri; 9:30am–12:30pm Sat.

One of the most historically significant buildings in the city, this was the place where Trujillo's independence from Spanish rule was planned, declared, and spearheaded by the Marquis of Torre Tagle in 1820. Also known as Casa Rossel-Urquiaga, after the family that owned the house from 1884 to 1944, it was the first seat of government and Congress in Peru.

In the mid 20th century, BBVA Banco Continental bought and restored the building as its head office in the city. The main courtyard and entrance exhibit a symmetrical and austere design and the wide gallery contains impressive marble flooring. There are a few interesting 18th-century murals depicting peasant life. The plans and the history of the house are displayed alongside permanent exhibitions on the life of iconic poet César Vallejo (1892–1938) and Bishop Baltazar Martínez de Compañón y Bujanda (1737–97), who, as he moved around his diocese, painted numerous watercolors that reveal the customs and lifestyle of the period.

🏛 Palacio Iturregui
Pizarro 688. **Tel** 044 244 434.
Open 11am–6pm Mon–Sat. 🚫

Occupied today by the Club Central, an exclusive social center for Trujillo's upper classes, this early 19th-century Neo-Classical mansion was home to General José Manuel Iturregui y Aguilarte, father of Peruvian independence. He bought it from the Marquises of Bellavista in 1841. Situated two blocks east of the Plaza de Armas, the so-called palace has three large patios encircled by beautiful halls and galleries embellished with gold moldings on the ceilings, tall, slender interior columns, and an open roof. There is restricted access, however, with only some parts open to tourists.

Frieze reproduction, Museo de Arqueología de la Universidad

🏛 Museo de Arqueología de la Universidad de Trujillo
Junín 682. **Tel** 044 249 322.
Open 9am–5pm Mon–Sat, 9am–1pm public hols. 🚫 🚫 🚫

Housed in what was once a splendid 17th-century Colonial mansion, the Museum of Archaeology of the University of Trujillo is remarkable for its large and comprehensive collection of thematic exhibits covering 12,000 years of the northern coast's history. This building has had many owners, including the Risco family who lived here until 1984, which is why it is also known as Casa Risco. After several years of state ownership, the mansion was handed over to the University of Trujillo in 1995, providing a permanent exhibition space for its large archaeological collection, begun in 1939.

Moche ceramic

Textiles, ceramic and metal objects, and other artifacts are on display. The most impressive are the Moche finds excavated from the Huaca de la Luna (see p227).

⛪ Iglesia y Monasterio del Carmen
Cnr of Colón & Bolívar. **Tel** 044 256 155. **Open** 9am–1pm Mon–Sat. 🚫 🚫 ⛪ 7–7:30am Sun.

This church and monastery was founded in 1759, though some historians claim it was established in 1724. Occupying an entire block, this is the

The historic Casa de la Emancipación

biggest religious complex in the city. Although severely damaged by earthquakes in 1759 and later in 1970, the complex has survived. Today, it is referred to as the "jewel of Colonial art in Trujillo".

The church and monastery houses the most important collection of Colonial art in Trujillo. The Pinacoteca Carmelita (Carmelite Painting Gallery) exhibits about 150 Baroque and Rococo paintings, most of them dating from the 17th and 18th centuries. Some of the finest examples include Flemish paintings, such as the *Last Supper* (1625), by Otto van Veen (1556–1629), one of Rubens' teachers, and the sculptured image of Joseph and Jesus crafted by Quiteño artist, Manuel Chili "Capiscara", in the late 18th century. At the end of the Pinacoteca, a room demonstrates the paintings' restoration process, although all explanations are in Spanish.

The church has other marvelous features, particularly the breathtaking central gilded altar, considered a masterpiece of the Churrigueresque style in Peru, created in 1759 by Fernando Collado de la Cruz, a free black Peruvian. Floral murals in soft pastel shades line each side of the single dome nave, with exquisite altars on either side and a fine gold-leaf pulpit.

The monastery has two cloisters, the processional and the recreational, both boasting superb vaulted arches and painted wooden columns. A fair portion of the convent's art collection is kept here, but it is not open to the public.

The Peruvian Paso

With Spanish horses such as the Berber, Spanish Jennet, and Andalusian as part of its lineage, the Peruvian Paso is an extraordinary, gentle creature. As an important Paso breeding stronghold, Trujillo hosts frequent festivals and competitions. The Paso horse has a unique gait: *paso llano*, a cross between a walk and a canter. This specially-bred characteristic enables the horse to cover long distances in a short period without tiring. The gait is inbred and requires no training. The gait of the pure-bred foals can be seen within a few hours of their birth. Another fundamental virtue is *término*: a loose action in which the front legs are rolled out as the horse strides forward, giving the mount balance.

The fine physique of a Paso horse

🏛 Museo del Juguete

Independencia 705. **Tel** 044 282 828.
Open 10am–6pm Mon–Sat,
10am–1pm Sun. 🗓 📷 💻

Inaugurated in 2001, this museum exhibits an unusual and fascinating collection of toys put together by Trujillo-born painter, Gerardo Chávez (b.1937). With about 1,000 pieces, including a 2,500-year-old Vicus whistle, pre-Columbian Chancay rag-dolls, genuine 18th-century French biscuit dolls, post-war metal cars, and battalions of diminutive tin soldiers, the museum aims to become the biggest private toy collection in Latin America. It is sponsored by Espacio Cultural Angelmira, headed by Chávez, which is located in the first floor, where a very discreet and smartly decorated café-bar offers drinks and snacks.

Numerous ceramics on display, Museo José Cassinelli

🏛 Museo José Cassinelli

Avenue Nicolás de Piérola 601.
Tel 044 203 433. **Open** 9am–1pm,
3–6pm Mon–Sat & 9am–1pm Sun;
can vary. 🗓 📷 by appointment.

Few could imagine that under a gas station there existed a "museum" of sorts. Owned by José Cassinelli Mazzei, a man of Italian descent born in Trujillo, this collection of artifacts reflects his abiding passion for pre-Columbian history. Despite its unusual setting, having Cassinelli, called "Pepe" by his friends, guide and explain the detail of each piece can be an unforgettable experience.

The collection of about 1,000 pieces includes ceramic whistling pots and other objects from the Chimú, Moche *(see p226)*, Vicus, and Recuay cultures.

Imposing façade of the Iglesia y Monasterio del Carmen

Moche Art

The Moche culture developed along the northern coast of Peru between 200 BC and AD 700. Archaeological sites reveal that their culture was sophisticated, however, they left no written records. Most of the information about the Moche society and religion is based on the illustrations found on their pottery. Their artifacts document a society which was highly class-based. These pieces depict everything from sexual acts to warriors, deities, and humans as well as hunting, fishing, war, and elaborate ceremonies. The predominant medium of the Moche was clay, however, copper, silver, and gold were also used. They were highly skilled in techniques of metalworking as splendid finds from the Lord of Sipán's *(see pp232–5)* burial site reveal.

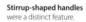

Stone inlay was an integral part of Moche art. Semi-precious stones such as lapis lazuli, shells, and metals were used to make mosaics, on discs made of gold, showing mystical creatures.

Ulluchu man is a 2-ft (0.6-m) high, gilded gold piece with the head and legs of a human and the caparace, legs, and claws of a crab. The odd-looking deity was found inside the Lord of Sipán's tomb.

Moche Pottery

There are two distinct types of pottery. One takes the form of animals or gods and is globular. The other shows elaborate scenes from battles or religious sites.

Black color vessels were rare; red was the predominant color.

Stirrup-shaped handles were a distinct feature.

Personal ornamentation was important as the large bracelets show.

Molds were used for mass production of pottery, bricks, and vessels. Makers' marks were very important and can be seen in a number of bricks.

Portrait vessels were made to order for men of social importance, emphasizing their most dominant characteristic.

Erotic figures of the Moche culture are famous for their explicit representation of sexual acts.

Daily life, scenes of significant events, as well as ceremonies were captured in ceramic by Moche artists.

View of the Huaca del Sol from the top of Huaca de la Luna

❷ Huaca del Sol y de la Luna

Road Map B3. 3 miles (5 km) SE of Trujillo along Panamerican Highway, detour on unpaved road. 🚕 Taxi from Trujillo. **Open** 9am–4pm daily. 🎨 📷 📖 📷

This archaeological complex includes two pyramids. The impressive Huaca del Sol (Temple of the Sun), at 148 ft (45 m), is the largest pre-Columbian adobe structure in the Americas. According to the Spanish chronicler, Antonio de la Calancha, it was built with 140 million blocks, by almost 200,000 workers around AD 500.

Close by is the Huaca de la Luna (Temple of the Moon), a smaller structure that contains six levels, built on top of the other during a 200-year span. It has interconnected rooms, and inner patios, with friezes of anthropomorphic figures.

❸ Chan Chan

Road Map B3. 3 miles (5 km) W of Trujillo. 🚕 Taxi from Trujillo. **Open** 9am–4pm daily. 🎨 📷 📖 📷

A part of the UNESCO World Heritage List since 1986, this enormous site covering almost 11 sq miles (28 sq km) is considered the largest adobe city in the world and one of Trujillo's major attractions. Chan Chan was built between AD 1100 and 1300 as the capital of the Chimú Empire *(see p49)* and residence of the Tacaynamu

dynasty. At the height of its glory, this pre-Columbian metropolis had a population of 100,000, comprising civilians, military personnel, as well as skilled artisans. The Chimú sovereigns surrendered to the Incas after a siege around 1470.

The complex is made up of nine sectors or citadels. The best preserved and most visited is Ciudadela Tschudi. A marked route leads through an amazing complex of large sunken plazas, chambers, restored corridors, temple cloisters, residential areas, and military barracks. Most have friezes depicting seabirds, fish, and other sea creatures. Unfortunately, many structures have been damaged by floods caused by El Niño in 1925, 1983, 1997, 1998, and 2003 as well as invaders and *huaqueros* (tomb-raiders).

Environs
Located about 2.5 miles (4 km) northwest of Trujillo, **Huaca El Dragón** is by far the best restored structure of the Chan Chan complex. It is also called Huaca Arco Iris (rainbow) after motifs found on its inner walls that can be traced back to the Nazca, Wari, or Tiahuanaco cultures. There is a small site museum too.

Between Chan Chan and Trujillo is **Huaca Esmeralda**, discovered in 1923. Excavations have revealed a temple enclosed by a defensive wall. It was probably part of the Chan Chan complex.

Maze of walls of the audience hall at Chan Chan

❹ Huanchaco

Road Map B3. 7 miles (12 km) NW of Trujillo. 🚍 38,000. ✈ from Lima. 🚕 Taxi from Trujillo. 🎨 Festival del Mar (Jul). 🌐 **huanchacoperu.com**

The best beach resort near Trujillo retains its quiet fishing village ambience. Although the water is too cold for swimming, it is perfect for surfers all year round. The town's 16th-century past is visible in the Baroque-style church of Virgen del Perpetuo Socorro, built in 1540 above a pre-Columbian temple, and various Colonial mansions. The major attractions, however, are the sea rafts or *caballitos de totora* which translate literally as reed horses. Locals still use them and are the only ones who can build these vessels, first used by the Moche culture some 2,500 years ago.

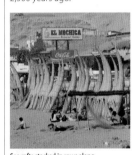

Sea rafts stacked in rows along Huanchaco beach

❺ Complejo Arqueológico El Brujo

Road Map B3. 28 miles (45 km) NW of Trujillo, off Panamerican Highway toward Magdalena de Cao. Taxi from Trujillo. **Open** 9am–5pm daily.

In 2006, archaeologists announced the discovery of a well preserved and tattooed 1,500-year-old mummy of a young woman. She was found in a mud-brick pyramid called Huaca Cao Viejo, a part of the El Brujo Moche complex. In the tomb with La Señora de Cao (The Lady of Cao), were funeral objects such as gold sewing needles, weaving tools, and metal jewelry.

Gallery display at the Museo Tumbas Reales de Sipán, Lambayeque

❻ Chiclayo

Road Map B3. 124 miles (200 km) N of Trujillo. 👥 798,500. ✈ from Lima. 🚌 from Lima & Trujillo. 🎉 Señor Cautivo de Monsefú (Sep).
ⓦ **lambayeque.com**

Founded in the mid-16th century as a rural Indian village that connected the Colonial towns of Zaña and Lambayeque with the port of Pimentel, Chiclayo is a commercial hub and northern Peru's second largest city after Trujillo. Major attractions here are the Neo-Classical style cathedral, built in 1869, and the Mercado Modelo (Central Market). The market is considered one of the most interesting in Peru, offering everything from herbs and healing charms used by *curanderos* and *brujos* (witchdoctors and healers), to mats, hats, woven straw baskets, and other products. Chiclayo serves as the most convenient starting point to visit all major archaeological and historical features in the area.

Gold jewelry, Museo Tumbas Reales de Sipán

Environs
About 6 miles (10 km) north of Chiclayo lies the 17th-century Colonial town of **Lambayeque**. It still retains houses with distinctive wooden balconies and wrought-iron, grillwork windows. Examples of fine architecture can be found along Calle 8 de Octubre or Calle 2 de Mayo, where Casa de la Logia o Montjoy boasts a 210-ft- (64-m-) long balcony, said to be the longest in Colonial America. The other big attractions here are the museums. **Museo Tumbas Reales de Sipán** is a state-of-the-art museum that exhibits the fabulous discovery of the Lord of Sipán's tomb *(see pp232–5)*. The **Museo Arqueológico Nacional Brüning** displays a fine collection of Sicán, Moche, Chimú, and Lambayeque archaeological artifacts collected by German engineer, Hans Heinrich Brüning

(1848–1928), and acquired by the Peruvian government in 1921. **Pimentel**, 6 miles (10 km) west of Chiclayo, has a nice beach with good waves for surfing. This coastal town has an old pier, which locals claim is one of the longest in South America, from where cotton and sugar were exported. The ghost town of **Zaña**, 32 miles (51 km) southeast of Chiclayo, was founded in 1563. The ruins of churches and buildings show evidence of this town's former opulence. Attacked by English buccaneers Edward Davis and Francis Drake, a flood destroyed Zaña in 1720 and it was abandoned.

Another museum worth a visit is **Museo Nacional de Sicán** in Ferreñafe, 11 miles (18 km) northeast of Chiclayo. On display here are golden artifacts, ceramics, and other utensils, found in the tombs at Batán Grande, they rival the Sipán finds.

🏛 **Museo Arqueológico Nacional Brüning**
Av. Huamachuco, Cuadra 8, Lambayeque. **Tel** 074 282 110. **Open** 9am–5pm daily. 🅿 📷 📹

🏛 **Museo Nacional Sicán**
Av. Batán Grande, Cuadra 9, Ferreñafe. **Tel** 074 286 469. **Open** 9am–5pm Tue–Sun. 🅿 📷 ✉ 📱 📹

❼ Museo Tumbas Reales de Sipán

See pp233–5.

The Peruvian Hairless Dog
Known as *perro sin pelo*, this ancient breed can be traced back to pre-Columbian times. Ceramic hairless dogs from the Vicus, Moche, Chimú, and Chancay cultures have been excavated along the north and central coast, offering evidence of its Peruvian origins. The Inca kept them as pets to please the Sun God and Moon Goddess. The Spanish conquest nearly caused the breed's extinction, but fortunately they survived in rural areas, where people believed in their magical forces. Smart, independent, and good with children, the breed's lack of hair has given them a reputation for being clean even though the skin has to be taken care of. The dogs vary in size from 10 inches (25 cm) to 26 inches (65 cm).

Peruvian hairless dog, declared a national heritage animal in 2000

Diorama of a shaman, Museo de Sitio Túcume

Túcume, built in 1991, exhibits the works of Heyerdahl and American archaeologist, Wendell C. Bennet, who was the first to scientifically excavate the site in 1936. Also on display are elements of the local *curanderismo* (the ancient art of healing), still performed around the site.

Museo de Sitio Túcume

At the entrance of the site. **Tel** 074 830 250. **Open** 8am–5pm daily. 🐾 📷 ♿ 🚻 🍴 🛍 🌐 tucume.com

❽ Túcume

Road Map B3. 21 miles (33 km) NE of Chiclayo on the Old Panamerican Highway to Piura. **Tel** 074 830 250. 🚌 from Chiclayo and Lambayeque. **Open** 8am–5pm daily. 🐾 📷 📱 🍴 🌐 tucume.com

Also known as the Valley of the Pyramids, this site is located in the plains of Túcume, in the Lambayeque Valley. The area was developed as the capital of the Lambayeque culture, which existed between AD 1000 and 1375. The settlement was occupied by the Chimú from 1375 to 1450, until the Incas conquered the Chimú kingdom and inhabited the city until 1532.

Replica of a frieze, Túcume pyramid

Túcume consists of 26 major adobe pyramids about 131-ft (40-m) high and other lesser buildings constructed around Cerro Purgatorio. This excellent 646-ft- (197-m-) high promontory lookout is also known as Cerro La Raya, after a sting ray fish that, according to legend, lives within it.

Túcume is thought to have been a center of pilgrimage which had high priests with great understanding of agro-astrology. The most relevant investigations carried out here were conducted between 1988 and 1994 by Thor Heyerdahl (1914–2002), the Norwegian ethnographer and explorer who led an expedition on a *kon-tiki* (balsa raft) from Peru to Polynesia in 1947. His studies concentrated on three major structures: Huaca Larga, Huaca 1, and the Templo de la Piedra Sagrada (Temple of the Sacred Stone). Heyerdahl discovered evidence of a pre-Columbian maritime culture, confirming theories that inspired his journey across the Pacific Ocean. Excavations have yielded details about the functioning and lives of the inhabitants. Evidence of the Chimú and Inca occupations of the region has been found in dedicatory offerings, burials, and ceramics. In Huaca Larga, for example, archaeologists found the lavish burial of a prominent Inca general. Some archaeologists believe that the fire that razed central Huaca Larga coincided with the beginning of the Colonial period in Peru. The **Museo de Sitio**

❾ Batán Grande

Road Map B3. 24 miles (38 km) NE of Chiclayo on the road to Ferreñafe. 🚕 Taxi from Chiclayo. 🐾 📷 📱 🍴 🛍 🌐 ⚠

An interesting blend of nature and history, Batán Grande consists of around 20 adobe pyramids situated in the heart of an ancient forest of *algarrobo* (mesquite) trees. Between 1978 and 2001, Japanese archaeologist, Izumi Shimada unveiled many tombs from the middle Sicán period (AD 900–1100). Some of the best gold artifacts found here are displayed at the Museo Nacional Sicán in Ferreñafe. The Sicán culture, which in Muchik language means "Temple of the Moon," arose after the Moche fell, but they left in the 12th century.

The **Santuario Histórico Bosque de Pomac**, protected since 2001, is home to 11th-century mesquite trees and 70 bird species.

Carob tree in the protected forest of Santuario Histórico Bosque de Pomac

The Cathedral, or Basilica Menor, in Trujillo's Plaza de Armas ▶

❼ Museo Tumbas Reales de Sipán

The pyramid-shaped Museum of the Royal Tombs of Sipán was inaugurated in 2002. Designed by architect Celso Prado Pastor, it is inspired by Huaca Rajada, a Moche mausoleum where the Lord of Sipán was buried 1,700 years ago. The pre-Columbian sovereign's tomb was discovered in 1987 by archaeologist Walter Alva and was dubbed "the richest tomb of the New World". This museum of monumental proportions has three floors and is divided into ten thematic sectors. The exhibits include 1,400 objects of gold, silver, copper, bronze, precious stones, and ceramics of extraordinary beauty and artisanship.

Pottery and Ceramics
The reconstructed old Lord of Sipán's tomb, which contains the pottery that was discovered.

★ Fully Costumed Moche High Priest
A human-sized mannequin of the high priest wearing a Mochica ceremonial outfit and jewelry. He watched over religious worship and rituals.

The High Priest's Tomb
has been reconstructed here. He was second in the hierarchy during the Lord of Sipán's reign.

The Octopus Pectoral
This impressive breastplate made of gilded copper and silver is shaped like the tentacles of an octopus that surround a funeral mask.

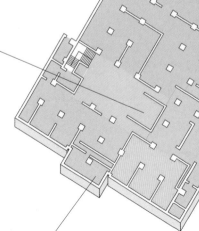

★ Lord of Sipán's Burial Chamber
This replica has been reconstructed exactly as it was found by archaeologists. The servants were buried along with the Lord *(see p235).*

First Floor

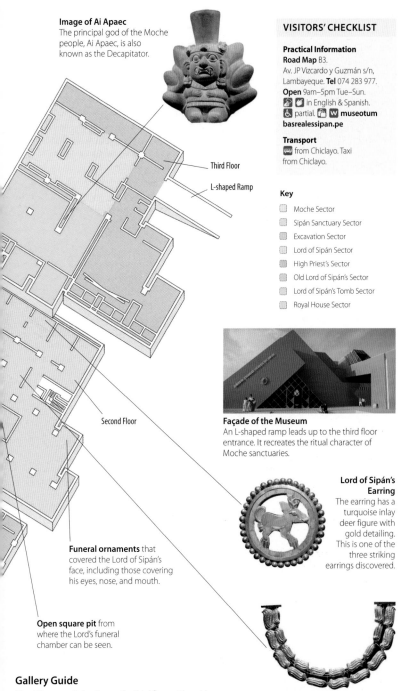

Image of Ai Apaec
The principal god of the Moche people, Ai Apaec, is also known as the Decapitator.

Third Floor

L-shaped Ramp

VISITORS' CHECKLIST

Practical Information
Road Map B3.
Av. JP Vizcardo y Guzmán s/n, Lambayeque. **Tel** 074 283 977.
Open 9am–5pm Tue–Sun.
🎥 🎧 in English & Spanish.
♿ partial. 📷 **W museotum basrealessipan.pe**

Transport
🚌 from Chiclayo. Taxi from Chiclayo.

Key
⬜ Moche Sector
⬜ Sipán Sanctuary Sector
⬜ Excavation Sector
⬜ Lord of Sipán Sector
⬜ High Priest's Sector
⬜ Old Lord of Sipán's Sector
⬜ Lord of Sipán's Tomb Sector
⬜ Royal House Sector

Second Floor

Façade of the Museum
An L-shaped ramp leads up to the third floor entrance. It recreates the ritual character of Moche sanctuaries.

Lord of Sipán's Earring
The earring has a turquoise inlay deer figure with gold detailing. This is one of the three striking earrings discovered.

Funeral ornaments that covered the Lord of Sipán's face, including those covering his eyes, nose, and mouth.

Open square pit from where the Lord's funeral chamber can be seen.

Gallery Guide

The visit unusually begins on the third floor with a video presentation of the Huaca Rajada excavations and Moche culture. A recreation of the original site and the repository is on the second, while the first floor focuses on the tombs of the Lord of Sipán and seven others.

★ Peanut Necklace
This 20-piece gold and silver necklace made from peanut-shaped pieces symbolizes Mochica duality.

Exploring Museo Tumbas Reales de Sipán

Entering one of Latin America's biggest museums through the apex of the building on the third floor, enables the visitor to experience seeing a tomb the way an archaeologist does: working down from the top, beginning with the most recent, general features, digging down to ever older, more specific findings, and ending at the dream find – an undiscovered royal tomb.

Gilded banner showing figure with turquoise bracelets

Third Floor

The entrance features a dark-glass antechamber which blocks UV rays and allows the eyes to adjust to the muted, sepulchral lighting. After a video presentation which is optional, the museum's **Moche Sector** gives an overview of that culture. It is followed by the **Sipán Sanctuary Sector** which details Sipán as an ancient site and explains life in the village today. Highlights on this floor include a fabulous collection of ceramics depicting various aspects of Moche life such as people working, playing musical instruments, making love, and so on. Plants and animals were also popular subjects for Moche potters, along with their many gods and related religious ceremonies.

Golden funerary mask

Second Floor

Much of this floor is dedicated to the **Lord of Sipán Sector**, where some of the most dazzling finds of the tomb are displayed. There are splendid adornments for the face and body of the Lord of Sipán, who archaeologists believe was a warrior-priest of high rank, including ear ornaments and a gold peanut necklace (see p233). Made principally of gold, silver, copper, and turquoise, this veritable treasure trove has been exhibited around the world. Equally interesting finds include funerary offerings such as over 1,100 miniature ceramic pots containing food and other items. The tomb of the guardian, discovered in a sitting position, is displayed here along with finds from the **High Priest's Tomb**.

First Floor

Finally, at the base of the museum, the **Lord of Sipán's Tomb** is displayed in all its splendour. The Lord was flanked by two warriors, one of whom was buried with his dog. The bodies of two young females were interred at his head and feet, and a small boy was found in a niche above the burial. One of the men and the women were missing their left feet – the reason for the amputation still remains a mystery. Two sacrificed llamas complete the burial entourage.

Nearby, another, older tomb was discovered. It contained a senior warrior-priest, dubbed the **Old Lord of Sipán**, who was buried along with several exceptionally well-crafted pieces including an octopus pectoral (see p232), a necklace of linked spiders, and an anthropomorphic crab, all displayed here.

On show today is a precise reproduction of the tombs with the original pieces.

A recreation of the Lord with his entourage

Huaqueros at Sipán

In Sipán, the *huaqueros* (robbers of *huacas* or shrines) first found a tomb in the pyramid known today as Huaca Rajada. In February 1987, the local police chief called Walter Alva to report that 33 antiquities had been found with a *huaquero*. Tense days followed and a *huaquero* was killed by the police. The villagers swore revenge but the situation was defused when local and international agencies provided financial backing and Alva hired *huaqueros* to work as excavators and guards. Four months later Alva came across the untouched tomb of the Lord of Sipán.

Excavation work at Huaca Rajada

Lord of Sipán's Burial Chamber

On the fiber-glass first floor lies a replica of the Lord of Sipán's coffin, which was surrounded by several other burials and offerings within a much larger burial chamber. The Lord was first clothed in a simple white undergarment and the body then adorned with splendid treasures of precious metals and gems combined with artistic ceremonial offerings. It was then wrapped in multiple shrouds and placed in a wooden coffin along with gold, silver, and copper ornaments. From his copper-sandaled feet to his feathered headgear, the ceremonial burial of the Lord clearly indicated his high stature in the Moche world.

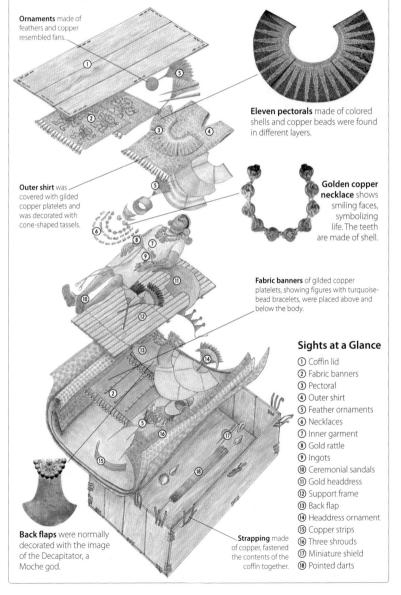

Ornaments made of feathers and copper resembled fans.

Eleven pectorals made of colored shells and copper beads were found in different layers.

Outer shirt was covered with gilded copper platelets and was decorated with cone-shaped tassels.

Golden copper necklace shows smiling faces, symbolizing life. The teeth are made of shell.

Fabric banners of gilded copper platelets, showing figures with turquoise-bead bracelets, were placed above and below the body.

Back flaps were normally decorated with the image of the Decapitator, a Moche god.

Strapping made of copper, fastened the contents of the coffin together.

Sights at a Glance

① Coffin lid
② Fabric banners
③ Pectoral
④ Outer shirt
⑤ Feather ornaments
⑥ Necklaces
⑦ Inner garment
⑧ Gold rattle
⑨ Ingots
⑩ Ceremonial sandals
⑪ Gold headdress
⑫ Support frame
⑬ Back flap
⑭ Headdress ornament
⑮ Copper strips
⑯ Three shrouds
⑰ Miniature shield
⑱ Pointed darts

Northern Beaches

Tumbes, the northernmost regional capital city of Peru, about 19 miles (30 km) away from the Ecuadorean border, is the starting point for traveling over 90 miles (150 km) to some of the finest beaches in the country. This relatively unexplored region has good waves to surf, attractive fishing villages, superb and spicy local food, unique wildlife enclosed in four protected areas, and the only stretch of Peruvian coast where the sea is really warm all year round.

① Santuario Nacional Manglares de Tumbes
The reserve is known for its red mangrove forest which houses 200 species of birds and 40 varieties of plants.

② Tumbes
This coastal city, with airport facilities, is the starting point for traveling down to the northern beaches. A number of wildlife reserves can also be visited from here.

③ Zorritos
This old fishing village used to be the favorite of the Tumbes aristocracy during the early 20th century.

PACIFIC OCEAN

Santuario Nacional Manglares de Tumbes
Puerto Pizarro
1A
Tumbes
Pedro Canga
Bocapán
Zorritos
Punta Sal
Reserva Nacional de Tumbes
Canoas
1A
Pampa El Toro
Catrina
Cap. Hoyle
CERROS DE AMOTAPE
Máncora Férnandez
Parque Nacional Cerros de Amotape
Vichayito
Los Organos
Nuro
Atascadero
Cabo Blanco
1A
Coto de Caza El Angolo

0 kilometers   20
0 miles   20

④ Punta Sal
The ideal spot for well-to-do Peruvians, this resort has extensive sands and warm waters. It is safe for swimming, fishing, and diving.

⑤ Máncora
The most-visited coastal resort with a lovely beach, Máncora is very popular with surfers, both local as well as foreign.

⑥ Vichayito
Located south of Máncora, it is a chic resort with stylish hotels built in front of a peaceful beach. Great spots for diving and kite-surfing have made it popular.

**⑩ Reserva Nacional
de Tumbes**
The Tumbes National Reserve
protects endemic species that
have adapted to the hot and
humid tropical conditions of
the surrounding area.

**⑨ Parque Nacional Cerros
de Amotape**
This park protects 225,607
acres (91,300 ha) of Equatorial
Dry Forest and a major part
of the Northwestern
Biosphere Reserve.

⑧ Coto de Caza El Angolo
A permit from SERNANP allows
hunting in this enclosed zone.
There is just one small lodge in
the Sauce Grande.

Key

━━ Major road

━━ Minor road

--- Park boundary

━•━ International border

⑦ Cabo Blanco
This was a popular resort
during the 1950s, mainly due
to the presence of writer Ernest
Hemingway and for its sport
fishing. Deep-sea fishing is also
possible here.

Banana harvest on the shores of Río Tumbes, Tumbes

⑩ Tumbes

Road Map B2. 90 miles (140 km) N
of Talara. 🚹 93,000. ✈ 🚌 from
Lima. 🎉 San Pedro in Puerto Pizarro
(Jun 28–29).

Tumbes is a small, peaceful city
which was originally inhabited
by the Tallanes, related to the
coastal tribes of Ecuador. The
Spanish conquistadores arrived
here in 1527. The city was also
the point of dispute in a border
war with Ecuador between
1940 to 1941 that was finally
won by Peru.

Environs
Located about 8 miles (13 km)
northeast of Tumbes, the
**Reserva de Biósfera del
Noroeste** (Northwestern
Biosphere Reserve), covering
702 sq-miles (1,818 sq-km),
comprises four protected areas
best accessed through a paved
road along the Tumbes River by
the town of Limon.

⑪ Zorritos

Road Map A2. 16 miles (28 km)
SW of Tumbes. 🚹 14,000. 🚌 Taxi
from Tumbes.

The area's biggest fishing village,
Zorritos has some great beaches
favored by locals. It is good for
fishing and because it is home
to many migratory birds, it is a
favorite with bird-watchers too.

Environs
About 6 miles (9 km) south of
Zorritos, at KM1232 of the
Panamerican Highway is
Bocapán, the turnoff to the hot
springs of **Hervideros** and the

main access road to the **Parque
Nacional Cerros de Amotape**
(Amotape Hills National Park).
Created in 1975, the park
conserves the extreme
northern environment of Peru
and protects many endangered
animals, including the Tumbes
crocodile *(Crocodylus acutus)*
and the South American
river otter *(Lutra longicaudis)*.
Visitors need to get permission
from the National Institute of
Natural Resources, SERNANP
to enter the park.

⑫ Máncora

Road Map A2. 14 miles (23 km) S
of Punta Sal. 🚹 9,000. 🚌 Taxi from
Tumbes. 🌐 vivamancora.com

Máncora is without doubt the
trendiest beach town in all of
Peru and attracts a mixed and
colorful crowd. Young surfers,
gringo backpackers, and well-
to-do Limeños, all head for this
town for its enchanting
beaches, mainly **Las Pocitas**,
3 miles (5 km) to the south. It is
a great surfing destination too,
easily rivaling those of Brazil and
Ecuador. It is renowned for its
lively bars and clubs, especially
in the summer months.

Environs
About 7 miles (11 km) to
the east are the **Baños de
Barro**, natural hot springs
with sulfurous waters believed
to have curative properties.
Beyond is the **Coto de Caza
El Angolo** (El Angolo Enclosed
Hunting Zone), where
hunting is allowed with a
SERNANP permit.

THE NORTHERN HIGHLANDS

Dominated by the great Amazonian rivers of Marañon and the Huallabamba, which cut through the towering Andes, the Northern Highlands is an ideal destination for the intrepid traveler. This remote, agriculturally rich, and extremely picturesque region is also well known for its vibrant tradition of crafts, a legacy that dates back to the pre-Inca Chachapoyan civilization.

Peru's Northern Highlands remain firmly off the beaten track. Yet this is one of the most exciting regions in the country. The provincial capital, Cajamarca, is renowned for its elegant Colonial architecture. From here, routes lead over the mountains to the beautiful cloud-clad region of Chachapoyas, with its famed ruins of Kuélap, and on to the jungle towns of Tarapoto and Yurimaguas in the Amazon, or else north towards Ecuador via Jaén, or south to Cajabamba.

The spectacular ruins of Kuélap are testimony to the skills of the Chachapoyas culture, which reached its "classic" period around AD 800 and grew to occupy a huge swathe of the northern Peruvian Andes. The wide range of habitat and climate allowed Chachapoyans to cultivate an extensive range of crops. They were skilled agriculturalists, carving terraces into mountain slopes and covering low-lying areas with intricately drained field systems. They were expert weavers as well and samples of their superb textiles are now on view at the community-run Museo Leymebamba.

The great Amazonian rivers, Marañon and Huallabamba, slice through the Andes, which rise here less dramatically than in the Cordillera Blanca. The area's remoteness has its advantages as well as disadvantages. On a positive note, there is an intrepid feel to exploring this hinterland, where tourists are few and far between and rural life continues as it has done for centuries. On the downside, infrastructure is creaky: buses are shabby, flights infrequent, journeys slow, and luxury hotels non-existent. One needs time and patience to explore the region in any depth, but the rewards outweigh the trials and tribulations.

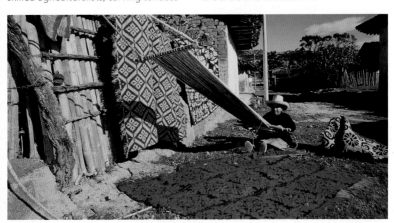

An Andean weaver at work in Cajamarca, provincial capital of the Northern Highlands

◀ Ruins of circular houses at Kuélap fortress, Chachapoyas

Exploring the Northern Highlands

This remote area sees few tourists and rural life continues as it has done for centuries. Heading inland from the coast, several routes connect the verdant countryside. The northernmost road loops up from Chiclayo to Jaén. From there, visitors can head south to Chachapoyas, past the Kuélap ruins, Gocta Falls, and on to Cajamarca. Most travelers with little time make a beeline for Cajamarca on the central route via an improved road from Pacasmayo (north of Trujillo) which winds its way up the beautiful Río Jequetepeque Valley. Cajamarca can be used as a base for visiting the thermal baths at Los Baños del Inca, the aqueduct at Cumbemayo, and the burial niches at Ventanillas de Otuzco. The southern route cuts east from Trujillo via Huamachuco and Cajabamba, then north to Cajamarca – or even south to the Cordillera Blanca.

Locator Map
Area Illustrated

Sights at a Glance

Towns and Cities
1 Cajamarca pp242–3
5 Leymebamba and La Laguna de los Cóndores
9 Karajía
8 Levanto

Archaeological Sites and Ruins
2 Cumbemayo
3 Los Baños del Inca

4 Ventanillas de Otuzco and Combayo
6 Revash
7 Kuélap pp248–50

Area of Natural Beauty
10 Cataratas Gocta

0 kilometers 25
0 miles 25

Jaén
Chamaya
Río Chamaya
Santo Domingo
Cutervo
Cochabamba
3N
Laja
Santa Cruz
Catache
La Florida
San Miguel De Pallaques
San Pablo
Río Jequetepeque
CUMBEMAYO
Tembladera
Contumazá
Pacasmayo, Trujillo
San Benito
Cascas

Key
— Main road
=== Untarred minor road
--- Track
— Regional border

Burial niches carved into the mountains, Otuzco

Model of the Karajía statues displayed in the Leymebamba Museum

Stairs leading up the Santa Apolonia hill to a small chapel, Cajamarca

Getting Around

There are only a few daily flights from Lima to Cajamarca (the region's sole airport with scheduled flights), so plan in advance. By bus, it takes up to 14 hours direct from Lima to Cajamarca via Trujillo and Pacasmayo. From Trujillo, it takes about 7 hours by bus to Cajamarca; from Chiclayo, it takes about 6 hours. Going via Huamachuco and Cajabamba, the journey takes two days. To get to Chachapoyas from Cajamarca, the journey is done in two legs: first to Celendín where you change and then take another bus. Check bus timings before starting since they are infrequent. Most of the roads except the road from Pacasmayo are in poor condition. With public transport erratic and uncomfortable, consider renting a high-clearance 4WD car in Lima, Trujillo, or Chiclayo.

For map symbols *see back flap*

① Cajamarca

Laid out in a traditional Spanish grid plan, the provincial Andean capital of Cajamarca has been a favorite haunt of travelers since Inca times. This is where the Inca emperor Atahualpa was captured by conquistador Francisco Pizarro. Its Colonial- and Independence-era architecture rivals that of Cusco and Arequipa for elegance. The main thoroughfare is Amalia Puga, with the Plaza de Armas at the city's historic heart. Cajamarca also makes a very pleasant base from which to explore the countryside renowned for its cheese and other dairy products. The best time to visit is during what is considered Peru's most raucous celebration, Carnaval, when the city pulsates with music, fireworks, and parades.

Beautiful interior of Iglesia de San Francisco

Baroque architecture of the Cathedral, Plaza de Armas

🏛 Museo Arqueológico

Del Batán 289. **Open** 8am–2:30pm Mon–Fri. **Closed** pub hols. 📷

Run by Cajamarca University, the Archaeological Museum consists of an informative run-through of archaeological finds in this north Andean region from around 3,000 years ago to the recent past. The display ranges from ceramics and textiles to black-and-white photographs and mummies, drawings of the Cumbemayo petroglyphs (see p246) and a collection of carved stones. Of note are the paintings by local artist, Andres Zevallos. The center also stocks good leaflets on the sights in the area.

🏛 Cathedral

Plaza de Armas. **Open** 7am–7pm. ♿ 🕐 7 & 8am.

On the northwest of the Plaza de Armas – with its lawns, benches, and imaginatively-trimmed topiary – rises the Cathedral. Begun in the 17th century, it was not consecrated until 1762. Its fine carved-stone façade is a beautiful example of the Baroque style championed in Colonial Peru. The main altar is in the imposing Churrigueresque style, covered tip-to-toe with gold leaf. The walls of the Cathedral incorporate a large amount of Inca masonry.

🏛 Iglesia de San Francisco

Plaza de Armas. **Open** 3–6pm. 🏛 museum only. 📷 ♿

The church and convent of San Francisco, erected in the 17th and 18th centuries, rivals the Cathedral with its Neo-Classical appearance. The priests left the belfries half-done to dodge the tax levied by Spanish authorities on religious buildings and they were only completed in 1951. This Franciscan church catered to the poor and non-whites and is also known as Iglesia de los Indios (Indians' Church). It has a fine altar, catacombs, and a religious art museum. To the right of the church is the **Capilla de la Virgen de Dolores**, the city's prettiest chapel, housing a statue of the town's patron saint, La Virgen de los Dolores, which is carried around the town during religious celebrations.

🏛 Ransom Chamber

Amalia Puga 722. **Open** 9am–1pm, 3–6pm Tue–Sat, 9am–1pm Sun. **Closed** public hols. 🏛 📷

An unpretentious house, the Ransom Chamber is none-theless a worthy port of call when visiting Cajamarca. It is the only remaining Inca building in the town, displaying their typical, earthquake-proof trapezoidal niches and doors, and some original masonry.

However, the 17-ft (5-m) wide and 22-ft (7-m) long chamber has far more historical significance than its appearance suggests. There are two historical versions regarding its use. One claims that the room was the place where Atahualpa, the last sovereign Inca ruler, was held captive by the Spaniards following his downfall. The other says it was the room which the Inca promised to fill with gold up to the height of his outstretched arm and twice

Original Inca masonry still on view, Ransom Chamber

with silver as ransom for his freedom. The chamber is decorated with murals by two famous local artists, Camilo Blas and Andres Zevallos.

🏛 El Complejo de Belén
Calle Belén. **Open** 9am–1pm, 3–6pm Tue–Sat, 9am–1pm Sun. **Closed** public hols. 🎫 🚫

This Colonial-era complex spreads across a group of buildings with several handsome patios and a number of institutions. These include the tourist office, the Institute of Culture (INC), part of the university administration, a small medical museum, two former hospitals, and one of Cajamarca's finest churches, the **Iglesia Belén**.

Ornate cupola with cherubs, Iglesia Belén

The church is regarded as one of Peru's best examples of the Baroque style, with its beautifully carved wooden pulpit, extravagant gold-leaf altars, and a delightfully ornate cupola complete with oversized cherubs holding an elaborate centerpiece made up of flowers.

The interesting **Museo Arqueológico y Etnográfico** lies across the street (at Junín y Belén) from the rest of the complex, in what once served as the Women's Hospital and morgue. The museum houses a wide collection of objects, with ceramics and weavings from the surrounding region as the highlight. Some jungle items are also on display.

VISITORS' CHECKLIST

Practical Information
Road Map B3. 532 miles (856 km) N of Lima. 🚇 190,000. 🛈 El Complejo de Belén, Calle Belén 631; 076 822 997. 📅 daily. 🎭 Carnaval (before Lent). 🌐 cajamarcaperu.com

Transport
✈ 2 miles (3 km), 076 822 523. 🚌 from Lima & Trujillo.

🏛 Cerro Santa Apolonia
SW of Plaza de Armas. 🚌 🎫
The hill of Santa Apolonia overlooks Cajamarca's historic heart, making it a great spot for getting a feel of the city. The hill can be explored via a series of walks through gardens with native plants, leading up to the peak from where the Spaniards, under Francisco Pizarro, aimed their cannons on the Inca army below. Also located here are the remains of Chavín- and Inca-era stone carvings. One of the rocks, popularly known as the Silla del Inca (the Seat of the Inca), is shaped like a throne and the Incas are said to have reviewed their troops from here.

Cajamarca City Center

① Museo Arqueológico
② Cathedral
③ Iglesia de San Francisco
④ Ransom Chamber
⑤ El Complejo de Belén
⑥ Cerro Santa Apolonia

0 meters 100
0 yards 100

Shepherdess in the Cumbemayo mountains near Cajamarca

❷ Cumbemayo

Road Map B3. 13 miles (20 km) SW of Cajamarca. Taxi from Cajamarca.

The mountainous region of Cumbemayo, situated to the southwest of Cajamarca *(see pp242–3)*, is famous for the canal and aqueduct carved from rock and pieced together by deft stonemasons with great skill. The structure is thought to be about 2,000 years old and perhaps had ritual as well as practical significance, due to the great effort that went into its construction. It originally carried water from the Atlantic water-shed over to the Pacific side through an intricate system of tunnels and canals, some of which are still in use.

To one side of the aqueduct is a rock, shaped like a face, into which a man-made cave has been carved. Inside the cave, with the aid of a torch, one can make out 3,000-year-old petroglyphs which bear feline features. This is a hallmark of the Chavín style which dominated this part of Peru at that time. There is a small museum at the site, but sometimes the guardian of the museum may have to be located to get it opened.

On the way from Cajamarca, before Cumbemayo, an odd natural rock formation known as the **Bosque de Piedras** (Stone Forest), is clearly visible. The limestone rock masses have eroded, forming tapered shapes which are reminiscent of the human form, thus giving it their Spanish name, *los frailones* (the big monks).

❸ Los Baños del Inca

Road Map B3. 3 miles (5 km) E of Cajamarca. Taxi from Cajamarca. **Open** 5am–6:45pm daily.

A pleasant way to spend an afternoon is to wallow in the thermal baths at the Baños del Inca, just a short taxi or bus ride from Cajamarca. The baths date back to pre-Inca times. It is believed that the last Inca, Atahualpa, and his army had camped at the baths when Spanish conquistador, Pizarro, arrived giving the place its name.

The resort is popular at the weekends, but it is probably best avoided then as it can be quite an experience sharing the bath with dozens of strangers. There are various pools at varying temperatures and prices. The best time to visit is in the morning when they are the cleanest. The complex has a modest restaurant and hotel, and is equipped with a sauna. The recreational complex is a huge attraction.

❹ Ventanillas de Otuzco and Combayo

Road Map B3. 5 miles (8 km) NE of Cajamarca. Taxi from Cajamarca. **Open** 9am–5pm daily. not official.

One of the oldest cemeteries in Peru, the Ventanillas de Otuzco date back about 3,500 years. The necropolis comprises a series of burial niches carved into the volcanic rock of the cliff, some of which are decorated with carvings. The chieftains of Cajamarca were buried in these niches. From a distance, they look like windows, hence the Spanish name *ventanillas* (little windows). An extensive collection of these niches can

Hot spring pools at Los Banos del Inca, near Cajamarca

Ancient burial niches in the cliff face at Otuzco

be found at Combayo, located 18 miles (30 km) southeast of Cajamarca. Both the sites can be visited on a tour from Cajamarca. Otuzco is a 90-minute walk from Los Baños del Inca.

❺ Leymebamba and La Laguna de los Cóndores

Road Map B3. 50 miles (80 km) SE of Chachapoyas. 🚗 🏔

The small and attractive market town of Leymebamba, about an 8- to 10-hour drive from Cajamarca, is not covered by most travel itineraries of Peru. However, the surrounding countryside is wonderful for exploring on foot as well as on horseback. Close to the town are many small archaeological sites of tourist interest, including **Museo Leymebamba**, built and run by the community.

The museum is located at San Miguel, the site of the original Leymebamba town which was evacuated following a yellow fever epidemic in the 1600s. It houses the amazing archaeological finds from the nearby Laguna de los Cóndores. The mummies and artifacts recovered from the cliff tombs in 1997 were moved to the museum to protect them from *huaqueros* (tomb-raiders). The Leymebamba museum and all the materials used in its construction, such as timber, stone and *tapia* (mud walls), were made by

local craftspeople using traditional construction techniques. Among the 5,000 artifacts on display are almost 150 well-preserved mummies, and there is an ethnographic display on life in the region. The museum also has a colorful orchid garden housing more than 100 native species of beautiful flowers.

The town has very basic facilities, and is best visited on a day trip from Chachapoyas. The trip to the Laguna, however, is for the adventurous as the route on foot or horseback climbs up to 12,139 ft (3,700 m) before descending to the spellbinding lake. There is a basic lodge here with minimum facilities, and if you bring food, the family will cook it for you. The journey takes about 10 to 12

Karajia-style statue, Museo Leymebamba

hours so it is best to plan it as a three-day trip.

🏛 **Museo Leymebamba**
Av. Austria s/n, San Miguel, Leymebamba. **Open** 9:30am–4:30pm Tue–Sun. **Closed** public hols. 🐾 📷
🌐 **centromallqui.org.pe**

❻ Revash

Road: **Map** B3. 37 miles (60 km) S of Chachapoyas, nr Santo Tomás. 🚌 Taxi from Chachapoyas. 📷

Named for the Revash culture, contemporary with the Chachapoyans *(see p250)*, this site is famed for its *chullpas* (funerary chambers). These small, multi-hued buildings perch precariously on ledges high up on the limestone cliffs. They are made from mud and stone walls, then plastered over and painted, and topped with peculiar gabled roofs. The *chullpas* have been looted, but a dozen burials and accompanying funerary offerings were discovered by archaeologists. A variety of pictographs can be seen on the cliff behind the structures.

There are daily minibuses from Chachapoyas to Santo Tomás. Visitors can disembark at the Santo Tomás turnoff. Allow 3 hours for the steep climb up to the ruins. Near Santo Tomás, the village of Yerbuena has a busy Sunday market.

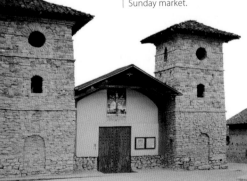
Building with local architectural features on the central square of highland town Leymebamba

⓿ Kuélap

The imposing fortress of Kuélap is the main attraction of the Chachapoyas region. It ranks among the finest and most impressive ruins in Peru. The structure occupies a perfect vantage point, set on a dramatic ridge high above the Río Utcubamba amid verdant, rolling countryside. Reclaimed by the surrounding forest for more than 300 years, it wasn't until 1843 that the site was rediscovered by a local judge, and it wasn't truly explored until the late 19th and early 20th centuries. Local experts claim the fortress contained three times more stone than the Great Pyramid at Giza in Egypt.

Bromeliads
The cloudforest is ideal for bromeliads and orchids to thrive. They can be seen growing on the ruin walls.

Outer Wall of Fortress
The huge perimeter wall, made of giant limestone blocks, was perhaps built for defense purposes. In some places the wall reaches a height of 36 ft (11 m) and encircles the entire site.

El Tintero
On the southern side of the citadel, a mysterious inverted cone-shaped structure, El Tintero (inkwell) rises 18 ft (5.5 m) high.

★ Main Entrance
The funnel-shaped defensive entrance is still used today. There are only three entrances to the fortress.

Surrounding Area
Located on a limestone ridge which runs north–south, the fortress was built to maximize the natural topography of the area against enemy raids.

Restoration Work
A recovery project to restore some of the ruins has been going on at the site since 1999.

★ Torreón
The great tower at the northern end is one of the main features at the ruin. It's a D-shaped lookout tower.

★ Circular Houses
Hundreds of round stone houses are scattered randomly throughout the site. They were once about 13-ft (4-m) high and had thatched roofs.

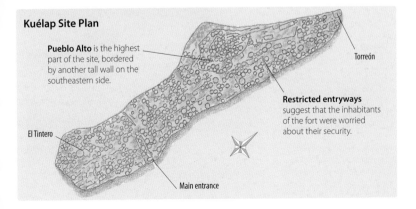

Kuélap Site Plan

Pueblo Alto is the highest part of the site, bordered by another tall wall on the southeastern side.

Torreón

Restricted entryways suggest that the inhabitants of the fort were worried about their security.

El Tintero

Main entrance

Exploring Kuélap

Ceramics discovered in Kuélap indicate that the area had been inhabited since AD 500, but the majority of construction occurred between AD 900 and 1100. The result is a fortress bigger than any other single structure in Peru. The complex had an outer wall protecting over 400 circular houses, thought to have been home to 3,500 people. It also had terraces, outlying settlements, and burial areas outside the main walls. When the Incas arrived around 1470, they found that Kuélap, full of fierce Chachapoyan warriors, was no easy place to conquer. They were unable to conquer the fort properly and only five Inca buildings have been found among the hundreds of structures in the fortress.

One of the original entrances to Kuélap

Main Entrance

There are actually three main entrances, all very similar to each other, however, only one is in use today. The funnel-shaped entrance leads into the fortress and becomes narrower the farther in one goes, until eventually it is wide enough for only one person. The solid walls rise high above the head. The construction of the entrance is a clear pointer to the fact that no one could have gained entry into the fortress without the inhabitants allowing them admission.

El Tintero

It is the most popular structure within the walls. The word means "inkwell" because of the structure's shape, an inverted cone, not because of any reference to ink since the Chachapoyans did not have a written language. Early surveys gave a variety of functions to this building, ranging from a water reservoir to a jail – even a torture chamber and a cemetery. However, studies now suggest that the building had astronomical functions, since the small entrance lines up with the sun at the most favorable times for planting crops. In reality, the purpose of this strangely shaped structure still remains a mystery. A small human face carved in low relief into a limestone block can be seen on the eastern side of El Tintero.

Circular Buildings

Unlike almost all other buildings in Peru, the Chachapoyans left circular structures for posterity to admire and ponder over. No one knows why they were circular. A few have been restored in Kuélap and elsewhere. Most researchers agree that the buildings had steep, conical thatched roofs designed to ward off torrential cloudforest downpours. In Kuélap, some of the buildings have walls 20 inches (50 cm) thick. The apparently random order of these buildings is quite deceptive. Archaeologists claim the design is quite rational, with the buildings being distributed either along corridors or arranged with the patios facing each other.

Torreón

This 23-ft (7-m) high tower at the north end of Pueblo Alto gave views in every direction. Archaeologists found an arsenal of broken stone axe heads and 2,500 stones piled on the floor, of a perfect size to fit in the slingshots that defenders would have used.

Water Channels

Stone channels have been found leading archaeologists to believe they may have led to a spring at the top of the ridge, which must have provided the fortress with a permanent source of water.

The Chachapoya People

The name Chachapoya is commonly believed to come from the conflation of two Quechua words, *sacha* and *puyu*, literally forest-cloud. The Chachapoyans were famous for their white skin and beauty. They were a fierce community and it took the Incas many men to conquer the region. They were also famous shamans, known as great sorcerers and herbalists. The people were skilled agriculturalists and also renowned for their weaving. The finds displayed at the Museo Leymebamba testify to the beauty of the imagery and the wide variety of techniques used, including plain weaves, tapestry, brocades, and embroidery on a single textile. They also produced a wide range of pottery.

Chachapoya people from the village of Cruzpata

A view of the sleepy town of Levanto

❽ Levanto

Road Map B3. 14 miles (22 km) S of Chachapoyas.
🚌 Taxi from Chachapoyas.

An original and unrestored Inca road joins Chachapoyas with Levanto, which was first settled by the Spanish in 1532. Despite its history it remains a small village with only a few remnants of its Colonial past.

A few miles away is the overgrown site of **Yalape** (built AD 1100–1300) which has classic circular buildings embellished with geometric friezes, and the remains of an irrigation system. This is part of the second largest known Chachapoyan fortress after Kuélap, with other sites nearby.

Most visitors make it a day trip, arriving by the morning bus uphill from Chachapoyas and returning along the Inca road downhill on foot.

❾ Karajía

Road Map B3. 30 miles (48 km) NW of Chachapoyas, near Luya. 🚌 from Chachapoyas. 🚕 Taxi from Luya.

Oversized, colorfully painted vertical sarcophagi made of earth, wood, and straw, decorated with faces, were the final resting places of important members of the famous Chachapoyan culture. Many of these coffins have been discovered

and the ones found at Karajía are the easiest to visit from Chachapoyas. The site is reached by minibuses from Chachapoyas to Luya, from where it is a 3-hour hike. Tours from Chachapoyas are also available. Karajía is a 45-minute walk from Cruzpata.

Environs

Gran Vilaya, a three-day trek from Karajía, is a large area with some 30 archaeological sites. The best way to explore them is by taking an organized tour from Chachapoyas.

Cavernas Quiocta near Lamud can be combined with a visit to Karajía. Located one-and-a-half hours by road from Karajía, this series of caves contain Inca remains, pools, and splendid geological formations. Visitors need to ask for a guide in Lamud.

❿ Cataratas Gocta

Road Map B2. Near San Pablo. Taxi from Chachapoyas or Pedro Ruíz. 📷 🏕 camping allowed but no facilities.

In 2002 it was discovered that this huge waterfall, hidden in the cloud forest and known only to the locals, was one of the highest in the world. Stefan Ziemendorff, a German hydro-engineer saw the falls on the Río Cocahuayco and did preliminary measurements – an astounding 2,531 ft (771 m) in height. Initially, the fall was touted as the third

highest in the world, but sceptics have pointed out that it is a two-tiered fall. However, the two tiers are close enough to one another and the World Waterfall Database considers them to be one waterfall, and rates them among the top ten in the world.

Gocta is on the east of the main Chachapoyas-Pedro Ruíz road. Taxis from either town can be taken for San Pablo, where informal guides take visitors on a trail which lasts 1–2 hours to a view of the upper falls. En route, views of both tiers are available. To see the falls from the bottom, it is necessary to backtrack and take another taxi to the smaller hamlet of Cocachimba, and walk about 3 hours through the cloud forest.

The magnificent Cataratas Gocta, rated amongst the world's highest waterfalls

THE AMAZON BASIN

The fabulous Amazonian rainforest is home to more species of animals than any other area on earth. This is where visitors may see monkeys and macaws, army ants and armadillos, thousands of butterfly species, 900 bird species, and a variety of trees and plants. National reserves protect the flora and fauna, and provide inaccessible areas where indigenous tribes live untouched by the 21st century.

The original rainforest inhabitants are separated into dozens of groups speaking distinct languages, but united by an ability to thrive in this difficult environment. Using local materials, people still build thatched wooden houses along constantly shifting riverbanks, carve canoes, and hunt using blow pipes and poison-tipped darts.

Little is known about their history. At the height of the Inca Empire, the upper Amazon Basin was incorporated into Antisuyo (the empire's eastern quarter) and the Indians traded scarlet macaw feathers and jungle fruits for metal tools. After the conquest, the Spaniards concentrated on the coastal and highland regions. A few ill-fated Amazonian expeditions were foiled by the Indians. The Spaniards' greatest impact was in the unintended introduction of diseases, to which natives had no resistance. Millions died of smallpox, influenza, or other illnesses.

In the 16th century, Colonial outposts were established in places such as Moyobamba, but the Amazon was not permanently occupied until a few missions were built in the 18th century. With the 1870s rubber boom the population exploded. Four decades later, the boom collapsed and the once-opulent towns survived by logging, exploitation of jungle crops, and export of animals for zoos.

The discovery of oil in the 1960s fueled another population boom, soon followed by a nascent tourism industry. Slowly, cities such as Iquitos, Pucallpa, and Puerto Maldonado gained renewed importance, and mestizo ribereños (river-dwellers) began to clear forests for agriculture.

Although over half of Peru lies in the Amazon, barely 5 percent of the population lives there. Visiting this wilderness, where few roads penetrate, can be a thrilling adventure.

The jaguar, the most prized wildlife sighting in the Amazon

◄ Black caiman in one of Oxbow lakes, Manu

The Amazon Basin

The rainforest is the overwhelming attraction, with jungle towns being essential gateways. River travel is customary and is a highlight of a visit. For premium wildlife viewing, a tour and rainforest lodge stay is ideal. In the south lies the Reserva de la Biosfera de Manu, difficult and expensive to reach but one of the world's most protected rainforest reserves. Nearby, the Ríos Tambopata and Madre de Dios converge at Puerto Maldonado, a remote jungle town with access to some of Peru's best rainforest lodges. The central part has the best road links with Lima and offers opportunities for those on a tight budget; reasonably priced tours can be taken from Chanchamayo, Tarapoto, and Yarinacocha. Iquitos, the area's most interesting city, is located in the north. It can be reached by riverboat from Pucallpa or Yurimaguas, and offers access to the Amazon's longest canopy walkway.

Sights at a Glance

Towns and Cities

1 Iquitos
2 Pevas
4 Ucayali River Towns
6 Yurimaguas
7 Moyobamba and Alto Mayo
8 Tarapoto
9 Pucallpa
12 Oxapampa

Areas of Natural Beauty

3 Reserva Nacional Allpahuayo-Mishana
5 Reserva Nacional Pacaya-Samiria
10 Yarinacocha
11 Chanchamayo Region
13 Reserva de la Biosfera de Manu
14 *Ríos Tambopata and Madre de Dios Area pp266–7*

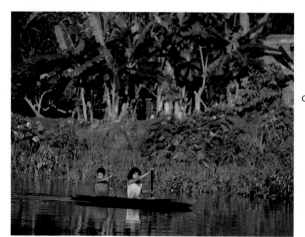

Children of the Bora tribe paddling in a dugout canoe

For hotels and restaurants in this region see pp274–9 and pp288–97

0 kilometers   150

0 miles   150

Getting Around

Iquitos, Peru's major Amazon city, is the world's largest with no access by road, and can only be reached by river or air. Other cities with regular flights from Lima include Pucallpa, Tarapoto, and Puerto Maldonado. Traveling between areas nearly always necessitates a return to Lima. Almost all Amazonian national parks and jungle lodges are best reached by a combination of air and river travel. The Chanchamayo area is the most accessible by road from Lima (8 hours) but gives the scantest taste of the Amazon Basin.

Chapawanqi Falls near Tarapoto

Napo

Curaray

Copal Urco

Vidal

Francisco
de Orellana

Mazán

T O

Rio Amazonas

2 PEVAS

IQUITOS **1**

Nauta

3 RESERVA NACIONAL
ALLPAHUAYO-MISHANA

Leticia,
Colombia

Tabatinga,
Brazil

Requena

4 UCAYALI RIVER
TOWNS

5

RVA NACIONAL
CAYA-SAMIRIA

RINACOCHA

? PUCALLPA

erto
gre

Puerto
Putaya

to
ao

San Luis

ruya

oresta

Rio Ucayali

El
ran
ional

Atalaya

UCAYALI

Puerto
Varadero

Rio Curanja

Cocama

Esperanza

Shepahua

Alerta

Rio Las Piedras

Rio Yaco

Noaya

26B

MADRE DE DIOS

Fitzcarrald

Rio Manu

RESERVA DE LA
BIOSFERA
DE MANU

13

Manu

Madre de Dios

Providencia

Rio Manuripe

Soledad

Rio Madre de Dios

Puerto
Maldonado

26B

RÍOS TAMBOPATA
AND MADRE DE
DIOS AREA

14

_Parque Nacional
Bahuaja-Sonene_

Rio Tambopata

Key

— Main road

--- Untarred main road

::: Untarred minor road

--- Track

▬ International border

▬ Regional border

A dry season view of Belén Village along Río Itaya, Iquitos

❶ Iquitos

Road Map D2. 373 miles (600 km) NE of Pucallpa. 🚹 450,000.
✈ from Panama only. 🚤 from Lima.
🚢 from Pucallpa or Yurimaguas. 🅇
Plaza de Armas, Napo 232, 065 236 144.
📅 Founding of Iquitos (Jan 5), San Juan (Jun 24). 🕸 iquitos-peru.com

Jesuit missionaries founded this major Amazonian port in 1757. Iquitos led a precarious existence until the rubber boom of the 1880s changed it from a village of 1,500 to a city of 25,000. The rubber export to Europe made it more connected to that continent than to Lima, and the city soon boasted opulent houses, decorated with tiles from Portugal, Spain, and Italy. Calle Prospero, south of Plaza de Armas, is lined by these old tiled buildings.

A block east is the Malecón Tarapacá, the river boulevard built during the rubber boom. One side has river views, while the other has tiled buildings and the **Amazon Museum**. The Museum provides a chance to view the interior of a late 19th-century building with photographs and paintings of early Iquitos. The most interesting exhibits are life-sized statues of indigenous tribespeople made of molds obtained by plastering live models. A military museum shares the same building.

The boulevard's north end becomes Malecón Maldonado, where weekend nights are busy with locals watching street performers. To the south is the outdoor Belén market, which stretches for many blocks. Famous for its huge

variety of jungle produce, on sale are dozens of fresh fish, thick home-rolled cigars, illegally hunted jaguar skins, live turtles, and caiman steaks. Ask for the Pasaje Paquito, an alley filled with unique medicinal products "guaranteed" to treat all kinds of ailments.

Behind the market is **Belén Village**, where thousands of people live in wooden huts which float for over half the year when the river rises during the rainy season. Locals offer boat tours to see, what they call, the Venice of the Amazon.

The absence of roads connecting Iquitos to the rest of the world gives it a sassy, friendly atmosphere. Iquiteños' infectious friendliness

Motocarro on the road

is unparalleled. The city is frenetically noisy because of the numerous motorcycles. Three-wheeled *motocarros* or motor-cycle rickshaws outnumber other vehicles and it is an inexpensive and popular mode of public transport.

🏛 **Amazon Museum**
Malecón Tarapacá 386. **Tel** 065 234 221. **Open** 8:30am–1pm, 2:30–5pm Mon–Sat. 🎫 ✅ ♿

❷ Pevas

Road Map D2. 90 miles (145 km) downriver from Iquitos. 🚹 3,000.
🚢 from Iquitos. 🛥 daily.

The oldest town on the Peruvian Amazon, Pevas today is made up of wooden structures, many with thatched roofs. Founded by missionaries in 1735, the town sadly has no buildings left of that era. Most of the friendly inhabitants are mestizos or natives of the Bora, Huitoto, Yagua, or Ocainas groups. The most famous resident of the town is artist, Francisco Grippa, whose unique works can be seen in the towering hilltop studio and gallery where he lives. Visitors are welcomed and served beer and bananas, instead of wine and cheese.

Canopy Walkway

In the 1990s, biologists at Explorama's Field Station constructed the canopy platforms linked by hanging bridges near the Río Napo, 100 miles (160 km) from Iquitos, to study life on the treetops. It is one of the world's longest canopy walkways with 14 platforms supporting a 550-yard (500-m) long series of suspension bridges, 115 ft (35 m) above the ground. The walkway, approached via a staircase, gives a superb view of the rainforest canopy. It is a highlight of any Amazon visit and the chances of seeing unusual birds, lizards, and orchids are excellent.

Canopy walkway enclosed in transparent netting

River Travel

It is impossible to visit the Amazon Basin without getting on a boat. Other than expensive cruises designed for tourists, the possibilities are endless and range from a 10-minute ferry crossing of the Río Madre de Dios at Puerto Maldonado to a week or more on a commercial boat from Yurimaguas or Pucallpa to Iquitos and beyond. Boarding a boat opens the traveler's eye to local life: be it on a tiny canoe or a majestic three-decked vessel, the *ribereños* (river-dwellers) can be seen traveling, working, cooking, washing, fishing, and getting on with life.

Iquitos to the Pacaya-Samiria area is the most common route taken by tourists. Boats stop at the national park and take a week to return. Another week-long cruise goes to the border and back.

Tips for Travelers

Commercial routes: Pucallpa to Iquitos (3–6 days), Yurimaguas to Iquitos (2–4 days), and Iquitos to Brazil/Colombia border (2–3 days).

Getting there: Destination and departure date is written in front of each boat. Tours can also be arranged (*see p307*).

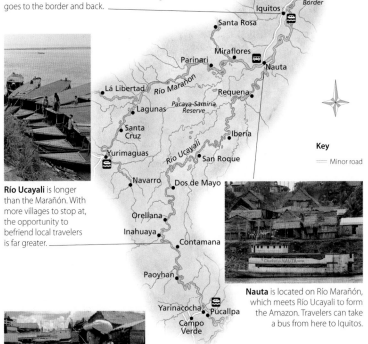

Río Ucayali is longer than the Marañón. With more villages to stop at, the opportunity to befriend local travelers is far greater.

Nauta is located on Río Marañón, which meets Río Ucayali to form the Amazon. Travelers can take a bus from here to Iquitos.

Dugout canoes are the main means of travel for the locals, especially those living in remote areas. They are used for myriad jobs: river taxis, fishing, cargo, as well as selling food.

Key
===== Minor road

Map locations: Mazán, Brazil/Colombia Border, Iquitos, Santa Rosa, Miraflores, Parinari, Nauta, Lá Libertad, Río Marañón, Requena, Lagunas, Pacaya-Samiria Reserve, Santa Cruz, Iberia, Yurimaguas, Río Ucayali, San Roque, Navarro, Dos de Mayo, Orellana, Inahuaya, Contamana, Paoyhan, Yarinacocha, Pucallpa, Campo Verde

0 kilometers 100
0 miles 100

White quartz sand soil visible in a forest clearing

❸ Reserva Nacional Allpahuayo-Mishana

Road Map D2. 16 miles (25 km) from Iquitos. 🚌 🚕 Taxi from Iquitos. **Tel** 065 265 515. ℹ️ Oficina IIAP, Av. A Quiñones KM2.5, Iquitos. 🅿️ 🌐

The Allpahuayo-Mishana Reserve is known for its unusually high levels of biodiversity. Covering an area of 142,520 acres (57,677 ha), the reserve is home to flora and fauna found nowhere else. It is a region of diverse soil-types ranging from the remarkable white-sand jungles to clay licks, which are a concentration of minerals deposited by rivers. Allpahuayo-Mishana was officially recognized as a reserved zone in 1999 making it Peru's only protected white-sand forest.

Bird-watchers are drawn to the 500 species found here, four of which are found only in the reserve – the Allpahuayo antbird, the ancient antwren, the Mishana tyrannulet, and the vibrantly colored pompadour cotinga.

Allpahuayo-Mishana also has a record number of 120 species of reptiles and 83 species of amphibians. About 150 mammal species, including the rare equatorial saki monkey and the Lucifer titi monkey, have also been spotted here. The 65 bat species found here make for the highest bat density in Peru. New plant and insect species are still being discovered as scientists comb through these protected riches that are unique in the Peruvian Amazon. Though easily accessible by bus along the Iquitos-Nauta Road, the infrastructure within the reserve is limited. Visitors should carry water, mosquito repellents, and wear sturdy footwear.

❹ Ucayali River Towns

Road Map C3. Btwn Pucallpa & Iquitos. 🚤 from Iquitos or Pucallpa.

For decades, the main waterway linking Iquitos (see p257) with the rest of Peru has been along the Río Ucayali from Pucallpa. Two- and three-decked riverboats ply the river between Pucallpa and Iquitos, delivering everything from motorcycles to medical equipment, to the villages and small towns in between. The riverboats also provide passenger transport to locals, most of whom hang their own hammocks on the second or third deck, while hot, stuffy cabins with a couple of bunk beds are also available for extra charge. Basic on-board meals are also provided on these boats. The boats stop frequently at the many small villages along the river. Passengers in a hurry can get a speed boat for a choppy ride, however, the slow riverboats are much more fun. The trip from Pucallpa to Iquitos, with the current, takes around four days, while the return, against the current, can take as long as six days. The faster *expreso* boats take one or two days to ferry passengers.

The main towns on the route are **Contamaná** and **Requena**, both of which have basic hotel and restaurant facilities. Contamaná, located 267 miles (430 km) from Iquitos, is known for its hot springs and a macaw clay lick that can be reached by car via a 14-mile (22-km) dirt road.

A growing town, Requena lies 100 miles (160 km) from Iquitos. It boasts of a small cathedral and Laguna Avispa, which is at a distance of 5 miles (8 km) by boat. This is a popular spot with the locals for fishing, both with lines and nets, and swimming in the calm, warm lake waters. Birdwatchers enjoy the small Laguna Avispa, not for any rare species, but for chances to observe some of the best-known Amazonian birds in their natural surroundings. Watching long-toed jacanas running speedily over the tops of the water lillies and other aquatic vegetation is a beautiful sight for any birdlover. Female jacanas mate with several partners, moving on after each laying and leaving the males to take

Pompadour cotinga

Harbor at Requena, one of the towns on Río Ucayali

Shoreline forest, lit by sunlight, inside Reserva Nacional Pacaya-Samiria

on the majority of hatching duties, a feature which is extremely rare among birds.

❺ Reserva Nacional Pacaya-Samiria

Road Map C2. 190 miles (306 km) SW of Iquitos. ☎ **Tel** 065 223 555. 🔢 SERNANP, Calle Jorge Chavez 930, Iquitos. 🔲 🔲

Lying mainly in the crook of the Ríos Ucayali and Marañón, this 8,031-sq-mile (20,800-sq-km) reserve is Peru's largest. Officially, it is inhabited by almost 450 species of birds, 102 species of mammals, and 256 species of fish, some of which are on the endangered list. This protected wildlife reserve includes jaguars, several species of monkeys, two types of turtles, giant river otters, and the huge paiche fish which, at over 7 ft (2 m) in length, is one of the largest freshwater fish in the world.

Even after the region was declared a reserve in 1982, the Indian and mestizo communities have been allowed to continue living here as before. Today, the 42,000 people living in the reserve, belonging to 94 different communities, survive on hunting, fishing, and gathering.

Entrance to the reserve is not easy for tourists. A paid permit is officially required ahead of time from SERNANP. Tourists are stopped for checking at ranger stations along the rivers, although gun-toting locals are

allowed to pass through. The best option is to take a local guide from a small town such as Lagunas, on the Río Huallaga, or join an organized tour from Iquitos and stay at the private Pacaya-Samiria Jungle Lodge on the banks of the Marañón.

A tour boat on the Río Yanuyacu in Reserva Nacional Pacaya-Samiria

❻ Yurimaguas

Road Map C2. 240 miles (390 km) from Iquitos. 🔢 35,000. 🚌 from Tarapoto. 🔲 🔲 Fiesta de la Virgen de las Nieves (Aug 5–15).

Founded by a Jesuit priest in 1710, the city derives its name from two indigenous groups, the Yoras and the Omaguas. These groups no longer exist though there are reports that some Omaguas still live in the more remote jungle regions.

It remained a tiny outpost until the rubber boom, and the tilework from its early days can be seen along the east end of Avenida Arica. Life in Yurimaguas still revolves around the colorful river port. The frenetic 20th-century growth visible in Iquitos and Pucallpa has passed the town by.

Popularly known as the Pearl of Huallaga, Yurimaguas is the main port on the Río Huallaga. It is the last motorable point with onward transport possible only by boat or chartered light aircraft. Despite being closer to Iquitos, Yurimaguas has been the forgotten option, while Pucallpa has long been considered the shortest and best route from Lima to the Amazon. Highways from the coast through Tarapoto to Yurimaguas are being paved and improved and locals hope that the city will now become more important.

River Dolphins

Two species of dolphin live in the fresh waters of the Amazon. While the smaller grey dolphin (*Sotalia fluviatilis*) is found throughout the Amazon and parts of the Atlantic Coast, the larger pink dolphin (*Inia geoffrensis*) is found only in the Amazon. Predominantly found in northern Peru, dolphins are spotted near tributaries where the merging waters attract fish on which they feed. An ideal place to see the dolphins is in their natural habitat at the Muyuna Amazon Lodge (*see p284*), near Iquitos. Tribal folklore of Peru abounds with stories revolving around the pink dolphin. The stories vary but are united by the common thread that dolphins change into handsome young men.

Pink river dolphin, a species exclusive to the Amazon

Locals crossing a weathered bridge over Río Mayo near Moyobamba

❼ Moyobamba and Alto Mayo

Road Map C3. 99 miles (160 km) E of Chachapoyas. 🚶 35,000. 🚌 from Chacapoyas. 🌐 **moyobamba.com**

Located on the edge of the Amazon Basin, the small town of Moyobamba was established by the Spaniards soon after the conquest of the region in the 1540s. Despite devastating earthquakes in 1990, 1991, 2001, and 2005, it has recovered and provides good access to the high subtropical jungle. The locals proudly call it the City of Orchids.

Moyobamba is the oldest city in Peru's Amazon region and, according to some, it was Tupac Yupanqui *(see p173)* who penetrated this area and made it a base from which the Incas made incursions into the surrounding areas. The name Moyobamba derives from the Quechua word *muyupampa*, which means a "circular plain."

Located on the upper Río Mayo basin, known as Alto Mayo, Moyobamba's main attractions are essentially water-related. The hot springs, popular with the locals, are just to the south of town and can be reached on foot or by a *motocarro* (a motorcycle rickshaw). Just an hour's drive from Moyobamba are the **Cataratas del Gera**, most popular amongst the many falls in the region.

❽ Tarapoto

Road Map C3. 72 miles (116 km) from Moyobamba. 🚶 100,000. ✈ 🚌 from Moyobamba or Chiclayo. 🚌 🎉 Fiesta Patronal (mid-Jul), Tarapoto's Anniversary (Aug 20). 🌐 **tarapoto.com**

The friendly and bustling town of Tarapoto is the largest and fastest growing city in the Department of San Martín. Located at a height of 1,181 ft (360 m), it is a place for fishing, swimming, and relaxing. Also dubbed as the Land of Waterfalls, it has some of the finest falls in the entire country. The Río Mayo, 19 miles (30 km) away, offers white-water rafting options to adventurous visitors from June to October.

Tarapoteños enjoy a good party, and their festivals feature street dances, folk music, costumed processions, and plenty of food. Among its many sought-after local drinks is *uvachado*, which is a potent brew made by soaking grapes in a cocktail of sugarcane alcohol, cinnamon, and honey for a month.

Environs

The famous Quechua-speaking hillside town of **Lamas** is located 18 miles (28 km) northwest from Tarapoto. The town is not built on the banks of any river, which is rare in the Amazon jungle. Recovering from the devastation of the 2005 earthquake, the village eagerly welcomes travelers interested in visiting the museum or experiencing the traditional dance, music, and folklore, seeing the thatch and mud-wall architecture, or buying arts and crafts. The colorful annual fiesta is held in late August. Guided tours are available from Tarapoto.

Of the many lakes in this area, the **Lago Sauce** is the most popular. Getting there is half the fun as taxis and minibuses have to cross the Río Huallaga on a balsa raft midway through the 32-mile (52-km) drive. A fish hatchery ensures abundant angling opportunities. Other relaxation comes in the form of boating and swimming. Hotel and camping facilities are available.

A view of the peaceful town of Lamas near Tarapoto

Visitors enjoying a *motocarro* ride through the mud streets around Pucallpa

9 Pucallpa

Road Map C3. 178 miles (288 km) NE of Lima. 290,000. from Lima & Iquitos. from Lima. from Iquitos. San Juan (Jun 24), Regional celebrations (Aug 20–22). **pucallpa.com**

A late-blooming city of the Peruvian Amazon, Pucallpa is now amongst its fastest growing. In 1900, it had a population of just 200. The highway from Lima came in 1930, changing Pucallpa into a major logging center of the country. Exploration for oil, gas, and gold has further boosted the city's economy, making Pucallpa the most important port on the Río Ucayali.

Not attractive in the traditional sense, Pucallpa is a city of modern buildings encircled by mud streets. Most travelers move on to nearby Yarinacocha or take a boat for a trip to Iquitos.

For artistically inclined visitors, an essential stop is the gallery in the **Home of Agustín Rivas**, a famous local woodcarver, whose pieces grace many public buildings in the town. Another is **Usko Ayar Museum and Amazonian School of Painting**, where shaman and painter Pablo Amaringo teaches, works, and exhibits his esoteric and visionary pieces inspired by rainforests.

Home of Agustín Rivas
Tarapaca 861. **Tel** 061 571 834.
Open 10am–noon, 2–5pm Mon–Sat.

Usko Ayar Museum and Amazonian School of Painting
Sánchez Cerro 465. **Open** 10am–5pm Mon–Fri.

10 Yarinacocha

Road Map C3. 6 miles (10 km) NE of Pucallpa. Taxi from Pucallpa.

Just 6 miles (10 km) northeast of downtown Pucallpa, this lovely, tranquil oxbow lake is a world away from city bustle. *Cocha* is the Quechua Indian word for lake, so the locals simply call it Yarinacocha.

Visitors arrive at **Puerto Callao**, a ramshackle lakeside village to the south. It has several basic hotels and many inexpensive restaurants. Worth a visit is the thatched warehouse called Maroti Shobo, which sells renowned Shipibo Indian ceramics with their characteristic geometric designs. This cooperative shop collects handmade pieces from about 40 Shipibo villages of the region.

Boats are readily available for those wanting to see the dolphins in the lake. Trips are organized to visit the verdant

Chullachaqui botanical garden, which includes a 45-minute boat ride followed by a 30-minute hike. Sloths and green iguanas can be spotted here.

Several Shipibo villages can be visited, of which **San Francisco** and **Santa Clara** to the west are the best known. The Shipibo is a matriarchal society and many continue to live traditionally in thatched, open-sided huts that are raised on stilts.

Adventurous overnight expeditions, during which travelers can sleep in Indian huts, can be arranged with the help of local guides. The few lodges offering comfortable accomodation are a short boat ride away.

Sloth climbing a tree in the Chullachaqui botanical garden

Bends in the Nanay River, a tributary of the Amazon River ▶

Andean spectacled bears can be spotted in Yanachaga Chemillén

⓫ Chanchamayo Region

Road Map C4. 190 miles (305 km) NE of Lima. 🏔 30,000. 🚌 from Lima.

The Yanesha and Ashaninka indigineous groups were the first inhabitants of this region, named for the Río Chanchamayo, when the valley was mainly a cloud forest zone. Since then much of the land has been cleared and the region is now famous for its coffee and fruit plantations. The small towns of **La Merced** and **San Ramón** are excellent bases for visiting the nearby area, which is known for its picturesque landscape. The region is full of rivers, waterfalls, and fruit orchards.

La Merced is the larger of the two towns, with a better choice of restaurants and accommoda-tion. It is the gateway for trans-portation to Puerto Bermúdez and Oxapampa, and for visiting remote **Ashaninka** communities such as in Marankiari Bajo, 16 miles (26 km) from La Merced. The drive to Puerto Bermúdez takes around 8 hours by bus.

Environs
Parque Nacional Yanachaga Chemillén covers an area of 47 sq miles (122 sq km) and protects several ecological zones, including the famous cloud forests of Peru, which are home to the endangered Andean spectacled bear. It has

a ranger station 5 miles (8 km) outside Oxapampa and some basic camping areas between Oxapampa and **Pozuzo**.

Pozuzo, settled in 1857 by Austrian and German families, is the real heart of the Teutonic settlement. Reached by a ser-pentine, unpaved 50-mile (80-km) road which passes through a section of the Chemillén National Park, Pozuzo is surrounded by steep hills and waterfalls. The road is sometimes closed by landslides in the rainy season. Pozuzo's founding is

celebrated with German music, dancing, costumes, and food.

✉ Parque Nacional Yanachaga Chemillén
Tel 063 462 544. ℹ SERNANP, Prolongacion Pozuzo 156, Oxapampa. **Open** 8am–1pm, 2:30–5:30pm Mon–Fri. 🏔 🌐 sernanp.gob.pe

Ashaninka
Carretera tramo via La Merced a Satipo KM26. **Tel** 064 766 373. 📷 🎭 July 25–30. 🚌 🏔 🌐 ashaninka-ciamb.site40.net

⓬ Oxapampa

Road Map C4. 50 miles (80 km) SW of Chanchamayo. 🏔 10,000. 🚕 Taxi from Chanchamayo. 🌐 oxapampaonline.com

Calling itself the geographical center of Peru, Oxapampa is a popular logging, ranching, and coffee-growing hub. Founded in 1891 by German settlers from Pozuzo, it has a hint of the Teutonic life in most of its festivals and architecture. Occasional blonde-haired, blue-eyed Peruvians attest to its original heritage. Connected to Chanchamayo by unpaved road, Oxapampa retains a friendly frontier atmosphere, as yet the town is little-visited.

The Ashaninka

The Ashaninka is the largest Amazonian indigenous group in Peru, with 55,000 members living in over 200 communities along several central Amazonian rivers. They depend mainly on subsistence agriculture, using age-old slash and burn techniques. Most of them do not speak Spanish and retain a traditional lifestyle. Their recent history is frightful. During the 1980s, the Sendero Luminoso (see p199) forcefully recruited Ashaninkas. In turn, the Peruvian army entered Ashaninka lands in pursuit of the guerillas, and the tribespeople were caught between the two. Since the capture of Sendero leaders in the 1990s, peace has returned to the tribe. They have begun claiming title to their land to protect themselves from incursions by oil and logging companies. Today, several communities have ecotourism projects and welcome visitors who stay in villagers' homes, learn about traditional customs, enjoy local music, and buy crafts. The Albergue Humboldt hotel in Puerto Bermudez organizes tours to visit Ashaninka communities.

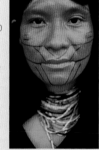
Ashaninkas use native fruits to color their faces

⓲ Reserva de la Biosfera de Manu

This UNESCO World Heritage Site covers almost 7,700 sq miles (20,000 sq km) of the Manu Basin. It drops vertiginously from 1,120 ft (4,000 m) above sea level north of Cusco, through remote cloud forests containing some of the most diverse bird populations on earth, to lowland rainforests which are home to various Indian groups and a proliferation of jungle flora and fauna. The reserve has three zones. Over 80 percent of the reserve lies in the intangible zone, the abode of natives who have almost no contact with the outside world; travelers are prohibited. The reserved zone allows tourism *(see p305)* and camping on beaches is permitted with authorized guides. The multiple use zone is where the one road from the highlands enters, and has several villages and cloud forest lodges.

Cloud Forest

The wide-ranging elevations create ideal environments for birds and new species are discovered here often. Mixed feeding flocks of dozens of bird species are a highlight and hikers on precipitous trails are rewarded with sightings of woolly monkeys and brown capuchins.

Toucans live in groups and are mainly fruit eaters but may use their bill against small prey.

Paradise tanager is a beautiful, bright bird popular for its seven-colored plumage.

Woolly monkeys live in groups and have a prehensile tail which can be used to hold objects.

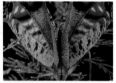

Giant katydid is one of the thouands of insect species found in Manu.

Reserved zone

This is the relatively flat rainforest of the Río Manu. Canopy platforms and towers are available for visitors, and over a dozen monkey species roam the forests here. Meandering in huge curves, the river sometimes leaves behind oxbow lakes known as cochas.

Hoatzins and horned screamers, both known for their ornate head plumes, live around oxbow lakes.

Oxbow lakes are the haunt of the rare giant river otters and some spectacular waterbirds.

Río Manu flows across the reserve which is home to a vast variety of flora and fauna.

⑭ Ríos Tambopata and Madre de Dios Area

The beautiful rivers, pristine lakes, and primary rainforests of southeastern Peru are teeming with wildlife. This is the most biodiverse area of Peru's Amazon and has the highest concentration of jungle lodges, staffed by naturalist guides and reached only by river. Most of the land south of Río Madre de Dios is protected by national parks. The vibrant frontier city of Puerto Maldonado sits conveniently at the confluence of the Madre de Dios and Tambopata rivers, and is the best base for visiting the area. Most visitors reach Puerto Maldonado on daily flights from Cusco and Lima. However, there is also an unpaved 310-mile (500-km) road which takes two to six days from Cusco depending on the season.

A family of capybaras, the world's largest rodents

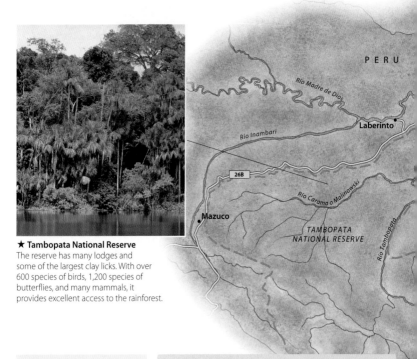

★ Tambopata National Reserve
The reserve has many lodges and some of the largest clay licks. With over 600 species of birds, 1,200 species of butterflies, and many mammals, it provides excellent access to the rainforest.

KEY

① **Río Madre de Dios** flows from the highlands near Manu Biosphere Reserve into Bolivia. A major trade route, it has a lot of traffic, gold dredging, and settlements.

② **Río Heath** is slowly being discovered and is becoming popular for ecotourism.

③ **Río Tambopata** is a tributary of Río Madre de Dios. The river is most likely to yield wildlife sightings.

Carlos Fitzcarrald (1862–97)

Fitzcarrald made a fortune during the rubber boom in the 1880s. He discovered that the Ucayali and Madre de Dios river basins were separated by a short finger of the Andean foothills. Enslaving hundreds of indigenous people, he moved a steamship piece by piece over the isthmus, and traveled down Madre de Dios past what would later become Puerto Maldonado. Werner Herzog's film, *Fitzcarraldo* was inspired by his story.

Scene from the film *Fitzcarraldo* (1982)

★ Puerto Maldonado

After the rubber boom, this town (with a population of 67,600) turned to logging, rainforest agriculture, and gold panning. The market has Brazil nuts, coffee, and tropical fruits on sale.
A 98 ft- (30 m-) high tower provides views of the ubiquitous corrugated-metal roofed buildings.

0 kilometers 20
0 miles 20

Las Piedras

26B

Lago Valencia ①

Lago Sandoval

Puerto Maldonado ✈

Infierno

Río Heath

BOLIVIA

BAHUAJA-SONENE NATIONAL PARK ②

③
Tambopata

Lago Sandoval
Surrounded by towering palms, this lake is home to the endangered giant river otters. It is possible to make a day trip from Puerto Maldonado to this impressive lake.

Key

= Minor road
--- Park boundary
—•— International border

★ Clay Licks
Riverside mud cliffs with abnormally high salt content attract hundreds of parrots and macaws who nibble on the clay to obtain essential minerals. The brilliantly colored macaws and parrots make it a spectacular sight indeed.

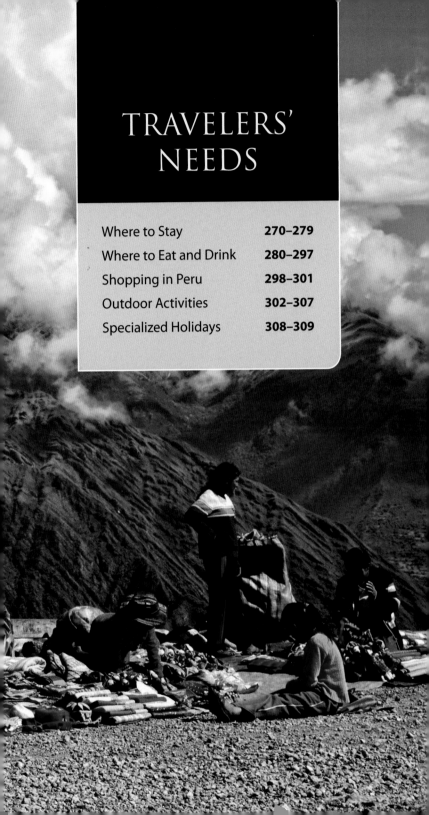

TRAVELERS' NEEDS

WHERE TO STAY

Despite the large variety of archaeological and natural treasures in Peru, it is only in the past 10 years that the number of visitors to the country has grown considerably. Consequently, there is no shortage of good quality accommodations but the standard can fluctuate, especially in more remote areas. Price is not always a reliable indicator of quality or facilities. Hotels are usually the best bet, *hostales* have fewer facilities, and campgrounds exist solely on treks. Room rates soar during local festivals, national holidays, and the high season, when advance bookings are a good idea as demand is huge. The listings on pages 274–9 include hotels that suit every taste and budget.

An inviting room with views from the balcony at the Sheraton Lima *(see p274)*

Grading

Peruvian hotels are graded using the international star system, although the standards within a rating can vary sigificantly. Establishments are awarded stars on the basis of meeting certain criteria such as providing color TV, parking, washing, and ironing services, rather than for the levels of luxury they provide.

The Peruvian government requires signage to be put up to identify types of accommodations: H for hotel; Hs for *hostal*, R for resort located in a holiday area, such as on a beach or by a river; AH for apart-hotel with kitchen facilities; E for eco lodge which promotes ecotourism; and A for *albergue* usually run by the state of church.

Prices

Hotel rates in Lima and other popular tourist areas, such as Cusco and Iquitos, are more expensive than in the rest of Peru. Whatever the star rating of a hotel, prices will rise in the peak season from June to September and for important festivals such as Inti Raymi in Cusco, Easter Week in Ayacucho, or national holidays such as Fiestas Patrias *(see pp38–41)*.

Booking

It is advisable to book accommodations well ahead of the visit, especially if traveling during the high season from June to August. In cities such as Cusco, Lima, Arequipa, and Trujillo it is difficult to get reservations during the festivals of Inti Raymi, Semana Santa *(see p198)*, and Fiestas Patrias when demand is very high.

Mountains form the backdrop to the Sanctuary Lodge, Machu Picchu *(see p276)*

◀ Local women selling handicrafts at the Sacred Valley, Inca Heartland

Spacious bathroom with hot tub at Casa Andina Private Collection *(see p273)*

If you have made the bookings using the Internet, do expect to pay for the privilege. Often, walk-in rates are cheaper, although a reservation removes the need to trudge unknown streets trailing heavy bags.

Hotel Chains

International chains such as the **Hilton**, **Marriott**, **Sheraton**, **Starwood**, and **Swissôtel** have properties in Lima, with tariffs in the high-end range. Restaurants, bars, swimming pools, and fitness centers are all standard facilities.

The **Orient Express Hotels** group operates six deluxe hotels in Peru: the Miraflores Park *(see p274)* in Lima, one in the heart of the Cañón del Colca, another in the Sacred Valley, the Palacio Nazarenas and the Monasterio *(see p276)* in Cusco, and the Sanctuary Lodge *(see p276)* in Machu Picchu. Top-end hotels charge an 18 percent sales tax on their room rates, but they will refund this to foreigners who can prove that they live outside Peru. Some charge a 13 percent service tax also.

Regional cities are the domain of hotel chains such as **Casa Andina** and **Libertador**, as well as **Sonesta**, all of which run mid-level and more expensive properties. The Casa Andina Private Collection properties, in Cusco, the Sacred Valley, Puno,

and on Lake Titicaca's Suasi Island are the upmarket version of their hotels, while the Libertador's more exclusive properties, in Puno, Arequipa, Cusco, and Paracas are linked with the **Starwood** luxury hotels chain. They also have hotels in Lima including the 29-story Westin *(see p274)*, the city's most modern hotel.

Mid-Range Accommodations

Standards do vary and despite ritzy reception areas, rooms in these hotels can sometimes be a letdown in comparison to their European, Asian, or North American counterparts. Private bathrooms, cable TV, minibars, telephones, and in warmer climates, fans or air-conditioning are normally the rule, although these facilities may be difficult to come across in remote jungle lodges.

Lima, Cusco, and Arequipa have a wide range of options available. In remote areas, the best hotel in town may bill itself as a four- or five-star but don't be surprised if the facilities are just mid- to low-range.

Budget Accommodations

There are innumerable inexpensive hotels in towns across Peru, but before booking, always ask to see the room.

While 24-hour hot and cold water is required by law for *hostales* and hotels from one star up, the supply of hot water is often limited. Some turn it on only at particular times of the day, or may need notice to do so. Ask before you check in. Guests may also be asked to throw toilet paper in a basket to avoid blocking the drain.

A *hostal* is not the same as a hostel in English. Instead, it denotes a small hotel or inn that is usually cheaper than a hotel and has fewer facilities. By law, *hostales* must have no less than six rooms.

The word *albergue* was traditionally used to describe shelters, such as those run by a religious order, or a simple guesthouse, but today the term encompasses a range of accommodation options in rural Peru. From coastal cabanas to smart hotels, their uniting feature is the local ambience and location.

Conventional *albergues*, similar to bed-and-breakfasts, still exist in Peru. Those that meet the minimal government regulations imposed upon them – such as a separate toilet for guests or emergency exits – are permitted to display a sign. Economical *pensiones* and *hospedajes* (guesthouses) are found throughout the major cities and towns. Often they do not display signs but rely on word of mouth.

Lodge accommodations at the Tambopata Research Center, Amazon Basin *(see p279)*

A room with a view at the Hotel Monasterio, Cusco *(see p276)*

Youth Hostels

There are more than 30 youth hostels in Peru, offering accommodations with dormitory, single, twin, or double rooms, some with private bathrooms. They usually have a bar, café, kitchen, and many come with a computer with Internet access. The website of **Hostelling International Peru** has information on hostels. Chains such as Loki *(see p274)*, have hostels in several cities.

Jungle and Eco Lodges

There are a range of options at varying prices in Peru's jungles, and advance reservations are recommended. River transport is included as lodges are usually a few hours upriver; tours and guides are often included too. Most lodges have offices in the capital city of Lima, and some in the Madre de Dios area have offices in Cusco.

Ceiba Tops, run by **Amazon Explorama Lodges**, is more of a resort than a lodge. Located near Iquitos, it has luxury rooms with screened windows, satellite TV, swimming pool, and large bathrooms with hot showers. The Wasai Eco Lodge in Puerto Maldonado *(see p279)* offers stilted wooden bungalows and a fine jungle introduction

on the Río Madre de Dios. **Inkaterra** is another organization that has luxury eco lodges, including two in Ríos Tambopata. Rustic options abound around Madre de Dios, with palm-thatched roofs, cold water, mosquito nets, and kerosene lanterns or candles. The focus here is on nature and wildlife, rather than luxury.

In keeping with government regulations, eco lodges must be constructed of natural material from the area. They should be built in harmony with the environment and preferably use natural energy sources such as solar or wind.

Homestays

Travelers can stay in the homes of villagers on the islands of Taquile, Amantani, and Anapia on Lake Titicaca *(see p151)* for a small price; conditions, however, are basic. **All Ways Travel**, which promotes social development with these communities, organizes stays on the islands. Vicos, near Huaraz, is the first Peruvian community to own the title to their lands. Ten families host travelers and tourists who then live and work alongside locals for stays of between two to five days. You can book your stay with them through **Yachaqui Wayi**.

Some families in Cusco also offer homestay programs. Contact **Homestay in Cusco** for more information.

Specialist Holidays

Many tour operators who concentrate on holidays in Peru also offer specialist tours *(see pp307–308)* for those interested in a particular activity. Trekking, rafting, mountain-biking, bird-watching, butterfly-watching, and culinary tours are common. Some visitors also choose to camp high up in the Andes or in the Amazon Basin, or head out for jungle trips to Iquitos in the north or Manu in the south. Several jungle tour operators have interests in lodges and tours are usually all-inclusive. For example, **Inkanatura Travel**

Trekkers camping during their journey through the Cordillera Blanca

Inner courtyard, Hotel Monasterio, Cusco *(see p276)*

is the profit-making branch of the Peru Verde or Green Peru conservation program, which part-owns the Reserva de la Biosfera de Manu *(see p265)*.

Travelers with Disabilities

Only the more upmarket, modern, or recently renovated hotels cater to travelers with disabilities, and most of these are located in Lima, Cusco, Trujillo, Iquitos, and Aguas Calientes. A few jungle lodges have facilities for disabled clients. Telephones for hearing impaired travelers are almost unknown in Peru. However,

some hotels are moving to install visual alarms and expand facilities for disabled clients. The hotel staff, in general, will do whatever is possible to assist any guests with disabilities.

Recommended Hotels

A variety of lodging options from cozy, family-owned inns and boutique hotels in the cities to relaxing beachfront resorts and Amazon and Andean eco lodges have been listed in this guide. These have been selected on two main criteria – location and services, and feature a wide selection

of options to suit every budget and requirement. Select from a list of the best Eco lodge, B&B, Budget, Luxury, Boutique, Resort, Chain, and Historical hotels in Peru.

For the best of the best, look out for hotels highlighted as the DK Choice. These establishments have been selected for their exceptional quality and charm. They may be set in a stunning location, boast a notable history, or offer an inviting atmosphere and excellent service. The majority of these are exceptionally popular, so be sure to make a reservation in advance.

DIRECTORY

Hotel Chains

Casa Andina
Tel 86 220 4434 (US),
888 350 6263 (Canada),
08 082 343 805 (UK).
w casa-andina.com

Hilton
w hilton.com

Libertador
w libertador.com.pe

Marriott
w marriott.com

Orient Express
Tel 800 237 1236 (USA
& Canada),
20 7960 0500 (UK).
w orient-express.com

Sheraton
Tel 01 315 5000.
w sheraton.com.pe

Sonesta
w sonesta.com

Starwood
Tel 1800 937 8461.
w starwoodhotels.com

Swissotel
Tel 01 611 4400.
w swissotel.com

Youth Hostels

**Hostelling
International Peru**
Av. Casimiro Ulloa 328,
Miraflores, Lima.
Tel 01 446 5488.
w hostellingperu.
com.pe

Jungle and Eco Lodges

**Amazon Explorama
Lodges**
Tel 065 252 530,
1800 707 5275 (USA).
w explorama.com

Inkaterra
Tel 01 610 0410, 1800 442
5042 (USA & Canada),
0 800 458 7806 (UK).
w inkaterra.com

Homestays

All Ways Travel
Casa de Corregidor,
Calle Duestua 576, Puno.
Tel 051 353 979.
w titicaperu.com

Homestay in Cusco
Tel 084 242 562.
w homestayincusco.
com

Yachaqui Wayi
Jr. Gabino Uribe 650,
Huaraz.
Tel 043 426 538.
w yachaquiwayi.org

Specialist Holidays

Inkanatura Travel
Manuel Bañon 461, San
Isidro, Lima.
Map 2 C2.
Tel 01 440 2022 /
422 8114.
w inkanatura.com

Where to Stay

Lima

Central Lima

Hotel España ⓢ
B&B **Map** 1 F2
Jirón Azangaro 105
Tel *01 427 9196*
ⓦ hotelespanaperu.com
A 19th-century building tastefully furnished. Dorms and private rooms with shared bathrooms.

Gran Hotel Bolivar ⓢⓢ
Historical **Map** 1 E2
Jirón de la Union 958
Tel *01 619 7171*
ⓦ granhotelbolivar.com.pe
Declared a historical icon of Lima, this hotel has clean, spacious rooms and friendly service.

Sheraton Lima ⓢⓢⓢ
Luxury **Map** 1 E3
Paseo de la Republica 170
Tel *01 315 5000*
ⓦ sheraton.com
Opulent hotel conveniently located near main art museums. Free shuttle service to Miraflores.

Miraflores

Hostal El Patio ⓢ
B&B **Map** 4 B1
Diez Canseco 341
Tel *01 444 2107*
ⓦ hostalelpatio.net
Charming *hostal* offering mini-suites with kitchenettes. All rooms open on to a verdant terrace.

Loki Hostel ⓢ
B&B **Map** 4 A1
Jose Galvez 576
Tel *01 651 2966*
ⓦ lokihostel.com
Dorms and rooms with private baths, and a roof garden.

Colonial façade of the Country Club hotel in San Isidro

Casa Andina Centro ⓢⓢ
Chain **Map** 3 D5
Av. Petit Thouars 5444
Tel *01 213 9739*
ⓦ casa-andina.com
Pleasant, sizable rooms, and good service at this hotel.

Hotel Antigua ⓢⓢ
Boutique **Map** 4 B1
Av. Grau 350
Tel *01 201 2060*
ⓦ antiguamiraflores.com
A large 1920s house with Peruvian art and antiques. Suites with cable TV, a Jacuzzi, and kitchenettes.

La Hacienda & Casino ⓢⓢ
Luxury **Map** 4 B2
Av. 28 de Julio 511
Tel *01 213 1000*
ⓦ hoteleslahacienda.com
Comfortable, luxurious hotel with all modern facilties and a casino.

J.W. Marriott ⓢⓢⓢ
Room with a view **Map** 4 B2
Malecon de la Reserva 615
Tel *01 217 7000*
ⓦ marriott.com
Set on the cliffs overlooking the ocean and the Larcomar complex.

Miraflores Park ⓢⓢⓢ
Room with a view **Map** 4 C3
Malecon de la Reserva 1035
Tel *01 610 4000*
ⓦ mirafloorespark.com
This boutique hotel has opulent rooms with stunning views of the Pacific, and a rooftop pool.

San Isidro

Foresta Hotel & Suites ⓢⓢ
Luxury **Map** 2 C3
Calle Los Libertadores 490
Tel *01 630 0000*
ⓦ foresta-hotel.pe
Well-appointed suites with fully equipped kitchenettes. Located in a residential area.

Country Club ⓢⓢⓢ
Luxury **Map** 2 A3
Los Eucaliptos 590
Tel *01 611 9000*
ⓦ hotelcountry.com
This 1920s hacienda-style hotel boasts antique furnishings and rooms with marble bathrooms.

Los Delfines ⓢⓢⓢ
Luxury **Map** 2 A3
Los Eucaliptos 555
Tel *01 215 7000*
ⓦ losdelfineshotel.com.pe
Los Delfines offers a full business centre, heliport, spa, casino, and views of the Lima golf course.

Price Guide

Prices are for a standard double room per night in high season, inclusive of all taxes and service charges.

ⓢ	up to S/200
ⓢⓢ	S/200 to S/450
ⓢⓢⓢ	over S/450

NM Lima Hotel ⓢⓢⓢ
Luxury **Map** 2 C4
Av. Pardo y Aliaga 300
Tel *01 612 1000*
ⓦ nmlimahotel.com
Contemporary design hotel with a calm atmosphere. Close to the ancient Hualla Pucllana site.

Sonesta Hotel El Olivar ⓢⓢⓢ
Room with a view **Map** 2 C3
Pancho Fierro 194
Tel *01 712 6000*
ⓦ sonesta.com/lima
Pleasant rooms at this hotel overlooking the Bosque El Olivar.

Swissotel ⓢⓢⓢ
Chain **Map** 2 B3
Av. Santo Toribio – Via Central 150, Centro Empresarial Real
Tel *01 421 4400*
ⓦ swissotel.com
Elegant hotel with a spa, beauty salon, and tennis court. Business facilities available.

DK Choice

Westin Lima ⓢⓢⓢ
Luxury **Map** 3 D2
Calle Las Begonias 450
Tel *01 201 5000*
ⓦ starwoodhotels.com/westin
Set in a 29-story glass skyscraper with vibrant, contemporary interiors, Westin is located in the heart of the financial and shopping district. Top-notch amenities include a luxury spa and an indoor pool, executive meeting areas, and a fully equipped business centre.

Barranco

3B ⓢⓢ
B&B **Map** 4 C4
Jirón Centenario 130
Tel *01 247 6915*
ⓦ 3bhostal.com
Boutique B&B offering well-appointed rooms with high-quality custom furnishings.

Second Home ⓢⓢ
Room with a view **Map** 4 C4
Domeyer 366
Tel *01 247 5522*
ⓦ secondhomeperu.com
The former home of acclaimed

Aerial view of the scenic Colca Lodge at Cañón del Colca

Peruvian sculptor Victor Delfín, this guesthouse has airy rooms and offers superb ocean views.

The Southern Coast

CHINCHA ALTA: Wakama ⑤⑤
Eco Lodge   Map C5
Panamericana Sur Km 174
Tel *998 386 154*
ⓦ wakamaecoplaya.com
Charming, rustic bamboo and eucalyptus bungalows next to the beach. Barbecues, hammocks, campfires, and games for children.

HUACACHINA: Hosteria Suiza ⑤
B&B   Map C5
Balneario de Huacachina 264
Tel *056 238 762*
ⓦ hosteriasuiza.com.pe
Nestled within a sandy landscape, this B&B offers cheerful rooms, good home cooking, and a pool.

DK Choice

**ICA: Hotel Viñas
Queirolo**
Luxury   Map C5
Carretera a Los Molinos Km 11
Tel *056 254 119*
ⓦ hotelvinasqueirolo.com
Built to replicate the 19th-century farmhouse that once stood on this site, this hotel is set in the vineyards that produce the Intipalka wines. Spacious, modern rooms and grand spaces overlooking 1.56 sq miles (4 sq km) of farmland. Facilities include a play area for children, a pool, a spa and wine tastings.

ICA: Las Dunas ⑤⑤
Resort   Map C5
Av. La Angostura 400
Tel *056 256 224*
ⓦ lasdunashotel.com
Set among sand dunes, Las Dunas offers excellent amenities. There are three pools to choose from.

NAZCA: Hotel Alegria ⑤
Budget   Map C5
Calle Lima 166
Tel *056 522 702*
ⓦ hotelalegria.net
Clean and comfortable rooms. Convenient for the airport.

NAZCA: Hotel Majoro ⑤⑤
Resort   Map C5
*Panamericana Sur Km 453,
Vista Alegre*
Tel *056 522 490*
ⓦ hotelmajoro.com
A richly decorated 17th-century convent with a relaxed ambience.

PARACAS: El Mirador ⑤
Budget   Map C5
Av. Paracas Km 20
Tel *056 545 086*
ⓦ elmiradorhotel.com
Basic, but rooms are comfortable. Facilities include children's play area, restaurant, and snack-bar.

**PARACAS: Double Tree
Hilton** ⑤⑤
Resort   Map C5
Lote 30–34, Urb. Santo Domingo
Tel *016 171 000*
ⓦ doubletree3.hilton.com
A four-star hotel near the Reserva Nacional de Paracas.

**PARACAS: Hotel
Paracas** ⑤⑤⑤
Luxury   Map C5
Av. Paracas 173
Tel *056 581 333*
ⓦ starwoodhotels.com
Five-star oceanfront hotel with contemporary furnishings.

Canyon Country

**AREQUIPA: Colonial
House Inn** ⑤
Budget   Map D6
Calle Puente Grau 114
Tel *054 223 533*
ⓦ colonialhouseinn.pe
Sprawling centuries-old house

known for its helpful staff. Basic and spacious rooms. Breakfast on the lovely rooftop terrace.

AREQUIPA: La Casa de Melgar ⑤
Budget   Map D6
Calle Melgar 108
Tel *054 222 459*
ⓦ lacasademelgar.com
A historic home of thick volcanic rock walls and vaulted ceilings with monastic simplicity in the rooms. Indoor patios and café.

AREQUIPA: Libertador ⑤⑤⑤
Luxury   Map D6
Plaza Bolívar s/n, Selva Alegre
Tel *054 215 110*
ⓦ libertador.com.pe
Arequipa's only five-star hotel is situated in a spacious republican-style building. Large rooms, sauna, and outdoor pool with Jacuzzi.

**AREQUIPA: Sonesta Posadas
del Inca** ⑤⑤⑤
Chain   Map D6
Portal de Flores 116
Tel *054 215 530*
ⓦ sonesta.com
One of the city's best hotels, with modern rooms and a restaurant overlooking the main plaza.

**CAÑÓN DEL COLCA: La Casa
de Mamayacchi** ⑤
B&B   Map D6
Pueblo de Coporaque
Tel *054 241 206*
ⓦ lacasademamayacchi.com
A delightful lodge with bright rooms, and superb views of the canyon's volcanoes.

DK Choice

**CAÑÓN DEL COLCA: Colca
Lodge** ⑤⑤
Eco Lodge   Map D6
Fundo Puye s/n, Yanque
Tel *054 531 191*
ⓦ colca-lodge.com
Relax in comfort at this hotel on the Colca River offering rooms with thatched roofs, adobe-and-stone walls, geothermal heating, and views of the valley. There is also an eco-spa with hot springs. Lodgings include standard rooms with terraces, quadruple rooms with lofts, and family suites. Ideal base for family holiday.

**ISLA SUASI: Casa Andina
Private Collection** ⑤⑤⑤
Eco Lodge   Map E6
Av. Sesqui Centenario 1970, Puno
Tel *01 213 9739*
ⓦ casa-andina.com
Built of local stone and adobe, this hotel has spacious rooms with views of Lake Titicaca.

For more information on types of hotels *see pages 271–2*

LAMPA: La Casona de Lampa ⓢ
B&B   Map E5
Jirón Tarapaca 271
Tel *054 345 844*
Clean, simple rooms with en suite
bathrooms. Charming owner.

PUNO: Plaza Mayor Hotel ⓢⓢ
Inn   Map E6
Jirón Deustua 342
Tel *051 366 089*
Ⓦ plazamayorhotel.com
Large modern baths and cozy
beds guarantee a good rest. Ask
for a room away from the road.

**PUNO: Taypikala
Hotel & Spa**
Room with a view   Map E6
Panamericana Sur Km 18, Puno
Tel *051 792 252*
Ⓦ taypikala.com
A roadside hotel festooned with
jagged faux rocks. Rooms face
Lake Titicaca or the garden.

PUNO: Libertador ⓢⓢⓢ
Room with a view   Map E6
Isla Esteves
Tel *051 367 780*
Ⓦ libertador.com.pe
A five-star hotel with a wellness
center. Rooms have splendid
views of Lake Titicaca.

The Inca Heartland

CUSCO: Amaru Hostal ⓢ
Historical   Map D5
Cuesta de San Blas 541
Tel *084 225 933*
Ⓦ amaruhostal.com
Colonial town house in the artists'
quarter, with a cheerful café.

CUSCO: Hostal Corihuasi ⓢ
Historical   Map D5
Calle Suecia 561
Tel *084 232 233*
Ⓦ corihuasi.com
Old world charm in a renovated
18th-century house. Comfortable
beds and tasteful decor.

CUSCO: Los Aticos ⓢ
B&B   Map D5
Calle Quera, Pasaje Hurtado 253
Tel *084 231 710*
Ⓦ losaticos.com
Centrally located, family-run B&B
with 24-hour kitchen facilities.

CUSCO: Hotel Monasterio ⓢⓢ
Historical   Map D5
*Calle Palacios 136, Plazoleta
Nazarenas*
Tel *084 604 000*
Ⓦ monasteriohotel.com
A plush hotel set in a restored
17th century monastery with
Spanish Colonial decor.

A warm, welcoming room at Hotel Monasterio, Cusco

DK Choice

**MACHU PICCHU: Inkaterra
Machu Picchu Hotel** ⓢⓢⓢ
Luxury   Map D5
Railroad Km 110, Cusco
Tel *084 211 122*
Ⓦ inkaterra.com
This secluded paradise has 85
bungalows nestled against the
mountainside in expansive
gardens and stone pathways.
Choice of warmly decorated
rooms, *casitas* (cottages), and
two villas with private terraces
and plunge pools. Enjoy the
excellent facilities at Unu spa.

**MACHU PICCHU:
Sanctuary Lodge** ⓢⓢⓢ
Room with a view   Map D5
Machu Picchu ruins
Tel *084 211 038*
Ⓦ sanctuarylodgehotel.com
Pricey but worth it for the
unparalleled sunrise and sunset
views over Machu Picchu.

**OLLANTAYTAMBO:
El Albergue** ⓢⓢ
B&B   Map D5
Train Station
Tel *084 204 014*
Ⓦ elalbergue.com
Spacious rooms simply furnished
in dark wood furniture, and
handwoven Andean textiles.

URUBAMBA: La Quinta ⓢⓢ
B&B   Map D5
Calle Arenales 105
Tel *084 201 448*
Ⓦ laquintaecohotel.com
Eco-friendly lodgings with bikes
for hire. Rooms have balconies.

**URUBAMBA: Monasterio
de la Recoleta** ⓢⓢⓢ
Historical   Map D5
Jirón Recoleta s/n
Tel *084 201 666*
Ⓦ hotelessanagustin.com.pe
Tastefully restored 15th-century
monastery with pleasant rooms.

Central Sierra

AYACUCHO: Tres Mascaras ⓢ
B&B   Map D5
Jirón Tres Máscaras 194
Tel *066 312 921*
Ⓦ hoteltresmascaras.galeon.com
Centrally located *hostal* offering
basic but clean rooms. Lovely
plant-filled patio.

**AYACUCHO: Hotel El Marques
de Valdelirios** ⓢ
Budget   Map D5
Alameda Bolognesi 720
Tel *066 318 944*
A grand Colonial-style building
decorated with local artwork.
Warm, spacious rooms.

AYACUCHO: Hotel Santa Rosa ⓢ
Historical   Map D5
Jirón Lima 166
Tel *066 314 614*
Ⓦ hotel-santarosa.com
A 17th-century building with
clean, large rooms and a lovely
courtyard.

**HUANCAVELICA: Hotel
Presidente** ⓢⓢ
Chain   Map C5
Plaza de Armas s/n
Tel *064 452 760*
Ⓦ huancavelicaes.hotel
presidente.com.pe
Light, airy rooms with cable TV
and Wi-Fi. Central heating.

HUANCAYO: Hotel Confort ⓢ
Budget   Map C4
Ancash 237
Tel *064 233 601*
Large hotel with sparse but
comfortable rooms. Friendly staff.

HUANCAYO: Hotel Turismo ⓢⓢ
Chain   Map C4
Jirón Ancash 729
Tel *064 231 072*
Ⓦ turistas.hotelpresidente.com.pe
A beautiful 1950s Colonial-style
building with nice, comfortable
rooms and grand common areas.

DK Choice
HUANCAYO: Tuki Llajta Pueblo Bonito Hotel
Eco Lodge   ⓢ ⓢ
     Map C4
Av. Centenario s/n, San Jeronimo de Tunan
Tel *064 797 107*
🆆 tukillajta.com
Located in the countryside, this lodge offers suites and family bungalows with fireplaces and impressive views of the Mantaro Valley. Amenities include Wi-Fi, conference room, and a good restaurant. There is a telescope available for star-gazing.

HUÁNUCO: Casa Hacienda Shismay
B&B   ⓢ
     Map C4
San Sebastian de Shismay
Tel *062 963 367 734*
🆆 shismay.com
A restored 19th-century *hacienda* with breathtaking valley views, and a convivial atmosphere.

HUÁNUCO: Grand Hotel Huánuco
Chain   ⓢ ⓢ
     Map C4
Jirón Dámaso Beraún 775
Tel *062 514 222*
🆆 grandhotelhuanuco.com
This grand building is located on the town's main square. Pretty courtyard and large pool.

Cordillera Blanca

CARAZ: O'PAL Sierra Resort
Resort   ⓢ ⓢ
     Map B3
Carretera Pativilca Km 266.2
Tel *043 391 015*
🆆 opalsierraresort.com
An idyllic spot with comfortable bungalows set in a large garden. Excellent value.

Stone steps leading to the quaint O'PAL Sierra Resort in Caraz

CARHUAZ: El Abuelo ⓢ
Budget   **Map** B4
Jirón 257, 9 De Diciembre
Tel *043 394 445*
🆆 elabuelohostal.com
Modern *hostal* offering meals prepared with produce from their own garden. Rooms are simply furnished.

CHACAS: Hostal Pilar ⓢ
Budget   **Map** C4
Jirón Ancash 110
Tel *043 723 813*
🆆 huaraz.com/pilar
Spacious, tastefully furnished rooms around a flower-filled courtyard. Excellent restaurant.

CHAVÍN: Hotel Inca ⓢ
Budget   **Map** C4
Jirón Wiracocha 170, Plaza de Armas
Tel *044 754 021*
🆆 huaraz.com/hotelinca
Family-run hotel offering pleasant rooms with en suite bathrooms.

HUARAZ: Albergue Churup ⓢ
Budget   **Map** C4
Jirón Amadeo Figueroa 1257, Soledad
Tel *043 424 200*
🆆 churup.com
Cozy, colorful rooms and dorms plus open fireplaces at this family-run hotel. Wonderful breakfasts.

HUARAZ: Hotel Colombia ⓢ ⓢ
Inn   **Map** C4
Jirón Francisco de Zela 210
Tel *043 421 501*
🆆 huarazhotel.com
A remodeled *hacienda* with airy rooms, sports facilities and a children's playground.

DK Choice
HUARAZ: The Lazy Dog Inn
Eco Lodge   ⓢ ⓢ
     Map C4
Apartado 94, Serpost
Tel *051 943 789 330*
🆆 thelazydoginn.com
Set in the idyllic countryside 7.5 mile (12 km) outside Huaraz, this family-friendly establishment has a greenhouse, vegetable garden, sauna, and offers home-cooked meals. Choice of suites, cabins, or a room in the main house. The owners also offer horseback riding, trail-riding, and hiking. Stunning views.

HUARAZ: Andino ⓢ ⓢ ⓢ
Room with a view   **Map** C4
Jirón Pedro Cochachin 357
Tel *043 421 662*
🆆 hotelandino.com
Swiss-owned and run hotel featuring suites with Jacuzzis and fireplaces. Good restaurant.

MONTERREY: El Patio de Monterrey ⓢ ⓢ
Inn   **Map** B4
Carretera Huraz-Caraz Km 206
Tel *043 424 965*
🆆 elpatio.com.pe
Charming hacienda-style hotel near the Monterrey hot springs. Pleasant rooms, plus four bungalows with fireplaces.

The Northern Desert

CHICLAYO: Hotel Villa Rita ⓢ
Budget   **Map** B3
Av. Lora y Cordero 825
Tel *074 235 892*
🆆 hotelvillaritachiclayo.com
Comfortable rooms as well as business facilities and a cafeteria. Helpful staff and excellent value.

CHICLAYO: Garza Hotel ⓢ ⓢ
Resort   **Map** B3
Av. F. Bolognesi 756
Tel *074 228 172*
🆆 garzahotel.com
This hotel, near the main square, has spacious rooms, restaurants, bars, and a casino.

HUANCHACO: Huanchaco International ⓢ
Resort   **Map** B3
Av. La Marina 466, Playa Azul
Tel *044 461 754*
🆆 huanchacointernational.com
Bungalows with beach views and cable TV. Large pool also on site.

HUANCHACO: La Casa Suiza ⓢ
B&B   **Map** B3
Los Pinos 451
Tel *044 461 285*
🆆 casasuiza.com
Small, Swiss-owned *hostal*; some rooms have private baths. Table games, barbecue area, plus breakfast, and laundry service.

DK Choice
LAMBAYEQUE: Chaparrí Ecolodge
Eco Lodge   ⓢ ⓢ
     Map B3
Reserva Ecológica Chaparrí
Tel *051 984 676 249*
🆆 chaparrilodge.com
This lodge – 47 miles (75 km) east of Chiclayo – provides a serene escape in the splendid countryside. Relax in wonderful adobe-and-stone cabins with hot water and electricity from solar panels. Home to the country's first spectacled bear rescue centre, and a herpitarium, Chaparrí has excellent walking trails and offers wildlife and bird-watching opportunities.

LOS ORGANOS: Soleil Bungalows ⓢⓢ
Resort   **Map** A2
Av. Ribera del Mar, Punta Veleros
Tel *073 257 637*
Ⓦ soleilbungalows.com
Charming bungalows on white-sand beaches; ideal for families. Excellent facilities.

MÁNCORA: Sol y Mar ⓢ
Resort   **Map** A2
Av. Piura s/n
Tel *073 258 106*
Ⓦ solymarmancora.com
Máncora's longest-established lodging has clean, bright rooms, a pool, bars, and a restaurant.

MÁNCORA: Sunset ⓢ
Boutique   **Map** A2
Panamericana Norte Km 1,196
Tel *073 258 111*
Ⓦ sunsetmancora.com
A B&B with oceanview rooms and warm, personal touches. Superb restaurant.

PUNTA SAL: Hotel Caballito de Mar ⓢⓢ
Resort   **Map** A2
Panamericana norte Km 1,187
Tel *072 540 058*
Ⓦ hotelcaballitodemar.com
Suites and bungalows with ocean-view terraces. Pool with Jacuzzi, massages, and surfing lessons.

PUNTA SAL: Punta Sal ⓢⓢ
Resort   **Map** A2
Panamericana norte Km 1,192
Tel *072 540 088*
Ⓦ puntasal.com.pe
Oceanfront hotel with all modern amenities, and activities such as jet-skiing and yacht sailings.

TRUJILLO: Mochica's Inn ⓢ
Budget   **Map** B3
La Arboleda E-19
Tel *044 328 457*
Ⓦ mochicasinn.com
Small, friendly hotel offering bright rooms with private bathrooms. Community kitchen.

TRUJILLO: El Brujo Hotel ⓢⓢ
Inn   **Map** B3
Santa Teresa de Jesús 170, La Merced
Tel *044 223 322*
Ⓦ elbrujohotel.com
Modern hotel in a quiet, safe locality near the historic centre.

TRUJILLO: El Gran Marqués Hotel & Spa ⓢⓢ
Luxury   **Map** B3
Díaz de Cienfuegos 145, La Merced
Tel *044 481 710*
Ⓦ elgranmarques.com
Variety of rooms and suites, Tussen spa with dry and steam saunas, hair salon, and buffet breakfasts.

TRUJILLO: Costa del Sol ⓢⓢ
Chain   **Map** B3
Av. Los Cocoteros 500, Urb. El Golf
Tel *044 484 150*
Ⓦ costadelsolperu.com
Elegantly decorated rooms with all amenities. Spa, massage room, and restaurant. Superb value.

TUMBES: Costa del Sol ⓢⓢ
Chain   **Map** B2
Jirón San Martin 275
Tel *072 523 991*
Ⓦ costadelsolperu.com
This hotel has a pool, sauna, a gym, barbecue area, and casino. Two blocks from the main square.

VICHAYITO: El Mirador de Vichayito ⓢⓢ
Resort   **Map** A2
Panamericana norte Km 1,155
Tel *01 271 6751*
Ⓦ elmiradordevichayito.com
Spacious and colorful suites and private bungalows at this laid-back resort. Pool and restaurant.

The Northern Highlands

CAJAMARCA: Hostal Portada del Sol ⓢ
B&B   **Map** B3
Jirón Pisagua 731
Tel *076 363 395*
Ⓦ hostalportadadelsol.com
Restored Colonial house with period furniture and a stone courtyard. Helpful owners.

CAJAMARCA: El Portal del Marqués ⓢⓢ
Historical   **Map** B3
Jirón del Comercio 644
Tel *076 368 464*
Ⓦ portaldelmarques.com
Centrally located Colonial mansion with a restaurant, conference room, and Internet café.

Palm tree-lined promenade with an ocean view at the Punta Sal Resort, Punta Sal

CAJAMARCA: Laguna Seca ⓢⓢ
Luxury   **Map** B3
Av. Manco Cápac 1098, Baños del Inca
Tel *076 584 300*
Ⓦ lagunaseca.com.pe
Countryside spa hotel with in-room thermal tubs as well as outdoor pools, and Turkish baths.

CELENDÍN: Hostal Celendín ⓢ
B&B   **Map** B3
Jirón Unión 305
Tel *076 555 041*
Ⓦ hostalcelendin.com
Located on the Plaza de Armas, this friendly *hostal* has simple rooms and a great restaurant.

DK Choice

CHACHAPOYAS: Casa Vieja ⓢ
B&B   **Map** B3
Jirón Chincha Alta 569
Tel *041 477 353*
Ⓦ casaviejaperu.com
Built in the late 1800s, this charming two-story house has been turned into an attractive, family-owned hotel. The cozy, individually decorated rooms have whitewashed walls, folk art, and dark wooden beams; one room has a fireplace. There is a library with local information, and a beautiful courtyard.

CHACHAPOYAS: Hostal Revash ⓢ
B&B   **Map** B3
Jirón Grau 517
Tel *041 477 391*
An over 300-year-old building on the Plaza de Armas. Rooms with en suite baths. Good value.

CHACHAPOYAS: Casa Andina Classic ⓢⓢ
Chain   **Map** B3
Carretera Pedro Ruiz Km 39,
Tel *041 965 339 840*
Ⓦ casa-andina.com
This hotel, surrounded by green hills, offers spacious rooms.

KUÉLAP: Marvelous Spatuletail Lodge ⓢ
B&B   **Map** B3
Kuelap Road, Choctamal, Levanto
Tel *041 995 237 268*
Ⓦ marvelousspatuletail.net
Popular with international bird-watching groups, this lodge has all modern comforts.

LEYMEBAMBA: La Casona ⓢ
B&B   **Map** B3
Amazonas 223
Tel *041 830 106*
Ⓦ casonadeleymebamba.com
Clean rooms with wooden balconies and whitewashed walls. Orchid nursery.

The Amazon Basin

IQUITOS: Casa La Pascana
B&B   Ⓢ   **Map** D2
Calle Pevas 133
Tel *065 235 581*
🆆 pascana.com
Popular, family-run hotel with small, neat rooms along a garden with shaded tables. Free Wi-Fi.

IQUITOS: El Dorado Plaza
Luxury   ⓈⓈ   **Map** D2
Jirón Napo 258
Tel *065 222 555*
🆆 grupo-dorado.com
The city's most opulent hotel has big rooms, pool, and Jacuzzi.

IQUITOS AREA: Muyuna Lodge
Eco Lodge   ⓈⓈⓈ   **Map** D2
87 miles (140 km) upriver from Iquitos on Río Yanayacu
Tel *065 242 858*
🆆 muyuna.com
Stilted, thatched bungalows with balconies and hammocks. Meals and tours are included.

LA MERCED: Fundo San José Lodge
B&B   ⓈⓈ   **Map** C4
Circunvalación s/n, Pampa del Carmen
Tel *064 531 816*
🆆 fundosanjose.com.pe
Modern bungalows set in an old coffee plantation perched on the hillside. Great valley views.

LAGO SANDOVAL: Sandoval Lake Lodge
Eco Lodge   ⓈⓈⓈ   **Map** E5
20 miles (30 km) from Puerto Maldonado
Tel *01 440 2022*
🆆 inkanatura.com
Set deep in the Reserva Nacional Tambopata, this lodge has cozy rooms and bungalows, and offers unique sightings of lake wildlife.

MOYOBAMBA: Puerto Mirador
Chain   ⓈⓈ   **Map** C3
Calle Sucre s/n, Barrio de Zaragoza
Tel *042 562 050*
🆆 hotelpuertomirador.com
Rooms in bungalows set around two pools in large grounds. Abundant orchids and birds.

OXAPAMPA: Albergue Turístico Bottger
Room with a view   Ⓢ   **Map** C4
Jirón Mariscal Castilla block 6
Tel *063 462 377*
🆆 oxapampaonline.com/bottger
Family-run *hostal* offering wood paneled rooms with full baths. Beautiful mountain views.

Simple and rustic decor at the Tambopata Research Center, Río Tambopata

PUCALLPA: Hotel Sol del Oriente
Inn   ⓈⓈ   **Map** C3
San Martín 552
Tel *061 575 154*
🆆 soldelorientehoteles.com
One of Pucallpa's best hotels features a pool, sauna, and beauty salon. Pricier rooms have a Jacuzzi.

PUERTO BERMÚDEZ: Albergue Humboldt
B&B   Ⓢ   **Map** C4
Puerto de la Rampa
Tel *963 722 363*
🆆 alberguehumboldt.com
Charming lodging on the Río Pachitea deep in lush Ashaninka territory. Accommodations include rooms, hammocks, and camps.

PUERTO MALDONADO: Hotel Don Carlos
Room with a view   ⓈⓈ   **Map** E5
Av. León Velarde 1271
Tel *082 571 029*
🆆 hotelesdoncarlos.com
This hotel has wood-paneled or tiled rooms with TV, mini-fridge, and views of Río Tambopata.

PUERTO MALDONADO: Wasai Eco Lodge
Eco Lodge   ⓈⓈ   **Map** E5
Jr. Billinghurst s/n costado Plaza Grau
Tel *082 572 290*
🆆 wasai.com
Stilted, thatched bungalows and a terraced restaurant overlooking the Río Madre de Dios.

RESERVE DE LA BIOSFERA DE MANU: Manu Lodge
Eco Lodge   ⓈⓈⓈ   **Map** E4
Cocha Juarez Lake, 1/2 mile (1 km) from Río Manu
Tel *084 252 721*
🆆 manuperu.com
This well-established lodge is the only permanent accommodation within the reserve. Comfortable rooms; shared bathrooms.

RÍO HEATH: Heath River Wildlife Center
Eco Lodge   ⓈⓈⓈ   **Map** E5
4 hours by boat from Puerto Maldonado
Tel *01 440 2022*
🆆 inkanatura.com
Palm-thatched bungalows with hot showers, and tree-top bird-watching platform in a remote area on the Peru-Bolivia border.

DK Choice

RÍO TAMBOPATA: Tambopata Research Center
Eco Lodge   ⓈⓈⓈ   **Map** E5
8 hours up the Tambopata River
Tel *01 719 6422*
🆆 perunature.com
This comfortable lodge's remote location, steps away from the largest known macaw clay-lick in the Amazon, makes it a favored choice with visitors as well as biologists, ecologists, and other researchers. Rooms are simple, separated by cane thatching and connected by a boardwalk, with shared bathrooms and hot showers. Airy, spacious common areas include a bar and lounge.

TARAPOTO: Río Shilcayo
Inn   ⓈⓈ   **Map** C3
Pasaje Las Flores 224
Tel *042 522 225*
🆆 dmhoteles.pe
Set in delightful, flower-filled grounds. Choice of colorful standard rooms or bungalows.

YURIMAGUAS: El Naranjo
Inn   Ⓢ   **Map** C2
Calle Arica 318
Tel *065 352 650*
🆆 hostalelnaranjo.com.pe
One of the best lodgings available in town due to central location and cheerful decor.

For more information on types of hotels *see pages 271–2*

WHERE TO EAT AND DRINK

Peruvian cuisine is said to be one of the world's finest. French culinary master Auguste Escoffier (1846–1935) ranked it third behind French and Chinese food. The country's huge biodiversity produces an assortment of fresh ingredients from the mountains, the jungle, and the coast, and its cultural mix – a hybrid of Andean and Spanish traditions with Japanese, Chinese, Italian, and African influences – lends the cuisine its distinctive edge. Regional food on offer includes the coastal Creole cooking *cocina criolla*, the Peruvian-Japanese fusion *nikkei*, and *novoandina*, the new Andean cuisine that melds native ingredients with new recipes.

Restaurants and Bars

Lima offers the greatest choice of places to eat, with something to suit every taste. There are elegant restaurants headed by lauded chefs as well as traditional family-run eateries, and no shortage of restaurants and bars offering a fixed-price *menú*, usually including a *causa* (cold potato salad) or soup, main course, a small dessert, and a drink. Arequipa is also famous for the standard and variety of its restaurants and produce, and Cusco has an increasingly wide variety of choices.

Head to a *cebichería* to try seafood, while *anticucherías* specialize in grilled kebabs, *pollerías* serve roast chicken, and *sangucherías* offer Peruvian-style sandwiches. *Picanterías* are traditional home-style eateries found in Arequipa, while *chifas* fuse Peruvian and Chinese flavors. The country also has the highest number per capita of Chinese restaurants in Latin America. Buffets are a popular option in both *chifas* and Creole restaurants, with Sundays drawing large family groups.

Welcoming entrance of La Trattoria del Monasterio, Arequipa *(see p291)*

Huariques, or hiding places, which are usually known only to locals, are small family-run establishments in which the cook has perfected one or two signature dishes, perhaps a *cebiche* (see p283), a sandwich or a spicy one-pot stew, and their modest appearance belies the quality of the food served. It is advisable to go with someone in the know.

Most restaurants are casual, without a strict dress code, particularly outside Lima, but a jacket is advisable when going to higher-end restaurants.

Chain Restaurants

Most of the principal American fast-food chains are represented in Peru, including Pizza Hut, KFC, McDonald's, Burger King, and Dominos, as well as two Tony Roma's in Lima. There are also a number of homegrown alternatives including Bembos (hamburgers), D'nnos and La Romana (pizza), and Pardo's and Caravana (roast chicken).

Lima's upmarket café chains, San Antonio, La Baguette, and Café Café serve sandwiches, salads, and hot snacks from morning to night, while T'anta offers more expensive and substantial meals. There are several branches of Cebicherías Punta Sal, Señor Limon, and Segundo Muelle across Lima.

Food Hygiene

Health standards can vary, especially outside major cities, and it is worth taking a few precautions. Avoid salads and uncooked vegetables in all but the best restaurants and cafés; creamy mayonnaise is a favoured dressing and as it is often prepared well ahead, it is best to steer clear of it. Peruvians tend to eat *cebiche* for lunch when they believe it is at its freshest.

Avoid undercooked meat. Remember to peel all fruit, or wash it in a bacterial disinfectant available from supermarkets. Open-air markets and street stalls should be treated with caution, especially home-made ice-cream vendors who are known to refreeze thawed wares. Drink only purified water, canned or bottled still or carbonated drinks, spirits, or hot drinks.

Busy dining room at *cebichería* La Mar in Miraflores, Lima *(see p288)*

When to Eat

Restaurants in general don't open before 8am – except in Cusco and Iquitos where tourist schedules may dictate early starts – so early risers in search of *desayuno* (breakfast) should head for an international hotel or high-end cafés. Breakfast consists of bread, jam, and coffee, or sandwiches, although on weekends, most families will sit down to a *tamale* (steam-cooked corn dough with or without filling), or *chicharrón* (deep-fried pork and rind) with Creole onions.

Lunch, or *almuerzo*, is eaten late, usually from 1:30pm. Most *cebicherías* only open for lunch. For most Peruvians, lunch is the main meal of the day and consists of a first course followed by a fish or meat dish with rice. The Peruvian version of English late afternoon tea, *lonche*, has more substantial food such as lamb *brochettes*, *empanadas*, triple-decker sandwiches, door-stop cake wedges or pie, and a pisco sour or thick hot chocolate. Some Lima restaurants offer special promotions for *lonche*. Peruvians rarely make *cena* (dinner) reservations earlier than 9pm. If invited for drinks or dinner, locals seldom arrive on time, displaying a more relaxed Latin attitude.

Paying and Tipping

Restaurants in Peru are required to publish their prices, including taxes and a 10 percent service charge, but they don't always do so. The service charge is indicated by the words *propina* or *servicio* near the bottom of the bill. Things such as bread or live entertainment can incur an extra charge. Peruvians do not normally tip and tourists are not obliged to, but for good service, add 5–10 percent to the 10 percent already charged. Credit cards are accepted and many restaurants accept payment in US dollars.

Alcohol

Restaurants and cafés usually have licenses to sell alcohol, and top-end restaurants have good wine lists, with many international options. Naturally, Argentinian and Chilean labels are prominent, along with local Peruvian brands. Bringing your own is not generally an option, although some restaurants will allow it and will charge a corkage fee.

Sale of alcohol is not permitted, even in supermarkets, during federal and local elections due to a *ley seca* (dry law), which runs from Thursday night through to Sunday night when the voting booths have closed.

Wheelchair Access

Few restaurants in Peru have special facilities for wheelchair users. Access is difficult and assistance is required. Toilets that can accommodate a wheelchair are rare.

Children

The majority of Peruvian restaurants welcome children, especially family-run ones. Most well-off parents, however, bring their nannies along to take care of them. Usually, there is little room for strollers. Child portions are not that common but the staff are happy to provide an extra plate so children can share.

Recommended Restaurants

The restaurants featured in this guide are spread across a wide price range and have been selected for their value, good

La Rosa Náutica restaurant in Miraflores, Lima *(see p289)*

food, location, and atmosphere. From authentic, no-frills eateries to the pricey temples of the Peruvian culinary boom, these restaurants run the gamut across all price levels and cuisine types. Reservations are neither needed nor customary at middle- to lower-priced restaurants, but some higher-end venues may host private events at certain times of the year, or close unexpectedly for certain holidays, so it is always wise to consult a restaurant's website or call before visiting.

For the best of the best, look out for the restaurants under the heading DK Choice. These establishments have been highlighted in recognition of an exceptional feature – a celebrity chef, exquisite food, or an inviting atmosphere. Many of these are exceptionally popular among local residents and visitors, so get there early.

Plant-filled terrace at Arequipa's Crepísimo crepe café

The Flavors of Peru

Peruvian cuisine is one of the world's most varied and delicious. Staples such as potatoes, corn, peanuts, chilies, quinoa, and fresh seafood pre-date the Incas, while chicken, beef, pork, citrus fruits, olives, wine, cinnamon, and cloves came courtesy of the Spanish. The blending of Spanish, African, and Andean ingredients resulted in what's known as *comida criolla* (Creole food). Later waves of immigrants, including Chinese, Japanese, and Italians, added their own flavors. Peru boasts some 400 versions of the iconic dish *cebiche*, a testament to its culinary creativity.

Quinoa

Ripe corn cobs in different colors piled on a roadside stall

Peruvian Produce

Peru is home to 84 of the world's 114 biological zones, which results in a cornucopia of fresh ingredients. The Pacific Ocean is the source of superb fish and seafood. From the Andes come an astonishing range of potatoes and peppers. Wild mushrooms are grown in the Sacred Valley. The Amazon harvest includes bananas and manioc. Juicy prawns are caught in the Arequipa rivers. Mangoes, asparagus, limes, and black scallops, all thrive in the northern valleys and lakes.

Top Peruvian chef Gaston Acurio claims to be able to choose from 60 different varieties of fresh fruit and vegetables and 70 different types of seafood when he visits a Lima market. While the cuisine varies from region to region, reflecting local produce and culinary traditions, the use of native *aji* (dried Peruvian chilies) and aromatic herbs such as coriander, basil, *hierbabuena* (mint), and oregano, is a common thread. Ancient ceramics, with their images

Avocado Prickly pears Granadilla Limes Papaya Cape gooseberries Bananas

Selection of luscious Peruvian tropical fruits

Peruvian Dishes and Specialties

Peruvian meals begin with *piqueos* (snacks) such as *anticuchos* (grilled beef heart kebabs marinated in vinegar), *conchitas a la parmesana* (scallops with Parmesan), *humitas* (savory mashed corn steamed in corn husks), *causa* (cold mashed potato), or *tiradito* (similar to *cebiche*). Pachamanca may feature pork, lamb, beef, potatoes, broad (fava) beans, and corn wrapped in banana leaves, buried in a pit with white hot rocks, and steamed. Other main dishes include *adobo* (a pork stew with corn beer and spices, cooked in a clay pot), and Chinese-influenced *chaufa* (beef, rice, onions, tomatoes, peppers, and soy sauce). For dessert, the caramel-flavored fruit *lúcuma* is delicious in mousses or ice cream, while *picarones* (sweet pastries dunked in sugar syrup) are a popular treat.

Chilies

Cebiche is chunks of raw fish marinated in lime juice, onions, and chilies, served with corn and sweet potato.

Traders thronging the lively and vibrant market stalls in Cusco

of native fruit and vegetables and daily cooking rituals, detail Peruvians' enduring love for preparing food.

Legacy of the Incas

Inca dishes have survived through the centuries. *Pachamanca* (the Peruvian underground barbecue) and *carapulcra* (dehydrated potato stew with pork), are cooked much as they were 500 years ago. The ancient Peruvians freeze-dried potato to make *chuño*, and llama and alpaca meat to produce *charqui*, akin to a beef jerky. Both remain popular today.

Maiz (corn) is still a mainstay of the Peruvian diet. In pre-Hispanic times, as today, it was toasted, boiled, or made into *humitas* (mashed corn dumplings). *Cuy* (guinea pig) has been an essential source of

protein in Central Peru for 5,000 years. "Raise guinea pigs and eat well," proclaims an Inca saying. *Cuy* is omnipresent at Andean fiestas, and is still used by healers to diagnose illnesses. Peruvians consume some 22 million *cuys* a year.

In upmarket restaurants throughout Peru, new uses are being found for the ancient grain quinoa, known to the Incas as the "mother of all grains." Today, its mild, nutty flavor may

Tending a *pachamanca*, underground barbeque

turn up in dishes like *quinoto* (risotto) or added to *arroz con leche*, a rich rice pudding.

Out of Africa

Cinnamon and cloves, synonymous with Creole desserts, were brought to Peru by the Spanish but they initially came from the Moors who occupied southern Spain for 700 years. Later, African slaves in the kitchens of Peru's plantation houses made the most of discarded ingredients, such as filleting and marinating beef hearts to make the now ubiquitous *anticuchos* (kebabs), and creating *tacu-tacu* (spicy fried patties) as a way of using leftover beans and rice.

THE STORY OF CEBICHE

Pre-Hispanic cultures started Peru's *cebiche* tradition – "cooking" their fish using the juices and flesh of the *tumbo* (a type of passionfruit). Later, the Incas marinated fish in *chicha* (corn beer), and also salted their catch for transport into the mountains. The Spanish brought lemons and onions to the dish. The Japanese popularized scallops and prawns so much that they now rival Peruvian *corvina* (sea bass) and *lenguado* (sole) as *cebiche* staples. Peruvians hail the leftover *cebiche* juice, called *leche de tigre*, as the perfect cure for a hangover.

Lomo saltado features strips of beef, sautéed with onions, chilies, garlic, tomatoes, spices, and fried potatoes.

Rocotos rellenos are roasted red peppers stuffed with meat, tomatoes, raisins, and olives, served with a spicy sauce.

Suspiro a la limeña is a blend of condensed milk, egg yolks, cinnamon, and port, topped with meringue.

Flavors of Peru: the Potato

As Francisco Pizarro navigated the Andes intent on conquering the Incas, he probably gave little thought to the *papa* (potato) plant he trampled beneath his feet. Yet it was to be one of the most significant treasures the Spanish uncovered in Latin America. The potato is thought to have reached Europe in the 1560s on board Spanish galleons. A dozen ancient varieties still grow in the Canary Islands, relics of that first voyage. Europe now grows the highest number of potatoes, but Peru has the most varieties and has been dubbed the "Potato Capital of the World."

Sweet potatoes

Cooking potatoes on an open fire in Arequipa province

Gold of the Andes

The potato was first domesticated more than 6,000 years ago near Lake Titicaca, where the greatest diversity of wild species is still found. The Incas cultivated more than 1,000 varieties and, of the 3,000 types currently identified, hundreds are still commonly available in Andean markets. The potato is known by countless names in the Andes. To people in the highlands each potato is distinct – they will eat one kind for breakfast, a different one for lunch, and yet another variety for dinner. Like their ancestors before them, they revere the earth and, for them, the potato is its consummate blessing. Centuries ago, harvested potatoes were reburied among hot stones as an offering so that Pachamama (Mother Earth) could eat before the farm workers. This practice gave rise to the method of roasting food underground, still in use today, the *pachamanca*.

Andeans have also found many non-dietary uses for the potato, from curing ulcers and dissolving kidney stones with raw potato juice, to soothing burns with raw potato compresses, and even patting on a mashed potato beauty mask at night.

Potatoes are used in a large variety of Peruvian dishes, from *papas rellenas* (potato croquettes) to *chupe de camarones* (seafood chowder). Potatoes is even the key ingredient in a few local desserts.

Waka kkallu · Puku tarma · Luntus · Yana allkkay warmi · Milagro · Puka pina · Yana warmi

Some of the many varieties of Peruvian potato

Peruvian Potato Dishes and Specialties

For Limeños summer wouldn't be summer without a *causa rellena*. Cold, mashed yellow potato is layered with avocado, mayonnaise, poached fish or chicken, and topped with prawn tails. *Causa de pulpo* is stuffed with octopus in olive mayonnaise, and *causa verde* is tinted green with spinach and parsley and layered with crab meat. *Papa a la huancaína* pairs potatoes with a spicy cheese sauce garnished with black olives and hard-boiled egg. Creole influence is apparent in *papa rellena*, which is served with a *salsa criolla* of sliced onions, vinegar, and chili. African cooks influenced one of Peru's preferred sweet treats, *picarones*, replacing the wheat flour with mashed sweet potato and pumpkin and dipping them in a cinnamon-orange syrup.

Papas rellenas, potato croquettes, are filled with meat, egg, olives, tomatoes, onions, and paprika.

Reading the Menu

The list below gives the most common dishes and main ingredients, in alphabetical order, that visitors are likely to encounter on a Peruvian menu, both in Lima and regionally. However, not all dishes will be available in every region. *Cuy* (guinea pig) for example, is a specialty of the Central and Southern Highlands, while fish dishes will feature more strongly (and be better and fresher) near the coast. General vocabulary that will be useful when eating out can be found in the *Phrase Book* on pages 346–8.

Cilantro (coriander)

Aji de gallina chicken stew made with milk, Parmesan, bread, chilies and walnuts.
Ajis chilies, including *amarillo* (yellow), *panca* (purple), *mirasol* (orange).
Albahaca basil.
Alfajores wafer-thin discs of shortbread dusted with icing sugar, filled with caramelized condensed milk or honey.
Anticuchos beef heart kebabs.
Arroz con camarones river prawns with rice, seasoned with chili, paprika, and coriander.
Arroz con pato duck and rice cooked with beer.
Caldo de cabeza ram's head soup flavored with mint and chili.
Cancacho roasted pork or lamb marinated in chili and oil.
Cancha fried corn kernels.
Carapulcra boiled, dehydrated potato stew with pork, chicken, chilies, garlic, and spices.
Cau-cau tripe stew with potatoes, mint and *palillo* (a turmeric-like spice).
Causa rellena (see opposite).

Deep-fried *cuy* (guinea pig), the centerpiece at a village fiesta

Field worker prepares a meal of maize and potatoes

Chicharrones pork rinds fried in their own fat.
Chicharrones de pescado fried pieces of fish.
Chifles fried banana chips.
Chimichurri olive oil, parsley, and garlic sauce.
Chirimoya custard apple.
Choclo corn on the cob.
Chuño lawa beef soup with rice, *garbanzos* (chickpeas), and dehydrated potatoes.
Chupe de camarones chowder of river prawns, fish, milk, eggs, potatoes, chilies, and oregano.
Chupe de cangrejo crab chowder.
Conchitas negras black scallops.
Cuy chactado guinea pig fried under a stone.
Escabeche fish or chicken marinated in vinegar and steamed with onions.
Juane rice (seasoned with *palillo*) and chicken or fish cooked in banana leaves.
Lechón suckling pig.
Mani peanuts.
Maracuya passionfruit.
Mariscos shellfish.
Mazamorra morada purple corn pudding.

Mero grouper fish.
Ocopa boiled potatoes with cheese sauce, lima (butter) beans, onions, olives, and *rocoto*.
Palta avocado.
Parihuela de mariscos seafood soup.
Pesque de quinoa mashed quinoa with milk and cheese.
Picante de cuy guinea pig stew with peanuts and chilies.
Pollo a la brasa spit-roasted chicken.
Pulpo al olivo octopus in black olive mayonnaise.
Rocoto hot, red pepper.
Salsa criolla (see opposite).
Seco de cabrito stew of roasted kid marinated in corn liquor, with beans.
Solterito salad of cheese, lima beans, red onions, black olives, corn, and *rocoto*.
Sopa a la criolla mildly spicy noodle soup with beef, milk and peppers, often with a fried egg on top.
Tacu-tacu "pancake" of fried pork-flavored beans and rice, topped with steak, onion, salsa, and sometimes a fried egg.
Timbuche concentrated fish and coriander broth.
Tiradito very thin slices of raw fish, doused in lime juice and chili salsa.
Tres leches three layers of sponge cake soaked in condensed and evaporated milk and cream or milk.
Tumbo type of passionfruit.
Tuna prickly pear fruit.
Turron de Doña Pepa aniseed-flavored layered biscuit in fruit syrup.
Yuca cassava root.
Zapallo pumpkin.

What to Drink in Peru

The wide variety of drinks on offer in Peru range from the non-alcoholic, blindingly yellow Inca Kola to the national favorite, the potent pisco sour, a cocktail invented in the early 20th century in Lima's Maury Hotel's Rojo Bar. As a rule, never drink tap water and avoid fruit juices and other drinks in places where cleanliness levels are suspect. It is better to stick to pre-packaged drinks. Bottled *agua sin gas* (still water) or *agua con gas* (sparkling water) are readily available in reliable shops.

Classic poster of Coca wine, a popular tonic in the 1870s

Beer

Cerveza (beer) has existed in Peru for hundreds of years. Home brewed *chicha* (corn beer) is often sold at markets or during festivals. There are *chicherias* (corn beer bars) in northern towns. Other forms include *chicha de molle*, made from pepper tree seeds, and *chicha de siete semillas*, made from corn, wheat, barley, and chickpeas. The best-known beer brands of Peru are Cristal, Cusqueña, and Pilsen. Sweet dark beer, called *malta* or *cerveza negra*, is also available all over the country.

Cristal and Cusqueña beer

Other Alcoholic Drinks

Pisco is the undisputed king of Peruvian alcohol, appearing in the celebrated pisco sour, as well as variations such as a piscopolitan (with cranberry juice), *algarrobina* (with carob syrup), and pisco puro (straight). Other drinks include *masato*, made from fermented yuca, with sweet potato or with some sugar.

Pisco sour   Piscopolitan

Wines

The first vineyards in Peru were planted in the 1550s. Grapes from the principal vineyards *(see p126)*, located near Ica on the Southern Coast, go into making pisco. However, the vineyards of Tacama and Tabernero are also serious about wine-making. Tacama has had a French wine-maker at the helm of the harvest since 1961 and several wines from both producers have garnered international praise. Ocucaje also makes wine. Naturally, given the proximity, Chilean and Argentine imports abound.

Wine from Tacama

Cold Drinks

The bubble-gum flavored Inca Kola has been Peru's top-selling drink since 1935. But there are others, including Real Kola. Almost as popular is *chicha morada*, a non-fizzy drink made from boiled purple corn, apple peel, pineapple, and cloves. *Ponche*, common in the Central Highlands is a milk-based drink flavored with sesame seeds, spices, nuts, and grated coconut. *Chapo*, a banana and sugar juice, is a favorite in the jungles of Peru.

Inca Kola bottle

Hot Drinks

Matés (herbal teas), served black with lemon and sugar, are more popular than plain tea in Peru. *Manzanilla* (camomile) and *anís* (aniseed) are quite prevalent in the towns and cities of the country. *Maté de coca* (coca leaf tea) is believed to help in altitude sickness and is considered emblematic of the highlands. *Café americano* (medium- to low-strength filter) or instant coffee is common, although espressos and cappuccinos are also available in most major cities.

Coffee

Coca tea   Camomile

Pisco: Peru's Miracle Drink

Hailed as the miracle of the desert, pisco is Peru's national drink. Writer Ricardo Palma dubbed it as his "rousing pick-me-up." When Peruvian wine exports were banned by Spain, wine-makers here began to increase production of grape brandy, shipping it from the port of Pisco. Exports reached their height in the 17th–18th centuries. Pisco is considered a symbol of Peruvian resilience. Despite the Spanish embargo, the Chilean army's systematic destruction of cellars during the War of the Pacific *(see pp54–5)*, and failed agrarian reforms in the 1970s which saw some vines cut up for firewood, pisco has survived. As the Peruvians say, "Pisco is Peru."

How pisco is made

Pisco, a clear grape brandy or aguardiente, is distilled from fresh grape must in stills. The final product should be transparent without any kind of additives. It takes almost 13 lb (6 kg) of grapes to make one bottle of pisco.

Grapes were brought from the Canary Islands to Peru's arid south coast. Aided by the knowledge of ancient peoples who had worked out how to irrigate the desert, locals started making pisco.

Pisco in Quechua means bird and a valley. The potters who made the large conical vessels, in which the liquor was, and sometimes still is, stored, were also called piscos.

Distillation takes place in steel or copper stills. Then pisco is aged in clay barrels or other neutral containers for three months. No distilled water is added to alter its consistency.

Bottling is done with the same level of alcohol as when it was produced, officially 38-48 percent. The flavor comes from the fruit itself; there is no aging in oak barrels.

Pisco was recognized to be of Peruvian origins in 2005 by the World Intellectual Property Organization after a prolonged dispute with Chile.

How to drink Pisco

Pisco can be chilled and sipped straight. However, most Peruvians prefer it in the form of the pisco sour. All you need is three parts pisco mixed with lime juice, sugar syrup, egg white, ice cubes, and some Angostura bitters. Just bear in mind that the bitters are to be added right at the end. Peruvians are very serious about their national drink and the national Pisco Day is celebrated on February 8, every year.

Pisco sour

Where to Eat and Drink

Lima

Central Lima

L'Eau Vive ⓥ
French   Map 1 F1
Jirón Ucayali 370
Tel *01 427 5612*   **Closed** *Sun*
A French order of nuns serves
delicious cooking in a restored
18th-century home. The fixed-
price lunch is a bargain while the
à la carte dishes are slightly
pricier. Proceeds go to charity.

DK Choice

Café del Museo Larco ⓥⓥ
Peruvian
Av. Bolívar 1515, Pueblo Libre
Tel *01 462 4757*
A pleasant hacienda-style
restaurant in the Museo Larco
grounds with pre-Hispanic
and Colonial decor. The menu
includes a variety of appetizers
and larger servings. Try the
delicious deep-fried squid and
vegetarian lasagna. The
children's menu has pastas and
hamburgers. The café is also ideal
for after or pre-dinner drinks.

Sankuay (Chez Wong) ⓥⓥ
Seafood   Map 3 D1
Calle Enrique Leon Garcia 114
Tel *01 470 6217*   **Closed** *Sun*
This 10-table restaurant at Chef
Javier Wong's home has no menu.
He decides what to cook from the
freshest flounder and octopus.
Book two days ahead.

Miraflores

El AlmaZen ⓥ
Vegetarian   Map 4 B1
Recavarren 298
Tel *01 243 0474*   **Closed** *Sun*
Fresh, organic produce sourced
from local farms is used to create
tasty and creative vegetarian and

vegan dishes at this informal
restaurant. Wonderful lemonade,
plus raw and cooked salads.

Pastelería San Antonio ⓥ
Bakery/Café   Map 4 C2
Av. Vasco Nuñez de Balboa 770
Tel *01 626 1313*
Part of a patisserie chain founded
over 50 years ago, San Antonio
offers fresh fruit juices, excellent
salads and sandwiches, signature
pastries, and heavenly ice cream.

Brujas de Cachiche ⓥⓥ
Peruvian   Map 4 A1
Calle Bolognesi 472
Tel *01 447 1883*   **Closed** *Sat*
Traditional Peruvian dishes
including *anticuchos* (grilled
skewered meat), and *cabrita
norteña* (goat stew in coriander
with beans and rice). Try the
sophisticated lobster *au gratin*.

La Mar ⓥⓥ
Seafood   Map 2 B5
Av. La Mar 770
Tel *01 421 3365*   **Closed** *Dinner*
No reservations at this trendy
eatery, so reach by noon or be
prepared to queue up at the bar.
Raw and cooked seafood is pre-
pared and served in many ways.

Madam Tusan ⓥⓥ
Fusion   Map 2 C5
Av. Santa Cruz 859
Tel *01 505 5090*
Chinese cuisine with a Peruvian
twist that upgrades the standard
chifa classics. Great dim sum,
roast duck, sweet barbecued
pork, deep-fried spicy chicken,
and fortune cookies.

Pescados Capitales ⓥⓥ
Seafood   Map 2 A5
Av. La Mar 1337
Tel *01 421 8808*
The name of this restaurant is a
play on the words *pescado* (fish)
and *pecado* (sin), as reflected in

the "deadly fins" menu. Superb
cebiche, raw fish in citrus juice.

DK Choice

T'anta ⓥⓥ
Bistro   Map 4 C2
Av. 28 de Julio 888
Tel *01 447 8377*
An upscale delicatessen by
Astrid Gutsche, wife of world-
renowned Peruvian chef Gastón
Acurio. Come here for cool
cocktails or coffee, wonderful
light meals, sandwiches, and
rich desserts. Pick up sun-dried
tomatoes and special breads, or
a few sautéed beef *empanadas*
to take home.

Wa Lok ⓥⓥ
Fusion   Map 2 C5
Av. Angamos Oeste 700
Tel *01 447 1314*
The hybrid Cantonese-Peruvian
cooking at Wa Lok includes crispy
roast duck, whole fried fish, sweet
and sour pork, and *chaufa* (fried
rice). Family menu options for
five are a good bargain.

Astrid & Gastón ⓥⓥⓥ
Novoandina   Map 4 C1
Calle Cantuarias 175
Tel *01 242 4422*   **Closed** *Sun, Mon*
Celebrity Chef Gastón Acurio and
his wife Astrid's first restaurant
ranks among the top 50 in the
world. New Peruvian cooking
combining Andean ingredients
and contemporary trends.

Central Restaurante ⓥⓥⓥ
International   Map 2 A4
Calle Santa Isabel 376
Tel *01 242 8515*   **Closed** *Sun*
The menu here changes six times
a year and offers the chance to
sample much of Peru's cuisine.
Try a plate of Arapaima fish, from
the Amazon jungle, or *chuno* (a
potato dish) from the Andes.

Costanera 700 ⓥⓥⓥ
Fusion   Map 2 B5
Av. El Ejercito 421
Tel *01 421 4635* **Closed** *Sun dinner*
Chef Humberto Sato is a legend
of Japanese-Peruvian fusion
cooking. The menu includes beef,
goat, and wild duck dishes but

Modern interior of T'anta, Lima

the emphasis is on fish – raw and cooked, plus sashimi and sushi.

La Trattoria di Mambrino ⊚⊚⊚
Italian   **Map** 4 B1
Calle Manuel Bonilla 106
Tel *01 446 7002*
Rated as one of Lima's best Italian restaurants. Savor delicious spaghetti with crayfish, pappardelle with rabbit ragout, and New York-style raspberry cheesecake.

Brightly colored decor in one of the dining rooms at Laeñe, Lima

---

DK Choice

Laeñe ⊚⊚⊚
Mediterranean   **Map** 4 B1
Av. Dos de Mayo 220
Tel *01 447 4807*   **Closed** *Sun dinner*
Classic Spanish and other Mediterranean cuisine served in a colorfully refurbished 19th-century house with a choice of three dining rooms. The menu includes oxtail stew, Valencia-style *paella*, tender Segovia-style roast pig, and rich desserts. Enjoy drinks and tapas in the bar or on the terrace.

La Rosa Náutica ⊚⊚⊚
International   **Map** 4 A2
Espigón 4 beach circuit
Tel *01 445 0149*
Built on a pier jutting out into the sea, this restaurant offers great seafood, tournedos, duck magret, and wonderful desserts. Stop by for lunch, drinks at sunset, or dinner. Extensive wine list. Fixed-price dining in the evenings.

Rafael ⊚⊚⊚
International   **Map** 4 B2
Calle San Martin 300
Tel *01 242 4149*   **Closed** *Sat lunch; Sun*
Chef Rafael Osterling is a culinary artist and ranks among the best cooks in the world. His unique creations include crispy fish in Thai curry sauce, goat baked in Madeira, and duck with cilantro rice. Excellent wine list.

San Isidro

San Ceferino ⊚⊚
Italian   **Map** 2 B2
Av. Dos de Mayo 793
Tel *01 422 8242*
This popular hunting-lodge style trattoria offers a wide variety of Peruvian and Mediterranean fusion dishes including fresh pastas, risottos, seafood, meats, and wood-fired pizzas.

Segundo Muelle ⊚⊚
Seafood   **Map** 3 D2
Av. Rivera Navarrete 530
Tel *01 717 9997*   **Closed** *Dinner*
Choose from a wide selection of fresh seafood including scallop *cebiche*, tuna and octopus *carpaccio*, and wok-fried Chinese vegetables with fish, calamari, and prawns at this local favorite.

Toshiro's Sushi Bar ⊚⊚⊚
Japanese   **Map** 2 C3
Av. Conquistadores 450
Tel *01 221 7243*   **Closed** *Sun*
Chef and owner Toshiro Konishi is a master of authentic Japanese cuisine, to which he adds Peruvian ingredients. A haven of delicious miso soups, sashimi, tempura, and *teishoku* (set meals).

Barranco

Las Mesitas ⊚
Café   **Map** 5 D4
Grau 341
Tel *01 477 4199*
A small, pleasant place with wood-paneling and marble-top tables. Serves generous portions of tasty regional home cooking. The Peruvian desserts are popular with the locals.

Rustica ⊚
Peruvian/Italian   **Map** 4 C4
Parque Municipal 105–7
Tel *01 247 9385*
This branch of a restaurant chain is located on a beach. Opt for the large lunchtime buffet of tasty *criollo* dishes or select from the à la carte menu, which is also available in the evening.

Sonia ⊚
Seafood   **Map** 5 D5
Agustin Lozano La Rosa 173
Tel *01 249 6850*
Wooden tables, a polished cement floor, a bamboo roof, and fishing paraphernalia are the backdrop for healthy portions of fresh seafood including *cebiche*, fried calamari, and prawn risotto.

Costa Verde ⊚⊚
International   **Map** 4 C4
Playa Barranquito s/n
Tel *01 247 1244*
The sumptuous lunch buffet is a popular draw at this seashore restaurant. À la carte dishes include Peruvian cuisine, *maki*, sushi, and other international fare. Fixed-price buffet also available.

El Hornero ⊚⊚
Grill   **Map** 5 D5
Av. Malecón Graú 983
Tel *01 251 8109*
This classic grill, overlooking the bay of Lima, offers grilled mushrooms, Angus beef, salmon, and suckling pig. The pepper steak sauce is especially flavorsome. The restaurant has a range of Spanish, Chilean, and Argentinian wines.

Cala ⊚⊚⊚
International   **Map** 4 C4
Playa Barranquito, Espigón B-2, Circuito Vial Costa Verde
Tel *01 252 9187*
Sleek decor and ocean views set the tone for sophisticated fare. Seafood, meats, rice, pasta, and rich desserts, all made with Peruvian flair. The trendy bar serves *maki* and other appetizers.

The Southern Coast

CHINCHA ALTA: El Batán ⊚⊚
Peruvian   **Map** C5
Panamericana Sur Km 791
Tel *056 268 050*
This spacious, cafeteria-style eatery is a great pit stop en route to the south. Choose from delicious freshwater *camarones* (shrimps), good pastas, soups, and salads.

For more information on types of restaurants *see page 280*

HUACACHINA:
Hotel Mossone ⓢⓢ
Peruvian/International **Map** C5
Balneario de Huacachina s/n
Tel *056 213 630*
Hotel Mossone's restaurant has excellent regional cuisine and also specialises in seafood. There is indoor seating, a pleasant veranda, and a wood-paneled bar.

ICA: Anita ⓢ
Café **Map** C5
Calle Libertad 133
Tel *056 218 582*
Anita serves sandwiches, generous portions of regional mains including chicken, beef and seafood, plus delicious desserts, cakes, and pies. Stop by for breakfast or the fixed-price lunch.

ICA: El Paraíso ⓢ
Vegetarian **Map** C5
Calle Loreto 178
Tel *056 228 308* **Closed** *Sat*
Vegan and vegetarian dishes served in a small, two-room restaurant. Good, classic Peruvian cooking using soy instead of chicken or beef. Pies, puddings, and a set lunch menu available.

DK Choice

ICA: El Otro Peñoncito ⓢⓢ
Peruvian **Map** C5
Calle Bolivar 255
Tel *056 233 921*
Three generations of kitchen expertise makes this a local favorite for lunch or an intimate dinner. Come here for large pisco sours, excellent seafood, and pastas. Regional specialties include *pollo a la Iqueña* (chicken in a rich pecan, pisco, and spinach sauce), and *lomo saltado* (beef stir-fry).

ICA: Pizzeria Venezia ⓢⓢ
Italian **Map** C5
San Martin 1229
Tel *056 210 372*
Italian family-owned eatery serving home-made gnocchi, ravioli, and other pastas, soups, salads, and steak. Choose from a variety of pizzas, including vegetarian options.

ICA: Las Dunas ⓢⓢⓢ
International **Map** C5
Av. La Angostura 500
Tel *056 256 224*
Classic Peruvian dishes with contemporary flair, fantastic cocktails, and delectable desserts. There is a lunch buffet on Sunday and weekend shows.

NAZCA: Don Hono ⓢ
Regional **Map** C5
Calle Maria Reiche 112
Tel *056 506 822*
Reliably good and hearty portions of regional dishes including stir-fried shrimp and lima beans with breaded steak. Served in a large dining room.

NAZCA: El Portón ⓢ
Italian/Regional **Map** C5
Calle Ignacio Morsesky 1260
Tel *056 523 490*
Renowned for its delicious pastas, including a seafood lasagna. El Portón also offers pizzas and a buffet of regional dishes such as *ají de gallina* (creamy chicken curry).

NAZCA: Los Angeles ⓢ
Peruvian/Vegetarian **Map** C5
Bolognesi 266
Tel *056 431 688*
A no-frills, great-value restaurant offering tasty Creole-style food. Soups, salads, a wide variety of vegetarian dishes, plus meat and seafood on offer. The owner is fluent in English and French.

PISCO: Puro Pisco ⓢⓢ
Seafood/Peruvian **Map** C5
Av. Genaro Medrano 460, San Andrés
Tel *056 542 384*
This restaurant offers a sophisticated touch to the fresh and tasty coastal dishes of Peru. The menu includes sole, sea bass, and shellfish, plus classic Peruvian beef and chicken options.

Canyon Country

AREQUIPA: La Cantarilla ⓢ
International/Peruvian **Map** D6
Calle Tahuaycani 106
Tel *054 251 515*
Arequipa's favourite open-air restaurant is a bastion of regional cuisine including *rocotos rellenos*

(stuffed peppers). Freshwater shrimps is the key ingredient in many dishes.

DK Choice

AREQUIPA: Crepísimo ⓢ
Creperie **Map** D6
Santa Catalina 208
Tel *054 206 620*
Owned by the Alliance Française, this informal café is set in a Colonial house. The menu has over 100 varieties of sweet and savory crepes, as well as fruit juices, frappés, coffee, and South American and European wines. The outdoor terrace has great views. There is a lounge with books and parlor games.

AREQUIPA: Laksmivan ⓢ
Vegetarian **Map** D6
Calle Jerusalén 402
Tel *054 228 768*
A good option for vegetarians with an extensive array of salads and fruit juices, as well as dishes such as spinach lasagna, and *paella*.

AREQUIPA: Mixto's ⓢ
International **Map** D6
Pasaje La Catedral 115
Tel *054 205 343*
A diverse menu with classic regional dishes, Spanish tortillas, pizzas, pastas, and good pisco sours. Located in a pedestrian alley behind the cathedral.

AREQUIPA:
El Mesón del Virrey ⓢⓢ
Peruvian **Map** D6
San Francisco 305
Tel *054 202 080*
Spacious restaurant with upscale Spanish Colonial decor. The varied menu includes octopus in olive sauce, quinoa with shrimp or honey,

Crepísimo, a popular creperie in Arequipa

Arched dining area with stained-glass windows in the background at Zig Zag, Arequipa

alpaca steak, and trout and asparagus lasagna.

AREQUIPA: El Viñedo
Grill　　　　　　Map D6
Calle San Francisco 319
Tel *054 205 053*
Grilled alpaca and lamb, wood-fired oven pizzas, pastas as well as regional cuisine at this sprawling place with a garden courtyard. Has a salad bar as well. Good choice for groups.

AREQUIPA: Sol de Mayo
Regional　　　　Map D6
Calle Jerusalen 207, Yanahuara
Tel *054 254 148*
Traditional Andean cooking served on tables with parasols in a sunny garden. Appetizers, soups, and main courses created with local ingredients. Coastal cuisine available as well. Music and dance shows on weekends.

AREQUIPA: Chicha
Fusion/Novoandina　Map D6
Calle Santa Catalina 210, Interior 105
Tel *054 287 360*
A modern space in a Colonial building, where the chef Acurio whips up innovative cuisine using regional ingredients. Soups, salads, pastas, stews, meats, and desserts on offer.

AREQUIPA: La Trattoria del Monasterio
Italian　　　　　Map D6
Santa Catalina 309
Tel *054 204 062*　**Closed** *Sun dinner*
Three cozy, elegant dining rooms in former monastery cloisters. Sophisticated Italian fare including spaghetti with *camarones*, risottos, osso buco, and tortellini stuffed with ricotta and asparagus.

AREQUIPA: Zig Zag
Peruvian　　　　Map D6
Zela 210, Cercado
Tel *054 206 020*

Warm, colorful restaurant with an antique iron staircase designed by Gustave Eiffel. The cuisine is a blend of Alpine and Andean gastronomy. The menu includes appetizers, meats, and salmon cooked on volcanic stones.

PUNO: Casa del Corregidor
Café　　　　　　Map E6
Jirón Deustua 576
Tel *051 35 1921*
Simple café fare, beer, and world-class local Tunki coffee served in the cozy setting of a historic 17th-century home. A sunny courtyard with umbrella-topped tables.

PUNO: Pizzeria El Buho
Italian　　　　　Map E6
Jirón Libertad 240
Tel *051 356 223*
Popular with locals and visitors alike, El Buho offers 23 varieties of pizza, cooked in an adobe wood-fired oven, as well as lasagna, cannelone, and fettucine. Good beer and wine list.

The Inca Heartland

CUSCO: Greens Organic
Organic　　　　Map D5
Santa Catalina Angosta 135
Tel *084 254 753*
Sit on a balcony with a view and choose from a large menu of home-made granola, fruit, and vegetable juices, and eggs Benedict. Serves alpaca with ratatouille, quinoa and spinach ravioli, wraps, and Brazil nut pie.

CUSCO: Inkazuela
International　　　Map D5
Plazoleta Nazarenas 167
Tel *084 234 924*　**Closed** *Sun*
Enjoy Peruvian and Latin American flavors in a colorful setting. The menu features tasty soups and stews cooked in clay

pots, fresh tuna, and dishes that consist of several varieties of potatoes.

CUSCO: La Bodega 138
Italian　　　　　Map D5
Herrajes 138
Tel *084 260 272*　**Closed** *Sun*
A family home converted into a relaxed restaurant. Feast on delicious wood-fired, thin-crust pizzas, spaghetti carbonara, ravioli with ragout or ricotta and kale, and tagliatelle with mushrooms.

CUSCO: La Pizza Carlo
Pizzeria　　　　Map D5
Calle Maruri 381
Tel *084 247 777*
Highly rated thin-crust pizzas, good lasagna, and calzone at this small, friendly eatery. Toppings and fillings include the classics: try the cheese and *rocoto* (pepper).

CUSCO: Pachapapa
Peruvian/Italian　Map D5
Plazoleta San Blas 120
Tel *084 241 318*
Peruvian specialties including roasted guinea pig (pre-orders necessary) and *lomo saltado* (beef stir-fry) served in a pleasant heated courtyard.

CUSCO: Baco
International　　　Map D5
Calle Ruinas 465
Tel *084 242 808*
A refined setting with dark wood furniture, colorful walls, modern art, and a cozy bar. Savor grilled alpaca, Argentinian steak, and gourmet pizzas. Good wine list.

CUSCO: Deva Restaurant
Regional/Vegetarian　Map D5
Calle San Agustín 280
Tel *084 247 727*
Regional cuisine with a modern twist. Consistently good hearty soups, *quinotto*, alpaca and guinea pig stews . Good Peruvian wines.

Bright decor and comfortable seating at Greens Organic, Cusco

For more information on types of restaurants *see page 280*

Elegantly laid out table at Inka Grill, an upscale restaurant in Cusco

CUSCO: Olas Bravas
Seafood   Map D5
Av. La Cultura, Mariscal Gamarra 11A
Tel *084 439 328*
Come here for generous servings
of *cebiche* (raw fish cured in citrus
juice) and other coastal seafood
dishes. Fresh fish is flown in daily
from Lima.

CUSCO: Cicciolina   ⓢⓢⓢ
International   Map D5
Calle Triunfo 393
Tel *084 239 510*
Fine dining in a chic restaurant
and tapas bar, with its own bakery
that opens for breakfast. The
menu includes duck and alpaca
dishes, trout, beetroot ravioli, and
risotto. Extensive wine list.

CUSCO: Incanto   ⓢⓢⓢ
Peruvian/Italian   Map D5
Calle Santa Catalina Angosta 135
Tel *084 254 753*
Modern bistro with Inca-style
architectural features. Specialties
include tenderloin in Marsala
wine, squid ink pasta, and
fettuccini with smoked sausage.
Relish the chocolate cake in
orange syrup.

CUSCO: Inka Grill   ⓢⓢⓢ
Regional   Map D5
Portal de Panes 115
Tel *084 262 992*   **Closed** *Sun*
A spacious, attractive restaurant
on the main square. Salads include
trout or quinoa-crusted shrimp
and avocado. Order criollo platter
followed by grilled or roasted
guinea pig, alpaca, or trout.

CUSCO: Map Café   ⓢⓢⓢ
Novoandina   Map D5
Plazoleta Nazarenas 231
Tel *084 242 476*
An elegant space in the Museo
de Arte Precolombino, offering
exquisitely prepared food. Ideal
for lunch or dinner after a visit to
the museum.

CUSCO: Marcelo Batata ⓢⓢⓢ
Fusion   Map D5
Calle Palacio 121, 2nd floor
Tel *084 222 824*
Innovative use of local
ingredients in dishes such as
smoked guinea pig ham, lamb
ribs and three cheeses, and
smoked trout causa. A selection
of pisco cocktails on offer.
Fantastic views from the terrace.

DK Choice

CUSCO: Tunupa   ⓢⓢⓢ
International   Map D5
Portal Confituria 233
Tel *084 252 936*
Experience the full flavor of
Cusco, both in food and music,
with pretty views of the Plaza
de Armas from the balcony.
The extensive buffet features
traditional Andean dishes as
well as Thai and Japanese
starters and desserts. Try
the alpaca *carpaccio* or Andean
ravioli trilogy from the à la
carte options.

OLLANTAYTAMBO: El Albergue
Restaurant   ⓢ
Peruvian/European   Map D5
Estación de Tren
Tel *084 204 014*
This rustic yet elegant
restaurant has an open kitchen
and serves dishes made with
organic produce from its own
farm. Favorites include barbecue
pork ribs, cheese-stuffed
peppers, and alpaca in
elderberry sauce. The brownies
are excellent.

URUBAMBA: El Huacatay ⓢⓢ
Peruvian fusion   Map D5
Jirón Arica 620
Tel *084 201 790*   **Closed** *Sun*
Gourmet food in a relaxed
family restaurant. Innovative
creations include purple corn

and chicken soup, parmesan-
stuffed potatoes, red vegetable
curry with coconut rice, and
alpaca lasagna.

Central Sierra

AYACUCHO: El Monasterio ⓢ
Peruvian   Map D5
Jirón 28 de Julio 178
Tel *066 312 343*
Regional dishes and large portions
of excellent roast chicken and
fried potatoes served in the
pleasant Colonial courtyard
of the Centro Cultural.

AYACUCHO: La Casona   ⓢ
Grill   Map D5
Jirón Bellido 463
Tel *066 312 733*
Light and airy eatery set around
a pretty courtyard. Generous
portions of Andean specialties as
well as grilled meats, trout, and
wood-fired roast pork.

AYACUCHO: Lalo's Café ⓢ
Café   Map D5
Jirón 28 de Julio 178
Tel *066 311 331*   **Closed** *Sun*
A popular venue in the
Centro Cultural courtyard with
a well-stocked bar. A large
selection of sandwiches and
light meals including salads,
pastas, local favourites, delicious
cakes, and pastries.

AYACUCHO: Pizzeria Italiana ⓢ
Italian   Map D5
Jirón Bellido 490
Tel *066 317 574*
A large wood-fired oven warms
up this small and cozy
restaurant. Serves excellent
thin-crust pizzas, cheese-stuffed
garlic bread, lasagna,
fettuccine, ravioli, and jugs of
good sangria.

The glassed-enclosed dining space at
Map Café, Cusco

DK Choice

AYACUCHO: ViaVia Café ⓢ
Café   **Map** D5
Portal Constitución 4
Tel *066 312 834*   **Closed** *Sun*
This bright travelers' café overlooking the Plaza de Armas, is a part of a chain of cafés across Africa, Asia, and Europe. It is inexpensive and offers a variety of breakfasts and fixed price four-course menus. Choose from soups, salads, *lomo saltado* (beef stir-fry) and Belgian stew made from local produce. Also a good range of cocktails, Belgian beer, and delicious fruit juices.

**HUANCAVELICA: Café
Restaurante Joy** ⓢ
Regional   **Map** C5
Jirón Virrey Toledo 230
Tel *067 752 860*
Small café with a limited menu of well-prepared dishes served in generous portions. Excellent grilled trout, fried chicken, and classic Peruvian dishes include soups and stews with rice.

**HUANCAVELICA: Fuente de
Soda La Española** ⓢ
Café   **Map** C5
Jirón Virrey Toledo 283
Tel *067 751 407*
Located just off the Plaza de Armas, this café serves regional dishes such as roast and deep-fried guinea pig, *lomo saltado* (beef stir-fry), sandwiches, fruit juices, breakfasts, and desserts.

**HUANCAVELICA:
La Olla de Barro** ⓢ
Regional   **Map** C5
Av. Agustín Gamarra 305
Tel *067 752 593*
Regional specialties such as *el patachi* (meat stew), trout, and guinea pig, plus well-prepared Creole dishes including beef stews and coriander chicken served with rice. Good service and pleasant atmosphere

**HUANCAVELICA: Mochica
Sachún** ⓢ
Regional   **Map** C5
Jirón Virrey Toledo 303
Tel *067 752 613*
Simple, hearty regional fare and sandwiches served at this cheerful place. Excellent-value lunch set menu including soup, a main course and a dessert.

HUANCAYO: Coqui ⓢ
Bakery/Café   **Map** C4
Puno 296
Tel *064 234 707*

Modern bakery and coffee shop serving sandwiches, empanadas, pastries, fruit juices, ice cream, and good coffee. Pizzas, salads, and main courses as well. A block away from Huancayo's main square.

HUANCAYO: Huancahuasi ⓢ
Regional   **Map** C4
Av. Mariscal Castilla 2222, El Tambo
Tel *064 244 826*
Generous servings of tasty dishes including duck with coriander rice, and *patasca* (maize and beef stew). Guitar music and *pachamanca* on weekends. Sit at a patio table or in the large, airy dining room.

**HUANCAYO: Olímpico
Restaurant** ⓢ
Peruvian   **Map** C4
Giraldez 199
Tel *064 291 515*
A family business since 1941, this restaurant has a modern decor, an open kitchen and a bar, and remains busy from breakfast through dinner. Offers great sandwiches, pastas, Creole dishes, and a Sunday lunch buffet.

HUÁNUCO: Chifa Khon Wa ⓢ
Fusion   **Map** C4
General Prado 816
Tel *062 513 609*
Large portions of Peruvian-Cantonese classics including wonton soup, spicy chicken fried rice, sweet-sour pork and a variety of stir-fries. Play area for kids

**HUÁNUCO:
Pizzeria Don Sancho** ⓢ
Pizzeria   **Map** C4
General Prado 645
Tel *062 516 906*
A vast range of wood-fired pizzas as well as pancakes, sandwiches, and good desserts make this a popular spot with tourists and young locals. Friendly service.

ViaVia Café, a Belgian run café-restaurant in Ayacucho

Cordillera Blanca

CARAZ: Café de Rat ⓢ
Café   **Map** B3
Jirón Sucre 1266, Plaza de Armas
Tel *043 391 642*   **Closed** *Sun*
Warm, friendly spot with a fireplace, music, a bar, and a balcony overlooking the main square. Serves sandwiches, large pizzas, pancakes, and a generous buffet breakfast.

CARAZ: Café La Terraza ⓢ
International   **Map** B3
Jirón Sucre 1107
Tel *043 301 226*
This large, cheerful place offers a tasty, great-value lunch menu. Stop by for pizzas, sandwiches, good espresso, and home-made Italian-style ice cream.

CARAZ: La Punta Grande ⓢ
Regional   **Map** B3
Daniel Villar 595
Tel *043 391 131*
A spacious restaurant with garden. Good Andean fare including guinea pig, beef, pork, chicken, and venison from locally raised deer. A 10-minute walk from downtown.

CARAZ: Pollería Jeny ⓢ
Peruvian   **Map** B3
Jirón Daniel Villar, Plaza de Armas
Tel *043 391 101*
Located on the main square, this well-established eatery serves scrumptious roast chicken along with traditional rice and meat dishes. Steak and trout are pricier.

CARHUAZ: Café El Abuelo ⓢ
Café   **Map** B4
Plaza de Armas
Tel *043 394 149*
A small café serving breakfasts, sandwiches, fresh coffee, and interesting ice cream flavors. Uses organic ingredients from the fruit and vegetable garden at El Abuelo *hostal*.

HUARAZ: Bistro de los Andes ⓢ
International   **Map** B4
*Jirón Julián de Morales 823,
Plaza de Armas*
Tel *043 726 249*
The multilingual owners offer a menu with French and Peruvian influence. Good wine menu and great views.

HUARAZ: California Café ⓢ
Café   **Map** B4
Jirón 28 de Julio 562
Tel *043 428 354*
A friendly place serving California-style breakfasts all day, as well as freshly roasted coffee, herbal teas, light meals, and salads. There is also a book exchange and a music collection.

Warm decor and candles on the bar at Trivio, Huaraz

A block away from the main square, this popular restaurant is ideal for the adventurous. Try the *chirimpico* – goat offal and coriander stew – a traditional breakfast.

CHICLAYO: El Huaralino ⑤
Regional   Map B3
Libertad 155
Tel *074 270 330*
Seafood, chicken, turkey, and duck are the basis for tender stews and rice dishes using summer squash, cilantro, corn, and yucca. Well-prepared, and elegantly served classic north coast cuisine.

DK Choice

HUARAZ: Café Andino ⑤
Café   Map B4
Jirón Lucar y Torre 530
Tel *043 721 203*
A relaxed, informal place with views over the Andes from the balcony. The extensive menu comprises special teas, freshly roasted coffee, and a selection of food including waffles, pastas, hamburgers, and desserts. Pick up an international magazine, a newspaper, or a book from the library and read by the fireplace or play a board game.

HUARAZ: California Café ⑤
Café   Map B4
Jirón 28 de Julio 562
Tel *043 428 354*
A warm, friendly, popular place serving California-style breakfasts all day, as well as freshly roasted coffee, herbal teas, light meals, and salads. Book exchange and a music collection.

HUARAZ:
Sabor Salud Pizzeria ⑤
Vegetarian   Map B4
Av. Luzurriaga 672
Tel *043 423 443*
Try vegetarian meals with an Italian twist including pizzas, spinach lasagna, pastas, and garlic bread at this charming eatery. Salads, yogurt, omelets, muesli, and soy burgers are also available.

HUARAZ: Chilli Heaven ⑤⑤
International   Map B4
Parque Ginebra
Tel *043 396 085*
The Anglo-Peruvian couple that own this restaurant cook exceptionally good food including biryani, Thai curry, chicken masala, burritos, and delicious home-made pastas. English ale also available.

HUARAZ: Creperie Patrick ⑤⑤
International   Map B4
Av. Luzurriaga 422
Tel *043 426 037*
Savory and sweet crepes are the stars but the resident French chef also serves delicious onion soup and fondues. Enjoy breakfast on the rooftop patio.

HUARAZ: El Horno
Pizzería Grill ⑤⑤
International   Map B4
Parque del Periodista,
Av. Luzurriaga 6th cuadra
Tel *043 424 617*
Gorge on tasty dishes from the extensive menu, such as pizzas, pastas, *anticuchos* (grilled skewered meat), pepper steak, and grilled meats. Good Peruvian wines. Lively terrace.

HUARAZ: Inka Pub
Monte Rosa ⑤⑤
International   Map B4
Jirón José de la Mar 661
Tel *043 421 447*
The Swiss owner offers an enticing menu of raclette, beef Stroganoff, vegetarian and Provençale pizzas, and cheese fondue in a chalet-style ambience.

HUARAZ: Trivio ⑤⑤
International   Map B4
Parque del Periodista, Av. Luzurriaga
Tel *051 943 919 840*
Salads, fresh pastas, pepper steak, and chocolate mousse on offer at this taproom-restaurant. Serves Sierra Andina beer. Live music and jazz evenings occasionally.

The Northern Desert

CHICLAYO: Bar Restaurante
Romana ⑤
Regional   Map B3
Av. Balta 512
Tel *074 223 598*

DK Choice

CHICLAYO: Fiesta Restaurant
Gourmet ⑤⑤
Regional   Map B3
Av. Salaverry 1829
Tel *074 201 970*
This top-end chain opened in 1983 has two other restaurants in Lima and Tacna. The specialty is the traditional cuisine of Lambayeque, cooked by age-old methods and served in a contemporary gourmet style, featuring free-range duck and baby goat, seafood, plus tasty rice dishes. The coriander-seasoned *pato con arroz* (duck with rice) is a must-try.

HUANCHACO: Casa Tere ⑤
Italian   Map B3
Jirón Larco 280, Plaza de Armas
Tel *044 461 197*
Casa Tere is a pretty restaurant set in a late 19th-century summer home decorated with antiques and old photographs. Serves pastas, pizzas, and great desserts.

HUANCHACO: Lucho del Mar ⑤
Seafood   Map B3
Av. Victor Larco 602
Tel *044 461 460*
One of the several restaurants in Huanchaco overlooking the beach, Lucho del Mar serves generous portions of excellent *cebiche* (raw fish cured in citrus fruit), and grilled, steamed, or deep-fried fish and shellfish.

HUANCHACO: Otra Cosa ⑤
Vegetarian   Map B3
Av. Victor Larco 921, Urb. El Boquerón
Tel *044 461 346*
Run by a Dutch-Peruvian couple, Otra Cosa is the only vegetarian restaurant in Huanchaco. Good coffees, juices, salads, fruits, desserts, and ice creams. Visit for energizing breakfasts, as well as delicious lunches and dinners.

HUANCHACO: Big Ben ⓢ
Seafood **Map** B3
Av. Larco 1884, Urb. El Boquerón
Tel *044 461 869*
Located in a three-story set of shaded terraces overlooking the ocean. Specialties include grilled Parmesan scallops and tasty *parihuela* (soup with crab, fish, shellfish, and seaweed).

HUANCHACO: Club Colonial ⓢⓢ
Peruvian/International **Map** B3
Av. de La Rivera 514
Tel *044 461 015*
The terrace-restaurant at the Club Colonial hotel offers great sea views. Classic Peruvian and tasty international dishes, including chicken in tarragon and mushroom sauce.

LAMBAYEQUE: El Rincón del Pato ⓢ
Regional **Map** B3
Av. Augusto B. Leguía 270
Tel *074 282 751*
Duck cooked in more than 25 ways is the specialty; try the ragout with peas. Chicken and fish dishes available. Perfect for lunch after a visit to the Museo Tumbas Reales de Sipán.

MÁNCORA: Angela's Place ⓢ
Peruvian/Austrian **Map** A2
Av. Piura 396
Tel *073 258 603* **Closed** *Sat*
Angela Schwitzberger offers excellent options for vegetarians and non-fish eaters, including smoothies and exotic pizzas. Also serves an excellent beef goulash. Friendly atmosphere.

MÁNCORA: Bananas Café ⓢ
Café **Map** A2
Av. Piura 224
Tel *01 968 769 702*
Order the good-value breakfast special comprising two large vegetarian sandwiches and a tall glass of fresh fruit juice. Drop in for pizzas in the evenings.

MÁNCORA: Pipo's Pizza ⓢ
Seafood/Italian **Map** A2
Av. Grau 149
Tel *073 411 333* **Closed** *Wed lunch*
Pipo Lombardi serves classic beachside fish starters and main courses include pastas with chicken and beef, and a variety of pizzas served in a cozy dining room.

MÁNCORA: La Sirena d'Juan ⓢⓢ
Peruvian/International **Map** A2
Av. Piura 316
Tel *073 258 173* **Closed** *Sun*
Savor tuna sashimi, lobster, prawns, freshly made pastas, and passion fruit cheesecake by Cordon Bleu-trained chef Juan Seminario. Good wine list.

TRUJILLO: Café Restaurant El Romano ⓢ
Café **Map** B3
Pizarro 747
Tel *044 252 251*
Established over 50 years ago, El Romano has a well-earned reputation for serving the best espresso and cappuccino in town. A wide variety of classic dishes, plus sandwiches, salads, soups, and desserts available.

TRUJILLO: Chia Ah Chau ⓢ
Chinese **Map** B3
Gamarra 769
Tel *044 243 351*
A plain doorway and a hand-painted sign leads to booths with trendy paneling. The restaurant serves Cantonese dishes with a Peruvian touch – big portions and exquisite flavors.

TRUJILLO: El Romano Criollo ⓢ
Regional **Map** B3
Estados Unidos 162, Urb. El Recreo
Tel *044 244 207*
This welcoming restaurant offers more than 200 traditional coastal dishes. Do not miss the delicious *cabrito a la norteña* (marinated goat), served with beans and rice.

TRUJILLO: Los Herrajes ⓢ
Seafood **Map** B3
Av. 9 de Octubre 893, Las Quintanas
Tel *044 204 846*
Owned by the Goicochea Cruz family that revived forgotten traditional seafood recipes of northern Peru. Great *cebiches* (raw fish cured with citrus juice), soups, hot and cold entrées, and deep-fried fish.

TRUJILLO: Chelsea ⓢⓢ
International **Map** B3
Estete 675
Tel *044 257 032*
Chelsea's diverse menu features salads, seafood, beef, pastas, smoked salmon, grilled meats, kebabs and more. Piano bar or live music and dancing from Thursday to Saturday nights.

TUMBES: Restaurant Latino ⓢ
Peruvian **Map** B2
Bolivar 163, Plaza de Armas
Tel *072 523 198*
Basic but clean, Latino serves a wide selection of Peruvian dishes, particularly seafood and regional specialties. Good soups and spicy stews of prawns, scallops, and crabs.

TUMBES: Bilbao Restaurante ⓢⓢ
Peruvian/Basque **Map** B2
Bolognesi 422
Tel *949 664 828*
A simple setting belies the sophisticated fare at this Basque outpost that offers imaginative variations of Peruvian dishes and Basque seagood classics. Try the flavorful *cebiche crocante* (deep-fried fish cured in citrus juice).

ZORRITOS: El Brujo ⓢⓢ
Peruvian **Map** B2
Av. Faustino Piaggo s/n
Tel *072 544 140* **Closed** *Mon*
A large restaurant on the beach with superb ocean views. Serves generous portions of fresh, award-winning Peruvian fare.

Well-stocked bar at the classy Chelsea restaurant, Trujillo

For more information on types of restaurants *see page 280*

The Northern Highlands

CAJAMARCA: Cascanuez
Café　　　　　　　　Ⓢ
Map B3
Puga 554
Tel *076 366 089*
The best place in town for the sweet-toothed, Cascanuez serves good coffee and home-made pastries and pies, as well as sandwiches and main courses. Popular with locals for a late afternoon or after dinner dessert.

CAJAMARCA: Don Paco
Regional　　　　　　Ⓢ
Map B3
Puga 726
Tel *076 362 655*
Simple eatery, just off the Plaza de Armas. Slow service, but delicious *novoandina* food including fried trout and duck magret in gooseberry sauce with fettucine. Vegetarian options available.

CAJAMARCA: El Batán
Peruvian　　　　　　Ⓢ
Map B3
Jirón Del Batán 369
Tel *076 346 025*　　**Closed** *Mon*
A delightful restaurant-cum-art-gallery set in a renovated 18th-century mansion. Choose from a set menu or dine à la carte. Folk music performances on weekends.

CAJAMARCA: Salas
Regional　　　　　　Ⓢ
Map B3
Puga 637
Tel *076 342 2867*
A mainstay of the Cajamarca dining scene for over six decades, Salas offers a true local experience. The huge menu features *sesos* (cow brain) omelet, *cuy* (guinea pig), *tamales* (steamed corn-based dough), and chicken and chips.

**CAJAMARCA:
El Cajamarqués**
International　　　　ⓈⓈ
Map B3
Amazonas 770
Tel *076 342 128*
This restaurant features white-washed walls, beamed ceilings, and caged birds in the adjoining courtyard. It offers a local and international selection of dishes, and a wide choice of meats.

**CAJAMARCA:
El Querubino**
International　　　　ⓈⓈ
Map B3
Puga 589
Tel *076 340 900*
Tiled and brightly painted, the Querubino is among the most stylish and popular eateries in town. The meat-heavy menu includes sweetbreads as well as seafood and pastas. Acoustic music adds to the ambience.

Colorful, simply furnished Café Fusiones

DK Choice
**CHACHAPOYAS:
Café Fusiones**　　　　Ⓢ
Café　　　　　　　　**Map** B3
Jirón Chincha Alta 445
Tel *041 479 170*
Started by young entrepreneurs focused on regional organic products and the slow food concept, Fusiones offers salads, sandwiches, and desserts in a colorful and simply furnished coffee shop. The highlight of the menu is organic coffee from the Guayabamba Valley – roasted and grounded on site. Also promotes and sells fair-trade folk art.

CHACHAPOYAS: El Tejado
Peruvian　　　　　　Ⓢ
Map B3
Grau 534
Tel *041 477 592*
Situated on the second floor of an old Colonial building, this restaurant serves mainly Peruvian-Creole food including several good chicken dishes. Great-value set lunches.

CHACHAPOYAS: La Tushpa
Grill/Italian　　　　Ⓢ
Map B3
Jirón Ortiz Arrieta 769
Tel *041 477 478*
This simply decorated restaurant offers excellent beef steak, sirloin, and grilled sausages. Superb pastas, pizzas, salads, and fresh fruit juices. Fresh bread baked on the premises.

**CHACHAPOYAS:
Terra Mía Café**　　　　Ⓢ
Café　　　　　　　　**Map** B3
Chincha Alta 557
Tel *041 477 277*
A comfortable restaurant in a colorfully decorated, charming old building. The fare includes waffles, local rice and maize *juanes* (boiled parcels), and wonderful desserts.

The Amazon Basin

IQUITOS: Ari's Burger
American/Regional　　Ⓢ
Map D2
Próspero 127
Tel *065 231 470*
This brightly lit place on the Plaza de Armas is nicknamed "gringolandia" for its popularity with travelers. Plenty of American choices, some local dishes, and good ice creams.

IQUITOS: Chifa Long Fung
Chinese　　　　　　Ⓢ
Map D2
San Martín 458, Plaza 28 de Julio
Tel *065 233 649*
The restaurants extensive menu offers delicious chicken won ton soup, *arroz chaufa* (stir-fried rice), and other Cantonese classics. Fantastic vegetarian options.

**IQUITOS:
Dawn on the Amazon**　　Ⓢ
International　　　　**Map** D2
Malecón Maldonado 185
Tel *065 234 921*　　**Closed** *Sun*
With a view of the boulevard and the river, this restaurant offers some of the best food in the city. Great breakfasts, regional dishes and salads, frosty tropical juices, and good vegetarian options.

IQUITOS: El Mesón
Regional　　　　　　Ⓢ
Map D2
Malecón Maldonado 153
Tel *065 231 857*
Set in a stunningly white building, El Mesón serves tasty regional dishes, and standard fare with less exotic ingredients. Outside tables with a river view.

IQUITOS: Fitzcarraldo
International　　　　Ⓢ
Map D2
Napo 100
Tel *065 236 536*
An riverfront restaurant in a 19th-century building. The menu includes salads and pizzas, as well as local and international mains.

IQUITOS: Huasai ⓢ
Meats **Map** D2
Fitzcarrald 131
Tel *065 242 222* **Closed** *Sat*
Huasai is the name for the "heart of palm" tree. Excellent regional dishes and vegetarian options. A good-value lunch draws the local business crowd. Daily specials, regional breakfasts, and dinner grills available.

DK Choice

IQUITOS:
Al Frio y Al Fuego ⓢⓢ
Regional **Map** D2
Av. La Marina 138
Tel *965 607 474*
This floating restaurant on the Itaya river offers an exceptional experience, and provides boat access from its own dock. Offers creative meals with fresh local ingredients including fish and exotic fruits. For lunch or dinner, sit under a palm-thatched roof on the top or lower decks and enjoy magical views. Sip a cocktail in or by the pool.

IQUITOS: Amazon Bistro ⓢⓢ
French **Map** D2
Malecón Tarapacá 268
Tel *065 600 785*
A French bistro in the Amazon with 19th-century Austrian tile floors and marble-topped tables. French cuisine made using regional ingredients. Meals and snacks from dawn to midnight.

LA MERCED: Los Kokis ⓢ
Peruvian **Map** C4
Tarma 381
Tel *064 531 536*
One of the favorites on the main square and a classic for regional cuisine. Los Kokis offers fruit juices, fish dishes, tasty *juanes* (boiled parcels of rice and other ingredients), and roast and cured meats including venison.

LA MERCED:
Shambari Campa ⓢ
Regional **Map** C4
Tarma 389
Tel *064 531 425*
A long-established restaurant on the main square featuring interesting old photographs and graffiti. An extensive menu and good-value set lunches.

MOYOBAMBA:
La Olla de Barro ⓢ
Regional **Map** C3
Pedro Canga 383
Tel *042 563 450*
One of the best Amazonian restaurants in town. Menu highlights include grilled venison and stewed *paca*. There are also vegetarian and Italian dishes, as well as refreshing fresh fruit juices.

OXAPAMPA: El Trapiche ⓢ
Regional **Map** C4
Av. San Martin 1ra, Cuadra
Tel *963 645 868*
A wooden lodge on the town's outskirts, with an emphasis on grilled and smoked Austro-German meats. Peruvian-style *pachamancas* on weekends.

OXAPAMPA: Oasis ⓢ
International **Map** C4
Bolognesi 120
Tel *063 762 206*
A simple albeit varied menu influenced by Peruvian-style Chinese and Italian cuisine. Great sandwiches, trout, delicious fruit juices, and more. All well-prepared and filling.

PUCALLPA: El Golf ⓢⓢ
Regional **Map** C3
Jirón Huascarán 545
Tel *061 574 632* **Closed** *Mon*
Creative regional and Peruvian-Creole dishes. Savor fish grilled in *bijao* leaves, *inchicapi* (chicken and peanut soup with coriander), fish in coconut cream, and desserts made with exotic fruits.

PUERTO MALDONADO:
La Casa Nostra ⓢ
Café **Map** E5
Velarde 515
Tel *082 573 833*
A small, friendly, family-owned café serving some of the best coffee in town. Generous breakfasts, regional dishes, *tamales* (steamed corn-based dough), snacks, hamburgers, good sandwiches, exotic fruit juices and salads, and desserts.

PUERTO MALDONADO:
Wasai Eco Lodge ⓢⓢ
International **Map** E5
Plaza Grau
Tel *082 572 290*
This terrace restaurant sits above the riverbank at the Wasai Eco Lodge and offers wonderful views. Serves chicken *pizzaiola* (cooked with peppers, tomatoes and olive oil), fish, and local specialties.

SAN RAMÓN: El Parral ⓢ
Grill **Map** C4
Uriarte 355
Tel *064 331 128*
Located in the El Parral hotel, El Parral serves a selection of different grilled meats including *anticuchos* (grilled skewered meat), rump steak, filet mignon, chicken, and pork chops. Salads, chips, and wine are the classic accompaniments.

TARAPOTO: Café d'Mundo ⓢ
Italian **Map** C3
Jirón Alegría Arias de Morey 157
Tel *042 503 223* **Closed** *Lunch*
This café offers pastas, pizzas, delicious lasagna, and has a full bar. Dine in cozy candlelight lounges or on the patio under the stars.

TARAPOTO: La Patarashca ⓢ
Regional **Map** C3
Lamas 261
Tel *042 528 810*
Award-winning regional cooking at its best and healthiest. Savor grilled and steamed Huallaga River fish, plantains, palm heart salads, and exotic fruits. Pleasant interior and terrace tables.

YARINACOCHA: La Maloka Eco Lodge ⓢ
International **Map** C3
Malecón Yarinacocha s/n, Puerto Callao
Tel *061 596 900*
Good regional and international cuisine for breakfast, lunch, and dinner. Opt to sit on the terrace overlooking Lake Titicaca for sublime views.

Poolside seating at the floating restaurant Al Frio y Al Fuego, Iquitos

SHOPPING IN PERU

Peruvian crafts are exquisite and few visitors leave without a souvenir. Upscale boutiques in the larger cities stock stylish silver jewelry and elegant alpaca shawls and jumpers, while street stalls in small northern beach towns brim over with shell necklaces and sarongs. Craft markets in Peru are loaded with alpaca knits, pottery, ceramics, handwoven textiles, baskets, and painted and carved wood. There are separate markets for fruits and vegetables. Bargaining is acceptable at street stalls but not in established shops. When buying directly from craftsmen, remember that profits are already low. Although illegal, piracy of DVDs, books, CDs, alcohol, and branded clothes is rampant, especially in Lima. It is illegal to export archaeological or valuable historical artifacts.

Shop filled with products in a handicraft market in the Inca Heartland

Opening Hours

As a general rule, shops, shopping centers, and handi-craft markets are open daily, from 9am to 8pm. Small boutiques and shops may close for lunch, between 1 and 3pm. Large super-markets, which exist only in Lima *(see pp104–5)* and in summer at Asia Beach, about 62 miles (100 km) south of Lima, do not close for lunch, remaining open until 10pm.

Payment and Prices

Major credit cards such as VISA, MasterCard, and to a lesser extent, American Express, are accepted in larger shops in major cities. However, most market stall-holders prefer to be paid in cash, either soles or US dollars. Credit cards may be rejected in small villages or rural areas, so always remember to carry cash. Stalls selling large ticket items in tourist centers accept payment by credit card. Some businesses add a surcharge of up to 12 percent for credit card purchases. Always check before paying. A value added tax (IGV) of 18 percent is added to all services and goods. A certain amount of bargaining is expected at craft markets. Local artisan cooperatives, such as those on Taquile Island on Lake Titicaca *(see pp150–1)*, have fixed prices with profits shared amongst the villagers. In other village co-ops, a portion of the profit goes directly to the craftsmen. In general, large galleries and shops arrange the shipping.

Samples of handwoven textiles with traditional patterns

General Stores

Most shopping malls, department stores, expensive boutiques, and supermarkets are located in Lima, but more key cities in the provinces now have Saga Falabella and Ripley department stores.

Towns are the domain of craft markets, small shops, and produce markets. Clothing boutique, Alpaca 111 *(see p105)*, and silverware shop, Ilaria *(see p105)*, operate branches in top-end hotels in the provinces, such as Cusco and Puno, and some airports.

Clothing

Alpaca clothing abounds in the form of jumpers, coats, shawls, caps, and gloves. Garments are also available in soft baby alpaca and vicuña, considered to be the world's finest wool. Arequipa is the center of the wool industry, and has no shortage of shops.

Designer handbags

Imported designer labels can be found at a few select boutiques in Lima. Max Mara has its own shop in San Isidro and Hugo Boss has one in Jockey Plaza. Department stores Ripley's and Saga Falabella stock a range of less expensive clothing, including popular surf labels, jeans, and mid-level brands. Designer labels available on the streets are certain to be fakes.

Expert tailors can whip up a suit in a week, and shops in the center of Lima can make leather jackets in various colors in the same time. The garment district of Gamarra is full of inexpensive fabrics, dressmakers, and tailors, as well as racks of ready-to-wear clothing. It is a poor neighborhood and travelers should exercise care.

Villages in the highlands near Cusco are the best places to buy embroidered clothing or textiles. The straw hats of Celendín, near Cajamarca, are considered the best in the entire country.

Craft Markets

The largest selection of handicrafts from across the country can be found in the strip of mini-malls that make up the indigenous markets in Miraflores *(see p81)* in Lima.

The daily market in Pisac *(see p173)*, near Cusco, is one of the best known, with Sunday being the busiest day. Colorful stalls fill the main plaza and adjacent streets, offering rugs, hats, alpaca ponchos, musical instruments, jewelry, and *mates burilados* or engraved gourds *(see p300)*.

Chinchero market in the Sacred Valley is a mix of a fruit, vegetable, and handicraft market. Artisans sporting traditional felt hats, with a secret fold that doubles as a purse, line their wares of painted wooden plates, hand-woven textiles, dolls, and colorfully beaded hats on the ground and weave while they wait for customers. Andean condor feathers are sometimes on sale, but it is illegal to buy or sell them.

Hand-painted carved wooden plates, Chincero, Inca Heartland

Textiles and ceramics made by the Shipibo community are a specialty of the Mercado Artesanal de San Juan in Iquitos *(see p256)*. The Shipibo community that lives along the Ucayali River in Peru's Amazon region, is known for their geometric designs.

In the northern surfing town of Máncora, street stalls are piled high with jewelry, beachwear, shell chimes, wooden carvings, and chandeliers.

Regional Products

Every region in Peru has its specialties and, often, it is more interesting and much cheaper, in terms of quality and variety, to buy locally.

Ayacucho's Barrio Santa Ana *(see pp196–7)* is filled with craft workshops devoted to weaving tapestries and carving *huamanga* stone. The town is also famous for its *retablos*, or the boxes depicting events and customs.

Quinua is known for its *iglesias de quinua* (miniature clay chapels) which Andeans put on their roofs for good luck. The pottery of Pampa, Pucará, and Chulucanas is also renowned.

Entire villages within the Mantaro Valley focus on one particular craft: Silver filigree in San Jerónimo de Tunán, woollen tapestries in Hualhuas, and engraved gourds in Cochas Grande and Cochas Chico.

The San Blas quarter in Cusco is home to candle-makers and the famous woodcarvers responsible for richly painted statues of the popular long-necked Virgins, saints, and chubby cherubs.

Colorful tapestry depicting a local vegetable market

Food and Drink

Olive oils and juicy olives from Ica and Tacna can be bought from small local shops, markets, and supermarkets. The grape brandy, pisco *(see p287)*, which originates in both areas, is found in supermarkets and *vinotecas* (bottle shops), as well as individual wineries.

Anis Najar, a liqueur made from aniseed oil, along with La Iberica's chestnut marzipan fashioned into mini fruit, are Arequipa specialties. They are sold in shops in the center of the city and at the airport.

Ajis (dried Peruvian hot chilies) can be found in fruit and vegetable markets such as Lima's Mercado Surquillo, while jars of chili salsa are available at supermarkets.

Tourist browsing through a local indigenous craft market

Buying Peruvian Folk Art

Folk art is an essential part of the country's religious, ceremonial, and everyday life with techniques passed down from generation to generation. Artisans use symbols and geometric designs in textiles as well as ceramics, and carve vivid portraits of rural life on to *mates burilados*. Textiles and clothing are made using alpaca wool, woven and spun by women in the highlands. Gold- and silversmiths create artifacts using old models and techniques. Spanish influence is evident in religious wooden carvings with Baroque flourishes and the depiction of the divine and daily life in *retablos*.

Detail on a handcarved gourd, *mates burilados*

Mates Burilados

Gourd carving has existed for many centuries in Peru. Different styles and techniques were developed as a result of trade between villages. The green outer skin is removed and the gourd is sun-dried. A design is then sketched on the gourd and carved by hand using a small wooden chisel. The uncarved area is finally burnt to get the colored effect.

Huamanga Stone Carvings

Statues made of Ayacucho's white alabaster, known as *piedra de huamanga*, became popular during Colonial times. The reason for this popularity was a shortage in porcelain and marble. Early works were religious in nature but now they encompass a range of different subjects.

Retablos

Retablos are filled with figures made of potato dough. The upper level represents heaven while the lower level depicts earthly events showing daily activities. *Costumbrista retablos* portray bullfights, dances, condor hunts, markets, religious festivals, and scenes showing the making of musical instruments and hats. The upheaval in Ayacucho, the home of *retablos*, especially during the time of the violent Sendero Luminoso (Shining Path) guerrillas *(see p199)*, is

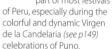

White alabaster statue

portrayed in *Testimonials*. The Jimenez family *retablistas (see p93)* from Ayacucho, are one of the leading exponents.

Woodwork

Churches and convents built in the Colonial era created a demand for elaborate wood-work including pulpits, choir-stalls, and religious statues. The craftsmen in the San Blas *(see p163)* district of Cusco still produce fine examples of local Baroque carving.

The town of Molinos near Huancayo *(see p191)* is famous for its wooden utensils and carved toys including animals, imaginary creatures, and acrobats.

Sarhua in the Ayacucho department is renowned for its *tablas* (painted boards) containing text and illustrated stories depicting everyday practices and customs. Originally the stories were drawn on the roof beams in homes. Masks are an integral part of most festivals of Peru, especially during the colorful and dynamic Virgen de la Candelaria *(see p149)* celebrations of Puno.

Silverwork

Artisans in the departments of Junín, Huancavelica, Cusco, and Ayacucho produce a range of silverwork, from religious icons to ornate frames. *Tupus*, or elaborate pins, are used to fasten shawls, a tradition left over from the Colonial era.

The town of Catacaos, in the Piura region, is famous for its delicate silver filigree. Silver and gold are thinned out, and the super-fine threads curled and beveled into jewelry and figures.

Textiles

Weaving is Peru's oldest art form, dating back some 3,000 years. At one point, woven clothes were used as a form of payment to Inca rulers. The best weavers are found in Ayacucho,

Colorful *retablo* depicting everyday life in a Peruvian village

Textiles and handicrafts on sale in a roadside marketplace in the Inca Heartland

Puno, Cusco, Junín, Apurímac, and Lima. Each village has its own technique and pattern, producing a rich variety of *chullos* (woollen caps with earflaps), bags, ponchos, scarves, rugs, and garments.

Weaving is largely done by women, but the men of Taquile Island are famous for their *chullos* and *chullis* (cummerbunds). Weavers of Ayacucho specialize in weft and warp textiles featuring abstract patterns. The weavers of Hualhuas make tapestries and rugs from hand-spun wool. Yarn is traditionally dyed using indigenous plants and insects. Pink cochineal is extracted from drying insects that feed on cacti.

Women in the village of Chucuito in Puno come from a long line of knitters. Today, they are known for their beautiful finger puppets, depicting the widlife of Peru, such as condors, llamas, pumas, and even pop cultural icons such as Spiderman.

Arpillera or *tapiz* is the term applied to appliquéd tapestries made by Peruvian women. Some of these record village events while others portray idyllic scenes from the urban and traditional life of the ordinary people of Peru.

Local weavers give daily demonstrations in the Centre for Traditional Textiles of Cusco, showing how ancient

techniques have been revived. The sales revenue from these products goes to the villagers who produce the brilliant textiles.

Baskets

Colorful baskets woven from native reeds of the area are produced mainly in the departments of Cajamarca, San Martín, and Piura, where they weave brightly colored baskets of all shapes and sizes. These baskets are easy to carry and can be used for decorative purposes. They are the perfect souvenirs of Peru.

Pottery

Pottery is one of the most common crafts practiced in the country. In the Northern Desert, Chulucanas potters do not use the potter's wheel, instead they hand-turn the clay, using a wood paddle and stone to make thinner pieces. The vases are then smoked in burning mango leaves to give them light and dark contrasts. The traditional geometric patterns of the Shipibo potters living in Peru's Amazon region are said to be copied from the skin of the giant anaconda, and astrological signs.

Painted ceramic plates from Pucara

The *torito* (Pucará bull), which is a hollow ceramic flask shaped like a bull, made by the potters in the Puno area, is an essential

ritual part of the cattle branding ceremony. It is filled with *chicha* (*see p286*) and buried as an offering to the gods for increased herds. Pairs of these bulls are placed on the rooftops of Puno homes. Variations of *toritos* are found in Ayacucho, which is famous for its clay churches.

Leather

Leather chests, armchairs, and riding apparel with Baroque motifs were first made during Colonial times. Armchairs, tables, and chests bearing traditional patterns are still made today.

Candles

An immense number of colorful, decorated candles are produced in areas such as Cusco, Ayacucho, Huaraz, Arequipa, and Lima. Festooned with articles such as flowers, leaves, angels' faces, and geometric patterns, they are used during religious festivals.

Elaborately decorated candles on sale in a local shop

OUTDOOR ACTIVITIES

Peru offers a multitude of outdoor activities to suit everybody's interests, abilities, fitness, and wallet. One highlight is a trek, a multiday camping and hiking expedition surrounded by the world's highest tropical mountains. Others include mountaineering, river rafting, mountain-biking, surfing, or watching wildlife in the Amazon Basin. Sand-boarding,

an unusual sport, is possible only on the huge dunes around Huacachina on the south coast. From the hundreds of outfitters and travel agencies that exist, we have selected ones that provide several kinds of services. Many visitors start with the South American Explorers (SAE), based in Lima or Cusco, which has information related to outdoor activities.

Mountain climbers on a glaciated peak, Cordillera Blanca

Trekking and Mountaineering

Trekking and mountaineering are extremely popular among visitors to Peru, especially during the dry season from May to September. The best base for trekking in the Andes is Huaraz. Nearby, Cordillera Blanca contains scores of glaciated mountains and is the best-known trekking area. The highlight is Huascarán, which at 22,205 ft (6,768 m) is the world's highest tropical mountain. With trails crossing passes at up to 16,405 ft (5,000 m) and camping spots commonly around 13,124 ft (4,000 m), these adventures are for fit, acclimatized visitors with good equipment. Both day trips and overnight treks, ranging from three to 12 days, can be arranged. More strenuous treks, lasting for 14 days, circumnavigate Cordillera Huayhuash, Peru's second highest range.

Mountaineers have a choice of towering icy summits, ranging from the relatively easy

Pisco to the symmetrical Alpamayo, or the challenging Artesonraju. All require technical ice- and snow-climbing equipment, which can be rented in Huaraz. The climbing season is from June to August. Some visitors opt to backpack alone while others hire guides, cooks, or *arrieros* (donkey drivers). Reliable information is available from the **Casa de Guías**, headquarter of the Peruvian Mountain Guide Association. Many rental places such as **MountClimb** and **Andean Kingdom** rent and sell gear and also arrange reasonably priced tours. **Peruvian Andes Adventures** is a top-notch outfitter in Huaraz with English- and German-speaking guides specializing in trekking and mountaineering. **Skyline Adventures** arranges treks, climbs, and mountaineering courses. **La Cima Logistics**, headquartered in

Mountaineering gear

Huaraz's Café Andino, specializes in personalized information and arrangements in the Cordillera Huayhuash. **Pony's Expeditions** in the village of Caraz, 42 miles (67 km) north of Huaraz, is a great choice for the north end of the Cordillera Blanca.

Cusco, with its fabled Inca Trail *(see pp174–7)* to Machu Picchu, is also the center for several other marvelous treks. As the Inca Trail is now highly regulated, trekkers need to plan their trips months in advance in order to obtain a permit during the dry season. Other treks are equally gorgeous and require less advance notice. The six-day circuit of Ausangate (20,906 ft/6,372 m) with glorious mountain views herds of alpacas, and natural hot springs, is highly recommended. Several treks often end up at Machu Picchu via routes other than the more famous Inca Trail.

Ecologically-minded **Ecoinka** offers their comfortable tented Camp Veronica with excellent meals, hot showers, sauna, and views of the glaciated Veronica (18,865 ft/ 5,750 m), as a base camp to the Inca Trail, a llama trek, and other trips in the surrounding region. **Explorandes** is a local pioneer and offers first-class trips. **Amazonas Explorer** organizes high-quality trekking, mountain-biking, and rafting trips. Fully guided expeditions of the highest distinction, including international guides, and first-class hotels, are arranged by **Wilderness Travel**, which has

A trekkers' camp at Laguna Carhuacocha in Cordillera Huayhuash

been trekking in Peru since the 1970s. **High Places** and **Wildland Adventures** are two other preferred international outfitters. Of dozens of mid-range local trek operators, **SAS Travel**, **Q'ente Adventures**, **Liz's Explorer**, and **Inca Explorers** are recommended.

The Arequipa area offers some unique adventures. A trek into two of the world's deepest canyons, the Colca (see pp146–7) and the Cotahuasi (see p148), can be arranged. Both have great scenery, condor-spotting opportunities, and remote

Hikers in Urubamba valley, near Maras, Inca Heartland

villages. Among the best out-fitters is **Colca Trek**, run by Vlado, an experienced English-speaking local guide.

Another special experience is climbing the arid Volcán Misti (19,101 ft/5,822 m) which dominates Arequipa's skyline. Some of the best guides are with **Zárate Adventures**, who pioneered climbing in the area and also offer ascents of higher peaks.

Mountain-Biking

The mountain trails with their jaw-dropping scenery are the perfect getaway for adventure lovers. They provide a stark contrast to the flat desert of the Panamerican Highway. Single track dirt roads crisscross the Andes, and a vehicle or a donkey are required to take you up for a descent of 9,843 ft (3,000 m). Rental bikes are quite good, but if you require top-of-the-line wheels, it is best to bring your own. Most international airlines allow passengers to carry them.

In Huaraz, **Mountain Bike Adventures** is the best choice, with short trips and multiday expeditions throughout the Cordillera Blanca region. The

friendly English-speaking owner, Julio, is a fine guide and bike mechanic and knows the sport inside out.

In Cusco, a good choice for planning your trip is **Ecotrek Peru** which has one- to six-day trips, some visiting Inca sites. The international outfitter, **BikeHike Adventures**, offers multisport excursions as their name implies. **Backroads** is a highly reputable company which arranges premier bike and trek tours in the Sacred Valley. A list of international biking outfitters offering luxurious personalized tours is available online on the **Adventurebiketours** website.

Mountain-bike rider on a rugged mountain trail

Rafters in action during a white-water rafting expedition

River-Running

The rugged high Andean rivers are the best place for white-water kayaking and rafting. Trips range from a few hours to over a week of descending through mountain canyons into the Amazon rainforest *(see p260)* and camping in the wilderness. Outfitters can be found in Arequipa and Huaraz, but Cusco has the best selection.

Short floats can be done in Class II and III rapids on the Río Urubamba in the Sacred Valley *(see p172)*, while longer trips descend the Ríos Tambopata *(see p266–7)* and Apurímac into the Amazon with rapids reaching Class IV and some very challenging Class V ones. Most are navigated by rafts with experienced guides; kayakers can also join a rafting expedition.

Companies with an emphasis on white-water trips include **Mayuc**, which has pioneered river-running in Peru and includes descents of the Colca Canyon as well as trips to the Cusco area. Also recommended is **Southern Rivers Expeditions**, which runs the Cotahuasi Canyon. Check with trekking companies as some of them also arrange personalized river-running.

Surfing

With almost 1,864 miles (3,000 km) of Pacific coastline, Peru offers great waves. The far north has the best and warmest conditions, with sea temperatures around 70°F (21°C) for most of the year. Temperatures at the beaches around Lima *(see p103)* drop to as low as 56°F (13°C) in the coldest months of April to December, when wet suits are mandatory. For an overview of dozens of surfing beaches, visit the website **Perú Azul**. For information about the competitive surfing scene go to the website of **Bodyboard Nation Peru**. The beaches in Peru are dry desert, unlike typical tropical beaches.

Lima fronts on to numerous beaches, on the Coste Verde, and surfers are seen through the year in Miraflores *(see p83)*. To avoid the crowds, surfers head to Punta Hermosa, about 25 miles (40 km) south of Lima, where several good breaks are found and international competitions are held. **Peru Surf Guides**, a local surf-board shop, sells, shapes, rents, and repairs boards, and doubles as a surfers' information center.

Puerto Chicama, near Trujillo and 380 miles (610 km) north of Lima, has the longest lefts in the world, but the infrastructure is limited to basic hostels. May to August are the best months for wave action. Farther north, at 721 miles (1,160 km) north of Lima, the pretty village of Máncora has warmer water, good surfing, and a variety of hotels in all classes. Check the Viva Máncora website *(see pp236–7)* for surfing conditions, which are best from November to February.

The challenging sport of kitesurfing is popular in Paracas, 149 miles (240 km) south of Lima. **PeruKite** offers equipment and lessons.

Scuba Diving

The waters off Peru are marked with cold currents and steep drop-offs. As a result, the long Pacific Coast does not offer coral reefs, but it has its own attractions for divers. Prime among these is Paracas *(see p127)*, where divers can swim with sea lions in their natural habitat. The warmest waters are near the Ecuadorian border, where fish are more visible. **Peru Divers** is an experienced company which sells gear, arranges tours, and provides international PADI certification courses for much less than what you would pay in Europe or North America.

Scuba diver

Surfers riding the fast waves of the Pacific Ocean

Forest along an Amazonian riverbank inside the Reserva Nacional Pacaya-Samiria *(see p259)*

Rainforest Exploration

A wildlife-watching expedition into the Amazon rainforest is an all-time adventure for those visiting Peru. Most visitors to the Amazon Basin will see sloths, monkeys, parrots, dolphins, piranhas, and a vast array of insects and plants, depending on the part of the basin they visit.

In the southern rainforests, riverside cliffs of salt-laden mud attract macaws and parrots intent on feeding on the minerals. Soon after dawn, large flocks of the colorful birds arrive to squabble and squawk over a particular area – a sight which delights bird-watchers and photographers alike. On a longer trip into remoter areas of the rainforest, glimpses of jaguars or tapirs are feasible. A good look at capybaras, anteaters, armadillos, giant river otters, and peccaries is possible as well.

Wildlife-watching is not the only highlight of the rainforest. The sounds of the jungle, from the dawn bird chorus to the nighttime frog, toad, and insect concertos, are hauntingly beautiful. Also, visiting an Indian village or climbing into the canopy are unforgettable experiences that visitors cherish for a lifetime.

Agouti, Amazon

From Iquitos, visitors can take a cruise of several days on a small ship featuring private, air-conditioned cabins and a naturalist guide with **Amazon Tours & Cruises**. The most expensive and luxurious trips are with **International Expeditions**. **Green Tracks** emphasizes biology on some of their voyages. Budget travelers can ride as hammock passengers in cargo boats *(see p257)* leaving regularly from the major ports of Iquitos, Pucallpa, or Yurimaguas.

Camping in the Amazon Basin is very popular in the Manu area *(see p265)*, where **Manu Ecological Adventures** has set up semi-permanent campsites in prime locations. **Manu Expeditions** offers tours with a mixture of camping and lodge nights and is known for its expertise in bird-watching. A good mid-priced company is **Pantiacolla Tours** which camps on different beaches. Visitors need to bear in mind that even though these are camps, the logistics of getting into such remote areas means that the expeditions are not cheap, and independent travelers are not allowed.

Another option for rainforest exploration is to stay in a lodge, such as Manu Lodge *(see p279)*. Some of these lodges have canopy platforms or walkways which are an adventure in their own right. Others, such as the Heath River Wildlife Center, provide a closer view of the riverside clay licks covered with hundreds of spectacularly colorful macaws and parrots.

Tourists on a wildlife-watching trip in the Amazon rainforest

Visitors enjoying a paragliding flight over the Costa Verde, Lima

Paragliding and Bungee Jumping

Adrenaline-pumping aerial adventures such as paragliding and bungee jumping are very much part of the Peruvian sports scene. Professional as well as amateur pilots glide by the Larcomar Mall *(see p83)* in Lima, around the Paracas Peninsula, and in the Sacred Valley area near Cusco. Facilities for tandem flights with experienced pilots, as well as training courses, are available from **PerúFly** and in Cusco from **Action Valley**, which has rentals for licensed pilots. Action Valley also caters for bungee jumping and slingshot, a catapult variation of bungee.

Horseback Riding

Peru is famous for its *paso horses (see p225)*, which have been bred for over 400 years to produce the smoothest gait in the world. **Cabalgatas** offers exhibitions and horseback tours using these horses. **Equitours** is a recommended international wrangler offering tours in the Sacred Valley. Several trekking companies also offer riding, but not always on *paso* horses. Beware that some horses offered cheaply are poorly looked after.

Sand-Boarding

The unusual sport of sand-boarding is a cross between snow-boarding and surfing with a huge sand dune thrown in. It is a popular pastime as the sand never melts and enthusiasts do not need to wait for the perfect wave. Sand-boarding is possible at any time, in any season, which makes it appealing for Peruvians.

Rain is almost unheard of in the coastal desert of Peru and even bad weather cannot stop the action. In the 1980s, the heart of the sand-boarding scene was the desert-lake oasis of Huacachina, a tiny village a 4-hour drive south of Lima. During earlier days, boards

looked like short surfboards, candles were used as wax, and riders sat or lay on the boards as they rode down the sand dunes encircling the lake.

Extreme boarders use equipment looking more like snowboards, with foot bindings allowing a controlled ride. More than 40 countries now boast boardable dunes, and sand-boarding competitions are held for international experts who ride, jump, spin, somersault, and flip their way down the dunes. Companies do not offer organized trips but a handful of hotels and shops in Huacachina offer old-fashioned and modern boards for rent. Boarders trudge slowly up the dunes, slipping back two steps for every three made forward, or they hire a driver and beach buggy to take them to the top. This is repeated for as long as their energy lasts.

Horseback riding

Huacachina remains the favored spot and is the easiest place to rent a board for about US$3 a day. Today dunes near Huacachina *(see p125)*, Trujillo *(see pp222–4)*, and even in the environs of Lima, are attracting boarders. See the **Peru Adventure Tours** website for information.

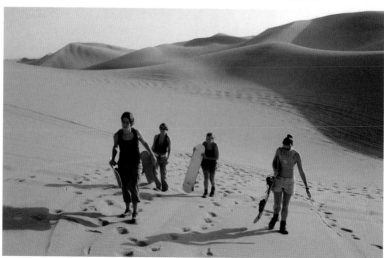

Sand-boarders trekking across sand dunes

DIRECTORY

General Tour Advice

SAE Clubhouse
Calle Enrique Palacios 956, Miraflores, Lima.
Tel 01 445 3306.
W saexplorers.org

Peru Adventure Tours
W peruadventures tours.com

Trekking and Mountaineering

Amazonas Explorer
Collasuyo 910, Miravalle, Cusco. Tel 084 252 846.
W amazonas-explorer. com

Andean Kingdom
Parque Ginebra 120, Huaraz. Tel 043 425 555.
W andeankingdom. com

Casa de Guías
Parque Ginebra 28 G, Huaraz. Tel 043 421 811.
W agmp.pe

Colca Trek
Jerusalén 401-B, Arequipa.
Tel 054 206 217.
W colcatrek.com.pe

Ecoinka
Maruri 288, Oficina 404, Cusco. Tel 084 224 050.
W ecoinka.com

Explorandes
Garcilaso 316-A, Cusco.
Tel 084 238 380.
W explorandes.com

High Places
Tel 0845 257 7500.
W highplaces.co.uk

Inca Explorers
Calle Peru W -18, Urb. Ttio, Cusco. Tel 084 241 070.
W incaexplorers.com

La Cima Logistics
Lucar y Torre 530, 3rd floor, Huaraz. Tel 043 721 203. W cafeandino.com

Liz's Explorer
Calle del Medio 114 B, Plaza de Armas, Cusco.
Tel 084 246 619.
W lizexplorer.com

MountClimb
Mariscal Cáceres 421, Huaraz. Tel 043 426 060.
W mountclimb.com.pe

Peruvian Andes Adventures
José Olaya 532, Huaraz.
Tel 043 421 864.
W peruvianandes.com

Pony's Expeditions
Sucre 1266, Caraz.
Tel 043 391 642.
W ponyexpeditions. com

Q'ente Adventures
Choquechaca 229, 2nd floor, Cusco.
Tel 084 222 535.
W qente.com

SAS Travel
Calle Garcilaso 270, Cusco.
Tel 084 249 194.
W sastravelperu.com

Skyline Adventures
Tel 043 427 097.
W skyline-adventures. com

Wilderness Travel
Tel 510 558 2489.
W wildernesstravel. com

Wildland Adventures
Tel 206 365 0686.
W wildland.com

Zárate Adventures
Santa Catalina 204, Oficina 3, Arequipa.
Tel 054 202 461.
W zarateadventures. com

Mountain-Biking

Adventure-biketours
W perubikingtours. com

Backroads
Tel 510 527 1555.
W backroads.com

BikeHike Adventures
Tel 604 731 2442.
W bikehike.com

Ecotrek Peru
Urb. Quispicanchi Jirón Panamá F-3, Cusco.
Tel 084 247 286.
W ecotrekperu.com

Mountain Bike Adventures
Lucar y Torre 530, Huaraz.
Tel 043 424 259.
W chakinaniperu.com

River-Running

Mayuc
Portal Confiturías 211, Plaza de Armas, Cusco.
Tel 084 232 666.
W mayuc.com

Southern Rivers Expeditions
Plateros 361, Cusco.
Tel 084 255 049.
W southernrivers.net

Surfing

Bodyboard Nation Peru
Tel 01 985 622 422.
W bodyboardnation. com

Perú Azul
W peruazul.com

PeruKite
Paracas, Ica.
Tel 01 959 524 940.
W perukite.com

Peru Surf Guides
Contact: Raul Delgado.
Tel 997 753 573.
W perusurfguides.com

Pukana Surfer School
Tel 01 994 264 815.
W pukanasurferschool. com

Scuba Diving

Peru Divers
Av. Huaylas 175, Chorrillos, Lima.
Tel 01 251 6231.
W perudivers.com

Rainforest Exploration

Amazon Tours & Cruises
Requena 336, Iquitos.
Tel 065 231 611.
W amazontours.net

Green Tracks
Tel 970 884 6107.
W greentracks.com

International Expeditions
Tel 205 428 1700.
W ietravel.com

Manu Ecological Adventures
Plateros 356, Cusco.
Tel 084 261 640.
W manuadventures. com

Manu Expeditions
Calle Clorinda Matto de Turner 330, Urb. Magisterial 1a Etapa, Cusco.
Tel 084 225 990.
W manuexpeditions. com

Pantiacolla Tours
Calle Garcilaso 265, 2nd Floor, Cusco.
Tel 084 238 323.
W pantiacolla.com

Paragliding and Bungee Jumping

Action Valley
Calle Santa Tesessa 325, Plaza Regocijo, Cusco.
Tel 01 954 711 028.
W actionvalley.com

PerúFly
Jorge Chavez 666, Miraflores, Lima.
Tel 01 444 5004.
W perufly.com

Horseback Riding

Cabalgatas
Tel 01 221 4591.
W cabalgatas.com.pe

Equitours
Tel 307 455 3363.
W equitours.com

Sand-Boarding

Peru Adventure Tours
W peruadventurestours. com

SPECIALIZED HOLIDAYS

Peru, with its rich culture and biodiversity, is becoming a hotspot for those looking beyond conventional travel. Specialized activities such as butterfly- and bird-watching are increasingly popular. Staying with and working in the fields with an Andean community can be a life-changing experience. Learning the secrets of Peruvian cuisine, one of the most varied in the world, is possible through culinary courses or tours around local markets and gourmet restaurants. Lessons in complex Peruvian dances can be a thrill in a group or individual classes, while Spanish and Quechua lessons will always improve your chances of meeting Peruvians and enjoying both the social and cultural life.

Bird-watching, a fast growing tourist attraction in Peru

Bird-Watching

Peru ranks first in the world for bird species, with more than 1,800 of them. However, bird-watching is small here in comparison to neighboring countries, but is increasing fast with new companies emerging, led by a conservation-minded generation of local and foreign experts.

Kolibri Expeditions offers trips to various destinations with mid-budget alternatives. **Rainforest Expeditions** has many programs for bird-lovers. Bird-watching expeditions from three to eight days within the Tambopata National Reserve *(see pp266–7)*, are available. A six-night program, dedicated to observing parrots and macaws at the clay licks is also offered. **Manu Expeditions** *(see p307)* has excellent guides with a varied combination of programs. **Gran Peru** is headed by Peruvian ornithologist, Thomas Valqui. He leads tours mainly to the Tambopata and Manu regions and into the North-western Biosphere Reserve, home to no less than 1,400 bird species.

Another company focused in this area is **Ultimate Voyages**. **Birding Ecotours** provide tailor-made expeditions all around Peru for clients with particular birding interests. **Tanager Tours**, has birding programs in the Colca Canyon *(see pp146–7)* and other areas in Southern Peru.

Alejandro Tello, an expert ornithologist, often works as a freelance guide for some of the companies mentioned above, but can also arrange personalized expeditions. For more information about bird-watching in Peru consult the **Birdingperu** website or the bird-watching webpage of the **PromPerú** website.

Butterfly-Watching

Two major companies offer packages for butterfly-lovers in order to explore some of the 3,700 species existing in Peru. Manu Expeditions has a 17-day tour into some of the most pristine cloud forest spots in the Manu National Park, where butterflies can be spotted at diverse altitudes and habitats. A three-day package tour into the historic Machu Picchu sanctuary *(see pp180–5)* is also a good opportunity to watch butterflies in the awe-inspiring scenery of the Inca citadel.

Rainforest Expeditions has a three-night program that is combined with other tropical rainforest explorations in the Tambopata National Reserve in the Amazon Basin.

Music and Dance

Afro-Peruvian music and dance with its combination of Peruvian sounds and deep African influence attracts many travelers to Lima. The **Centro Cultural de la Pontificia Universidad Católica del Perú**, offers dance workshops and *cajón (see pp32–3)* lessons by María del Carmen Dongo, a respected percussionist who also offers lessons at her own school **Zonarte – Escuela de Percusión**.

White-breasted kingfisher

For those with a major interest in Latin rhythms, **El Sol – Escuela de Español** offers dance classes every Friday afternoon. They include salsa, *merengue*, and other groovy beats, taught by expert Latino dancers and trainers.

Visitors enjoy traditional rural life with Andean communities

Community-based Tourism

Sponsored by **The Mountain Institute**, community-based tourism aims to re-evaluate Andean culture and tradition.

Tilling the land and dyeing wool are part of the home-stay experience in Vicos or Humac-chuco, two Quechua communities in the Cordillera Blanca (see pp206–7). Similar homestay options are also available with the community in Lake Titicaca (see p151).

Ethnic and Medicinal Traditions

Etnikas Travel offers one-week retreats promoting the alternative healing traditions of Amazon and Andean shamans in the Sacred Valley. In Iquitos, **Latitud Sur** gives visitors the opportunity to help preserve primary forests and the ancient knowledge of medicinal herbs on tours into the Pacaya-Samiria Reserve.

Culinary Tours and Courses

Lima Tours (see p323) offers a six-day tour that combines sightseeing and Peruvian gastronomy in Lima and Cusco with visits to a selection of exquisite restaurants and countryside mansions. One-day tours within Lima that include a visit to a local produce market, lessons in making cebiche (see p282), and dinner at one of Lima's finest restaurants are also offered. **Le Cordon Bleu Peru** in the Miraflores district of Lima offers an intense five-day course where popular Peruvian recipes can be learnt.

Spanish and Quechua Classes

In Lima, El Sol – Escuela de Español, **Instituto Cultural Peruano Norteamericano**, and, in Cusco, **Centro Tinku** offer various language classes ranging from one to 20 weeks and up to a year. **Centro de Idiomas PUCP** also offers Spanish for foreigners and has one of the best Quechua learning programs in Peru.

DIRECTORY

Bird-Watching

Alejandro Tello
Tel 01 9665 6589.

Birding Ecotours
Tel 01 420 4448.
W birdingecotours.co.za

Birdingperu
birdingperu.com

Gran Peru
Tel 074 977 1575.
W granperu.com

Kolibri Expeditions
Tel 01 476 5016.
W kolibriexpeditions.com

PromPerú
W perubirdingroutes.com

Rainforest Expeditions
Tel 01 421 8347 (Lima), 084 24 6243 (Cusco), 082 52 2575 (Puerto Maldonado).
W perunature.com

Tanager Tours
Tel 054 42 6210.
W tanagertours.com

Ultimate Voyages
W ultimatevoyages.com

Music and Dance

Centro Cultural de la Pontificia Universidad Católica del Perú
Tel 01 616 1616.
W cultural.pucp.edu.pe

El Sol – Escuela de Español
W elsol.idiomasperu.com

Zonarte – Escuela de Percusión
W cajonperu.com

Community-based Tourism

The Mountain Institute
W respons.org

Ethnic and Medicinal Traditions

Etnikas Travel
W etnikas.com

Latitud Sur
W latitudsur.com

Culinary Tours and Courses

Le Cordon Bleu Peru
Tel 01 242 8222.
W lecordonbleuperu.edu.pe

Spanish and Quechua Classes

Centro de Idiomas PUCP
Tel 01 431 0052 / 423 8078. W pucp.edu.pe/eculpub/cipuc

Centro Tinku
W centrotinku.com

Instituto Cultural Peruano Norteamericano
Tel 01 706 7000.
W icpna.edu.pe/ingles

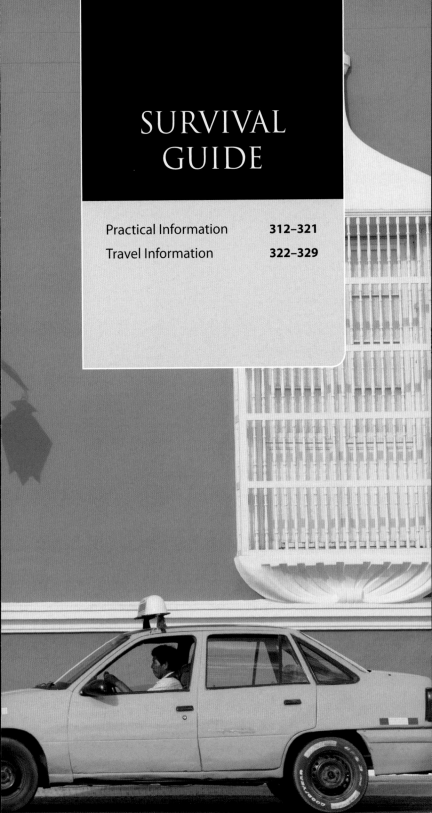

SURVIVAL GUIDE

PRACTICAL INFORMATION

In the last ten years Peru has made great progress in its tourism industry and today, it is much easier to travel around the country. There are some expert tour operators offering a range of options, from ecotourism and outdoor adventure to gastronomy and mysticism. Tourist offices, known as iPerú, are located in the larger cities, while in smaller towns, visitors can often obtain information from the *municipalidad* (town hall). Facilities in the more remote areas, however, may still be somewhat limited. Life is a bit laidback in Peru and everything takes a little longer, be it restaurants, offices, or shops, so bear in mind that patience is indeed a virtue.

June to August, the best time to visit Machu Picchu

When to Go

Most people visit Peru in winter, from June to August, when the weather is dry and sunny in the highlands and jungles. Prices for hotels rise during this period.

The wettest months are from December to March, which means muddy paths and cloudy skies for trekkers along with the water hampering outdoor activities.

The central and southern desert coast is shrouded in mist in winter, but sunny during the rainy season in the highlands. The north coast, however, has sun year round.

May, September, October, and November are good times to visit – the weather is fine, tourist routes are less crowded and prices are lower.

Visas and Passports

Citizens of Australia, Canada, New Zealand, South Africa, UK, USA, and most European and Latin American countries do not require a visa to visit Peru. The maximum stay is 90 days, although this can be extended at a *migración* (immigration) office in major cities. On arrival, visitors get a 30- or 90-day stamp on their passport and an embarkation card that has to be returned on leaving the country. All visitors should have a passport valid for six months from the date of travel.

Opening Hours

Museum opening hours can vary, but are generally from 10am to 5pm. Many post offices and banks are open all day while government offices open from 9:30am to 5pm, Monday to Friday. Shops and government offices usually close for lunch.

Entrance to a post office with the distinctive Serpost logo

Customs Information

Peru allows duty-free import of three liters of alcohol, 400 cigarettes or 50 cigars, and gifts worth up to US$300 or equivalent in other currencies. It is illegal to take out pre-Columbian artifacts, Colonial art, and animal products from endangered species, unless accompanied by documentation from Peru's National Institute of Culture (INC) indicating that the object is a reproduction. Coca leaves and coca tea are legal in Peru but not in most other countries.

At Lima international airport, all travelers have their luggage passed through an x-ray machine for checking, but the process is quite quick. Visitors are allowed to bring a laptop, camera, bicycle, and sports gear for personal use.

Language

Spanish and Quechua are the official languages of Peru but Spanish is the most widely used. Aymara, spoken mainly around Lake Titicaca, is also recognized by the state, along with 48 other native languages. English is spoken and understood by workers in tourism-related industries, and by members of Peru's upper socio-economic class. Outside large cities people have only a basic knowledge of English.

Social Customs

Peruvians are polite, and a bit formal. A handshake is exchanged at the beginning and end of a meeting. People who know each other greet with a single kiss.

◀ A vibrant, Neo-Classical façade in Plaza de Armas, Trujillo

Wear non-revealing clothes when visiting churches

When addressing people, use their title *(señor, señora, señorita)* or their professional title. Personal space is not a respected commodity – the buses as well as the streets are crowded.

Wearing revealing clothes or shorts in a church is considered disrespectful. Topless bathing should be avoided.

Observe signs that prohibit photography. Photography of airports, military bases, places near high-tension towers, and police stations is forbidden. Some indigenous people do not like to be photographed so ask permission first.

Women Travelers

It is generally safe for women to travel alone but be warned that Peruvian men are persistent in their attention. It is common for men to stare, offer *piropos* (unsolicited comments or come-ons), whistle, and catcall. Peruvian women ignore them, so do the same. Fair, blonde women come in for most attention. Wearing a wedding ring or traveling in a group can be a disincentive. Do not flag taxis in the street, avoid walking alone on tourist trails or dark streets, and stay in centrally located hotels.

Disabled Travelers

While facilities for disabled people are improving, they are still inadequate. Wheelchair ramps and disabled toilets are rare. Only high-end hotels such as the Marriott, Sonesta, and Casa Andina have specially designed rooms for disabled travelers. Many archaeological sites are accessible but only with some assistance.

Time

Five hours behind Greenwich Mean Time (GMT), Peru is in the same time zone as the east coast of the USA (and an hour behind during US daylight saving time). Peru only has one time zone, and daylight saving is not in use.

Electricity

The electric current outlets are 220 volts and 60 cycles AC. There are two-prong outlets that accept both flat and round prongs. Some large hotels also have 110-volt outlets.

Tourist Information

The official tourism body, **PromPerú**, has small offices in many cities and towns, including Arequipa, Ayacucho, Cusco, Huaraz, Iquitos, Lima, Puno, and Trujillo. Brochures, maps, and information are available. There is also a 24-hour information hotline to assist travelers. Visitors can file a complaint at tourist offices or get advice on what to do if documents have been lost or stolen.

Women travelers looking at articles in a local market

Personal Security

Crime has become a threat for visitors to Peru, so it is important to be alert and take precautions. Theft and pick-pocketing are common in the main tourist cities and on long-distance bus routes. Always keep cash in a moneybelt under your clothes and do not wear expensive jewelry. Use ATMs during the day when there are more people around. Avoid walking alone on deserted stretches at night and always remain careful. Do not hail taxis on the street as they are not reliable, instead use radio taxis. Carry copies of important documents, such as your passport and visa, all the time.

POLICIA DE TURISMO
TOURIST POLICE

A woman officer at a tourist police station

Police

Peruvian police are generally helpful, especially in larger cities. They are allowed to check your visa and passport, so always carry some identification. A certified copy of the photo-graph and visa page of the passport is also acceptable. The officers can be recognized by their dark-green uniforms. If a policeman tries to solicit a bribe, politely refuse or suggest a visit to the nearest police station. Police officials are paid poorly and bribes can be as little as S/5 or an Inca Kola.

If, for some reason, you are held by the police, do not make a statement or sign any document without seeing a representative from your embassy or consulate. Also, insist on the services of a reliable translator.

The government has set up tourist police, or *policía de turismo*, offices in a number of cities such as Ayacucho, Cajamarca, Chiclayo, Cusco, Huancayo, Huaraz, Iquitos, Ica, Lima, Nazca, Puno, Tacna, and Trujillo, as well as a 24-hour hotline for visitors. Tourist police offer emergency assistance, and also register complaints about tourist operators, airlines, customs, or police officials. The tourist police officers speak English as well as Spanish. They can easily be distinguished from normal police by their white shirts. The men in brown uniforms standing outside private homes, apartments, offices, and shops are private security guards or vigilantes. They are not affiliated to the Peruvian police or military and are not authorized to hold or question visitors.

General Precautions

Be alert and aware of your surroundings at all times, especially on busy city streets and markets, airports, and bus terminals. Pickpockets are common in buses and *combis* and in crowded marketplaces. Baggage theft is rife on long distance bus trips.

For a safe and happy trip bear in mind some general guidelines on safety. Do not carry your wallet or passport in your back pocket. Keep expensive cameras out of view. In restaurants or cafés, hold your bag, or use the "leashes" on the table or chairs which can be attached to the bag handle.

Most cases of thefts involve momentary distraction – spilling something on your clothes, spitting, or a sudden fall are all possible diversions.

Make copies of important documents such as passport and airline tickets. Use safety deposit boxes for your valuables where available.

Never accept drinks from strangers, especially in nightclubs; there have been cases of drinks being laced with tranquilizing drugs.

Drugs

Possession of, or trafficking in, illegal drugs is considered an extremely serious offence in Peru. If arrested on drug charges, there is a protracted pretrial detention in poor prison conditions. A minimum sentence can lead to a lengthy imprisonment of several years, and there is no bail for drug trafficking offences. Avoid conversations about drugs with people you have just met and under no circumstances accept presents from strangers. There are lots of scams involving drugs and people posing as police, whose sole aim is to relieve you of your money.

Lost and Stolen Property

If your belongings are lost or stolen, notify the police within 24 hours as you will need an official report to claim your insurance. If your passport is misplaced or stolen, contact your embassy or consulate immediately. Report lost credit cards to the relevant company (see p318).

Taxis

Signs at Lima airport warn travelers to use official airport taxis only. Several taxi companies have counters at the exit of the immigration area. Check their blackboards for service rates. Thieves working in conjunction with unlicensed drivers have been known to smash windows and grab bags when the taxi stops or slows down in heavy traffic. Visitors must avoid taking street cabs, especially at night. Telephone-dispatched radio-taxis are more expensive than the regular taxis but are far more trustworthy. Ask your restaurant or hotel to arrange one.

Street Hazards

Most roads in Peru have inadequate traffic signs and markings and lack guard rails. Peruvian drivers, particularly taxi and *combi* drivers, disobey stop signs and traffic lights, disregard traffic lanes, and never stop for pedestrians, so be extra careful while crossing roads. They are also known for their hostile attitude – speeding buses, minibuses, taxis, and cars are part of the normal landscape. A 2005 university survey of 640 taxi drivers in Peru found that almost 40 percent of them

Earthquake safe zone sign

showed psychopathic attributes including "agressive, anxious and anti-social behavior."

When walking, always keep a lookout for uneven pathways and potholes. Driving at night is not recommended because, apart from the risk of robbery, lighting is also inadequate. The potholes are unmarked, pedestrians and animals may be wandering on roads, and obstacles, such as rocks or truck tyres, are difficult to spot due to poor visibility.

Natural Disasters

Earthquakes are common in Peru and small tremors are frequent. In case of an earthquake, move away from windows or weighty objects and take shelter under a doorway or a strong table if you are indoors. Never take refuge under a staircase during an earthquake and do not use elevators. If outdoors, stand clear of electric wires and poles and any tall structures. Quickly move to the safe zone identified easily by the green-

and-white earthquake symbols. Most hotels and office buildings in Peru have these signs indicating the safe areas.

Avalanches, landslides, and mud slides are common in the highlands. They destroy roads and railroad lines during rainfalls every year.

Typical pedestrian and traffic movement in a busy plaza, Cajamarca

Health Precautions

When traveling to Peru, pack a small medical kit of essentials before you leave home. This should include things of every-day need such as bandages, tweezers, scissors, tape, anti-bacterial ointment, antibacterial hand gel, and insect clothing spray. Although Peruvian pharmacies are well stocked, explaining what you need if you don't speak Spanish, can be a trial. It is sensible to carry prescription or allergy medicines and water purification tablets, if visiting remote areas. If you wear contact lenses, do not forget to bring the solution. The sunlight can be severe in high altitudes, so bring a sunhat and strong SPF sunscreen. Wear long-sleeved shirts and full length pants to avoid mosquito bites.

Medical Treatment

Peru's health care system is considered quite good. There are several top-notch private clinics as well as public hospitals in Lima. Despite the sometimes-limited facilities in the latter, Peruvian doctors are renowned for their resourcefulness. Smaller cities also have public hospitals and private clinics, however, anyone with a serious medical complaint should travel to Lima, where the facilities are much better. There are many English-speaking doctors and dentists prac-ticing here. Contact the hotel or the tourist information hotline *(see p313)*, for a list of reliable doctors and related information. If the condition is serious get in touch with your embassy.

Pharmacies

Peruvian pharmacies, known as *farmacias* or *boticas*, are identified by a red or green cross. Generic medicines and antibiotics are readily available. They can be purchased over the counter without any formal prescription.

Altitude Sickness

Almost all people who visit Arequipa, Cusco, Puno, Huaraz, and Huancayo succumb to some form of altitude sick-ness. Some of the common symptoms include shortness of breath, fatigue, heartpounding, headache, appetite loss, insomnia, and nausea. The solution is to take it easy till you get accustomed to the altitude. Eat lightly, drink lots of water, and avoid intense exercise, especially on the first day in a place of high altitude. Do not consume alcohol, cigarettes or sedatives. If acute symptoms persist for more than 24 hours, descend to a lower altitude at the earliest oppor-tunity and seek medical advice immediately. The symptoms should not be ignored as severe altitude sickness can sometimes develop into high altitude pulmonary edema – which leads to fluid in the lungs. It can also cause high altitude cerebral edema where the brain starts swelling. Both these situations can become serious, therefore extra care should be taken. You can resume the hike or journey after taking complete medication and proper rest. Coca tea and bottled oxygen helps, as does acetazolamide. Locals also recommend Sorojchi pills for altitude sickness. It is wise to stock up before you start a trip to the areas at higher altitudes.

Altitude sickness pills

Coca tea sachets

Vaccinations and Insurance

No vaccinations are officially required for a visit to Peru. However, travelers planning a jungle visit should get yellow fever vaccination. Hepatitis A, typhoid, and rabies vaccinations are recommended for people intending to trek to remote areas. Hepatitis B is suggested for visitors who expect to stay more than six months, or who might be exposed to blood, such as doctors, nurses, and health care volunteers. It is always best to ensure that tetanus and diphtheria shots are up to date. Plan your trip to Peru well in advance, since it usually takes about two weeks for vaccinations to take effect. In addition to the vaccinations, malaria pills are strongly recommended if traveling in the jungle.

Travel insurance is very important. Almost all Peruvian hospitals adopt a pay-first policy, and treatment in a private clinic can be very

Entrance to one of the Peruvian pharmacy chains

Travelers wearing protective clothes and trekking boots

DIRECTORY

International Clinics

Clínica Anglo Americana
Alfredo Salazar, 350, San Isidro,
Lima. **Map** 2 B4.
Tel 01 616 8900.

SANNA Clínica El Golf
Av. Aurelio Miro Quesada 1030,
San Isidro, Lima. **Map** 2 A3.
Tel 01 635 5000.

SANNA Clínica San Borja
Av. Guardia Civil, 337, San Borja.
Map 3 F2. **Tel** 01 635 5000.

Vaccination Centers

**International Health
Department**
Jorge Chávez International
Airport (Piso 1), Lima.
Tel 01 575 1745.
(Yellow fever only)

**International Vaccination
Centers**
Av. El Ejército 1756, San Isidro,
Lima. **Map** 2 A5. **Tel** 01 264 6889.
In Cusco, go to a private clinic
w cuzco.info/hospitals.htm

expensive. Make sure that the insurance policy covers activities that can be dangerous, such as rafting and mountain climbing. It should also have the provision of supporting an ambulance or an emergency flight home.

Health Hazards

Mosquito-borne diseases such as malaria, yellow fever, and dengue fever are not common in Peru. Malaria is most prevalent in the jungles of northern Peru. Mosquitoes are usually at their worst at dawn and dusk. Use heavy-duty insect repellent, mosquito coils known as *espirales*, and a mosquito net at night. Squirt your clothes with a permethrin-based spray even during the day. Wear long pants, long-sleeved shirts, a hat, and shoes to protect yourself. If a bite becomes infected, see a doctor. Malaria pills are advised for travelers visiting the Amazon, however, there is no vaccination for dengue, a viral infection with flu-like symptoms.

Do not underestimate the power of the sun. Wear a sun hat, 15 or higher SPF sunblock, sunglasses, and avoid the midday sun. Even though it may feel cooler, the sun is more intense at high altitudes. Drink lots of water to guard against dehydration, and take time to acclimatize.

When hiking at very high altitudes, or even taking a long

bus trip through the mountains, make sure you are prepared. Have layers of clothing, including fleecy tops, a woolen hat, a rainproof jacket, as keeping dry is crucial, and a lightweight space blanket. Do carry a sufficient supply of food and water. Hypothermia might set in under extreme conditions. The symptoms include skin numbness, shivering, slurred speech, aggressive behaviour, cramps, and dizziness. If afflicted, get the person out of the weather and change their clothes if they are wet. Have high calorie food, such as chocolates, and any hot drinks for immediate nourishment. Rest until the temperature returns back to normal.

Tap water and ice is not safe. Take basic precautions with food *(see p280)* to avoid traveler's diarrhea. Do not feed or fondle animals, aside from domestic ones. They carry diseases and can react unpredictably. Any animal bite or scratch should be cleaned immediately with soap, water, and antiseptic. Contact the local health authorities in case you need follow-up rabies treatment.

Insect repellent

HIV and AIDS

While official statistics about HIV/AIDS, or SIDA in Spanish, are a little vague in Peru, the UN classifies it as a low level epidemic. Some 75 percent of people affected by HIV/AIDS live in Lima and Callao. Most are

men but the fastest-growing incidence of the illness is among women. The risk of infection is small, but take precautions. The concept of safe sex is not common in Peru.

Public toilet signboard in Spanish
as well as English

Public Toilets

There are public toilets in small towns, as well as petrol stations, bus and train terminals, and markets, but they are not always clean. Facilities in shopping malls, department stores, and large supermarkets are usually better, while toilets at airports and major tourist centers are generally adequate. Carry toilet paper; cubicles rarely have any, though some transport terminals have attendants who charge the visitors for providing a few sheets of toilet paper.

Banking and Local Currency

The unit of currency in Peru is the nuevo sol, although US dollars are widely accepted. Large hotels, shops, and restaurants in bigger towns and cities accept major credit cards. Carry cash in US dollars as other currencies are not always readily available, although the euro is fast gaining acceptance. Carry some coins and smaller notes for taxis, buses, and minor purchases as storekeepers and drivers rarely have sufficient change for larger denominations. The amount of money you may bring in or take out of the country is limited to $US 10,000.

A *casa de cambio* or foreign currency exchange booth

Banks and Moneychangers

The most well known banks in Peru are **Banco de Credito (BCP)**, **Banco de la Nacion**, **BBVA Banco Continental**, and **Scotiabank** which took over Banco Weisse Sudameris. Banking hours are normally between 9am and 6pm, weekdays, and almost all banks are open on Saturdays until noon.

Banks are the safest places to exchange money but their rates are generally lower than *casas de cambio* (foreign currency exchanges) or street moneychangers. Normal bank commissions can be anything from zero to three percent. Practice general precautions wherever you exchange money. Count your money in the presence of the cashier, never accept damaged bills, and always check the notes before you leave the counter. *Cambistas* (street moneychangers) usually loiter outside banks and *casas de cambio*. Although a badge and colored vest identify them as legal, these are not always an indication of their honesty. However, they do offer competitive rates and are open to bargaining but it is best to use them only when exchanging small amounts of cash. Check their calculations and the Peruvian notes before handing over money. Moneychangers are often the only option at border crossings.

Credit Cards and Traveler's Checks

Credit cards are accepted in all major cities of Peru, with VISA being the most popular. Many businesses add a surcharge of up to 12 percent for paying with a credit card, although high-end hotels and restaurants often waive it. Always check the amount you are being charged. In small towns and rural areas, credit cards are less likely to be accepted so always carry cash.

Traveler's checks are exchanged at fewer places these days, and the exchange rate is usually less than for cash. You will be asked for identification so carry your passport. **American Express** is the most recognized brand. Traveler's checks can be difficult to exchange in small towns and villages, and replacing them outside of Lima is almost impossible.

Logos of the major credit cards accepted in the main cities of Peru

ATMs

ATMs are easily found in major towns and cities. Look for machines with the Global Net sign, as some of the ATMs dispense money only to local account holders. Banks impose a fee each time a card is used at an

ATM (check with your bank before departing) and withdrawals are either in soles or US dollars. As a precaution withdraw money at ATMs inside banks or shops in shopping malls.

Cash and Electronic Transfers

US dollars are the easiest foreign currency to use in Peru. Most restaurants, hotels, and shops in the main cities accept them as payment. However, if you pay in US dollars, you will receive soles as change. Electronic money transfers can be arranged via Western Union or Moneygram to agents throughout Peru.

Money can be made available quickly but commission is charged. Home bank money transfers to Peru can be difficult, if not impossible.

Tipping and Taxes

While not compulsory, tips are appreciated by hotel staff, drivers, porters, and guides. Unofficial parking attendants watch over your car and expect a tip for doing so. All goods and services attract a 18 percent value added tax (IGV). Hotels and restaurants add a ten percent service fee. As per law, vendors are obliged to show the client the final price, including taxes.

Currency

The Peruvian nuevo sol is divided into 100 céntimos, and is represented by the symbol S/. It was introduced on July 1, 1991, to replace the highly inflated inti, which took over from soles in 1985. Counterfeit currency, in US dollars as well as nuevo soles, is in circulation in the country. Do not accept old, faded, torn, or taped bills as they are difficult to get rid of, although moneychangers may trade them. Shops and super-markets will routinely check S/100 bills, and these large bills can be hard to change in small towns.

Bank Notes

Peruvian nuevo sol notes are issued in five denominations – S/10, S/20, S/50, S/100, and S/200.

10 nuevo soles

20 nuevo soles

50 nuevo soles

100 nuevo soles

200 nuevo soles

Coins

There are seven coins – 5, 10, 20, and 50 céntimos and S/1, S/2, and S/5. The lower denominations are copper while 50c and S/1 are silver colored. S/2 and S/5 have a copper colored center with silver surround.

S/1   S/2   S/5

5c   10c   20c   50c

Communications

The telephone is the most popular form of communication in Peru. Public telephones, using either coins or pre-paid phone cards, are common in towns and cities. The postal service can be slow and large companies in Lima use a delivery service for more important correspondence. Low cost Internet kiosks are available throughout the country. Peru has several free-to-air television channels, cable TV service, and a number of national and regional radio stations. The leading daily newspaper is *El Comercio*.

Public Telephones

Public telephones are quite widespread in Peru; almost every main square across the country has one. Telefónica is the primary phone company and its mobile phone provider arm is known as Movistar. Claro and Nextel are other major mobile phone service providers.

Public phones accept coins (both céntimos and nuevo soles) and phone cards sold at kiosks, supermarkets, and pharmacies. Avoid buying cards from street vendors as they are often used cards being recycled. Pre-paid cards with a value of up to S/30 are available and are best used to make local calls. The most commonly used card in Peru is Tarjeta 147.

International calls can also be made from private *cabinas* (cabins) in Telefónica's main offices. Keep in mind that calls made from hotels incur very expensive surcharges and are best avoided. Major international phone cards can be used in Peru but make sure that you have the list of access codes available.

Internet to phone systems are available in a number of Internet kiosks, with cable connections that are usually clearer than telephone lines.

One of the colorful Telefónica booths found all over Peru

Using a Coin and Card Telephone

1 Lift the receiver and wait for the dial tone. The digital display will indicate that you have to insert a coin.

2 At least one 20 céntimos coin is required to make a call to a mobile phone or to a local number.

3 Dial 1-4-7 if using a 147 card. You will be directed in Spanish to dial the 12 digit code provided on your card. You will also be given details about the remaining value and time available for the call.

4 Dial the required number in the following order – country code, followed by area code and then the number. Once you finish the call, your card will automatically emerge.

Pre-paid card

Useful Dialling Codes

- To call Peru from abroad, dial your international access code, the country code, which is 51, followed by the area code minus the first 0, and the number.
- For international calls from Peru dial 00, followed by the country code, the area code, and the number.
- Codes: Australia 61; Canada and USA 1; Ireland 353; New Zealand 64; South Africa 27; UK 44.
- For long-distance calls in Peru, dial the three digit area code, followed by the number. For calls within the same department, omit the code.
- All areas other than Lima have a three digit area code begining with 0 and followed by a six or eight digit number.
- To make international reverse-charge or collect calls, dial 108 and ask for *llamada de cobrado revertido* and give the number. For national collect calls, dial 129.
- For directory enquiries, dial 103 and for national calls, dial 109 (in Spanish).
- For emergency assistance, dial 105 for police and 116 for medical assistance (in Spanish).
- Numbers beginning with 9 are mobile phone numbers.

Mobile Phones

Mobile phone use is widespread in Peru. Almost all carriers work in Lima and other major cities and tourist areas. Travelers with tri-band mobile phones can use them providing their plan has international roaming and their carrier has a partner in the region. It is possible to rent and buy pre-paid mobile phones (called cellulars in Peru). Sale counters are located inside the baggage hall at the airport, as international travelers exit passport control.

Internet

Cabinas (Internet cabins) are widely available throughout Peru, especially in major cities. Most of them consist of simple cubicles with terminals and sometimes printers. The hourly rates are quite inexpensive. Only the top hotels in Peru have in-room Internet connections. Wi-Fi is gradually gaining in popularity, particularly in Lima. In its Miraflores district, some public parks offer Wi-Fi. Hotel business centers usually charge high rates for Internet access.

Fax services are available at many hotels, but they are expensive. Some shops also have facilities for sending and receiving faxes.

Peruvian Addresses

Peruvian addresses list the street number after the street name. The *departamento* (apartment) number comes next, followed by the suburb and *código postal* (post code). For business centers, the *piso* (floor) and the number of the *oficina* (office) are included in the address. "Jr" is short for *jirón* (street) and "S/n" signifies *sin numero* meaning without a number.

Radio and Television

There are many radio stations in Peru, however, all of them broadcast in Spanish. There are seven free-to-air television channels. Cable TV is widely available, with Cable Mágico as the most popular provider.

Roadside kiosk packed with magazines and tourist information material

More than 100 channels in a variety of languages are available. Plus TV, which has a range of lifestyle shows, and news channel Canal N are the most famous Peruvian cable channels. High-end hotels offer in-room cable TV.

Postal Services

The Peruvian mail service is run by a private company, **Serpost**. International letters and postcards usually take a few weeks to reach their destination. A *certificado* (registered mail) service is also available. All major cities have a main post office, open from 8am to 8pm Monday to Saturday; some may open on Sunday morning. The fastest way to send important documents, letters, or packages is via courier. **DHL**, **FedEx**, and **TNT** have offices in Lima.

Newspapers and Magazines

The most widely read daily newspaper in Lima is the conservative *El Comercio,* which also has a Friday supplement

A standard red-and-white mailbox of the mail service, Serpost

on arts and entertainment with listings for Lima. *La República* is highly regarded for its investigative news coverage, while *Peru 21* is an easy-reading daily tabloid.

There are no English-language local newspapers in Peru. However, some kiosks in Lima stock international papers such as the *International Herald Tribune,* although they are usually a few days old. News magazines such as *Time* and *Newsweek* are also available. The most influential magazine in the country is *Caretas.*

TRAVEL INFORMATION

Peru is a large country and while the highway system and access to remote areas has improved, internal travel is not always as fast as you might hope. There are airports in the main cities, and flying is by far the most time-efficient way to travel. The air transportation system is well developed. Train travel is almost non-existent. The majority of Peruvians, and indeed many tourists, rely on buses to get around. Driving can be an alarming experience as road conditions are not good. The reward, on the other hand, is a glimpse of Peru that air travelers will never see. As there is no system of state public transport, a clutter of overcrowded minibuses, dilapidated buses, and battle-scarred taxis ply the streets of Peru's cities.

Domestic and international check-in desks at Lima's airport

Airports

Fourteen Peruvian airports are equipped to handle domestic flights and several are deemed to have inter-national capabilities. In reality, however, Lima's Jorge Chávez airport is the only fully equip-ped international airport and all international passengers must pass through it. Trujillo, Chiclayo, Piura, Tarapoto, Iquitos, Juliaca, Cusco, Tacna, Arequipa, and Cajamarca (*see p325*) among others, have respectable airport facilities but in more remote towns the runway may be nothing more than an isolated strip.

Arriving by Air

The key arrival point for interna-tional flights into Peru is Lima's **Aeropuerto Internacional Jorge Chávez**, 10 miles (16 km) northwest of the city. Flights from here connect other major cities and towns as well as inter-national destinations.

There are direct flights connecting Peru to various cities of North America such as Miami, the main hub for Latin America, as well as Atlanta, Dallas, Houston, Newark, and New York. The main carriers of this route are **American**, **Delta**, **Continental**, and **LanPeru/LanChile** (*see p325*). Airlines such as American, Delta, and Continental all fly to Peru from Canada, stopping at their hubs in the USA. **Air Canada** connects with other carriers in the USA, usually via Miami. LanPeru/LanChile stop in Los Angeles, New York, or Miami en route to Lima from Canada. There are no direct flights to

Lima from the UK or Ireland. Travelers must go via Europe or the USA. **Iberia** flies direct from Madrid to Lima, while **Air France/KLM** flies from Amsterdam and Lufthansa flies from Frankfurt. LAN flies direct from Lima to Madrid.

From Australia and New Zealand, travelers can fly via Buenos Aires on **Aerolíneas Argentinas** and then connect to Lima. **Qantas** and LAN have a code share agreement, so travelers can fly via Auckland and Santiago and connect with a flight to Lima, or travel via Los Angeles.

Aeromexico, **Tam**, Copa Airlines, **Taca** (*see p325*), and Avianca operate direct flights from Colombia, Brazil, Mexico, and some Central American cities, as well as Cuba.

Airline timetables are subject to change due to unpredictable weather conditions or other unavoidable situations, so reconfirm flight timings.

Arriving by Land

Visitors can enter Peru overland through Ecuador, Bolivia, or Chile. There are three border crossings for vehicles – from Huaquillas in Ecuador to Aguas Verdes in Peru, from Arica in Chile to Tacna in Peru, and from Desaguadero in Bolivia to Desaguadero in Peru.

A long-distance bus for visitors on an overland journey

Travelers from Quito in Ecuador will pass through the major northern coastal cities en route to Lima. From Bolivia, there is a frequent service from La Paz and Copacabana to Puno, and on to Cusco.

From Chile, most buses travel from Arica to Tacna, connecting with buses to Arequipa or Lima. Since many visitors prefer to enter and leave Peru by bus, companies such as **Expreso Internacional Ormeño**, Cruz del Sur, and **Caracol** run services linking Peru with neighboring South American countries.

Arriving by Boat

Peru is an important stop on the itineraries of several international cruise lines. Several cruise boats stop off in the port of Callao, near Lima. Passengers are permitted to disembark for excursions in the surrounding areas. **Princess**

Cruises also stops off in the port of Salaverry in Trujillo for visits to the nearby Mochica temples.

Peru can be accessed from Brazil by boat on the Amazon River via the border crossing from Manaos, on the Brazilian side, to Iquitos in Peru. Smaller ports, such as Santa Rosa, Tabatinga, and Leticia, at the tri-border between Peru, Brazil, and Colombia, are connected by ferries.

Organized Tours

Agents in Australia, Europe, and North America offer organized tours to Peru. Nature trips geared towards bird-watching, wildlife-viewing, or jungle treks are popular. Others include visiting archaeological sites, trekking through the Andes,

Tour operator sign board

white-water rafting, mountain climbing and biking, as well as surfing. A range of Peruvian holidays are available via members of the **Latin American Travel Association (UK)**, Australia's **Peregrine Adventures**, and the **South and Central American Travel Association (Nth America)**. Within Peru, **Explorandes** and **Lima Tours** offer a variety of organized tours focusing on special interest (*see pp308–9*). The peak tourist season is from May to November.

Departure Tax

All travelers leaving Peru are required to pay a mandatory departure tax, however this fee is now included in the price of outbound plane tickets so there is no longer a need to pay it at the airport.

DIRECTORY

Airports

Aeropuerto Internacional Jorge Chávez
Callao, Lima.
Tel 01 511 6055 (flight information).
W lap.com.pe

Airlines

Aerolineas Argentinas
Av. Dean Valdivia 243, Oficina 301, San Isidro, Lima. **Map** 3 D2.
Tel 01 513 6565, 0800 52 200 (free call).
W aerolineas.com.ar

Aeromexico
Av. Pardo y Aliaga 699, Of. 501, San Isidro, Lima. **Map** 2 C4. **Tel** 01 705 1111, 0800 53 407 (free call).
W aeromexico.com

Air Canada
Calle Italia 389, Lima.
Map 4 A1.
Tel 01 626 0900, 0800 52 073 (free call).
W aircanada.com

Air France/KLM
Alvarez Calderón 185, Oficina 601, San Isidro, Lima. **Map** 2 B4.
Tel 01 213 0200.

American Airlines
Av. Jorge Basadre 265, San Isidro, Lima. **Map** 2 C2. **Tel** 01 211 7000, 0800 40 350 (free call). **W** aa.com

Delta
Av. Victor Andres Belaunde 147, San Isidro, Torre Real 3 Oficina 701.
Map 2 C3. **Tel** 0 800 50861/ 211 9211. **W** delta.com

Iberia
Av. Camino Real 390, Oficina 902, Lima. **Map** 2 C2. **Tel** 01 411 7801.
W iberia.com

Qantas
Av. Conquistadores 256, Oficina 601-B, Lima. **Map** 2 C4. **Tel** 01 221 4444.
W qantas.com.au

Tam
Av. Jose Pardo 513, Miraflores, Lima.
Map 4 B1. **Tel** 01 213 8300.

Arriving by Land

Caracol
Av. Brasil 487, Lima. **Map** 1 D4.
Tel 01 431 1400. **W** perucaracol.com

Expreso Internacional Ormeño SA
Av. Javier Prado Este 1057, Lima.
Map 3 D2. **Tel** 01 472 1710.
W grupo-ormeno.com.pe

Arriving by Boat

Princess Cruises
24844 Av. Rockefeller Santa Clarita, CA 91355. **Tel** 1 800 PRINCESS (USA). **W** princess.com

Organized Tours

Explorandes
Calle Aristides Aljovin 484, Miraflores, Lima.
Map 4 C2. **Tel** 01 200 6100.
W explorandes.com

Latin American Travel Association (UK)
W lata.org

Lima Tours
Av. Nicolas de Pierola 589 (at Hotel Crillon), Lima.
Tel 01 619 6900.
W limatours.com.pe

Peregrine Adventures
380 Lonsdale Street, Melbourne, VIC 3000. **Tel** 1300 85 44 44 (within Australia), 61 3 8601 4444.
W peregrineadventures.com

South and Central American Travel Association (Nth America)
W sata-usa.com

Domestic Flights

In a country with a vastly rugged terrain such as Peru, internal flights offer a convenient alternative to long and sometimes grueling bus journeys, especially for travelers with serious time constraints. While air travel is usually more expensive than bus travel, the smaller domestic airline companies such as Star Peru and Peruvian Airlines do offer deals from time to time, although their networks are limited. LanPeru provides a majority of the flights, servicing all the major centers. The flights often make a brief stopover at some of the other Peruvian towns.

		Llegadas Arrivals		
Hora *Time*	Procedencia *From*	Vuelo *Flight*	Estimada *Expected*	Observaciones *Remarks*
11:00	MALVINAS	06	1650	DELAYED
14:10	PUCALLPA	2I	3234	14:19 LANDED
14:20	CAJAMARCA	06	109	14:25 LANDED
14:40	CUSCO	06	221	14:35 LANDED
14:55	HUANUCO	LCB	1332	14:44 LANDED
15:20	CUSCO	LP	072	15:20 CONFIRMED
16:20	CUSCO	LP	028	LAN
16:45	CUSCO	LP	038	LAN
17:00	AREQUIPA	2I	1234	STAR PERU
17:00	ICA	06	1627	AEROCONDOR

Schedule board at one of the domestic airports

Domestic Airlines

International passengers arriving at Jorge Chavéz International Airport in Lima can connect with scheduled domestic flights. Flights leave frequently from the capital to all of Peru's major cities, although flight times can change without warning.

LanPeru, which is part of the Chilean owned LAN airline company, operates an extensive network with regular flights from Lima to Tacna, Arequipa, Cusco, Chiclayo, Piura, Iquitos, Pucallpa, Puerto Maldonado, Juliaca, Tarapoto, Trujillo, Cajamarca, and Tumbes.

Peruvian Airlines flies from Lima to Arequipa, Cusco, Pucallpa, Tarapoto, Iquitos, Piura, and Tacna.

Star Peru has flights from Lima to Cusco and Puerto Maldonado in the south, to Iquitos, Pucallpa, and Tarapoto in the jungle, and to Ayacucho and Huánuco in the Central Andes.

LC Peru currently flies small 19-passenger Fairchilds to Andahuaylas, Ayacucho, Cajamarca, Huaraz, Huánuco, Jauja, Pisco, and Tingo Maria. They also offer charter services. There are several daily flights to Cusco, however, most flights depart in the morning as weather conditions in the

Andes can change in the afternoon. Central America's **Taca** flies to many cities throughout Latin America and operates several daily flights between Lima and Arequipa, Chiclayo, Cusco, Juliaca, Piura, Puerto Maldonado, Tarapoto, and Trujillo.

Distant towns are reached via connecting flights. Flights from Lima to Juliaca, for example, stop in Cusco or Arequipa. Some flights from Lima to Puerto Maldonado stop in Cusco, and Arequipa is a pitstop on some flights to Juliaca. Small towns do not have daily services.

Reservations and Checking-In

Tickets can be purchased through travel agents, tour operators, or directly from the airlines on their websites.

Reservations should be made well in advance, especially during peak travel periods, such as May to November, Easter (Semana Santa), Christmas, and the national Fiestas Patrias (July 28 and 29). Fare prices are significantly higher during these times.

Flights are routinely overbooked so it is advisable to check in via the airline company's website no later than 48 hours before the flight. Flights are canceled or changed with annoying regularity. Passengers are advised to arrive for check-in at least 2 hours ahead of scheduled take-off, as long queues at the counters and baggage x-ray are routine. Airlines will often reallocate tickets if passengers have not checked-in at least 60 minutes before departure time on busy flights, or may refuse check-in.

Baggage being loaded on to a LanPeru aircraft

Perú Perú gift shop at Lima airport

The economy class baggage allowance for domestic flights is usually two pieces of luggage weighing a total of 51 lb (23 kg). For some international flights, passengers can carry only up to 51 lb (23 kg), although some airlines allow two pieces of luggage weighing 51 lb (23 kg) each. Business class flyers are allowed 71 lb (32 kg). Carry-on baggage is limited to one piece, weighing not more than 11 lb (5 kg). All airlines, domestic as well as international, do not allow passengers to smoke on board during the flight. A small domestic airport departure tax of a little more than US$6 is included in the price for all plane tickets.

Jorge Chavéz International Airport is renowned as one of the best airports in South America and is well regarded among travelers due to its good facilities and helpful staff. Travelers can access a wide choice of international food and drink outlets, and a hotel with business amenities and spa facilities. A good range of shops in the Peru Plaza shopping area sell Peruvian and international brand goods. Visitors cannot take Peruvian artifacts out of the country. Any replica items should be accompanied by a certificate, which may be requested at the airport.

Concessionary Fares

Infants under two-years can travel free on domestic flights, provided they do not occupy a seat of their own. Children over two years and under 12 years of age pay 50 percent of the full fare, which buys them a regular seat and standard baggage allowance.

Passengers waiting patiently at the check-in counter

DIRECTORY

Airlines

LanPeru
Av. José Pardo 513,
Miraflores, Lima.
Map 4 B1. **Tel** 01 213 8200. ⓦ lan.com

LC Peru
Av. José Pardo 269,
Miraflores. **Map** 4 B1.
Tel 01 204 1313.
ⓦ lcperu.pe

Peruvian Airlines
Av. José Pardo 495,
Miraflores. **Map** 4 B1.
Tel 01 716 6000,
01 715 6122.
ⓦ peruvian.pe

Star Peru
Av. Jose Pardo 485,
Miraflores, Lima.
Map 4 B1.
Tel 01 705 9000.
ⓦ starperu.com

Taca
Av. José Pardo 812,
Miraflores.
Map 4 B1. **Tel** 01 511 8222 (reservations).
ⓦ taca.com

Regional Airports

Aeropuerto Alfredo Rodríguez Ballon
Arequipa.
Tel 054 44 3459,
054 44 3464.

Aeropuerto Mayor General Armando Revoredo Iglesias
Cajamarca.
Tel 076 343 757.

Aeropuerto Alejandro Velasco Astete
Cusco.
Tel 084 22 2601.

Aeropuerto Capitan José Abelardo Quiñones Gonzáles
Chiclayo. **Tel** 074 23 6016.

Aeropuerto Inca Manco Cápac
Juliaca. **Tel** 054 32 8974.

Aeropuerto Coronel Francisco Secada Vignetta
Iquitos. **Tel** 065 22 8444.

Aeropuerto Capitán Mondes
Talara. **Tel** 073 38 5070.

Aeropuerto Capitán Guillermo Concha Ibérico
Piura.
Tel 073 34 8279.

Aeropuerto Coronel Carlos Ciriani Santa Rosa
Tacna. **Tel** 052 314 503.

Aeropuerto Comandante Guillermo del Castillo Paredes
Tarapoto.
Tel 042 53 2206.

Aeropuerto Capitán Carlos Martínez de Pinillos
Trujillo.
Tel 044 46 4224.

Corporación Peruana de Aeropuertos y Aviación Comercial (CORPAC) – Information on domestic airports and flights
ⓦ corpac.gob.pe

Traveling by Bus and Train

Buses are the most economical way of traveling around Peru. Deluxe bus services offer comfortable seats, air conditioning, and safe drivers, although you pay more for the pleasure. Avoid the bargain basement operators – their vehicles are usually lacking in the road-worthy stakes and drivers are not safety conscious. Trains in Peru are limited. There is a daily train service between Cusco and Machu Picchu, and a less-frequent service between Cusco and Puno.

A deluxe Cruz del Sur bus, ideal for long-distance travel

Buses and Terminals

While no one bus company services the entire country, the larger ones, including **Cruz del Sur** and **Movil Tours**, cover almost all the major areas. Each has its own office, either in the main long-haul bus terminal in regional areas or huddled together in one part of town. Buses depart Lima's **Plaza Norte** terminal station for many destinations within Peru, as well as to Buenos Aires in Argentina and Santiago de Chile in Chile. Do remember to check from which terminal the bus departs or arrives when buying the ticket.

Traditionally, bus terminals are in the poorer districts, particularly in Lima, and bag-snatchers and pickpockets are rampant. It is best to buy your tickets in advance, so that you do not have to worry about keeping an eye on your luggage at the same time.

Small pieces of luggage can be carried on board, larger ones are stowed in the luggage compartment. A baggage ticket will be provided for later retrieval. Make sure all bags are securely locked. Theft of carry-on luggage is common. Place luggage on a rack where you can see it. If traveling alone, try not to fall asleep. If traveling with a friend, take turns to watch the bags. The farther you travel away from the main cities, the worse are the roads, and the

poor conditions of the road can double travel time. Delays are very common during the rainy season in the highlands and the jungle.

Traveling at night is not recommended as some hijacks have occurred on buses along the deserted mountain roads, with passengers being robbed of cash, expensive items, and even passports.

Bus fares double during peak travel times, and tickets can be sold out weeks in advance. Tickets can be bought online from companies, or travel agencies, or directly on the bus.

Luxury Buses

For long-distance hauls, Peru's intercity luxury bus services are the way to go. They are more comfortable, much

safer, and more reliable than other services. The deluxe buses offer fully reclining bed-like seats, direct non-stop travel, all meals, air conditioning, videos, reading lamps, a hostess, and on-board toilets. One bus line even organizes a bingo game for passengers. Companies identify their top services with names such as Imperial, First Class, or Especial.

The next level is the business or *ejecutivo* class, which shares many features of the deluxe service, excluding the bed seats. Both deluxe and business services are much faster as they only make fuel stops, and buses travel with two drivers so that they can drive in 4-hour shifts. The buses have a controlled speed limit.

Economy services run by the large companies include comfortable seats, qualified drivers, and programmed toilet and food stops for long-haul trips. Many travelers, however, bring their own food, rather than rely on eateries in the middle of nowhere.

Trains

Perúrail, which is owned by the Orient Express group, runs daily train services from Cusco to Aguas Calientes, the station for Machu Picchu. Trains also depart from Ollantaytambo to Machu Picchu. Three trains depart from Cusco's Poroy station every morning for the four-hour trip: the mid-range Vistadome 1, Vistadome 2, and the budget Backpacker

Backpacker train to Machu Picchu, for those traveling on a budget

Passenger boat ferrying visitors to the islands on Lake Titicaca

train. The luxurious Hiram Bingham *(see p180)* departs daily from Poroy Station, outside Cusco. Perúrail also operates the upmarket Andean Explorer, and the Backpacker train from Cusco to Puno and back four times a week. They also run a train charter service on the route between Arequipa and Puno.

One of the highest railroads in the world operates intermittently from Lima to the Andean cities of La Oroya and Huancayo *(see p187)*. Information on its services are available from **Ferrovias Central Andina S.A.**

Boats

Slow-moving passenger boats ferry tourists to various islands on Lake Titicaca, however, there is no regular service to Bolivia. Many boat companies organize trips to the islands in Lake Titicaca.

Boats carry passengers as well as cargo along the Amazon. Boat names and departure times are displayed at ports. The timetables are flexible as the boats depart only when they have a full load of cargo. Do check with the harbor master, known as the *capitania*, for reliable information. Passengers either rent a cabin or carry a hammock and string it on the upper deck.

The most popular routes are from Yurimaguas or Pucallpa to Iquitos. Travelers can also cross over into Peru from Brazil via the river, landing in Iquitos.

Companies, such as **Amazon River Expeditions** also operate upmarket river cruises which explore the national reserves of Allpahuauyo-Mishana and Pacaya-Samiria, which is accessible only by boat. Visitors can fish the river or gently cruise the Amazon to the junction of the Marañón and Ucayali rivers. Rivers can swell greatly during the rains and become dangerous for boat travel.

Three-wheeled taxi

Taxis are plentiful on Lima streets but not all are licensed

Local Transport

The cheapest way to get around major Peruvian cities is via public transport. In Lima, that means taxis, buses, or minibuses known as *micros* or *combis* or *colectivos (see p329)*. Most of them are aging sedans imported from the US, though Japanese and Korean minibuses are taking over. *Colectivos* usually run on fixed routes throughout Peru, such as between Cusco and Pisac and from Huanchco to Trujillo. Taxis can be easily flagged down in the streets but they cannot be trusted. It is safer to call for a radio-taxi.

In provincial towns, *ticos*, which are tiny Korean-made cars and motorcycle rickshaws, known as *mototaxis* or *motokars*, are common. Not the safest means of transport, it is best to avoid them. A more convenient alternative is to contact your hotel or tour agency. Hire a car and driver, or a taxi by the hour or day.

DIRECTORY

Bus Travel

Cruz del Sur
Av. Javier Prado Este 1109,
La Victoria, Lima.
Map 3 F1.
Tel 01 311 5050.
w cruzdelsur.com.pe

Movil Tours
Av. Paseo de la República
749, Lima.
Map 1 F4.
Tel 01 716 8000.
w moviltours.com.pe

Plaza Norte Bus Terminal
Intersection of Panamericana
Norte with Av. Tomás Valle and
Av. Túpac Amaru, Independencia.

Train Services

**Ferrovias Central
Andina S.A.**
Av. José Galvez Barrenechea
566 (Piso 5), San Isidro, Lima.
Map 3 F2.
Tel 01 226 6363.
w ferrocarrilcentral.com.pe

Perúrail
Av. Pachacutec s/n, Cusco.
Tel 084 581 414.
w perurail.com

Boat Travel

Amazon River Expeditions
Av. Las Camelias 511,
Oficina 402, Lima.
Tel 01 421 9195/442 4515.
w amazonrex.com

Driving in Peru

Traveling around at your own pace in a car may seem like the most flexible way to explore Peru, however, you need to keep some general rules in mind. Poor road conditions, expensive fuel, scarcity of fuel stations, and aggressive drivers are just a few of the hazards. Consider renting a car at each destination and using it only in that area rather than traversing the entire country in one car. Driving at night can be dangerous in remote areas and robberies do occur.

Sign showing a speed limit on a highway

Rules of the Road

Peruvians drive on the right-hand side of the road and distances are measured in kilometers. Wearing of seatbelts is compulsory. Normal speed limits are 25 mph (40 km/h) in streets, 38 mph (60 km/h) in avenues, 50 mph (80 km/h) on expressways, and 19 mph (30 km/h) in school and hospital zones. The speed limit is 38 mph (60 km/h) on rural roads and 62 mph (100 km/h) on highways. Speeds are reduced to 34 mph (55 km/h) in residential areas and 22 mph (35 km/h) in commercial areas when a highway crosses a town. Traffic must come to a stop at all "Stop" (*pare*) signs. Usual international road signs are used.

Bump ahead sign

Road Network

Peru has over 48,000 miles (78,000 km) of roads, with 10,380 miles (16,705 km) of *carreteras* (national highways). The Carretera Panamericana Norte y Sur, or Panamerican Highway North, are the most important highway linking the towns along Peru's coast. The Carretera Marginal de la Selva connects towns in the northern jungle with those in the south, near the Bolivian border. The Carretera Central begins in Lima and cuts inland to the central highlands, climbing through the mountain pass of Ticlio, which at 15,810 ft (4,818 m) above sea level, is one of the world's highest railroad pass. Few roads, aside from the highways, have signposts. In towns, street names are rarely signposted. The percentage of unpaved roads increases with distance from main cities.

Road Maps

Pick up a road map prior to arriving as detailed versions can be hard to find. The **Instituto Geográfico Nacional** and the **Touring y Automóvil Club del Perú** sell them. Road maps are included in travel guides such as *Guía Toyota* and *Guía Inca del Perú*.

Fuel Stations

Fuel is expensive in Peru, with costs rising according to the grade, diesel being the cheapest. Fuel stations such as Repsol and Primax are plentiful in large cities and towns but less common in rural or jungle areas. Get the tank refilled whenever you get a chance. Stations are not self-service, therefore when the attendant asks "*cuánto*", either specify an amount or say "*lleno por favor*" (fill it up). Credit cards may not be accepted in remote areas.

Car and Motorcycle Rental

Car rental companies such as **American**, **Avis**, **Budget**, **Dollar**, **Hertz**, and **National** have offices in Lima and other major cities. All have 24-hour desks at Lima airport. Drivers must be at least 25 years of age and have a driving license from their own country or an International Driving Permit. Optional services, available for an additional charge, include theft and accident insurance, tow truck service, pick-up or drop-off in another city, and airport pick-up.

Make sure you understand the rental agreement and all costs involved before signing. Inspect the vehicle before accepting delivery to make sure it is in good condition. In the event of an accident obtain a copy of the police report. Always carry your driver's license and copies of your passport and the rental contract. Four-wheel drive vehicles are best for remote rural areas and motorcycle rental is usually limited to jungle towns.

Road Safety

Most roads in Peru have inadequate traffic signs and markings. Speeding buses, minibuses, taxis, and cars are part of the landscape. Driving at night in Peru is not recommended due to the number of obstacles. It is wise to sound the horn and flash your lights to indicate that someone can overtake, or cut in.

Getting Around Lima

The best way to explore Central Lima is on foot, although you need to take some form of transport to reach the suburbs of Miraflores and Barranco. Traffic is chaotic and congested, thanks to myriad taxis and minibuses, and is best avoided during rush hours. If you choose to drive, do so with the doors locked and the windows closed. Use guarded parking lots, rather than unattended on-street parking.

Walking

Walking is the best way to explore the heart of Lima's historic center, as well as other areas such as Barranco. The main pedestrianized thoroughfare in the center of Lima is Jirón de la Unión, which connects Plaza San Martín with Plaza Mayor.

Footpaths, however, are narrow and crowded, and pedestrians are often forced to step on the roadway, even when they are on an official crossing. This can be dangerous as traffic is heavy and drivers do not automatically stop for pedestrians.

Pickpockets operate in crowded places. Do not wear jewelry or dangle an expensive camera from your shoulder. Avoid walking across the Río Rimac to Convento de los Descalzos or Plaza de Acho as it is a poor area and robberies have occurred. Even though people congregate in and around Plaza Mayor at night, it is still safest in the daytime. Keep to busy, well-lit streets during night.

Stop sign, Lima

Taxis

Many unlicensed companies operate taxis in Lima and visitors are advised not to flag taxis on the street. Bright yellow taxis, registered with the Metropolitan Lima Taxi Service, hang around major hotels and shopping centers, such as Larcomar. As a rule call for taxis from companies such as **Taxi Real**, **Taxinet**, **Taxi Seguro** or **Taxi Satelital**. Radio-taxis cost 30 to 50 percent more than street taxis but are more reliable. The fare must be agreed upon in advance as taxis do not have meters.

A trip to or from the airport is almost always quoted in American dollars and ranges between US$15 to US$30, depending on the distance covered. Fares increase by 35 to 50 percent after midnight and on holidays.

Buses, Combis, and Colectivos

Buses are plentiful and cheap but painfully slow. There are buses and *combis*, *micros* or *colectivos*, all minibuses of varying size. Many *combis* charge a flat rate and follow fixed routes. Signs on windscreens indicate their routes. Conductors call out street names as the minibus hurtles along, and hold up fingers to show how many seats are available. They are frequently crowded and theft is common. *Colectivos* run in some Lima areas but are more popular in coastal and mountain towns.

DIRECTORY

Maps

Touring y Automóvil Club del Perú
Av. Cesar Vallejo 699, Lince, Lima.
Map 2 B2. **Tel** 01 614 9999.
W touringperu.com.pe

Instituto Geográfico Nacional
Av. Aramburu 1190, Surquillo, Lima. **Map** 3 E3. W ign.gob.pe

Car Rental Companies

American
Av. Nicolas Arriola 565, Santa Catalina, Lima. **Map** 3 E1.
Tel 01 472 5824.

Avis
Av. 28 de Julio 587, Miraflores, Lima. **Map** 4 B2. **Tel** 01 444 0450.
W avis.com

Budget
Av. Larco 998, Miraflores, Lima.
Map 4 B2. **Tel** 01 517 1880 (24-hours). W budgetperu.com

Dollar
Jr. Cantuarias 341, Miraflores, Lima. **Map** 4 C1. **Tel** 01 444 4920.
W dollar-rentacar.com.pe

Hertz
Jr. Diez Canseco 218, Miraflores, Lima. **Map** 4 B1. **Tel** 01 517 2402 (24-hours). W hertz.com.pe

National
Av. Costanera 1380, San Miguel, Lima. **Tel** 01 578 7878.
W nationalcar.com.pe

Taxis

Taxinet
Tel 01 578 3584.

Taxi Real
Tel 01 215 1414.

Taxi Satelital
Tel 01 355 5555.

Taxi Seguro
Tel 01 241 9292.

Jirón de la Unión, a pedestrianized pathway, Plaza Mayor, Lima

General Index

Acknowledgments

Dorling Kindersley would like to thank the many people whose help and assistance contributed to the preparation of this book.

Main Contributor

Australian-born journalist, Maryanne Blacker, moved to Lima in 2005. Prior to relocating to Peru, she lived for nine years in Paris specializing in food and travel writing. Her work has been published in diverse magazines, newspapers, and guidebooks worldwide including *Australian Gourmet Traveller*, *Elle*, *House & Garden*, the *Quantas* magazine, and *Vacations & Travel*. During a career which has taken her from her birthplace in outback Australia to Sydney, Paris, and Peru, she has also worked as a website bureau chief and news editor, newspaper sub-editor, public relations/press officer for a theater company, and as a book editor. She was also the editor of Australia's top-selling cookbook series. She holds a BA in Journalism and an MA in Applied History and is intrigued by Peru's complex and beguiling past, and its present.

Other Contributors

Rob Rachowiecki was born in England and moved to the Americas as a young adult. He has traveled from Alaska to Argentina and is the author of numerous guidebooks to several areas and countries in the Americas, especially about Peru where he works frequently as a leader of adventure travel vacations. Rob has a Masters degree in Ecology and Evolutionary Biology and currently makes his home in Arizona. He dedicates his work to his children: David, Alison, and Julia.

Joby Williams spent much of her childhood in Spain, and her early twenties traveling in Central and South America. She has an undergraduate degree in Hispanic Studies, an MA in Social Anthropology and has just started a PhD. Joby reviews books for the *Sunday Times* and is a regular contributor to guidebooks and other travel publications. She is also a part-time cheesemonger.

Jorge Riveros Cayo was born in Lima, raised in Canada, and lived his university student years in Chile. From being a French horn player, he shifted to journalism while studying in Santiago. On his return to Peru, he worked at a radio station and contributed to local newspapers and magazines. He has traveled extensively all over Peru and has written about travel, tourism, and conservation subjects. In 2003, he won the Biodiversity Reporting Award, granted by Conservation International. He has also contributed to many Latin American regional magazines, as well as to *Americas* and *National Geographic Traveler*. Currently he is in the process of starting his own travel company in Peru, specializing in gastronomic tourism.

Phrase Book
Lexus Ltd.

Fact Checker
Eleanor Griffis

Artwork Reference
Miles Buesst

Proofreader
Andy Kulkarni

Indexer
Ajay Kumar Lal Das

Design and Editorial
Publisher Douglas Amrine
Publishing Managers Jane Ewart, Scarlett O'Hara
Senior Editor Fay Franklin
Project Editor Alastair Laing
Project Art Editor Sonal Bhatt
Editorial Assistance Alexandra Farrell
Senior Cartographic Editor Casper Morris
DTP Designer Natasha Lu
XML Coordinator Bulent Yusuf

Revisions Design and Editorial
Emma Anacootee, Ines Contreras, Caroline Beactrice D'Cruz, Ryan Dube, Rupanki Kaushik, Emer FitzGerald, Eleanor Griffis, Priya Kukadia, Jude Ledger, Carly Madden, Hayley Maher, Alison McGill, Susie Peachey, Helen Peters, Lucy Richards, Susana Smith, Nikhil Verma, Sylvia Tombesi-Walton, Dora Whitaker.

Additional Picture Research
Ellen Root, Rachel Barber

DK Picture Library
Romaine Werblow

Production Controller
Linda Dare

Cartography
Base mapping for Lima and Peru derived from Netmaps

Additional Photography
Deni Bown, Peter Bush, Neil Fletcher, Philip Gatward, Nigel Hicks, Dave King, Bob Langrish, Jamie Marshall, Ray Moller, Gary Ombler, Matthew Ward. **Dorling Kindersley:** Tim Draper, Ian O'Leary, Suzanne Porter.

Special Assistance
Many thanks for the invaluable help of the following individuals and establishments: Lilian Delfín; Fernando I. López Mazzotti at PromPerú; Jonathon Miller W.

Photography Permissions
Dorling Kindersley would like to thank the following for their assistance and kind permission to photograph at their establishments:
Bodega El Catador; Bodega Tacama; Casa de Aliaga; Catedral de Arequipa; Catedral de Huamanga; Cebichería La Mar; Convento de los Descalzos; Don Bosco School; El Caravedo; El Complejo de Belén; Gonzalo Cilloniz at Hacienda San José; Hotel Monasterio; Huascarán National Park; La Candelaria; Miriam Holguin at La Catedral, Cusco; Larcomar; Eliana Romero at Monasterio de Santa Catalina; Hermano Ernesto Chambi Cruz at Monasterio at San Francisco, Lima; Sra Directora Rosa de Amano at Museo Amano; Dr Giuseppe Orefcici and Senorita Indara Chavez at Museo Antonini; Museo Arqueologia; Museo de Arqueología de la Universidad de Trujillo; Dr Giuseppe Orefcici and Senorita Indara Chavez at Museo de Archeológico Antonini; Sonia Moy at Museo de Arte de Lima; Museo de Arte Italiano; Museo de Arte Religioso; Neydo Hidalgo at Museo de la Electricidad; Enrico Poli at Museo Enrico Poli; Museo-Galería Arte Popular de Ayacucho; Museo Jose Cassinelli; Dr Sonia Guillen at Museo Leymebamba; Museo de la Nación; Senora Vitoria Mujica at Museo de Oro del Peru; Bernarda Delgado at Museo de Sitio Túcume; Doctora Carmen Arellano and Maria Elena Mayuri at Museo Nacional de Arqueología, Antropología e Historia del Perú; Mariana Watson at Museo Arqueologico Rafael Larco Herrera and Museo de Arte Precolombino; Pedro Gjurinovic at Museo Pedro de Osma; Museo Taurino; Director Walter Alva at Museo Tumbas Reales de Sipán; Carol Verde Cenas at Museo de Sitio Huaca Pucllana; Parque Municipal, Lima; Pueblo Eco Lodge; Rojo Bar; Santa Domingo; Santa Rosa de Ocopa Convent; Vista Alegre

Picture Credits
a-above; b-below/bottom; c-center; f-far; l-left; r-right; t-top.

Every effort has been made to trace the copyright holders and we apologize in advance for any unintentional omissions. We would be pleased to insert the appropriate acknowledgments in any subsequent edition of this publication.

The Publishers are grateful to the following individuals, companies, and picture libraries for permission to reproduce their photographs:

Works of art have been reproduced with the kind permission of the following copyright holders:

El Beso by Victor Delfin 34cl; *Chirapa Callo/Lengua de Arco Iris* by Don Pablo Amaringo 34bl; *L'abisso* by Pietro Canonica, Museo de Arte Italiano.

Al Frio y Al Fuego: 297bl

Alamy Images: AA World Travel Library 174cl, 174bl; Adams Picture Library t / a apl 119ca; AM Corporation 95bl; Amazon-Images 257crb; Arco Images 192tr; The Art Archive Gianni Dagil Orti 102bl; Suzy Bennett 186, 191br; John Bentley 22cr; Blickwinkel 267br; Tibor Bognar 41tc; Rachael Bowes 30clb, 257bl; Michelle Chaplow 283tl; Bruce Coleman Inc. 202bl; TS Corrigan 133cra; Lee Carruthers 257cl, 26-27c; China Span / Keren Su 28cl; Gary Cook 69tl, 175cr; Danita Delimont 23clb, 25crb, 303bl; Eagle Visions Photography / Craig Lovell 184bl; Emilio Ereza 12tr; Mark Eveleigh 205br; Michele Falzone 151tl; Federico Tovoli VWPics 16; Fabienne Fossez 198cra; Derrick Francis Furlong 256br; Furlong Photography 305br; Mike Goldwater 26bc, 264crb; Jeff Greenberg 54tr; Blaine Harrington III 116-117; Terry Harris 284cla, 285ca; Hemis 33br; Anthony Ibarra 64clb; Izel Photography 78; Janine Wiedel Photolibrary 151cr; Florian Kopp 58-59; Emmanuel Lattes 209cb; Jennie Lewis 160bl; Melvyn Longhurst 32crb, 32bl, 68bl, 138bl, 287bl; Mary Evans Picture Library 55tl, 286tr; mediacolor's 24br; Michele Molinari 90cl, 93tr; Magali Moreau 145br, 267tl; North Wind Picture Archives 29bl, 51bl; Chris Pancewicz 306b; Edward Parker 23bc, 264tl; Peter Arnold, Inc. 118cla; Photofrenetic 61tr, 68cl, 70br; Leonide Principe 259br; The Print Collector 65cra; Radius Images 207br; Rainer Raffalski 258c; Robert Harding Picture Library Ltd 147bl, 150tr; Pep Roig 246tl, 258br, 261t; Bert de Ruiter 24clb, 29tl, 209clb; Philip Scalia 130cla, 130cl, 131cr; Paul Springett 119br, 236bl; Sue Cunningham Photographic 232bl; Glyn Thomas 266tr; Mark Towner 238; Tribaleye Images / J Marshall 118clb, 285bl; Genevieve Vallee 257cla; Mireille Vautier 28clb, 44, 47bl, 49bl, 53br, 192bl, 282cl; Emil von Maltitz 208cla; Westend 61 42bl; Wietse Michiels Travel Stock 198br; Peter L. Wilson 149cl; World Religions Photo Library 60cl; Worldwide Picture Library 176c; Konrad Zelazowski 25cr.

Alfaguara: La Ciudad y Los Perros 35bc, Aves sin nido 35br, Maldita Ternura 35fbr.

ArchivoLatino: Adriana Orozco 27tl, 199tr.

Josh Armstrong: 169clb.

Jim Bartle: 204tl, 206bl.

Paul Beckers: 196cl.

The Bridgeman Art Library: War of the Pacific - Bombardment of the city of Iquique, Chile, by the Chilean Squadron on the night of 16th July 1879 (engraving) 54cl, Naval Combat beween the Peruvian Ship 'Huascar' against the Chilean 'Blanco Encalada' and the 'Cochrane' in 1879 54bl, Ricardo Palma (1833-1919) 1896 82bl, St. Jerome (oil on canvas) 171clb, Atahualpa (c.1502-33) 14th and last Inca King, mid-18th century (oil on canvas) 173br, Pottery portrait vessel, Mochica (earthenware & paint) 226bl

Miles Buesst: 64cl, 80cl, 81tl, 81cra.

Michel Burger: 203tr, 203cr, 207tc, 209crb, 217tr.
Cafe Fusiones: 296tr.

Casa Andina: 271tl.

Rolly Valdivia Chávez: 149c, 199br.

Chelsea PUB Restaurant: 295b.

Christie's Images Ltd: 171cr, 171bl.

Tom Cockrem: 250br.

Colca Lodge : 275tl.

Eva Ayllon's private collection: Rosa Rubalcava 33cr.

Corbis: 53crb; Archivo Iconografico, S.A. 226br; Yann Arthus-Bertrand 73crb; Sygma / Jean Louis Atlan 266br; Atlantide Phototravel 47tr, 224c, 226bc; Nathan Benn 48br, 226clb, 226crb; Bettmann 56tl, 56bc, 73cl; Bowers Museum of Cultural Art 48bc; Brooklyn Museum 28-29c, 34tr; Christie's Images 171br; Colita 35c; Colin Monteath Hedgehog House 214-215; Corbis Sygma / Balaguer Alejandro 57tr, 57bl,/ Arici Graziano 35tl,/ Alain Keler 55bl,/ Touhig Sion 27tr; Jay Dickman 254bl; dpa / Frank Leonhardt 21br; EFE / Paolo Aguilar 61ca, 84clb; Enrique Castro-Mendivil 244-245; EPA / Paolo Aguilar 29cr,/ Peruvian National Institute 216tr,/ Sergio Urday 19tl; Ric Ergenbright 201b; Jack Fields 65br, Michael & Patricia Fogden 23bl; The Gallery Collection 51tr; Paul Harris 262-263; Martin Harvey 23br; Jeremy Horner 157b; Hughes Hervé 164-165, 230-231; Charles & Josette 49bc; Steve Kaufman 87c; Kelly-Mooney Photography 161cra; Bob Krist 13t; Frans Lanting 265br; Danny Lehman 36-37c; Charles & Josette Lenars 28cr, 36cl; Richard List 22tr; Lorpresse / Corbis Sygma / J.C. Kanny 51tc; Giacomo Morini 2-3; Kazuyoshi Nomachi 27cr, 198bl; Gianni Dagli Orti 65crb, 100clb; Alex Robinson 200; Galen Rowell 211bl; Kevin Schafer 47br, 234bl; John Slater 19c; Greg Smith 73bc; James Sparshatt 18b; Hubert Stadler 67br; Stapleton Collection 52crb; George Steinmetz 216cra; Ivan Vdovin 156; Francesco Venturi 6-7, 161crb, 198crb; Brian A. Vikander 266cl; Werner Forman 36c, 48crb; Nik Wheeler 38cr, 38bl.

Crepísimo restaurant: 281br, 290br.

Cusco Restaurants: 291br, 292tl, 292br.

Danita Delimont Stock Photography: Jon Arnold 64tr; Keren Su 40tl.

Victor Delfin: 83br.

Dreamstime.com: Pablo Hidalgo 11b; Yeolka 11tr; Yulan 128-129; Michael Zysman 8bl.

FLPA: David Hosking 265clb; Frans Lanting 23cr, 255cr; Minden Pictures / Claus Meyer 265cb,/ Mark Moffett 265crb.
Sally Foreman: 175tl, 175br, 176tr, 177tc, 177cl, 177br.

Getty Images: AFP / Robert Atanasovski 33tr,/ Jaime Razuri 42c; Luis Davilla 134, 268-269; ilkerender 120; Image Source 178-179; Andras Jancsik 194-195; Rob Kroenert 152-153; LatinContent / Patricio Realpe 57bc; Photographer's Choice / Frans Lemmens 309t; Heriberto Rodriguez 107t; Niceforo Ruiz 33bl, 39tr, 95ca, 196tr; Michael Sewell 252; Stone / Alejandro Balaguer 73clb.

Go2peru.com: Jorge Mazzotti 187b, 242tr.

The Granger Collection, New York: 50cl, 50cb, 50bl, 50br, 50-51c, 51cra, 52c, 52bc, 52br, 53c, 53bl, 54-55c, Granger Collection, New York 28tr, 183br.

Instituto Fotografico E. Courret: 93br.

International Potato center : 284c.

John Warburton-Lee Photography: 219b, 220bl.

Laeñe restaurant: 289tr.

Lonely Planet Images: Mark Daffey 20tr.

Magical Andes Photography: James Brunker 143tl, 175bl, 176bl, 216cl, 217cla, 248br.

Mariri Magazine: Lorna Li 26cl.

Jorge Luis Montero: 55cr.

National Geographic Stock: Gina Martin 174tr.

naturepl.com: Hermann Brehm 265bl; Pete Oxford 267cr; Staffan Widstrand 23cl.

NHPA / Photoshot: Bill Coster 265c.

O'Pal Sierra Resort: 277bl.

Odyssey Productions, Inc.: Robert Frerck 25br, 48tl, 221tr, 221cr.

Carlos Olivares: 240bl.

Orient-Express Hotels Ltd: 272tl, 276tr.

perudelights.com: 283bc.

Photographers Direct: Ann Stevens Photography 61cr; Marmotta PhotoArt / Krys Bailey 136bl, 159t.

Photolibrary: Index Stock Imagery / Shirley Vanderbilt 20bl; Jtb Photo Communications Inc 32cr; Science Photo Library / Camacho Tony 23tc.

Photoshot / World Pictures: Walter Hupiú 149bl.
Heinz Plenge: 21tr, 22br, 23tl, 23tr, 24cl, 25tl, 32cl, 33tl, 33cl, 33bc, 40br, 47c, 67cl, 119tl, 125crb, 141br, 151br,236tr,

236cl, 237tr, 237cl, 239b, 253b, 308cl.

PromPerú: 67bl, 150cla, 304tl; Archivo 41br, 147br; Mylene D'Auriol 39b; Domingo Giribaldi 198cl; Anibal Solimano 211cr; Michael Tweddle 46t; Renzo Uccelli 209cl.

Punta Sal Club Hotel: 278bc.

Steve Raffo: 146-147c.

Reuters: Mariana Bazo 72bl; Ho New 57clb; Pilar Olivares 28br; STR New 324b; Str Old 56clb.

Robert Harding Picture Library: Michael DeFreitas 218; Robert Frerck 74-75; Derrick Furlong 65tl; Tono Labra 88; Jose Enrique Molina 96; Odyssey / David Dudenhoefer 22crb.

Clifford J. Schexnayder: 80bl.

John Servayge: 248clb, 251t.

Sheraton Lima Hotel & Casino: Sheraton Lima Hotel & Casino 270cl.

South American Pictures: Robert Frances 149crb; Kathy Jarvis 283cb; Tony Morrison 122tr, 130br, 131tl, 131bl, 149br.

Spectrum Photofile: Spectrum Photofile 21c.

SuperStock: age fotostock 62; Hughes Herv 310-311.

T'anta restaurant: 288bl.

Tambopata Research Center: 271br, 279tr.

Trivio restaurant: 294tl.

ViaVia Reiscafes: 293bc.

Wikipedia: 45bc, 22fbr, 23cb.

www.pabloamaringo.com: Painting / 34bl.

Zig Zag restaurant: 291tl.

Cover Picture Credits
Front Endpaper: Left -**Alamy Images:** Izel Photography c, Mark Towner tc; **Corbis:** Alex Robinson br; **Robert Harding Picture Library:** Michael DeFreitas tl, Tono Labra bc, Jose Enrique Molina bl; **SuperStock:** age fotostock cl. Right **Alamy Images:** Suzy Bennett tr; **Corbis:** Ivan Vdovin c; **Getty Images:** Luis Davilla cr, Michael Sewell tc, ilkerender br.

Jacket Images:
Front: **Alamy Images:** Gary Cook bl; **SuperStock:** Mike Theiss / National Geographic c.
Spine: **SuperStock:** Mike Theiss / National Geographic t.

All other images © **Dorling Kindersley**
For further information see:
www.dkimages.com

Phrase Book

In Peru, there are three main different forms of pronunciation of Spanish: variations from the Andes, from the coast (Lima being its center), and a combination of the two which has emerged during the last 50 years due to internal immigration.

In the variation from the Andes, sometimes the **e** and **o** become **i** and **u**; thus, **ayer** would be pronounced '**a-yeer**' and **por** is '**poor**'. There is often a distinction between **ll** and **y**, where the pronunciation would be like the English **y** for **yes** and **j** for **job** respectively. It is also common that **r** and **rr** are pronounced similarly.

In the variation from the coast, there is a clear distinction between **r** and **rr**. Sometimes the **s** becomes **h** before another consonant as in **pescado** 'pehka*do*'. In addition, the **ll** and **y** are pronounced the same, such as in the English **j** for job. Finally, the **d** at the end of the word may become **t** or may be omitted; for example, **usted** would be pronounced 'ooste**h**'.

In the variation which combines Andean and coastal pro-nunciations, there is also a clear distinction between **r** and **rr**. In this variation, the **ll** and **y** are also pronounced as in the English **j** for **job**. Besides, the sounds **b**, **d**, **g**, and **y** may become nonexistent between vowels; for example, **cansado** would be pronounced 'kansa-o'. Finally, the **s** may become **h** before another consonant as in **fresco** 'frehko'.

Some special Peruvian words

¡A la firme!	a la feermeh	Sure!
agua de caño	agwa deh kan-yo	tap water
bravazo	brabaso	wonderful
brevete	brebeteh	driving licence
carro	karro	car
chamba	chamba	job; work
chelear	cheleh-ar	to drink beer
chévere	chebaireh	cool, great
chibolo	cheebolo	young person
chorear	choreh-ar	to steal
coco	koko	dollar
del carajo	del karaho	excellent, very good
estar aguja	estar agoo-ha	to be skinny
estar con la	estar kon la	to have diarrhea
bicicleta	beeseekleta	
estar hasta la	estar asta la	to be fed up
coronilla	koronee-ya	
estar parado	estar parado	to be well off
estar piña	estar peen-ya	to be unlucky
feria	fair-ya	market
hacer cholito	asair choleeto	to deceive someone
a alguien	a algen	
los tombos	los tombos	the police
pan comido	pan komeedo	it is easy
pata	pata	pal, mate
pueblo jóven	pweblo hohven	shanty town
rubia	rroob-ya	beer
tener caldero	kaldairo	to be hung over

Emergencies

Help!	**¡Socorro!**	sokorro
Stop!	**¡Pare!**	pareh
Call a doctor	**Llamen un médico**	yamen oon medeeko
Call an	**Llamen a una**	yamen a oona
ambulance	**ambulancia**	amboolans-ya
Police!	**¡Policía!**	poleesee-a
I've been robbed	**Me robaron**	meh rrobaron
Call the police!	**Llamen a la policía**	yamen a la
		poleesee-a
Where is the	**¿Dónde queda el**	dondeh keda el
nearest	**hospital más**	ospeetal mas
hospital?	**cercano?**	sairkano?
Could you help	**¿Me puede ayudar?**	meh pwedeh a-
me?		yoodar?
They stole my...	**Me robaron mi...**	meh rrobaron
		mee...

Communication Essentials

Yes	**Sí**	see
No	**No**	no
Please	**Por favor**	por fabor
Pardon me	**Perdone**	pairdoneh
Excuse me	**Disculpe**	deeskoolpeh
I'm sorry	**Lo siento**	lo s-yento
Thanks	**Gracias**	gras-yas
Hello!	**¡Hola!**	houla
Good day	**Buen día**	bwen dee-a
Good afternoon	**Buenas tardes**	bwenas tardes
Good evening	**Buenas noches**	bwenas noches
Night	**Noche**	nocheh
Morning	**Mañana**	man-yana
Tomorrow	**Mañana**	man-yana
Yesterday	**Ayer**	a-yair
Here	**Acá**	aka
How?	**¿Cómo?**	komo
When?	**¿Cuándo?**	kwando
Where?	**¿Dónde?**	dondeh
Why?	**¿Por qué?**	por keh
How are you?	**¿Qué tal?**	keh tal
Very well,	**Muy bien, gracias**	mwee byen gras-yas
thank you		
Pleased to meet	**Encantado/mucho**	enkantado/moocho
you	**gusto**	goosto
It's a pleasure!	**¡Es un placer!**	Es oon plahcer
Goodbye, so	**Adiós, hasta luego**	ad-yos, asta lwego
long		

Useful Phrases

That's fine	**Está bien**	esta b-yen
Fine!	**¡Qué bien!**	keh b-yen
How long?	**¿Cuánto falta?**	kwanto falta?
Do you speak a	**¿Habla un poco**	abla oon pako deh
little English?	**de inglés?**	eengles?
I don't	**No entiendo**	no ent-yendo
understand		
Could you speak	**¿Puede hablar más**	pwedeh ablar mas
more slowly?	**despacio?**	despas-yo?
I agree/OK	**De acuerdo/bueno**	deh akwairdo/bweno
Certainly!	**¡Claro que sí!**	klaro keh see
Let's go!	**¡Vámonos!**	bamonos
How do I get to...?	**¿Cómo se llega a...?**	komo se yega a...?
Which way to...?	**¿Por dónde se**	por dondeh seh ba
	va a...?	a...?

Useful Words

large	**grande**	grandeh
small	**pequeño**	peken-yo
hot	**caliente**	kal-yenteh
cold	**frío**	free-o
good	**bueno**	bweno
bad	**malo**	malo
so-so	**más o menos**	mas o menos
mediocre	**regular**	regoolar
sufficient	**suficiente**	soofees-yenteh
well/fine	**bien**	b-yen
open	**abierto**	ab-yairto
closed	**cerrado**	serrado
entrance	**entrada**	entrada
exit	**salida**	saleeda
full	**lleno**	yeno
empty	**vacío**	basee-o
right	**derecha**	dairecha
left	**izquierda**	eesk-yairda
straight on	**(todo) recto**	rrekto
under	**debajo**	debaho
over	**arriba**	arreeba
quickly	**pronto**	pronto

early	**temprano**	*temprano*
late	**tarde**	*tardeh*
now	**ahora**	*a-ora*
soon	**ahorita**	*a-oreeta*
more	**más**	*mas*
less	**menos**	*menos*
little	**poco**	*poko*
much	**mucho**	*moocho*
very	**muy**	*mwee*
too much	**demasiado**	*demas-yado*
in front of	**delante**	*delanteh*
opposite	**enfrente**	*enfrenteh*
behind	**detrás**	*detras*
first floor	**primer piso**	*preemair peeso*
ground floor	**sotano piso**	*soutano peeso*
lift	**ascensor**	*asensor*
bathroom	**baño**	*ban-yo*
women	**mujeres**	*moohaires*
men	**hombres**	*ombres*
toilet paper	**papel higiénico**	*papel eeh-yeneeko*
camera	**cámara**	*kamara*
batteries	**pilas**	*peelas*
passport	**pasaporte**	*pasaporteh*
visa	**visa**	*beesa*
tourist card	**tarjeta turistica**	*tarheta tooreesteeka*

Health

I don't feel well	**Me siento mal**	*meh s-yento mal*
I have a stomach ache/ headache	**Me duele el estómago/ la cabeza**	*meh dweleh el estomago la kabesa*
He/she is ill	**Está enfermo/a**	*esta enfairmo/a*
I need to rest	**Necesito descansar**	*neseseeto deskansar*
drug store	**farmacia**	*farmas-ya*

Post Office and Bank

bank	**banco**	*banko*
I'm looking for a bureau de change	**Busco una casa de cambio**	*boosko oona kasa deh kamb-yo*
What is the dollar rate?	**¿A cómo está el dolar?**	*a komo esta el dolar?*
I want to send a letter	**Quiero enviar una carta**	*k-yairo emb-yar oona karta*
postcard	**postal**	*postal*
stamp	**estampilla**	*estampee-ya*
draw out money	**sacar dinero**	*sakar deenairo*

Shopping

I would like/ want...	**Me gustaría/quiero...**	*meh goostaree-a/ k-yairo...*
Do you have any...?	**¿Tiene...?**	*t-yeneh...?*
expensive	**caro**	*karo*
How much is it?	**¿Cuánto cuesta?**	*kwanto kwesta?*
What time do you open/ close?	**¿A qué hora abre/ cierra?**	*a ke ora abreh/ s-yairra?*
May I pay with a credit card?	**¿Puedo pagar con tarjeta de crédito?**	*pwedo pagar kon tarheta deh kredeeto?*

Sightseeing

avenue	**avenida**	*abeneeda*
beach	**playa**	*pla-ya*
castle, fortress	**castillo**	*kastee-yo*
cathedral	**catedral**	*katedral*
church	**iglesia**	*eegles-ya*
district	**barrio**	*barr-yo*
garden	**jardín**	*hardeen*

guide	**guía**	*gee-a*
house	**casa**	*kasa*
map	**mapa**	*mapa*
highway	**autopista**	*owtopeesta*
museum	**museo**	*mooseh-o*
park	**parque**	*parkeh*
road	**carretera**	*karretaira*
square	**plaza**	*plasa*
street	**calle, callejón**	*ka-yeh, ka-yehon*
town hall	**municipalidad**	*mooneeseepaleedad*
tourist bureau	**oficina de turismo**	*ofeeseena deh tooreesmo*

Transport

When does it leave	**¿A qué hora sale?**	*a keh ora saleh?*
When does the next train/bus leave for...?	**¿A qué hora sale próximo tren/bus a...?**	*a keh ora saleh el prokseemo tren/boos a...?*
Could you call a taxi for me?	**¿Me puede llamar un taxi?**	*meh pwedeh yamar oon taksee?*
airport	**aeropuerto**	*a-airopwairto*
railroad station	**estación de ferrocarriles**	*estas-yon deh fairrokarreeles*
bus station	**terminal de buses**	*tairmeenal deh booses*
customs	**aduana**	*adwana*
port of embarkation	**puerta de embarque**	*pwairta deh embarkeh*
boarding pass	**tarjeta de embarque**	*tarheta deh embarkeh*
car hire	**alquiler de carros**	*alkeelair deh karros*
bicycle	**bicicleta**	*beeseekleta*
rate	**tarifa**	*tareefa*
insurance	**seguro**	*segooro*
fuel station	**estación de gasolina**	*estas-yon deh gasoleena*
garage	**garage**	*garaheh*
I have a flat tyre	**Se me pinchó una llanta**	*seh meh peencho oona yanta*

Staying in a Hotel

I have a reservation	**Tengo una reserva**	*tengo oona rresairba*
Are there any rooms available?	**¿Tiene habitaciones disponibles?**	*t-yeneh abeetas-yones deesponeebles*
single/double room	**habitación sencilla/ doble**	*abeetas-yon sensee-ya/dobleh*
twin room	**habitación con camas gemelas**	*abeetas-yon kon kamas hemelas*
shower	**ducha**	*doocha*
bath	**tina**	*teena*
balcony	**balcón**	*balkon*
I want to be woken up at...	**Necesito que me despierten a las...**	*neseseeto keh meh desp-yairten a las...*
warm/cold water	**agua caliente/fría**	*agwa kal-yenteh/ free-a*
soap	**jabón**	*habon*
towel	**toalla**	*to-a-ya*
key	**llave**	*yabeh*

Eating Out

I am a vegetarian	**Soy vegetariano**	*soy begetar-yano*
Can I see the menu, please?	**¿Me deja ver el menú, por favor?**	*me deha ber el menoo por fabor?*
fixed price	**precio fijo**	*pres-yo feeho*
What is there to eat?	**¿Qué hay para comer?**	*keh I para komair?*
The bill, please	**la cuenta, por favor**	*la kwenta por fabor*

glass	**vaso**	*baso*
cutlery	**cubiertos**	*koob-yairtos*
I would like some water	**Quisiera un poco de agua**	*kees-yaira oon poko deh agwa*
wine	**vino**	*beeno*
The beer is not cold enough	**La cerveza no está bien fría**	*a sairbesa no esta b-lyen free-a*
breakfast	**desayuno**	*desa-yoono*
lunch	**almuerzo**	*almwairso*
dinner	**comida**	*komeeda*
raw	**crudo**	*kroodo*
cooked	**cocido**	*koseedo*

Menu Decoder

aceite	*asayteh*	oil
agua mineral	*agwa meenairal*	mineral water
ajo	*aho*	garlic
anticucho	*anteekoocho*	kebab
arroz	*arros*	rice
asado	*asado*	roasted
atún	*atoon*	tuna
azúcar	*asookar*	sugar
bacalao	*bakala-o*	cod
betarraga	*betarraga*	beetroot
café	*kafeh*	coffee
camarones	*kamarones*	prawns
carne	*karneh*	meat
carne de chancho	*karneh deh chancho*	pork
causa	*kowsa*	potato salad
cerveza	*sairbesa*	beer
chancada	*chankada*	maize cake
chifa	*cheefa*	Chinese food
choro	*choro*	mussel
dulce	*doolseh*	sweet
ensalada	*ensalada*	salad
fruta	*froota*	fruit
guargüero	*gwargwairo*	sweet fritter filled with fudge
helado	*elado*	ice cream
huevo	*webo*	egg
jugo	*hoogo*	fruit juice
langosta	*langosta*	lobster
leche	*lecheh*	milk
mantequilla	*mantekee-ya*	butter
marisco	*mareesko*	seafood
mazamorra	*masamorra*	pudding made with corn starch, sugar and honey
pachamanca	*pachamanka*	meat barbecued between two hot stones
pallar	*pa-yar*	butter bean
palta	*palta*	avocado
pan	*pan*	bread
papas	*papas*	potatoes
pescado	*peskado*	fish
picante	*peekanteh*	spicy meat stew
pisco	*peesko*	eau-de-vie made from grapes
plátano	*platano*	banana
pollo	*po-yo*	chicken
postre	*postreh*	dessert
potaje	*potaheh*	soup
puerco	*pwairko*	pork
queque	*kekeh*	cake
queso	*keso*	cheese
refresco	*refresko*	drink
sal	*sal*	salt
salsa	*salsa*	sauce
sopa	*sopa*	soup
té	*teh*	tea
té de yuyos	*teh deh yoo-yos*	herbal tea
tuco	*tooko*	tomato sauce
vinagre	*beenagreh*	vinegar
zapallo	*sapa-yo*	pumpkin

Time

minute	**minuto**	*meenooto*
hour	**hora**	*ora*
half an hour	**media hora**	*med-ya ora*
quarter of an hour	**un cuarto**	*oon kwarto*
week	**semana**	*simana*
next week	**la próxima semana**	*la prosima simana*
month	**mes**	*mes*
last month	**el mes pasado**	*el mes pasadou*
Monday	**Lunes**	*loones*
Tuesday	**Martes**	*martes*
Wednesday	**Miércoles**	*m-yairkoles*
Thursday	**Jueves**	*hwebes*
Friday	**Viernes**	*b-yairnes*
Saturday	**Sábado**	*sabado*
Sunday	**Domingo**	*domeengo*
January	**Enero**	*enairo*
February	**Febrero**	*febrairo*
March	**Marzo**	*marso*
April	**Abril**	*abreel*
May	**Mayo**	*ma-yo*
June	**Junio**	*hoon-yo*
July	**Julio**	*hool-yo*
August	**Agosto**	*agosto*
September	**Setiembre**	*set-yembreh*
October	**Octubre**	*oktoobreh*
November	**Noviembre**	*nob-yembreh*
December	**Diciembre**	*dees-yembreh*

Numbers

0	**cero**	*sairo*
1	**uno**	*oono*
2	**dos**	*dos*
3	**tres**	*tres*
4	**cuatro**	*kwatro*
5	**cinco**	*seenko*
6	**seis**	*says*
7	**siete**	*s-yeteh*
8	**ocho**	*ocho*
9	**nueve**	*nwebeh*
10	**diez**	*d-yes*
11	**once**	*onseh*
12	**doce**	*doseh*
13	**trece**	*treseh*
14	**catorce**	*katorseh*
15	**quince**	*keenseh*
16	**dieciséis**	*d-yeseesays*
17	**diecisiete**	*d-yesees-yeteh*
18	**dieciocho**	*d-yes-yocho*
19	**diecinueve**	*d-yeseenwebeh*
20	**veinte**	*baynteh*
30	**treinta**	*traynta*
40	**cuarenta**	*kwarenta*
50	**cincuenta**	*seenkwenta*
60	**sesenta**	*sesenta*
70	**setenta**	*setenta*
80	**ochenta**	*ochenta*
90	**noventa**	*nobenta*
100	**cien**	*s-yen*
500	**quinientos**	*keen-yentos*
1000	**mil**	*meel*
first	**primero/a**	*preemairo/a*
second	**segundo/a**	*segoondo/a*
third	**tercero/a**	*tairsairo/a*
fourth	**cuarto/a**	*kwarto/a*
fifth	**quinto/a**	*keento/a*
sixth	**sexto/a**	*seksto/a*
seventh	**sétimo/a**	*seteemo/a*
eight	**octavo/a**	*oktabo/a*
ninth	**noveno/a**	*nobeno/a*
tenth	**décimo/a**	*deseemo/a*

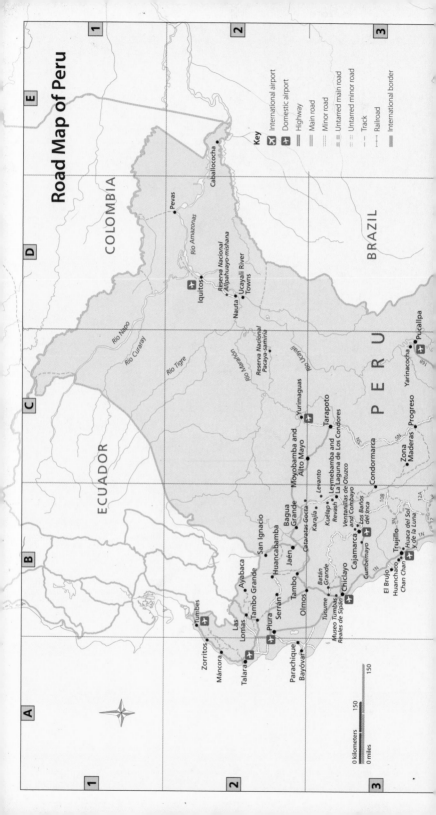

Road Map of Peru

Key

✈ International airport
✈ Domestic airport
━━ Highway
━━ Main road
═══ Minor road
═ ═ Untarred main road
= = Untarred minor road
- - Track
+++ Railroad
━━ International border

ECUADOR

COLOMBIA

BRAZIL

P E R U

Zorritos
Máncora
Talara
Tumbes
Las Lomas
Ayabaca
Tambo Grande
Piura
San Ignacio
Serrán
Huancabamba
Parachique
Bayóvar
Olmos
Tambo
Jaén
Bagua Grande
Túcume
Batán Grande
Museo Tumbas
Reales de Sipán
Chiclayo
Karajía
Cataratas Gocta
Kuélap
Revash
Leymebamba and
La Laguna de Los Condores
Levanto
Moyobamba and
Alto Mayo
Yurimaguas
Tarapoto
El Brujo
Huanchaco
Chan Chan
Trujillo
Huaca del Sol
y de la Luna
Cumbemayo
Cajamarca
Ventanillas de Otuzco
Los Baños del Inca
Condormarca
Progreso
Zona Maderas
Yarinacocha
Pucallpa

Pevas
Iquitos
Nauta
Caballococha
Ucayali River Towns

Rio Napo
Rio Curaray
Rio Tigre
Rio Marañón
Rio Amazonas
Rio Ucayali
Rio Huallaga

Reserva Nacional
Allpahuayo-mishana
Reserva Nacional
Pacaya-samiria

3N
1N
10B
12A
5N
8N
189

0 kilometers   150
0 miles   150